THE
EUROPEAN NOBILITIES
in the Seventeenth and Eighteenth Centuries

VOLUME ONE

WESTERN EUROPE

Also available:

The European Nobilities in the Seventeenth and Eighteenth Centuries. Volume II: Northern, Central and Eastern Europe
Edited by H.M. Scott

THE
EUROPEAN NOBILITIES
in the Seventeenth and Eighteenth Centuries

VOLUME ONE

WESTERN EUROPE

Edited by
H. M. Scott

LONGMAN
London and New York

Longman Group Limited,
Longman House, Burnt Mill,
Harlow, Essex CM20 2JE, England
and Associated Companies throughout the world.

Published in the United States of America
by Longman Publishing, New York

First published 1995

ISBN 0 582 08072 X CSD
ISBN 0 582 08066 5 PPR

British Library Cataloguing-in-Publication Data

A catalogue record for this book is
available from the British Library

Library of Congress Cataloging-in-Publication Data

The European Nobilities in the seventeenth and eighteenth centuries/edited by H.M.
Scott.
p.   cm.
Includes bibliographical references and index.
Contents: v. 1. Western Europe
ISBN 0-582-08072-X (v. 1 : csd). — ISBN 0-582-08066-5 (v. 1 : pbk)
1. Nobility—Europe—History—17th century.

2. Nobility—Europe—History–18th century. I Scott, H. M. (Hamish M.), 1946–   .
D247.E94 1994
929.7—dc20   93-47258
CIP

Set by 14B in 10 / 13 pt Garamond
Produced by Longman Singapore Publishers (Pte) Ltd.
Printed in Singapore

Contents

Preface

The editing of this collection has been a more extended process than first anticipated. My principal debt is to all the contributors both for their encouragement and forbearance during this delay and for their willingness not merely to produce their individual chapters but to undertake revisions with the aim of producing greater uniformity between the national surveys. I have been helped particularly by three friends: Robert Oresko and Isabel de Madariaga awakened my interest in Europe's nobilities and have subsequently provided both encouragement and practical advice, besides allowing me to draw on their profound knowledge of the subject; while Christopher Storrs has been an enthusiastic collaborator on our joint chapter and a fertile source of ideas and information. Helen Hyde translated the chapter on the Italian peninsula with speed and efficiency, and Claudio Donati undertook a careful revision of the English text: I am grateful to them both. Parts of the text were typed and revised by Nancy Bailey and Lucy Bosworth, without whose skill the collection could not have been completed. My greatest practical debt is to the staff at Longman, and especially to Andrew MacLennan, Joan Perry and Hilary Shaw, for the advice, encouragement and assistance they have generously provided throughout the whole project. Anyone who has been fortunate enough to publish a book with Longman will readily understand the extent of my obligation in this respect.

H. M. SCOTT
St Andrews

Glossary of Technical Terms

allodial: Of land, meaning full ownership, that is to say, not subject to a feudal superior, such as the king. During the seventeenth and eighteenth centuries, the greater part of the landed property held by the nobility in almost every European country was or became allodial.

derogation; dérogeance (French): During the early modern period many countries particularly in western and southern Europe possessed or acquired laws which prescribed loss (or, sometimes, suspension) of privileged status for a nobleman who engaged directly in commercial activities and especially in the retail trade. Such conduct, it was believed, derogated from noble status: the nobility was, in theory, expected to live solely on the income of its landed estates. In practice, however, such laws were not always implemented and by the eighteenth century they did little to prevent many noblemen engaging in a wide variety of commercial activities.

endogamy: The practice of choosing marriage partners exclusively from one's own social group. Strictly speaking endogamy means marriage within the kin or family group, but it has come to be used more loosely, for example, to cover marriage between members of the same social group such as the nobility. During the early modern period it was very widely practised among the European nobilities.

entail: A permanent and unbreakable legal trust covering landed property and, sometimes, moveable forms of wealth. This also regulated succession to the estate, which was normally by male primogeniture, and was therefore also referred to under the name '*majorat*' (French); '*maggiorasco*' (Italian); and '*mayorazgo*' (Spanish): (q.v.). The heir was not permitted to dispose of any of the entailed property, though he (or she) enjoyed the income during his (or her) lifetime. Entails became increasingly common during the early modern period, especially among the aristocracy and higher nobility and were frequently incorporated into wills or marriage settlements. Though there were technical differences between these forms of trusts, in practice these were unimportant and all can be referred to simply as 'entails'.

exogamy: The practice of marrying only outside one's own social group.

fedecommesso (Italian): See entail.

Fideikommiss (German): See entail.

mayorazgo: The form of entail (q.v.) prevailing in Spain, where it was widely adopted among the higher and lesser nobility. It had evolved during the Late Middle Ages and was codified in the Laws of Toro in 1505. In theory it could not be broken without specific permission from the Crown, and was thus a particularly rigid form of entail. In the second half of the eighteenth century it was subjected to increased criticism and some efforts were made to restrict its operation and further spread; it was finally abolished in 1836.

partible inheritance: The practice of dividing a father's landed and moveable property among all of his heirs. His sons would normally secure the largest share of the inheritance. During the seventeenth and eighteenth centuries this was increasingly superseded among the higher nobility and aristocracy by the practice of male *primogeniture* (q.v.).

patrilinear inheritance: The practice of dividing an inheritance among the father's male children.

primogeniture: Succession of, and inheritance by, the first-born child, who alone secured the title and even the landed property; *male primogeniture* (inheritance by the eldest son) became increasingly widespread among the higher nobility in seventeenth- and eighteenth-century Europe.

strict settlement: A form of property entail (q.v.) in England, where its increased use after the Restoration of 1660 was one factor in the rise of the great landed estates.

CHAPTER ONE

Introduction:
The Consolidation of Noble
Power in Europe, c.1600–1800

H. M. Scott and Christopher Storrs
Universities of St Andrews and Dundee

I

A striking feature of recent historical writing has been the widespread revival of interest in Europe's nobilities. Since the mid-1970s, scholars have rediscovered nobility as a historical phenomenon. This is true for all periods and for most countries. Medieval historians, most notably Georges Duby, have done much to clarify the development and characteristics of the élite which emerged in Europe during the centuries after c.1000, while later modern scholars, above all Arno Mayer and David Cannadine, have explored the enduring importance of the aristocracy in the nineteenth and even twentieth centuries. A stream of monographs, general studies and edited collections have appeared;[1] while an increasing number of academic conferences – those barometers of scholarly fashion – have been devoted to the élite.[2] This comes after a generation during which other social groups, in particular the peasantry and the middle class, secured the lion's share of attention. These were thought to be more worthy of study than a nobility assumed to be in long-term decline. This rediscovery has been

* This survey incorporates material collected in the course of a research project funded by the Leverhulme Trust. We are very grateful to the Trust for its generous financial support. We also thank Dr Derek McKay for his helpful comments on an earlier version of this introduction.

1. For example: A. J. Mayer, *The Persistence of the Old Regime: Europe to the Great War* (New York, 1981); David Cannadine, *The Decline and Fall of the British Aristocracy* (New Haven, Conn., 1990); Kristen B. Neuschel, *Word of Honour: Interpreting Noble Culture in Sixteenth-century France* (Ithaca, N. Y., 1989); H. Rössler, ed., *Deutscher Adel 1430–1555* (Darmstadt, 1963); H. Rössler, ed., *Deutscher Adel 1555–1740* (Darmstadt, 1964); R. Vierhaus, ed., *Der Adel vor der Revolution* (Göttingen, 1971). No attempt is made to provide a full bibliography in the footnotes to this introduction. For the period 1600–1800, an up-to-date survey of the literature available for each country is provided by the 'Guides to Further Reading' which conclude each volume.

2. See, for example, Philippe Contamine, *L'état et les aristocraties: XIIe-XVIIe siècle: France, Angleterre, Ecosse* (Paris, 1989); B. Köpecki and E. H. Balázs, eds, *Noblesse française, noblesse hongroise, XVIe–XIXe siècles* (Budapest and Paris, 1981); Armgard von Reden-Dohna and Ralph Melville, eds, *Der Adel an der Schwelle des Bürgerlichen Zeitalters 1780–1860* (Stuttgart, 1988); G. Delille, ed., *Les noblesses européennes au XIXe siècle* (Milan and Rome, 1988).

accompanied by a widespread recognition of the élite's crucial importance in all areas of human activity: social relations, political and religious life, central and local government, cultural patronage, even economic enterprise. Though this renaissance has been apparent from the Ancient World to the twentieth century, it has been especially evident in the study of the early modern period. It is unnecessary to be an apologist for the *ancien régime*, far less to be eager for its return, to recognize the crucial and wide-ranging importance of Europe's nobilities during the seventeenth and eighteenth centuries.

This shift no doubt owes something to the carousel of historical fashion: many topics experience periods of neglect followed by bouts of popularity and intensive study. But the current revival has far more fundamental causes. A major stimulus has been the re-evaluation of 'absolutism', with the recognition that traditional institutions and the élites who dominated them continued to play an important rôle in government throughout the early modern period. In many ways, however, the question is not why the nobility is once again in fashion, but why it was so seriously neglected, and for so long. Here the nobility's apparent eclipse during the twentieth century and even, to some extent, during the nineteenth as well, has exerted an important influence on subsequent historiography. Historians tend to study success, though this preference can often be subconscious. By that yardstick, the relative neglect of the nobility may be comprehensible for later modern history, but it is much less so for earlier centuries. It is difficult to escape the conclusion that the European nobility has suffered from an established tendency to write the whole of the continent's history in terms of economic progress, and the accompanying and irresistible advance of the middle class to social, economic and political power. The nobility has all too often seemed an anachronism in an industrial and democratic society, a reminder of a world that has been lost, and this has contributed to its neglect by modern scholars.

The topic poses certain other problems. All historians depend, to a very great extent, on the accidental survival of sources and especially written records. Here the situation regarding Europe's élite is contradictory. On the one hand, more records are likely to be available than for subordinate social groups, above all the peasantry. At the same time, however, the nobility presents source problems all of its own. The papers of many families simply do not survive, or where they do either remain inaccessible or have not been adequately catalogued, or are in fragmentary form.[3] This is usually due to chance, but sometimes to the dispersal and even deliberate destruction of records. It is especially the case in France, where the Revolution of 1789, with the destruction of seigneurial archives and the noble

3. For the barrier this presents to the study of the nobility, see for example the comments of Miguel Artola in his prologue to I. Atienza Hernández, *Aristocracia, Poder y Riqueza en la España Moderna: la Casa de Osuna, siglos XV–XIX* (Madrid, 1987): a study that was possible because when the family experienced acute difficulties in the nineteenth century, the twelfth Duke sold its papers (to raise much-needed cash!), and they ended up in the Archivo Historico Nacional in Madrid.

emigration that followed, caused particular problems. The Peninsular War and the later civil war in Spain both destroyed and dispersed valuable source material for the study of the Spanish élite. Similar difficulties were created by the political upheavals in Russia during and after 1917. These problems over sources have been exacerbated by later political developments, which have often contributed to the subject's neglect. One especially obvious example is the way that the nobility could not be studied directly in the USSR for more than seventy years after the Bolshevik Revolution of 1917:[4] as throughout Communist eastern Europe for four decades after 1945, until the disintegration of the Soviet bloc in 1989. This has been an especial barrier to our knowledge of the East European nobilities, to which the second volume of this collection is largely devoted. Here Western scholars, who have not been subject to the same political and ideological pressures, have been in the forefront of research.

In another sense, however, there is also the very opposite problem: too many studies of the nobility, but of the wrong type.[5] Traditionally, there had been two principal ways of writing about the European nobility. Family histories have been the most common. The nineteenth and early twentieth centuries were the heyday of works of family pride, with the publication of significant numbers of books inspired and frequently actually written by a descendant. Understandably such works celebrated the achievements of the house in general and glorified individual ancestors.[6] They were often principally and even entirely genealogical in nature. Though they have to be used with caution, they contain much valuable information and should certainly not be neglected, and they have continued to be produced, though in smaller numbers, until the present day.[7] The later nineteenth and twentieth centuries also saw some significant political and institutional studies of the nobility.[8] For the early modern period, these tended to focus on relations between the emerging modern State and the traditional social élite, who often appeared in the guise of inevitable victims of an irresistible historical process. These books suffered from perspectives that were blinkered and incomplete, rather than entirely flawed, and they too contributed to a developing understanding of the nobility.

The modern scholarly study of the European nobility, however, goes back no more than sixty or seventy years, and it has flourished especially during the past two decades. The inter-war period saw the established form

---

4. Cf. Professor de Madariaga's comments: Volume II, Chapter 8.

5. See, for example, the comments of Jean Meyer, that the available literature is both vast and – with the exception of a handful of titles – at the same time mediocre in nature: *La noblesse Bretonne au XVIIIe siècle* (2 vols, Paris, 1966), i. p. xxi.

6. For example, Jacob Falke, *Geschichte des Fürstlichen Hauses Liechtenstein* (Vienna, 1868–82).

7. For example, Fürst Karl zu Schwarzenberg, *Geschichte der reichsständischen Hauses Schwarzenberg* (Neustadt an der Aisch, 1963).

8. For example, G. d'Avenel, *La noblesse française sous Richelieu* (Paris, 1901) and E. Schwenke, *Friedrich der Grosse und der Adel* (Burg, 1911).

of historical writing, that of political narrative, slowly give way to the method of structural analysis, and an accompanying broadening of the range of topics studied by historians. This facilitated an increasing interest in the subject of nobility. Sir Lewis Namier's celebrated investigation of the political influence of the landed classes in mid-eighteenth century England was the best known of a series of analyses of the composition and rôle of élites which appeared in English during the 1920s and 1930s. In France the importance of the topic of nobility and the ways in which it could best be investigated were set out by Marc Bloch, the great historian and co-founder of the *Annales*, in a seminal article published in 1936.[9] Among continental scholars, one central text was Otto Brunner's *Land und Herrschaft*, the first edition of which was published in 1939.[10] Brunner's celebrated book was in the forefront of a widespread reaction against traditional legal and constitutional history, which focused almost entirely on the rôle of the monarch and of the State. Instead he emphasized the importance of lordship, in its widest sense, and redirected attention away from institutions and the centre to the nobility and the localities. *Land und Herrschaft* did much to establish the approach of the following generation of continental scholars and its influence has remained considerable until the present day.

The study of the European nobility has been firmly established by the explosion of research and publication during recent decades. The subject has been and continues to be approached in a plurality of ways, partly due to differences in national historical traditions and to the relative availability of sources. But certain broad problems and perspectives can be identified. One fundamental problem is that in most continental countries, the size of the early modern élite makes detailed and reasonably comprehensive studies of entire national nobilities very difficult and probably impossible, except within narrow geographical or social boundaries. Even if a reliable and extensive documentary base could be found, such studies are only feasible for relatively small élites, such as the Venetian nobility or the British peerage.

The past generation has seen certain broad types of detailed study establish themselves, though the distinctions between these are often blurred and the amount of overlap can be considerable. The first builds on the traditional concern with the fortunes of an individual family to produce scholarly studies of the trajectory of one noble House, often over an extended period of time. Outstanding recent examples of this *genre* are

---

9. *The Structure of Politics at the Accession of George III* (London, 1929); 'Enquêtes sur la noblesse', *Annales* 8 (1936), 238–55 and 366–78. Two review articles provide a helpful introduction to recent writing: Carlo Capra, 'La nobiltà europea prima della Rivoluzione', *Studi Storici* 18 (1977), 117–38, which provides a perceptive survey of work on the eighteenth-century nobility down to the mid-1970s; and K.-G. Faber, 'Mitteleuropäischer Adel im Wandel der Neuzeit', *Geschichte und Gesellschaft* 7 (1981), 276–96, devoted to publications of the 1970s.

10. For Brunner's influence, see the illuminating 'Translators' Introduction' to the recent translation (by Howard Kaminsky and James Van Horn Melton): *'Land' and Lordship: Structures of Governance in Medieval Austria* (Philadelphia, Pa., 1992), pp. xiii–lxi.

Ignacio Atienza Hernández's study of the changing fortunes of the Castilian House of Osuna across four centuries; Grete Klingenstein's examination of the rise at the Habsburg Court of the Moravian ministerial family of Kaunitz; Pierre Hurtubise's survey of the Salviati and their rise and fall at the Papal court; and Tommaso Astarita's monograph on the Caracciolo di Brienza in Spanish Naples.[11] These and similar works are broadly socio-economic in focus, paying considerable and occasionally overwhelming attention to the landed power base, but also finding space for some examination of leading members of the family. The particular merit of this approach is that it recognizes that the crucial unit of the early modern élite – and thus for its historian too – is the noble family, or House, which inspired the actions of individuals and provided the framework within which these took place.

Linked to this approach, though far less numerous, have been biographical studies of one especially prominent nobleman. A notable example is Rohan Butler's panoramic biography, still in progress, of the duc de Choiseul, who rose to be France's leading minister from 1758 until 1770.[12] Such studies, admirable in themselves, have tended to be more concerned with the individual's life than with his rôle within the nobility. They depend on the survival of adequate documentation and for this reason have mostly been of members of the aristocratic élite or the higher nobility. Occasionally, however, the fortuitous survival of sources has enabled a member of the lesser nobility to be examined in detail. The classic example here is Otto Brunner's remarkable study of the life and ethos of a member of the *Ritterstand* (knights or lesser nobility) of Lower Austria, Wolf Helmhard von Hohberg (1612–88).[13] In this case, Hohberg's authorship of the so-called *Georgica Curiosa* enabled Brunner to reconstruct the social and cultural milieu of a nobility in the twilight of its days. The case of Helmhard von Hohberg, however, is quite exceptional, and his world can only be reconstructed so minutely because of the unique nature of the available sources.

Studies of particular families are now less common than monographs devoted to regional nobilities or to prominent groups within a particular élite. In each case, the size of the nobility selected for investigation is such that, given adequate sources and an extended period of research time, a reasonably comprehensive investigation can be undertaken. French historians have been in the forefront of this approach. This is both because of the prevailing fashion for the regional monograph during the generation after the Second World War, under the influence of the *Annales* school of historians, and because the large-scale French *doctorat d'état*, only recently superseded, provided the space and time essential. The first such study,

11. *Aristocracia, poder y riqueza en la España moderna: la casa de Osuna, siglos XV–XIX; Der Aufstieg des Hauses Kaunitz: Studien zur Herkunft und Bildung des Staatskanzlers Wenzel Anton* (Göttingen, 1975); *Une Famille-Témoin: Les Salviati* (Vatican City, 1985); *The Continuity of Feudal Power* (Cambridge, 1992).

12. *Choiseul, Volume I: Father and Son, 1719–1754* (Oxford, 1980).

13. *Adeliges Landleben und europäischer Geist* (Salzburg, 1949); see Professor James Melton's essay, Volume II, Chapter 5.

and the model for those that followed, was Jean Meyer's remarkable thesis, published in 1966 and devoted to the nobility of eighteenth-century Bretagne. Other examples of this *genre* are Jean Nicolas's study of the Savoyard élite, Jean-Marie Constant's work on Beauce and, most recently, Calixte Hudemann-Simon's thesis on eighteenth-century Luxembourg (then part of the Austrian Netherlands).[14] These and similar works devote particular attention to the internal composition and demographic evolution of the élite and to its social position and economic activities. This approach has not been entirely the preserve of French historians. Heinz Reif's impressive and large-scale study of the Catholic nobility of Westphalia at the end of the early modern period and Eila Hassenpflug-Elzholz's statistically-orientated analysis of the mid-eighteenth century Bohemian nobility adopt a very similar approach.[15] On a more modest canvas, Dutch and American scholars have also produced socio-economic studies of regional or local élites.[16]

A broadly similar method has been that of focussing upon an especially important group within the nobility. Once again, the manageable size of the group studied and the availability of source material are important considerations. An outstanding example of this approach is Jean-Pierre Labatut's social study of the aristocratic élite of seventeenth-century France, the *ducs et pairs*.[17] Two American scholars of early modern Russia have adopted this perspective: Robert O. Crummey in his excellent monograph on the seventeenth-century *boyar* aristocracy and Brenda Meehan-Waters in her examination of the *generalitet*, the members of the first four divisions in Peter the Great's Table of Ranks.[18]

The final approach, which has become especially prominent during the past two decades, has been to study the élite's distinctive ethos and to explore changes in the concept of 'nobility' during the early modern period. This makes considerable use of contemporary literary evidence, and views the nobility through a socio-cultural lens. It also employs certain anthropological categories, above all the concern with identifying value-systems. The foremost exponent is the French scholar Arlette Jouanna, and this perspective has also been adopted by Italian and North American

14. Jean Nicholas, *La Savoie au XVIIIe siècle: noblesse et bourgeoisie*, 2 vols (Paris, 1978); Jean-Marie Constant, *Nobles et paysans en Beauce au XVIe et XVIIe siècles* (Lille, 1981); Calixte Hudemann-Simon, *La noblesse Luxembourgeoise au XVIIIe siècle* (Paris, 1985).

15. *Westfälischer Adel 1770–1860: Von Herrschaftsstand zur regionalen Elite* (Göttingen, 1979): it should be noted that this contains a significant amount of material on the decades *before* 1770; *Böhmen und die böhmischen Stände in der Zeit des beginnenden Zentralismus* (Munich-Vienna, 1982).

16. For example, H. K. F. van Nierop, *The Nobility of Holland: from Knights to Regents, 1500–1650* (1984; English trans., Cambridge, 1993); James B. Wood, *The Nobility of the Election of Bayeux, 1463–1666* (Princeton, NJ, 1980); Jonathan Dewald, *The Formation of a Provincial Nobility: the Magistrates of the Parlement of Rouen 1499–1610* (Princeton, NJ, 1980).

17. *Les ducs et pairs de France au XVIIe siècle* (Paris, 1972). Janine Fayard's model study of the Councillors of Castile adopts a similar approach: *Les membres du Conseil de Castille à l'époque moderne (1621–1746)* (Geneva and Paris, 1979).

18. *Aristocrats and Servitors: the Boyar Elite in Russia, 1613–1689* (Princeton, NJ, 1983); *Autocracy and Aristocracy: the Russian Service Elite of 1730* (New Brunswick, NJ, 1982). For the *generalitet*, see Volume II, Chapter 8.

historians.[19] These divisions are no more than broad categories and certainly are not mutually exclusive. Indeed, the best research is usually informed by a plurality of approaches: as, for example, in Maria-Antonietta Visceglia's remarkable studies of the traditional nobility of the Kingdom of Naples.[20]

The advances in our knowledge and understanding of the early modern nobility during this past generation have been very striking. Yet surprisingly little of this scholarship is accessible to an English-speaking readership, while the undoubted excellence of the detailed studies cannot hide the absence of a general picture of Europe's élite at a crucial point in its evolution. There appears to be no reasonably comprehensive and up-to-date study of the early modern nobility in any European language. Two pioneering syntheses were published in French in the 1970s, but both were very Francocentric and are now beginning to show their age.[21] The only comprehensive treatment of the eighteenth century is provided by a vintage collection of essays, but this is even older and inevitably is now seriously outdated in the information it contains and the approach it embodies.[22]

The present collection aims to fill this gap and to present an up-to-date picture of Europe's nobilities during the seventeenth and eighteenth centuries. By integrating the increasingly plentiful specialist research into studies of national élites, it seeks to carry forward the subject. The last generation has established certain broad approaches to the study of the nobility, and these are followed in the individual essays.

Certain limitations can be indicated at the outset. One has already been referred to in passing. This is that sources for the middle and especially upper ranks of the nobility are always likely to be more plentiful and our knowledge of these groups far more detailed and exact than of the much more numerous – though usually less important – lower nobility, which is difficult to study in any depth. The national essays are throughout more detailed on the aristocracy and the higher nobility, for whom the surviving evidence is always more abundant. A second limitation arises from the unequal state of development in the study of particular national nobilities. In certain countries, the scholarly study of the élite is still in its infancy.[23]

19. See especially Jouanna's thesis, *L'idée de race en France au XVIe siècle et au début du XVIIe siècle* (3 vols, Lille, 1976; reprinted in 2 vols, Montpellier, 1981) and her more broadly focused *Le devoir de révolte: la noblesse française et la gestation de l'Etat moderne, 1559–1661* (Paris, 1989); cf. André Devyver, *Le sang épuré: les préjugés de race chez les gentilhommes français de l'Ancien Régime (1560–1720)* (Brussels, 1973); C. Donati, *L'idea di nobiltà in Italia, secoli XIV–XVIII* (Bari, 1988); Neuschel, *Word of Honor*, Ellery Schalk, *From Valor to Pedigree: Ideas of Nobility in the Sixteenth and Seventeenth Centuries* (Princeton, N. J., 1986).

20. See especially *Il bisogno di eternità: Comportamenti aristocratici a Napoli in età moderna* (Naples, 1988) and *Territorio, feudo et potere locale: Terra d'Otranto tra Medioevo ed età moderna* (Naples, 1988) and her numerous articles.

21. Jean Meyer, *Noblesses et pouvoirs dans l'Europe d'Ancien Régime* (Paris, 1973); Jean-Pierre Labatut, *Les noblesses européennes de la fin du XVe siècle à la fin du XVIIIe siècle* (Paris, 1978).

22. A. Goodwin, ed., *The European Nobility in the Eighteenth Century: Studies of the Nobilities in the Major European States in the Pre-Reform Era* (London, 1953). A lightly-revised second edition was published in 1968.

23. Though there are even here some valuable recent contributions. The Southern Netherlands is a particularly interesting example: see Paul Janssens, 'L'évolution de la noblesse belge', in *idem* and L. Duerloo, *Armorial de la noblesse belge du XVe au XXe siècle*, vol. I (Brussels, 1992), pp. 17–28, which is a trailer for a major study by the same author of *La noblesse belge depuis la fin du moyen âge*.

This is especially true in Portugal, and explains why this collection contains no study of the Portuguese nobility. Finally, considerations of space mean that certain topics can only be dealt with in outline or have been neglected altogether. The principal *lacunae* – both the result of an editorial decision – in the national surveys that follow are the nobility's rôle in and links with the various European Churches, and its cultural activities, especially its rôle as artistic patrons.

One established theme of recent writing about the early modern nobility has been the manifold problems which it faced. Some historians have spoken of a seventeenth-century crisis of the élite, while others have seen a long-term decline in the face of the Leviathan State and the rising middle class which was a preparation for its subsequent eclipse. The nobility's problems during the seventeenth and eighteenth centuries have been viewed as the consequence of three interlocking developments. The first was economic, with a short-term and sometimes acute period of difficulties for the finances of many families during the seventeenth century and, in the longer perspective, a shift in the balance of wealth, which moved away from an increasingly indebted élite and towards the rising middle class. The nobility has been seen as losing its traditional authority: politically, to the centralizing State that was coming into existence at this time, socially to other groups in the community. Finally, the nobility has been viewed as having undergone a severe crisis of identity, as the moral basis of nobility itself was undermined. The élite suffered a collective loss of self-confidence and purpose, as its prestige waned and its political, economic and military rôles were undermined. This was compounded by its own failure to equip itself with the education that was essential if it was to retain power in a changing world.

The essays in this collection provide very limited support for such a pessimistic prognosis. Individual families and even whole sections of the nobility clearly experienced real economic difficulties, particularly during the seventeenth century, but the élite as a whole surmounted these problems and prospered during the decades of renewed economic expansion which followed (see below, section IV). The military and administrative changes at this time did not destroy the nobility's political rôle: on the contrary, in important respects it consolidated and even extended this (see below, section V). The ideological challenge would ultimately prove to be the most serious. Yet until the Enlightenment began to question the whole basis of privilege and the inequalities which sustained it, the notion of nobility itself rarely came under direct attack: except, of course, during the English Revolution of the mid-seventeenth century. The House of Lords had been abolished in 1649 and was restored at the Restoration of 1660 (this volume, Chapter 2). This was quite exceptional, at least until the French Revolution. Though in the longer perspective the doctrine of natural rights and the political changes which this inspired would eventually undermine the nobility, they had made next to no progress before 1800. The essays which follow make clear that the most appropriate descriptions of the élite's fortunes during these two centuries are not 'crisis' and 'decline', but 'consolidation' and 'transformation'. Whatever political, social and economic difficulties the nobility had faced in the decades since 1600, by the later-eighteenth century they were everywhere not only firmly entrenched but perhaps even in a more powerful position. The means by which noble power was consolidated and perpetuated provide the dominant themes in the essays that follow.

II

The concept of nobility had its origins in the celebrated, though idealized and somewhat theoretical, division of medieval society into three orders or Estates. Since the central Middle Ages the nobility's *raison d'être* – the justification for its privileged position in state and society – had been that it was the fighting class (*defensores* or *bellatores*). Whereas the First Estate, the clergy, prayed and the Third Estate worked (to provide for the other two in their more essential tasks) the Second Estate provided protection and military muscle. In some languages the very words for 'nobility', or parts of it, derived from this military function: for example, *cavalieri* (Italian), *chevalerie* (French) and *riddarskapet* (Swedish). The European nobility thus consisted originally of the men on horseback, the mounted knights who had formed the backbone of medieval armies. In return for this military service the nobles had been rewarded by lands and by certain political and social privileges, and slowly evolved into a separate group within society: a noble order had come into existence in France by the end of the twelfth century and throughout much of Europe by the end of the fourteenth century. Its origins were primarily, though not exclusively, military, and were accompanied by a distinctive lifestyle.

These notions remained alive in the early modern period. A good definition of what it meant to 'live nobly' was provided by the Dutch observer, Wouter van Gouthoeven, in 1620. 'Nobles', he declared, had to live

from their own income from lands, tithes and manors, and [refrain] from mercantile activities, and in particular shopkeeping; but practising war and serving in the Prince's court, or in some honourable office, and owing the country and other two [orders] protection with their weapons against the violence or attack of enemies, provided that they have commission from high authority.[24]

Noble status was acquired primarily by birth. Though this status was essential, however, it was not sufficient: it had to be defended and upheld

---

24. Quoted by van Nierop, *The Nobility of Holland*, p. 33.

by the maintenance of a lifestyle that was self-evidently noble. The nobility was further distinguished by being the only social group entitled to use titles, such as count, or duke, or prince. The importance of these designations would increase during the seventeenth and eighteenth centuries, as will be seen. Yet the essays in this collection make clear that, even in 1800, only a minority – and sometimes a very small minority – of the Second Estate possessed titles. In every continental country most members of the nobility were untitled, and distinguished only in nomenclature by the right to employ the operative participle: 'de' in French, 'von' and 'zu' in German. These and similar designations were the marks of simple nobility.

Another important badge of noble status was the ownership or occupation of landed estates. Yet though land and nobility often went hand in hand and new or aspiring noblemen were always keen to secure such property, the connection was far from exclusive. The nobility was always an important and sometimes a dominant landowner, but the king and the Church were also likely to control substantial estates. More importantly, many members of the lesser nobility all across Europe owned no landed property, though this in itself was not a barrier to the maintenance of their noble status. The attractions of a landed estate and the social and economic power that this conferred were, however, considerable and their possession everywhere the aim of the nobility as a whole.

The problems of terminology have aroused extended and sometimes heated debates, though these have so far been inconclusive. In particular whether the nobility can be accurately described as a 'class' remains to be proved, especially in view of the assumptions that now surround that term about the economic determination of social status. In the seventeenth and eighteenth centuries the 'nobility' was a distinct group within society distinguished primarily by the social and legal privileges which it enjoyed and by its position as an important and often dominant landowner. Terms such as 'order' or 'Estate' seem much more satisfactory than 'class' to describe this élite. The early modern nobility, moreover, was distinguished from the various élites that have existed at different periods of human history and in different countries and continents by the hereditary nature of its position and power. Noble status and wealth were transmitted across the generations by inheritance and did not depend upon external political and economic circumstances. These might change, but at least until the very end of the eighteenth century such alterations exerted little influence upon the position of the European nobility as an élite.

Nobility was thus essentially a status that was hereditary and one that conferred important privileges that were political, juridical and social in nature.[25] These privileges attached both to a nobleman's person and to his property. They were unequally distributed throughout the nobility as a

---

25. Here the best introduction is the remarkably comprehensive survey by Michael Bush, *Noble Privilege* (Manchester, 1983).

group. All noblemen and noblewomen possessed certain privileges: this was what distinguished them from the rest of society. But within the nobility the more powerful and wealthy individuals possessed additional privileges. These were often honorific in nature, such as the monopoly of certain titles or forms of clothing, or the right to be addressed in a particular way, and they marked out a hierarchy with the nobility itself. These privileges varied significantly in incidence and importance from one country to another and between regions of the same country, as the national essays make clear. The principal exception was Russia, where the nobility only secured the rights and privileges that their counterparts in other countries had long enjoyed in 1785 through Catherine II's celebrated Charter (in volume II, Chapter 8).

Noble privileges were many and varied. One important category was political in nature. These guaranteed the nobility's right to participate in and, in practice, to dominate public life. Where representative assemblies or Estates survived and continued to meet during this period, they were almost everywhere dominated by noblemen who either attended in person or chose a deputy as a representative. In most European countries, certain public offices were reserved for the nobility, either legally or in practice, while the élite also enjoyed preferential promotion to many other posts in government. Less formally, rulers all across Europe continued to consult the nobility both as individuals and as a group, and this practice survived down to 1800 and far beyond. Noblemen were long seen as the natural counsellors of kings and a source of authority within society at large.

The second kind of privileges were judicial in nature. Here there was a measure of variation from country to country. In general terms, however, the nobility was not subject to the same legal system and courts as the unprivileged groups within society. A nobleman accused of a crime could often claim special legal treatment. He would be tried in a separate court usually composed of his peers and, upon conviction, would be subject to a different range of punishments. If convicted of murder, or another capital offence, he could claim decapitation (usually by a sword) rather than hanging, which was the fate meted out to common criminals. A nobleman also enjoyed important privileges in civil law and often could not, for example, be successfully sued by his creditors: an important privilege for an élite that, during the seventeenth and eighteenth centuries, was increasingly indebted. Finally, the nobility itself played an important and continuing rôle in the administration of justice. In some countries nobles served in public law courts and other tribunals, but much more significant was their rôle in providing justice at the provincial and local level. Noblemen continued to supervise and sometimes actually to administer much of the law in their own locality to a surprisingly late date.[26] The growth of State-administered justice, and the codification of law which accompanied

26. See, for example, the recent study by Steven G. Reinhardt, *Justice in the Sarladais 1770–1790* (Baton Rouge, La., 1991).

this, were important developments during the early modern period. But though these trends limited the scope of private justice they certainly did not eradicate it. Until 1800 and beyond, noblemen continued to hold their own courts, now increasingly staffed by their own lawyers, and to admin-ister justice as they had long done. This was one dimension of a wider lordship which they exercised over their tenants and neighbours and which conferred considerable social prestige as well as bringing important income in the form of the profits of justice.

A third group of privileges were essentially fiscal. The most important, and also the most celebrated, was the nobility's supposed exemption from direct taxation. This has been a fertile source of misunderstanding and exaggeration, largely because of the success of the French nobility in de-fending its exemption from the *taille personnelle* (the principal direct tax in large areas of France) and the alleged rôle of this privilege in bringing about the Revolution of 1789. In fact, the fiscal position of the European nobilities was much more complex and generally less favourable to the élite. It also varied significantly between countries, and even within indi-vidual states, as the national essays make clear. Much depended on the nature of the fiscal system, and the élite clearly did not enjoy a generalized exemption from direct taxation. One crucial difference was between tax-ation of land and taxes levied on the person. A nobleman was much more likely to pay the former. Exemption from direct taxation was important and, where it existed, a significant privilege, but it was far from universal. The Second Estate, moreover, was not the only group within society to enjoy fiscal privileges, though it was the most important. During the sev-enteenth and eighteenth centuries some of the nobility's fiscal exemptions were undermined by financially hard-pressed States. Even where these priv-ileges survived, they were becoming more of a badge of social status than a real financial advantage by the closing decades of the eighteenth century.

The final group of privileges were social in nature. These were both a matter of law and of custom, and collectively they marked out the élite as a distinct and dominant group within society. Everywhere nobles pos-sessed and exercised extensive rights to hunt over the lands of their neighbours, tenants and peasants. A nobleman was often the only member of society who was legally entitled to carry arms in civilian life, in recog-nition of the élite's military origins and continuing rôle as the fighting class. The carrying of a sword remained a badge of nobility and was widely prized during the seventeenth and eighteenth century. It distinguished a nobleman from the common people: significantly, impoverished members of the nobility of Poland-Lithuania carried wooden swords as a symbol of their status, even though they were too poor to be able to acquire steel sabres.[27] The nobility alone were entitled to wear certain kinds of clothes, a privilege that was sometimes guaranteed by sumptuary legislation.

27. N. Davies, 'The Military Traditions of the Polish *Szlachta* 1700–1864', in B. K. Király and G. E. Rothenburg, eds, *War and Society in East Central Europe*, vol. I: *Special Topics and Generalizations on the 18th and 19th Centuries* (New York, 1979), pp. 37–46, at p. 43.

Noblemen could display their coats of arms, for example over the portals of their residences or on their carriages. They had the right to be addressed in particular ways: one of the most celebrated was the rise of the 'don' in seventeenth- and eighteenth-century Spain (this volume, Chapter 6). They alone could acquire designations of simple nobility (for example, 'von' in the German-speaking lands) and the higher titles (such as duke or count or baron) which were introduced or became more widespread throughout Europe during the early modern period. The nobility had a privileged position in any religious or secular ceremony or procession in which they took part. In church, for example, they would normally have their own pew and even private box or gallery, located prominently next to the pulpit and below the altar in order to underline their place at the top of the social hierarchy. Where – as often happened – more than one noble family attended the same church, fierce and prolonged disputes over precedence were common.[28]

The importance of such pre-eminence in a society in which visual impressions were all-important is obvious enough. At the local level, the nobility had a further series of privileges which were an important source of revenue and which largely proceeded from their dominant position as landlords and seigneurs. In certain countries, theoretically they alone among social groups possessed the right to own land, but this privilege was being eroded during the seventeenth and eighteenth centuries, when a small number of commoners clearly purchased estates. Noblemen, however, secured important income and privileges from their pre-eminent position as landowners. They could compel their tenants to use their mill, or oven, or wine-press, and to pay for the privilege. Local noblemen often possessed a monopoly over local hunting and fishing rights and over the natural resources of the estate, such as minerals. They also possessed important rights over their tenants, who were sometimes unable to move or to marry without the lord's permission. These were part of the wider lordship which the nobility had traditionally exercised over society at large and which it continued to enjoy.

These privileges belonged both to the nobility as individuals and as an Estate. The individual nobleman or noblewoman, however, was everywhere subordinate to the demands of the wider family or house. This is one of the dominant conclusions of recent scholarship concerning the early modern nobility, and it is crucial to any understanding of the subject. During the later modern period and especially the twentieth century, possessive individualism has come to the fore in all areas of human activity. By this is meant the pursuit of personal ambition and advancement, often at the expense of family cohesion and group solidarity, arising out of the central rôle played by economic considerations. The situation in the early modern period was quite different, especially among the élite for whom the

28. See the interesting article by Jan Peters, 'One's Place in Church: hierarchical attitudes in the Late Feudal Period', of which an abbreviated English translation was published in G. G. Iggers, ed., *Marxist History in Transformation: East German Social History in the 1980s* (New York and Oxford, 1991), pp. 161–87.

individual was always a representative of a wider grouping and where his – or her – interests were everywhere expected to take second place to those of relatives and of family and to advance the position, wealth and influence of the wider group or house. The overriding goal was always the success of the family and the increase of its fame and fortune – whether by an advantageous marriage, a successful military or political career, or simply the skilful management of the estates. A younger son might be deprived of an expected share of an inheritance, or pushed into the Church or army at someone else's expense, a daughter packed off to a comfortable seclusion in a nunnery, each prevented from marrying because family strategy dictated this course of action. Success and failure would determine the trajectory of the family within the nobility. The ultimate disaster, of course, was extinction: the 'name and arms' of the house ceasing to exist through a failure of heirs and especially of its male children.

This was a greater threat than might at first be realised. Since – except in Britain – all legitimate children of a nobleman were noble – and occasionally, as in Spain, illegitimate offspring too – the transmission of status and property should have been relatively secure. Usually, however, nobility descended primarily in the direct male line. This, together with the familiar demographic uncertainties of the early modern period, made succession a much less certain business. The pitfalls are graphically illustrated by the case of a Dutch nobleman, Johan Wolfert van Brederode (1599–1655). Brederode married twice and fathered no less than twenty-one children: twelve by his first wife, Anna Johanna, countess of Nassau-Siegen; and nine by his second bride, Louise Christina, countess of Solms-Braunfels. Such fecundity, it might be thought, would have ensured the survival of the House of Brederode. In fact, the outcome was very different. Seven of his twelve children by his first wife died in infancy; the remaining five were all daughters. His second marriage produced nine children: two did not survive infancy, four died around the age of twenty; and only three survived. Two of these were daughters, leaving a solitary son, Wolfert, to perpetuate the line. But Wolfert died childless in 1679 and took one of Holland's leading noble families to the grave with him.[29]

The extinction of the House of Brederode underlines both the fragility of the links between one noble generation and the next and the importance of extinction as a threat to the entire Second Estate. Though most of the nobility should have enjoyed better nutrition than the common people and with it an improved chance of survival and procreation, the hazard of childbirth and the threat of disease were ever-present in the early modern period and did not respect social hierarchies. Biological failure, that is to say the extinction of an entire family or House, was a permanent and ubiquitous danger for members of the Second Estate. Rates of such failure varied both from one country to another and within national nobilities. In

29. Van Nierop, *Nobility of Holland*, p. 65. The Brederode property presumably descended through the female line.

England, of sixty-three peerage families in 1559, only twenty-two with direct descent in the male line remained a century later, while in the duchy of Savoy, the rate of extinction may have been as high as 37 per cent over the period 1702–87.[30] Figures like these could be produced from all over Europe.[31] This was an especial problem for nobilities starved of new entrants: for example, the élite of the Dutch Republic after 1579, of Venice for much of the early modern period and of Denmark before 1660: in each case, a sharp numerical decline is visible (this volume, Chapters 3 and 7; Volume II, Chapter 3). But all noble families lived under the permanent threat of extinction, and for many it became a reality.

Such biological failure was not, of course, new: the typical noble family of later medieval France had seldom lasted longer than three or four generations in the male line.[32] It was not entirely the outcome of biological chance, though that clearly had much to do with it. Extinction also resulted from a number of demographic variables: the frequency and age of marriage, and the rates of fertility and child and adult mortality. Conscious choice also played a part. Many families, especially among the higher nobility, adopted strategies to overcome the economic difficulties which they faced during the later-sixteenth and early-seventeenth centuries (see below, section IV). These could actually increase the chances of extinction, though their objective and – in most cases – their effect was the reverse. The widespread adoption throughout much of southern and parts of central Europe of entail and primogeniture entrusted the family patrimony to one male relative, usually the eldest son.[33] This was often accompanied by a strategy of restricted marriage, by which younger sons and all the daughters might be prevented from leading an independent life and especially stopped from marrying. In this way primogeniture, by concentrating all the family's future prospects on the small number of males who did marry, heightened the importance of the fertility of particular unions and actually increased the possibility of extinction.

The individual chapters make clear that – with some important exceptions – the total numbers in national nobilities increased, sometimes quite sharply, over the seventeenth and eighteenth centuries as a whole, in line with the rapid expansion of the general population. Yet this expansion should not disguise the reality of extinction which faced many families at this time. This was a ubiquitous threat but not a universal fate. Many Houses whose nobility originated before 1600 survived and prospered into the nineteenth century and beyond. The expansion of the élite, however, was made possible by constant replenishment, with the entry of new families into the nobility. As families became extinct, others replaced them,

30. L. Stone, *The Crisis of the Aristocracy, 1558–1641* (Oxford, 1965), p. 769; Nicolas, *La Savoie au XVIIIe siècle*, i. pp. 21–2.

31. There are some good examples in M. Bush, *Rich Noble, Poor Noble* (Manchester, 1988), p. 97.

32. E. Perroy, 'Social mobility among the French noblesse in the later middle ages,' *Past and Present* no. 21 (1962), pp. 21 *et seq.*

33. See below, pp. 33–5, for more on this.

underlining once again that the Second Estate was itself constantly undergoing change. Such replenishment was crucial to the consolidation of noble power, and highlights the importance of the ways in which nobility itself could be secured.

Noble status could be acquired in a number of ways. The most important, which has been referred to already, was also the simplest: through birth. On the continent all the legitimate children – female as well as male – of a nobleman were themselves noble and occasionally illegitimate descendants too, while in certain countries and under particular circumstances a noblewoman could also transmit her privileged status to her children. The situation in Britain was rather different. Here only the eldest son of a nobleman received his father's status, the other children being in law commoners unless the family possessed additional titles which passed to one or more younger sons. This was quite exceptional in the context of continental Europe, where a father's noble status passed to all his legitimate children.

The second way in which nobility could be acquired was from a ruler, either by grant or sometimes purchase. During the seventeenth and eighteenth centuries, rulers continued to reward meritorious service by a patent of nobility or by advancing a nobleman within the élite through the award of a title or a higher rank than he possessed. The principal routes to such ennoblement continued to be military or administrative service. During the later seventeenth and early eighteenth centuries, monarchs in Denmark, Sweden and Russia in particular formalized this practice through the creation of Tables of Rank, the best known of which was introduced by Peter the Great in Russia in 1722 (Volume II, Chapters 2, 3 and 8). These tied noble status to service to the ruler and State, and provided that any individual who reached a particular rank in the army or grade in the administration would automatically be ennobled. Privileged status could also be acquired by purchase, either of a patent of nobility, of land that conferred noble status or by buying an ennobling office. This attracted a good deal of unfavourable comment from contemporaries, but the number ennobled in this manner was usually a relatively small proportion of the total. It was, however, of considerable importance in France where the numbers who secured the status of *noblesse de robe* were considerable, reflecting the scale of the sale of such *charges* and the way in which the system became systematized after the introduction of the *paulette* at the beginning of the seventeenth century (this volume, Chapters 4 and 5). The outright sale of nobility itself was much rarer in seventeenth- and eighteenth-century Europe. Occasionally a financially hard-pressed ruler would sell a favoured applicant the status of noble or a title which allowed him to rise within the élite. These were exceptional, and went almost invariably to individuals and families deemed well worthy of the honour in the first place.

The final way in which nobility might be acquired was by assuming the status and lifestyle of a noble and hoping it would be acknowledged by other members of society. A commoner who had acquired some wealth or land, or aspired to a position of standing within his local community, would simply begin to behave like a nobleman: by carrying a sword, by wearing noble dress, by claiming some of the other privileges of nobility and so forth. If he was able to secure acceptance of this status and especially of the privileges which accompanied it, particularly entry to the ranks of those who were exempt from taxation or other burdens imposed by the State, he might be able to establish himself as a member of the local lesser nobility and, in certain countries such as Spain, have his status formally acknowledged by a law court. The growing emphasis during the early modern period upon maintaining a noble lifestyle facilitated this way of entering the lesser nobility, which was in any case very difficult to detect. A man who was prepared to leave his own immediate locality and take up residence elsewhere would often be able to establish a claim to noble status in this way, especially if he possessed – or could pretend to – experience of military service: the connection between arms and nobility was still crucial. The essays in this collection suggest that the assumption of noble status was especially common in countries such as France and Spain, where the fiscal privileges of nobility were especially valuable, and in other countries which had a large and ill-defined lower nobility, such as Poland-Lithuania and Hungary. In certain states, the revenue lost to such 'false nobles' led the government to institute enquiries into the noble status of families within a particular region: these were especially common within seventeenth-century France, the so-called *'recherches de la noblesse'*, and within the eighteenth-century Habsburg Monarchy. Both rulers and the nobilities themselves were keen to prevent impostors securing noble status and in this way undermining the concept of nobility. Yet it was extremely difficult to prevent a wealthy and skilful commoner slipping into the lesser nobility and even rising within it: the barrier between the Second Estate and the rest of society was always permeable.

The reverse of this was the question of how and under what circumstances a nobleman might fall out of the élite. There was always a steady exodus out of the nobility and in the second half of the eighteenth century, this river became a torrent: it has recently been suggested that as many as one-third of the entire European nobility disappeared during the century after 1750.[34] Once again, such movement was largely concentrated at the bottom end of the nobility, with considerable movement out of the lesser nobility into the ranks of the commonalty. In the French province of Bretagne, for example, the size of the Second Estate dropped by perhaps as much as a half between around 1660 and the eve of the French Revolution, from some 40,000 to 20,000–25,000.[35] By far the majority who lost their élite status did so more or less willingly and largely because they were unable to support the lifestyle demanded of a nobleman. Even if the poverty of a member of the lesser nobility might be relative when

34. G. Delille, 'Introduction', in *idem.*, ed., *Les noblesses européennes au XIXe siècle* (Rome-Paris, 1988), pp. 1–12.

35. J. Meyer, 'La noblesse française au XVIIIe siècle: aperçu des problèmes', *Acta Poloniae Historica* 36(1977), 21–2.

considered against that of a peasant, it was still a formidable barrier for many lesser noblemen faced with the costs of supporting the style of life demanded by their status. Another way in which a member of the lesser nobility might fall out of the Second Estate was by contracting a marriage that was 'unworthy', that is to say, with a commoner. The conclusion of a *mésalliance* would often deprive a nobleman or noblewoman of their status and many who contracted such unions willingly dropped out of the nobility. This was strengthened by the growing preoccupation with lineage and untainted descent during the seventeenth and eighteenth centuries, especially but not exclusively in western Europe.

There were several other ways in which noble status might be lost, all involving action by the State. One has already been mentioned: the *recherches de la noblesse* by which the hard-pressed French State, especially during the seventeenth century, sought to reduce the number of 'false nobles' and the accompanying loss to the treasury of direct taxation. This became a significant factor in the numerical decline of the nobility during the following century, when both the Spanish and Austrian Habsburg governments also began to investigate and thus to challenge the nobility of significant numbers of the élites throughout their territories. In a more general way, it is clear that the early modern period saw an increasing body of legislation defining the nobility more precisely than medieval law codes had done and thus laying down what members of the Second Estate could – and could not – do. The actual impact of these new laws, however, is less easy to establish with any certainty.

A good example of this is provided by the concept of derogation. In theory, any nobleman who engaged in certain kinds of activities, principally commercial, put his noble status in jeopardy. Many States had or acquired such legislation during this period. Yet the practical effect of these legal provisions is less easy to establish. In the first place, noble status was often suspended, rather than forfeited altogether, and it could be recovered relatively easily. In some places – for example, Bretagne – a nobleman intending to establish or recover his family's fortunes by a successful career in commerce could put aside his noble status and simply resume it when convenient. The essays in this collection suggest that formal laws of derogation were neither a universal nor a very effective threat against noblemen engaging in commercial activities of all kinds. Indeed, as Dr Thompson points out, it is probably not legitimate to suggest a dichotomy between land and economic and commercial activities of all kinds.[36] It was always accepted that a nobleman could exploit his own landed estate, which in itself was likely to involve commercial activities of certain kinds. Many noblemen supported commercial enterprises and invested in a variety of financial opportunities either openly or through an intermediary, and very few suffered loss of status because of this.

One traditional way of losing noble status was becoming a thing of the

36. Below, pp. 229–32.

past during the seventeenth and especially the eighteenth centuries. This was through rebellion or treason. Occasionally this could still be a factor of importance. The unsuccessful Bohemian rebellion against the Austrian Habsburgs in 1618–20 led to significant numbers of the Kingdom's nobility losing their lands, their status and, in some cases, their lives, while many others were forced into obscure exile. This was followed by a significant reconstitution of the Bohemian élite, with the ascent and sometimes the arrival of many noblemen devoted to the House of Habsburg (Volume II, Chapter 5). A generation later, the English Civil Wars of the 1640s inflicted surprisingly little damage, at least in the long term, on the peerage (this volume, Chapter 2). Simultaneously, a significant minority of the Portuguese nobility remained loyal to Madrid during the extended rebellion (1640–68) by which Portugal regained its independence after sixty years of union with Spain. Though this group lost lands and were forced into exile, some of its members were subsequently rewarded by the Spanish king with grants of titles and of lands. A generation later, during Spain's War of Succession, some Castilian nobles – including four grandees of the first class – suffered for choosing the wrong side in the struggle between Habsburg and Bourbon at the beginning of the eighteenth century.

Such cases were becoming exceptional, and underlined that domestic politics were everywhere now less violent, as the nobility's own military power was reduced.[37] By the eighteenth century, noble rebellion had almost become a thing of the past. Treason was also now extremely rare, and seldom led to the permanent loss of noble status. The most celebrated case was that of the Portuguese Houses of Aveiro and Tavora, who were jointly implicated in an attempt to assassinate King José in 1758.[38] The retribution inflicted was severe: their estates were confiscated, their arms and residences destroyed, the very name of the Tavora temporarily expunged. Yet the family survived: Portugal's leading minister during the third quarter of the eighteenth century, the marquis of Pombal, who had himself carried out the judicial proceedings, subsequently married one of his daughters into the Tavora House. This highlighted a general trend: though individuals would occasionally suffer a severe fate for treason and occasionally rebellion, their families would frequently survive and, in time, flourish again. Nobility was too precious a plant for a single stem to be destroyed simply because one bud had failed to blossom.

The attempted regicide was significant in a second respect. During its severe judicial aftermath, members of the two noble Houses involved were treated with especial brutality. The duke of Aveiro and the marquis of Tavora were both broken on the wheel, their arms and legs being crushed, without first being strangled. The remaining members of the family who

---

37. See below, pp. 42–3, for more on this.

38. Kenneth Maxwell, 'Pombal: the paradox of enlightenment and despotism', in H. M. Scott, ed., *Enlightened Absolutism: Reform and Reformers in Eighteenth-Century Europe* (London, 1990), pp. 75–118, at p. 100.

were implicated were also broken on the wheel, but were first put to death. Such treatment was not unfamiliar in eighteenth-century Europe, but for common criminals, and not leading aristocrats, and the sentences were for that reason widely condemned. The episode underlined the extent of the privileges the nobility possessed and expected to enjoy: even when convicted of the crime of treason.

III

In 1600, the European nobility was the product of an evolution which extended back over five or six centuries, yet it was still in a state of flux. The nobilities of individual States were often surprisingly heterogeneous, reflecting the varied ways in which the status of nobility could be and had been acquired: this diversity is apparent in the essays which follow. The two principal paths into the nobility are best illustrated by the case of the Italian peninsula (this volume, Chapter 7). There was a traditional nobility created by service – and especially military service – to a sovereign, rewarded by grants of land, rights of lordship and other privileges, and a separate noble élite which had evolved out of the urban patriciates. The latter path was relatively unimportant outside Italy. Yet this is not the same thing as saying that the nobility was exclusively or even predominantly to be found in the countryside. One general conclusion of significance is that the world of the noble spanned town and country: particularly in the more urbanized parts of Europe, a significant proportion of the nobility ordinarily lived in towns. The possession of a landed estate and the rural lifestyle which accompanied this were, however, everywhere widely seen as desirable badges of noble status: determinedly defended by their fortunate owners, avidly sought by those who lacked them. Indeed one key development, for example in later sixteenth- and seventeenth-century Italy, was a search by the urban patriciates for landed property, where they might cultivate what they saw as the attributes of true nobility.

One conclusion which emerges from the national essays is that the European nobility was not evenly distributed, either between individual countries or within particular States. Each national élite had been shaped by a distinct historical evolution and this influenced both its size and composition. The individual essays provide such figures as are available for the size of particular nobilities, both numerically and as a proportion of that State's total population. In view of the significant variations between countries, any attempt to aggregate these totals to produce a figure for Europe as a whole would be misleading. There was rather a spectrum, ranging from those States – Britain, Denmark, Brandenburg-Prussia – where the nobility amounted to less – and sometimes much less – than 1 per cent of the total population, to the countries whose élites were a much higher proportion: in Hungary the corresponding figure was 5 per cent, in Po-land-Lithuania between 6 and 7.5 per cent, while in Spain it was even higher and at its peak may have approached 10 per cent. The remaining countries were located somewhere between these two extremes. One gen-eral conclusion of particular interest is that everywhere, as more detailed research is undertaken on the demography of the nobility, employing fiscal and other records, previous estimates are having to be revised downwards.

The Second Estate was not a consistent proportion of the population in a second important respect. It was never distributed evenly throughout a particular society. Within individual countries there were always signifi-cant regional variations. In early modern Spain noblemen were much more numerous in the north and relatively scarce in some areas of the south, because of the Iberian peninsula's distinctive historical evolution (this vol-ume, Chapter 6). Though this was the extreme case, the nobility was everywhere unevenly spread geographically. In parts of central and eastern Europe, it had been particularly easy to secure the status of noble, as medieval rulers sought to encourage colonization and settlement of inhospitable regions: this was why both Eastern Pomerania in Brandenburg-Prussia and Mazovia in Poland-Lithuania contained whole villages composed largely and occasionally entirely of impoverished nobles (Volume II, Chapters 4 and 7). There were parts of Poland-Lithuania, however, where noblemen were extremely scarce.

The nobility everywhere resembled a pyramid, though the steepness or otherwise of the sides varied according to the characteristics and the com-position of the particular élite. At its apex were a small number of wealthy and powerful families who together composed an aristocracy. Originally this word, of Greek derivation, had simply meant 'rule by the best'. But during the eighteenth century, it was increasingly used to describe the noble élite, in the sense of an order with immense social and political privileges.[39] This was an index of a process that was underway by which the élite of the nobility became more sharply differentiated from the middling and lesser nobility. At the very top of the noble pyramid there were a handful of magnate families enjoying immense wealth and power: sixteen in Hung-ary, around ten in the Austrian and Bohemian Lands, between twenty and forty in Spain. Below these came the rest of the aristocracy and higher nobility, families whose wealth and political influence were considerable. Though the aristocracy as a whole would retain some influence in at least one locality, its horizons were always national rather than regional. Below them were to be found the middle ranks of the nobility: families of stand-ing in their particular locality, but whose ambitions and perspectives occasionally moved upwards to the national level. The base of the pyramid would everywhere consist of a numerous and sometimes impoverished lesser nobility, whose interests seldom extended far beyond their own region and many of whom even lacked land. These divisions were fluid,

39. Jonathan Powis, *Aristocracy* (London, 1984), pp. 6–7.

yet are fundamental to an understanding of the structure of Europe's nobilities. In 1600, the élites in the western and southern European States were structurally rather more complex, with more levels separating the aristocratic élite from the mass of petty nobility, than those of countries lying to the north and east, reflecting their longer and more varied evolution. By 1800, however, the contrast was less clear cut, and the nobilities of central and eastern Europe in particular became increasingly stratified.

Though these horizontal divisions were important, there was always significant movement within the Second Estate. The rise and fall of individual families was a permanent feature, and it was probably more important than the movement into and out of the nobility which was discussed earlier. During the seventeenth and eighteenth centuries, the principal development, apparent in all European countries to some extent, was the increased degree of stratification within the nobility, with the aristocracy everywhere emerging as more wealthy, more powerful and more sharply differentiated from the rest of the nobility. This was often assisted by the State, which believed it could reinforce its own authority by elaborating the social hierarchy over which it presided. But it resulted primarily from the success of individual families in securing land, wealth and the political power that everywhere accompanied these and in this way rising out of the ranks of the nobility into the aristocratic élite.

The rivalries of individual families divided the nobility vertically, especially its middle and upper ranks. Emphasis on the elements which united the Second Estate – in particular, shared privileges and a common ideology – does not mean that it was a unified body. On the contrary: it was rather an aggregation of rival and fiercely competitive individuals, families and houses.[40] The great and middle-ranking nobility were engaged in a continuous struggle for advancement and a search for additional status and new economic and political opportunities for themselves and for their followers. Those families that were successful in this quest moved up the noble hierarchy, and the most successful entered the more clearly defined aristocratic élite that was emerging at this time.

In most countries, this élite was also distinguished and sometimes defined by its monopoly of certain hereditary titles. These were not of course an innovation in the early modern period, but they did become much more important and widespread. This is exemplified by the development of the title of 'duke' in England. Until the Glorious Revolution of 1688, this had been seldom granted, and then usually to members of the royal family or to particular favourites of the ruler of the day. Thereafter it was granted much more freely to favoured members of the peerage and helped to advance the stratification of the English nobility (this volume, Chapter 2). On the continent new titles were introduced and

---

40. For a striking recent demonstration that this was so, see the remarkable article by David Parrott, 'Richelieu, the *Grands*, and the French Army', in J. Bergin and L. Brockliss, eds, *Richelieu and his Age* (Oxford, 1992), pp. 135–73. This makes clear the sheer extent of the competition among leading families for commands in the army.

old ones revived or employed more freely, while simultaneously a more clear-cut hierarchy was taking shape, with a progression upwards from baron and count through earl and duke to the exalted, and very rare, status of prince. The possession of such ranks helped to differentiate the higher nobility from the rest of the Second Estate. The grant of a title was often a way for an impoverished ruler to reward a nobleman at little cost to himself, and this accelerated their diffusion at this time.

There were exceptions to this trend: the only titles in early modern Poland-Lithuania either had Lithuanian or Ruthenian origins or were foreign in origin. In neighbouring Russia the situation was particularly complex, with native princes but no other hereditary titles until Peter I sought – not altogether successfully – to introduce these as parts of his thoroughgoing attempt to create a Western-style nobility (Volume II, Chapters 7 and 8). In countries such as Sweden, Denmark and Brandenburg-Prussia, indigenous titles seem to have been a relatively late innovation and one that was of limited significance (Volume II, Chapters 2, 3 and 4). Elsewhere, however, they increased in number and in importance during the seventeenth and eighteenth centuries.

Titles were – as they had long been – a way of rewarding meritorious service and recognizing power and wealth. During the seventeenth and eighteenth centuries, however, they increasingly became a way of favouring and, at the same time, distinguishing the aristocratic élite and simultaneously advancing the growing internal stratification of the nobility. The classic example of this trend was the rise of the *ducs et pairs* in seventeenth-century France.[41] Successive kings sanctioned and, in some measure, created an élite of wealth and power at the top of the French nobility through the grant or extension of the title of *duc* and the privileges associated with this, together with gifts of lands and, occasionally, cash to the especially favoured (this volume, Chapter 4). A broadly similar process was underway in Spain, too, with the rapid increase in the number of grandees from forty-one (in 1627) to over 100 by the early eighteenth century (this volume, Chapter 6). Titles were everywhere important as a public mark of a family's power and achievements and of the esteem in which it was held. Promotion in the established hierarchy of titles was eagerly sought by families engaged in the ceaseless search for power and advancement. There was an element of social engineering in this: rulers such as Louis XIV were motivated in part by a desire to create a more stratified hierarchy both within the aristocratic élite and within the nobility as a whole.

The granting of such advancement, moreover, recognized an existing hierarchy more than creating a new one. It was very rare for a commoner and even a member of the lesser nobility to be honoured in this way. The award of a higher title was usually a simple recognition of social and political reality and of the distribution of wealth and power. It acknowledged a family's growing importance and, sometimes, its economic might, more

41. The fundamental study is Labatut, *Les ducs et pairs*.

than contributing to its rise. A notable example of this is provided by the Eszterházy family, whose seventeenth-century ascent from minor and impoverished Hungarian nobles to great aristocrats was the most remarkable success story of the age. It was brought about by a mixture of matrimonial and political skill, loyal service to the House of Habsburg and the rewards that brought, principally in the form of lands. This was climaxed in 1687 when a grateful Emperor created the Palatine Pál Eszterházy a prince of the Holy Roman Empire.

This section has emphasized the vertical and horizontal divisions within the early modern nobility and has outlined the different degrees of status, power and wealth. These were undoubtedly significant and became more so during the two centuries after 1600. Yet, at the same time, the European nobilities were also remarkably unified social groups, particularly in their dealings with other sections of society. The very concept of nobility was a powerful adhesive. By marking out who was, and therefore who was not, 'noble', it imparted considerable unity to the Second Estate. The process of consolidation was advanced by the development of clientage and patronage links among all Europe's nobilities during the early modern period. By this is meant a series of personal ties and networks that ran vertically through the noble élites in particular of all continental countries. These had existed in earlier periods, primarily for the purpose of self-defence. They now became more elaborate and extensive, and concerned principally with the advancement of nobles great and small. One element in the power of the great aristocrats was the links they established and cultivated with the middle and, indirectly, lower ranks of the nobility. An aristocratic patron would secure social and professional opportunities and advancement for his clients, who in return would provide loyalty, support and, sometimes, payments in cash or kind. This relationship was reciprocal, and it was continually nurtured by the distribution of all manner of favours and advantages to a patron's noble clients in the localities. These opportunities could take many forms: a fortunate marriage, a gift of lands, entry into or advancement within the army, government or (where this was present) the Roman Catholic Church. These vertical bonds did much to unify the Second Estate, and they were everywhere the means by which national aristocracies maintained important links with the regional nobilities.

IV

Wealth was an important accompaniment of nobility, enabling families to live nobly and so uphold their privileged status. Noble descent was only to be valued if accompanied by a life style that was visibly noble. Economic success was not essential, but economic failure might be fatal to a noble House. Individual families were concerned primarily to support that life style and thus their social position, and to maintain the lineage indefinitely. This meant that consumption was usually more important than production where their own finances were concerned, and long-term stability more important than short-term growth. The patrimony and the other sources of a family's income were valued principally for their ability to produce the income essential to maintain that lifestyle: be it the expenses of a marriage or a funeral (two occasions on which splendour would be essential to emphasize the honour and power of the family) or the cost of a dowry or a military commission for a younger son. Family finances were administered with these conservative and traditional ends in view, rather than the capitalist priorities of later centuries.[42]

Both collectively and individually, the nobility was the wealthiest group in society in every European country, with the important exception of the Dutch Republic. During the seventeenth and eighteenth centuries, there was surprisingly little change in the sources of that wealth, which remained overwhelmingly landed in origin and character. This is not to say that the élite was uninterested in commerce, finance or manufacturing: as has been seen, derogation was seldom much of a barrier to such activities, particularly by the eighteenth century. Their very wealth, moreover, often made nobles the only group within society with sufficient capital available for investment. Yet the principal origin of that wealth was always land, and the major element in noble fortunes, the estates which they controlled and exploited, together with the income generated from their rights of lordship. The importance of land for the élite makes the willingness of the Swedish aristocracy to submit to Karl XI's resumption of alienated Crown estates all the more remarkable (Volume II, Chapter 2). Though the scale of these transactions remains to be established, the episode is a unique example of significant losses of land by the nobility during the two centuries covered by this collection. Indeed, the nobility were usually anxious to increase the estates under their control. The Second Estate had done well out of the distribution of Church lands at the Reformation in the sixteenth century, while throughout the early modern period individual nobles successfully incorporated peasant holdings into their own properties on a considerable scale.

The economic health of the nobility as a group during the seventeenth and eighteenth centuries is a subject of crucial importance, yet one where satisfactory generalizations are especially difficult and perhaps impossible. Too often the short-term problems of one family have been used to support speculative theories about the entire élite. There is also a need to view developments in the long-term, where the resilience of individual families and the nobility as a whole is impressive. A family experiencing financial problems at one point could, a generation or two later, once again be prospering. A good illustration of this is provided by the changing fortunes of the Neapolitan Caracciolo di Brienza. This family experienced an extended period of economic difficulties during

42. See, for example, Atienza Hernández, *Aristocracia, poder y riqueza*, pp. 291 ff.

the second half of the seventeenth century, but recovered spectacularly during the following century. As landowners the Caracciolo – like most noble Houses – benefited from the eighteenth-century boom associated with population growth and price inflation.[43] Though some impressive studies have been published, there is still a need for much more detailed research into the finances of individual families and the economic circumstances of particular groups within national nobilities. One considerable barrier to such investigations is the paucity of surviving records, especially for families outside the higher nobility.[44] Even where the sources for such a study exist, the obstacles in the way of exploiting these records are still considerable.[45] Nevertheless, some tentative conclusions about the subject of noble finance are becoming possible. Once again, much more detailed information is likely to be available for the aristocratic élite than for other groups within the nobility, for whom generalizations are more problematical.

Different groups were clearly affected in different ways, while the chronology of decline and recovery also varied significantly, in line with the highly regionalized structure of the European economy as a whole. This is why it is impossible to be at all precise about the chronology of decline and recovery, since these varied not merely from country to country and region to region but from family to family. All that can be said with any certainty is that many noble families experienced periods of acute economic difficulties during the century after c.1580, and that the fortunes of the nobility as a group improved significantly during the extended period of economic expansion and increased prosperity which began in the decades around 1700. Throughout the nobility, moreover, individual families were prospering, maintaining their position or declining during this period not only or even principally because of economic factors. The trajectory of an individual noble House would frequently be determined not by trends in the economy but by variables such as the succession of a spendthrift heir or of a family head who was financially astute. Biological chance also played its part. Too many daughters, with dowries to be paid upon marriage or entry to the Roman Catholic Church, might help to undermine a family's finances. Conversely, too many sons who had to be launched on a career or provided with portions could impair the fortunes of a noble House. But these might also be retrieved – sometimes in the most spectacular fashion – by a son's fortunate marriage or dazzling success in military or State service, with the rewards these might bring.

There is, however, significant and accumulating evidence that in many countries sections of the nobility were facing serious economic problems

43. Astarita, *Continuity of Feudal Power, passim.*

44. This is a general problem facing all historians of the nobility: see, for example, Atienza Hernandez, *Aristocracia, poder y riqueza*, pp. 234–6; van Nierop, *The Nobility of Holland*, p. 96.

45. See, for example, the comments of Daniel Roche, 'Aperçus sur la fortune et les revenus des Princes de Condé à l'aube du XVIIIe siècle', *Revue d'histoire moderne et contemporaine* 14 (1967), 217–43, at 218–20.

in the decades around 1600.[46] One established explanation was that these difficulties were a delayed consequence of the sixteenth-century rise in prices, particularly of foodstuffs. The élite was squeezed between increasing costs, which resulted both from this inflation and from its own soaring expenditure, and incomes that were stable and sometimes decreasing. Its revenues were often fixed (particularly in the form of long-term leases of land) and could not easily be raised to cover the new costs. These problems were compounded by the widespread economic instability apparent during the later sixteenth and first half of the seventeenth century, with the end of the long period of economic and demographic expansion, stable prices and general prosperity. Members of the lesser nobility were particularly adversely affected and, in some countries, faced major economic difficulties by the decades around 1600.

One region where this was clearly the case was Lower Austria. Noble landowners, most of whom received over two-thirds of their incomes in the form of fixed feudal rents, services and other dues, were severely affected by the cumulative impact of the sixteenth-century Price Revolution. Unable to profit from the prevailing high prices for agricultural produce (since so little of their income came in that form), the nobility of Lower Austria, and especially the lesser nobles and younger sons, experienced severe problems between around 1580 and 1620.[47] These problems were exacerbated by the accompanying demographic expansion, which increased the numbers of landless nobles. By the final decades of the sixteenth century, significant numbers of poorer nobles in particular were facing severe economic problems all across Europe. The same broad process was underway in other countries such as Denmark and Scotland. In both the lesser nobility was trapped between incomes that were stable and even

46. These difficulties led an earlier generation of scholars to argue for a widespread economic 'crisis' of the nobility at this time. This was seen as part of the broader problems it faced during the century after c.1550, and was stimulated both by the response of continental scholars to the publication of Lawrence Stone's celebrated *The Crisis of the Aristocracy* in 1965 and by the simultaneous debate on the 'General Crisis of the seventeenth century'. The later 1960s and early 1970s saw several works on the 'crisis' experienced by individual national nobilities at this time, such as E. Ladewig Petersen, *The Crisis of the Danish Nobility 1580–1660* (Odense, 1967) and Davis Bitton, *The French Nobility in Crisis 1560–1640* (Stanford, Cal., 1969); there is a valuable and sceptical survey by François Billaçois, 'La crise de la noblesse européenne (1550–1650): une mise au point', *Revue d'histoire moderne et contemporaine* 23 (1976), 258–77. It is clear that sections of the nobility in many European countries experienced real economic difficulties at this time: see, for example, Charles Jago, 'The "Crisis of the Aristocracy" in seventeenth-century Castile', *Past and Present* no. 84 (1979), 60–90, and below, Chapter 6, for Spain. But such problems were far from universal and they inflicted surprisingly little lasting damage on the nobility as a whole. The prevailing trend in research is rather to emphasise its vitality and capacity to adjust to difficult circumstances: see, for example, the comments of Arlette Jouanna, *Le devoir de révolte*, pp. 92–8, on France, and van Nierop, *The Nobility of Holland*, pp. 93–6. A recent contribution to the 'crisis' literature is an essay on the Habsburg Monarchy by Thomas Winkelbauer, 'Krise der Aristokratie?: Zum Strukturwandel der böhmischen und niederösterreichischen Ländern im 16. und 17. Jahrhundert', *Mitteilungen des Instituts für Österreichische Geschichtsforschung* 100 (1992), 328–53.

47. Karin J. MacHardy, 'The Rise of Absolutism and Noble Rebellion in Early Modern Habsburg Austria, 1570 to 1620', *Comparative Studies in Society and History* 34 (1992), 407–38, esp. 411–15. On the decline of the lower nobility, see also the same author's 'Der Einfluss von Status, Besitz und Konfession auf das politische Verhalten der Niederösterreichischen Ritterstandes 1580–1620' in G. Klingenstein and Heinrich Lutz, eds, *Spezialforschung und 'Gesamtgeschichte'* (Wiener Beiträge zur Geschichte der Neuzeit, 8; Vienna, 1981), pp. 56–83. See below, Volume II, Chapter 5.

declining (as grain prices fell) and outgoings that were rising sharply.[48] Yet this trend was far from universal, nor in itself a complete explanation for the undoubted economic problems of many noble families at this time.

In the first place, there was widespread use of short-term leases, with rents which could readily be raised. A high proportion of noble income and sometimes the majority was likely to be paid in kind, and this offered some protection against inflation. The sale of agricultural surpluses, received as rent or dues, or produced by direct farming, also helped to cushion the nobility against increases in its own expenditure. One especially noteworthy example is provided by the Junkers of Brandenburg-Prussia who had prospered throughout the sixteenth century and continued to do so until the 1620s (Volume II, Chapter 4). Their wealth was based very largely on the profitable sale and export of grain, mainly produced by demesne farming involving serf labour, and was only undermined by the widespread destruction of the Thirty Years War, which devastated central Germany and Brandenburg in particular.[49] The economic problems of the Junkers owed everything to the dislocation and destruction caused by this fighting and to the residual problems after it ended in 1648. Yet that same conflict also enabled some Junkers to rebuild their fortunes through successful careers as mercenary soldiers. The near-continuous warfare of the later sixteenth and seventeenth centuries enabled many families to retrieve their economic position: many of the 'Military Enterprisers' active in Germany during the Thirty Years War were noblemen. The long period of civil war in France between 1562 and 1598, for example, exemplified exactly this combination of opportunities for enrichment and severe damage to the incomes of individuals and families caused by the disruption of their established agricultural profits.[50] This underlines once again that the fortunes of individual families and of groups within the nobility were determined by national and local factors as well as by European trends.

More important, however, is the growing consensus that the nobility's economic problems around 1600 were caused primarily by the new scale and purposes of expenditure being undertaken, especially but not exclusively by the aristocratic élite, rather than by the erosion of incomes by inflation. These soaring costs had several origins. The transformation of warfare during the early modern period (see below, section V) was accompanied by increased outlays on the part of every noble officer. Military careers might and sometimes did yield significant income, but the investment demanded had gone up substantially.

Changes in noble lifestyles were even more important. Conspicuous consumption, undertaken especially by élite families, in order to keep up

48. Petersen, *The Crisis of the Danish Nobility 1580–1660*, esp. pp. 25–7; Keith M. Brown, 'Aristocratic finances and the origins of the Scottish Revolution', *English Historical Review* 104 (1989), 46–87, esp. 51–9.

49. William W. Hagen, 'Seventeenth-century Crisis in Brandenburg: the Thirty Years' War, the destabilization of serfdom and the rise of absolutism', *American Historical Review* 94 (1989), 302–35; see Volume II, Chapter 4.

50. See the contributions by Philip Benedict and Mark Greengrass to Peter Clark, ed., *The European Crisis of the 1590s: Essays in Comparative History* (London, 1985), pp. 84–105 and 106–34.

appearances, was widespread. The importance now placed upon maintaining a lifestyle that was self-evidently noble was apparent in all these expenditures. By the decades around 1600 nobles were building more resplendent country residences, often with ornate – and costly – gardens, while the tendency for the higher nobility, particularly in France and Spain, to reside at or near to the royal Court for at least part of the year involved the running costs and sometimes the construction of a second major residence in the capital. A similar process was underway in the British Isles, where the Union of the Crowns in 1603 was followed by the migration of prominent Scottish aristocrats to James VI and I's Court in London. Though this brought new wealth, in the form of royal patronage and economic opportunities, it also increased expenditure sharply, and drawing up an overall balance sheet is difficult.[51] At the end of the seventeenth century, a similar evolution can be seen in the lands of the Austrian Habsburgs (Volume II, Chapters 5 and 6). The Austro-Bohemian aristocracy and, to a lesser extent, the Hungarian magnates were drawn to the Court in Vienna, where they built impressive town houses and then suburban palaces. Residences, entertainments, even clothes: all were becoming more resplendent and therefore expensive, particularly throughout western Europe.

Individual families and sometimes whole groups of the nobility were clearly experiencing significant financial problems throughout the later sixteenth century and the first half of the seventeenth century. The nobility, moreover, was not immune from the general economic difficulties of these decades, with – at the very least – the ending of the sixteenth-century expansion and the prosperity that it had brought. Yet the Second Estate, and especially the aristocratic élite, were frequently better placed than other groups to cope with these problems. This was principally because of their access to new sources of income and, more important, to credit, which often came from fellow noblemen. Spain provides a notable example of this. The first half of the seventeenth century saw something approaching a 'crisis' of the Monarchy's nobility. Most families overcame these problems, however, mainly at the expense of the State, by diverting its fiscal income into their own pockets and by extensive borrowing frequently facilitated by the Crown (this volume, Chapter 6). During this period borrowing and the resulting debts became an important feature of family finances across much of Europe and an important factor in the apparent prosperity of the higher nobility. Throughout Europe, the higher nobility benefited from the new financial and economic opportunities offered by the monarchical State. Pensions and cash gifts went to a favoured minority,[52] but land and advantageous economic opportunities were more widely distributed, while the salaries and other income available to the agents of the expanding State

51. Brown, 'Aristocratic Finances', esp. pp. 63–4; see now the same author's more detailed examination, 'The Scottish Aristocracy, Anglicization and the Court, 1603–38', *Historical Journal* 36 (1993), 543–76.

52. See, for example, their importance for the Bourbon-Conty during the eighteenth century: François-Charles Mougel, 'La fortune des Princes de Bourbon – Conty: revenus et gestion, 1655–1791', *Revue d'histoire moderne et contemporaine* 18 (1971), 30–49.

structures (section V) benefited the nobility not least. This access to the Court and the central government was also instrumental in securing essential loans, which were crucial in enabling the noble élite to survive the economic difficulties of the seventeenth century. The price of this survival all over Europe was a growing interdependence between rulers and their élites.

The nobility as a whole, and especially the aristocracy, prospered during the long economic recovery which began during the second half of the seventeenth century and continued almost until the end of the period covered by this collection. The downturn which had set in around 1600 now gave way to a renewed and, before long, spectacular period of expansion and prosperity. Prices stabilized and soon began to increase, trade and economic activity started to expand once again, and population rose. The nobility was well placed, as producers and landlords, to benefit from this recovery. Though the fortunes of individual families rose and fell, the nobility as a group did relatively well out of the long period of prosperity. Their estates were either farmed directly or leased out to tenants: here there was considerable variation from country to country and even from region to region, as the national essays make clear. The chapters in the second volume qualify the familiar emphasis on the distinction between western Europe and the lands lying to the east of the river Elbe. They make clear that throughout central and eastern Europe, demesne farming based on serf labour was certainly important, but it was far from universal. Here, too, some parts of the noble estate were leased out, rather than exploited directly by means of a subject peasantry.

At the top of the noble pyramid, the power of certain families was truly immense. A few individuals – notably the Eszterházy princes in northern Hungary and several magnate families, such as the Radziwill, in the eastern regions of Poland-Lithuania – ruled over what were in effect private kingdoms and maintained their own administrations, legal systems and even princely Courts. By the eighteenth century it was increasingly common for aristocratic estates to be professionally administered with the intention of maximizing the income which the family could enjoy. Profligacy and indifference had not been eradicated, but they seem to have become less common, especially among the higher nobility. These land holdings were at times as large as some of the smaller sovereignties within the Holy Roman Empire, and the authority of the ruling aristocrat was scarcely less complete, at least over his own peasants and tenants. Such power was certainly exceptional, but all across Europe, the seventeenth and eighteenth centuries saw the consolidation of great *latifundia*, large tracts of land owned and dominated by the noble élite: be it the feudal baronage in the Kingdoms of Naples and Sicily, the grandees in Spain or the aristocracy of the Austro-Bohemian lands. There were significant exceptions to this, as has been seen, but the general trend is clear.

These vast family estates were rarely territorially consolidated or fully contiguous: the pattern of land-holding in *ancien régime* Europe was a bewildering mosaic of small or medium-sized properties each with different owners. This reflected the impact of political and religious up-heavals, and also of inheritance practices, over several centuries. A territorially compact landholding of any size was difficult to create. One notable example of such consolidation was the Zamoyski entail in Poland-Lithuania, established in 1589. This extended over some 4,000 square kilometres and was located principally in the palatinate of Lublin in central Poland. By the 1770s, its population approached 100,000, with close to 100 manors, more than 220 villages and ten towns.[53] The relative compactness of the Zamoyski landholdings was unusual. The normal pattern was of groups of separate estates scattered across several regions and even different prov-inces. Though a significant proportion of these might lie close to the area where the family had originated and perhaps from where it derived its title, the obstacles to further rationalization were considerable. An outlying property might be sold and the income used to purchase lands closer to the centre of family power, though the higher nobility's increasing adop-tion of the practice of entail was a barrier to such transactions.[54]

The aristocratic owner of such a patrimony enjoyed considerable social and economic power but he was the preponderant influence in these re-gions rather than the sole or even the principal landowner, and he would also own or control many estates at a distance from the centre of his own power. Two examples will illustrate this crucial point. The Eszterházy fam-ily was the largest landowner in eighteenth-century Hungary, and one of the biggest in Europe as a whole. Its estates may have covered as much as one million acres when the first family entail was established in the mid-1690s. There were then no less than thirty-seven separate properties principally in Hungary and Transylvania, but also at Schwartzenbach in Lower Austria. During the eighteenth century, this total declined slightly, due to the alienation of some minor Transylvanian estates, but at the death of Prince Nikolaus the Magnificent (the celebrated Maecenas and patron of Joseph Haydn) in 1790, there were still twenty-nine separate proper-ties.[55] At the other end of Europe, the Spanish ducal House of Bejar, a prominent grandee family, had estates which in the seventeenth century were scattered all across Spain: from Bañares in the far north, close to the French frontier, to Cartaya in the extreme south-west.[56] In both cases, there was a central core of family possessions, together with some widely scattered properties distributed across a much larger area.

This reflected the way in which most great noble estates had been built

53. J. T. Lukowski, *Liberty's Folly: the Polish-Lithuanian Commonwealth in the Eighteenth Century 1697–1795* (London, 1991), p. 26. For the legal device of entail, see below, pp. 33–5.

54. See below, pp. 33–5.

55. János Harich, 'Das fürstlich Esterházy'sche Fideikommiss', *The Haydn Yearbook* 1 (1962), 5–27, at 5; Rebecca Gates-Coon, 'The Esterházy Princes as Landlords: Estate management in Hungary during the late eighteenth century', in *Studies in East European Social History*, ed. K. Hitchins, vol. II (Leiden, 1981), pp. 157–89, at p. 157; a relatively full list of the major properties is given on pp. 168–9 of the same author's unpublished PhD dissertation: 'The Esterházy Princes, 1760–1790' (University of Illinois, 1979).

56. See the map at p. 64 of Jago, 'The "Crisis of the Aristocracy" in Seventeenth-century Castile', *Past and Present* no 84 (1979), 60–90; cf. Nicolas, *La Savoie au XVIIIe siècle*, i. pp. 151–3, for the dispersal of noble lands in Savoy.

up in stages and over an extended period of time. They were created through skilful marriages, fortunate inheritance, shrewd property dealings and, occasionally, donations of land by a grateful ruler. The acquisition of new estates would increase the wealth and power of a noble House and was everywhere a dominant element in family strategy: land usually provided an accurate index of status. This meant that the landholdings of most successful noble families tended to grow, though usually very slowly and over several generations. The consolidation of aristocratic landed power was sometimes assisted and seldom opposed by early modern rulers: only in Russia does there appear to have been an established strategy of seeking to prevent members of the élite acquiring properties close to their existing estates and in this way strengthening their power in that locality.[57] This underlines the fundamental community of interests between royal and aristocratic power, an interdependence that increased during this period.

The consolidation of landed property, evident across most of Europe at this time, illustrates the immense importance of inheritance for the historian of the nobility. Once again, generalizations are difficult and even problematical, in view of the considerable diversity in legal provisions and customary practices evident at this time. There was immense variation not merely between individual territories and provinces, but also within the same region. Yet at the risk of oversimplification, certain broad points can be made about the situation during the sixteenth century. A distinction was made between 'real' (that is to say, landed) property and moveable wealth. With some significant exceptions, all sons would have a right to some share of their father's real property, which would normally be inherited principally and sometimes solely by his male descendants. There was considerable variation in the precise proportions inherited by each son. In Muscovy, for example, a father would divide his lands approximately equally among all his male children, and would also make some provision for his widow and any daughters.[58] This was unusual. It was much more normal for one son (usually the eldest) to inherit the majority of the landed patrimony, with the other male children and, less frequently, any daughters receiving their portions from the remaining estates and the moveable wealth. In a family where there were male heirs, any daughters would secure some share of their father's moveable wealth and in theory would be furnished with the necessary dowry when they married or entered a religious foundation. It was rather less common for daughters to inherit any of their father's land. One country where they did was Poland-Lithuania, where one-quarter of a father's inheritance was set aside to pay his daughters' dowries (Volume II, Chapter 7).

Partible inheritance of real property was an obvious obstacle to the consolidation of landed estates. If strictly observed, it would militate against the creation and survival of noble landed power by enforcing a division of the patrimony every generation. In this way, the continued existence of a

---

57. See Professor de Madariaga's comments: Volume II, Chapter 8.
58. Crummey, *Aristocrats and Servitors*, pp. 35, 113, 116–17, 171.

noble family would itself be threatened, and successive generations forced to engage in a continual scramble for new lands and other sources of wealth. Even before 1600, however, there is clear evidence that such legal provisions were in practice being circumvented. During the later Middle Ages and the sixteenth century, informal understandings and, sometimes, formal agreements were made between the surviving brothers in order to keep the family estate, or, the great part of it, together. A good example of the latter is the *fraterna* or 'fraternal partnership' to be found in the Italian peninsula. The fact that extended families were widespread among the higher nobility also meant that several brothers might continue to reside with the eldest. The strategy of restricted marriage would sometimes accompany such arrangements: as was the case, for example, among the patriciate of the Venetian Republic.[59] In its strictest form, only the son succeeding to the family lands would marry. If he remained childless or fathered only daughters, then another brother might be married, in order to perpetuate the line.

It is impossible to know exactly how widespread such inheritance practices were, even among well-documented families in the higher nobility during the early modern period. The essays in this collection, however, suggest that the creation of large estates and thus the consolidation of aristocratic power during the seventeenth and eighteenth centuries was facilitated by the widespread adoption, particularly among the noble élite, of succession arrangements favouring one son, almost invariably the eldest. This could be achieved by the head of a family customarily favouring the senior male heir in his will, and this was widespread in those regions where inheritance was normally regulated by testamentary disposition.[60] In the much larger areas of the continent where written law prevailed, often with a notably generous allowance for younger children, succession arrangements were increasingly controlled by the formal establishment of an entail, usually accompanied by the adoption of male primogeniture.

The legal device of entail had been familiar during the Middle Ages, but it became much more widely adopted between the mid-sixteenth and the mid-eighteenth century, particularly among the aristocratic élite of many European countries.[61] Simultaneously, nobles and their propagandists argued forcibly against dividing inheritances into ever smaller shares and in favour of some form of male primogeniture. The attraction of entails to the

59. See J. C. Davis, *The Decline of the Venetian Nobility as a Ruling Class* (Baltimore, Md., 1962), pp. 62–72.

60. Notably in areas where Roman law influences were strong: see the recent study by Donna Bohanan, *Old and New Nobility in Aix-en-Provence 1600–1675: Portrait of an Urban Elite* (Baton Rouge, La. 1992), pp. 63–78 *passim*. The father's will was also important in Savoy: Nicolas, *La Savoie au XVIIIe siècle*, i. pp. 373–4.

61. The only attempt at a comprehensive study is the remarkable article by J. P. Cooper, 'Patterns of inheritance and settlement by great landowners from the fifteenth to the eighteenth centuries', in J. Goody, J. Thirsk and E. P. Thompson, eds, *Family and Inheritance: Rural Society in Western Europe 1200–1800* (Cambridge, 1976), pp. 192–327; but this focused especially on England (with some attention to Western Europe) and is in any case now out-of-date. Among more recent historians, the Italian scholar M. A. Visceglia has been especially notable for her emphasis upon the crucial importance of entail. See, in particular, her 'Linee per uno studio unitaria dei testamenti e dei contratti matrimoniali dell'aristocrazia feudale napoletana tra fine Quattrocento et Settecento', *Mélanges de l'école Française de Rome: moyen âge et temps modernes* 95 (1983), 393–470.

higher nobility in particular was that they were a means by which the wealth and thus the glory and renown of a noble House could be secured and perpetuated. The Neapolitan Prince Guglielmo Ruffo di Scilla explicitly declared – when founding a second family entail in 1747 – that 'there is no other means to ensure the splendour of the great Houses than [to provide for] the continuation of their wealth'.[62]

Though there were significant variations in the form, nature and chronological and geographical incidence of entails, certain broad points can be made about their rôle and importance. Technically, an entail was an unbreakable legal trust covering the greater part of a family's landed property and regulating succession to it, usually by male primogeniture. Entails were frequently laid down in wills or marriage settlements. Newly acquired estates could subsequently be added, along with other family income and assets. The heir was not the owner of this patrimony but merely a temporary beneficiary who enjoyed the income during his own lifetime. He was also a trustee who was obliged to administer the property with care and to pass it on to his own heir in the condition that he received it. Only property not covered by the trust could be freely bequeathed by a father, usually to his younger children. Legally an entail, once established, could be broken only with considerable difficulty. This – like the formal creation of such a trust – usually required the ruler's formal sanction. In practice, however, it is clear that entails were not absolutely watertight and that some land was being taken out and sold or otherwise disposed of, while other estates were being added from time to time. Entails were a fertile source of litigation, both by disappointed younger children and by families suing for the full payment of dowries, which was being refused because the assets were protected by a trust. Such arrangements were themselves an effective legal defence of a family's wealth: it was very difficult for creditors to undertake successful court action for the payment of debts against a noble House whose property had been entailed.

Entail was far from ubiquitous, and it was most widely practised among the aristocracy and higher nobility. The national essays make clear that the device was most important in Spain and the Italian Peninsula, where it had existed during the later Middle Ages and became much more widespread in the sixteenth century (this volume, Chapters 6 and 7). Around 1600, entail spread north of the Alps, first to Poland-Lithuania, where a handful of magnate families adopted the device, and then to the Austrian Habsburg territories, where it was much more widely influential (Volume II, Chapters 5 and 7). In Great Britain, a form of entail, the so-called strict settlement, was clearly instrumental in the creation of the great aristocratic landed estates after the Restoration of 1660 (this volume, Chapter 2). Elsewhere, it did not become established to any great extent.[63] Peter I's attempt to introduce it into Russia through his Law of Single Inheritance in 1714 was widely unpopular among a nobility deeply attached to partible inheritance,

---

62. Quoted by Visceglia, 'Linee per uno studio unitaria . . .' p. 423.
63. Though it was important in Portugal, where the holder of an entailed estate was even distinguished by a specific title, that of 'morgado', while his wife was the 'morgada'.

and this measure was revoked after the *coup* of 1730 (Volume II, Chapter 8), while it was not until the nineteenth century that entail was at all widely adopted among the Prussian Junkers. Entails were also a relatively late arrival in Denmark. Legislation to make these possible was enacted after the introduction of absolute monarchy in 1660, as part of the Crown's attempt to create a new nobility of service, and entails were becoming widespread by the eighteenth century (Volume II, Chapter 3).

Further research is needed on the spread and function of entails: as Professor Donati wisely remarks, we must be careful not to exaggerate their rôle until much more detailed information is available.[64] Yet their central place in the consolidation of aristocratic landed power during these centuries seems established. One of the clearest demonstrations of their importance is provided by developments in Bohemia. There, the sixteenth century had seen larger estates continually broken up through the operation of partible inheritance. From around 1600, however, the introduction and rapid spread of the *Fideikommiss* immediately put a stop to this fragmentation. Instead, the seventeenth and eighteenth centuries saw the build-up of the impressive *latifundia* which were the basis of the power of the Bohemian aristocracy in particular (Volume II, Chapter 5). This was exactly why the Prussian king Frederick the Great advocated the practice of entail and unsuccessfully sought to persuade the Junkers to adopt it after the Seven Years War.[65]

The importance of entail underlines that the aristocracies which consolidated their power at this time were, first and foremost, landed élites. The great estates which they owned and exploited provided both income and social power. They also exercised authority in their own regions as the local agents of the king's government and, sometimes, in the central administration, too: here the continuity from earlier periods was striking. This was one dimension of what was always the key relationship: that between the nobility and the monarchical State.

V

One recurring theme of this collection is the extent and continuity of noble involvement at all levels of government. By the eighteenth century and especially the decades after 1750, this was coming to be reduced, as many monarchs acquired an increasing number of trained personnel to assist in ruling their states. Though the nobility's rôle was being diminished, it remained an important element in central and especially local administration in most European countries until the very end of this period. This was

64. See below, p. 255.
65. See his comments in the Political Testament of 1768: R. Dietrich, ed., *Die politischen Testamente der Hohenzollern* (Berlin, 1986), p. 500.

notably true of Spain, where during the seventeenth century the grandees were always influential and sometimes dominant in central government, particularly under Charles II, while their clients among the lesser nobility still controlled municipal administration, though this influence was declining. This situation was transformed after 1700, when the rôle of the Spanish aristocrats was sharply reduced by the new Bourbon régime and by the centralizing reforms it introduced (this volume, Chapter 6). In the States of the Italian peninsula, both the urban patriciates and the landed nobilities continued to play an important administrative role, though in some areas – particularly the Duchy of Milan – this was similarly reduced by centralising reforms introduced during the second half of the eighteenth century by the new Austrian Habsburg régime (this volume, Chapter 7).

In seventeenth-century France, the traditional military nobility (the *noblesse d'épée*) remained formally and informally involved in government, especially through the provincial governorships (this volume, Chapter 4). Indeed, one influential revisionist view has emphasized that the relative strength and success of Louis XIV's domestic régime during the first half of the Sun King's long personal rule after 1661 was due as much – if not more – to the policy of cooperation with established provincial élites as to the recent administrative innovation of the intendancies.[66] The traditional nobility's grip upon the key positions in central government certainly slackened, particularly after 1661, but it was reasserted after Louis XIV's death in 1715. The *noblesse d'épée* were usually well-represented and occasionally dominant in France's eighteenth-century ministries (this volume, Chapter 5). Even in the Dutch Republic, the landed nobility were influential in the local administration of all the provinces apart from Holland (this volume, Chapter 3). By the eighteenth century, Britain's political society was considerably more mature than that of most continental states, with a developing parliamentary system. Yet once again the peers' influence was considerable, both on political life and on central and local government (this volume, Chapter 2). The nobility's administrative rôle was even greater throughout northern, central and eastern Europe, as the essays in the second volume make clear.

This consensus reflects the direction of recent research, which views the relationship between Crown and nobility as one based on mutual dependence and necessary cooperation, rather than rivalry and conflict.[67] Yet it also represents a departure from an established interpretation which had seen absolutism as resting on the defeat of the aristocracy, and had assumed that the nobility as a whole were inevitable victims of the new administrative arrangements introduced at this time. It is certainly true, as will shortly be seen, that by the seventeenth century noble military power

66. William Beik, *Absolutism and Society in Seventeenth-Century France: State Power and Provincial Aristocracy in Languedoc* (Cambridge, 1985), pp. 333–4 and *passim*.

67. See the useful and wide-ranging survey by Jean Bérenger, 'Noblesse et absolutisme en Europe à l'époque de la Contre-Reforme', *Il Pensiero Politico* 11 (1978), 145–68. The notion of the interdependence of noble and State power is now established: see for example, Atienza Hernández, *Aristocracia, Poder y Riqueza*; and Astarita, *Continuity of Feudal Power.*

was ceasing to be much of a threat to the ruler and survived principally in some areas of central and eastern Europe. The seventeenth and eighteenth centuries also witnessed an expansion of government, driven principally by the need to raise the taxes and the men to support the incessant and new-scale warfare of the age. New institutions and novel methods of government enabled rulers to enforce their authority more effectively and to carry out a wider range of functions. These new tasks in turn required those who carried them out to possess more education, or at least training: administration now demanded an increasing degree of professionalism. The chronology and extent of these changes varied from country to country, and their overall impact has been the subject of much discussion: in particular whether they can be described as 'absolutism' in any meaningful sense has been hotly debated. Yet the impact of the administrative expansion on all sections of society cannot be doubted.

One prevailing interpretation saw the key development as being the emergence of bureaucracies, increasingly staffed by men of middle-class birth. This view had its origins in the writings of administrative and institutional historians during the later nineteenth and early twentieth centuries, strongly influenced by the great German sociologist, Max Weber, who saw bureaucracy as one of the principal agents of modernization. It was buttressed by the publication of documentary collections drawn substantially and sometimes exclusively from central State archives. The most notable of these was the celebrated series on the history of the eighteenth-century Prussian administration, the *Acta Borussica*. The result was a view of the early modern State as a centralized bureaucratic structure staffed by professional administrators who were everywhere replacing noblemen as the main agents of royal government.

This view was incomplete rather than totally wrong. It concentrated on central government and on institutions. The most serious omission was the key area of local administration, where only slowly did effective royal agents emerge to carry out decisions taken at the centre. Though the early modern period undoubtedly witnessed the emergence of new administrative agencies staffed by men with more training and from a different social background, such changes were mainly in central government. There were also important continuities from earlier centuries, particularly at the provincial level. There the established administrative structures, dominated by local élites, were in practice only slowly overlaid, and never entirely replaced, by the institutions of the emerging absolutist State. In seventeenth- and eighteenth-century Hungary, for example, the lesser nobility continued to control the Kingdom's distinctive local administration, the system of the counties, and were even successful in resisting Joseph II's centralizing measures during the 1780s (Volume II, Chapter 6).

The limitations upon monarchical régimes, and the need to view government as a matter of personalities as well as institutions, are now fully recognized. This has been accompanied by renewed attention to the regional and local dimension of absolutism and a corresponding appreciation of the nobility's continuing role. In a seminal essay, the distinguished German historian, Gerhard Oestreich, wrote of this process that

an entirely different world is revealed within absolutism itself: the old world of the European nobility, shaped by the ideal notion of the three estates and by ancient aristocratic tradition. It was a world at once uniform and diverse, which continued to be the dominant force not only in spiritual, social and economic life, but also in the political shaping of absolutist society.[68]

These continuities were most important in local government and were a corollary of the nobility's social, economic and political power in the provinces. At the centre, the picture is less uniform. There is evidence both of the aristocracy's continuing influence in central government and of its replacement by a new breed of professional administrator. Yet nowhere was it completely excluded from power.

This enduring rôle resulted from three related considerations. The most important was the composite nature of all early modern States.[69] Undoubtedly royal authority increased during these centuries. This expansion, however, and the territorial integration which accompanied it, both fell far short of that achieved by the unified nation-State which first came into existence during the nineteenth century. Early modern States, by contrast, were never fully integrated. They consisted of a number of provinces and even semi-independent kingdoms, not yet fully unified and sometimes only recently united. Such polities were really only groups of territories under one ruler, and in one or two cases – notably Brandenburg-Prussia and the seventeenth-century Spanish Monarchy – the constituent parts were actually separated by land or even by sea. Full incorporation of distant provinces was seldom attempted and even more rarely achieved. The slowness and unreliability of communications, and the relative smallness of all administrations at this time, were further barriers to unification. Within these composite monarchies each particular territory sought to defend its own institutions, legal and fiscal privileges and way of life, and did so with tenacity and surprising success during the seventeenth and even the eighteenth centuries.

Such integration as took place was usually achieved by means of compromise and cooperation with the existing agencies of government and the established political élites: in each case largely composed of regional nobilities. Everywhere rulers were forced into partnership with noblemen who enjoyed significant power in their own localities. Great nobles continued to exercise their traditional authority in their own regions, where their own

---

68. 'The Structure of the Absolute State', in his *Neostoicism and the Early Modern State*, eds B. Oestreich and H. G. Koenigsberger (Cambridge, 1982), pp. 258–72, at p. 262.

69. For which see especially H. G. Koenigsberger's 1975 inaugural lecture, '*Dominium Regale* or *dominium Politicum et Regale*: monarchies and parliaments in Early Modern Europe', reprinted in the same author's *Politicians and Virtuosi: Essays in Early Modern History* (London, 1986), pp. 1–26, esp. pp. 12 *et seq.*, and the recent discussion by J. H. Elliott, 'A Europe of Composite Monarchies', *Past and Present* no. 137 (1992), 48–71.

kin and their clients provided a secure base for political power. One way in which their influence could be exercised was through representative assemblies.[70] Membership of such bodies was usually an important privilege for the higher nobility and sometimes a defining characteristic: as it was, for example, in early modern Hungary, where the aristocracy was distinguished by the possession of titles and by its right of personal attendance at the Diet (Volume II, Chapter 6). There is no doubt that the power of provincial and national Estates declined during the early modern period and, in some countries, such assemblies even ceased to meet: as did the Russian *Zemsky Sobor* after the later seventeenth century and the Estates-General in France between 1614–15 and the eve of the French Revolution. Extinction, however, was an unusual fate. More normally, the power of such Estates might be reduced, but they continued to play a rôle in local administration, often through their influential committees.[71] Here too the power of regional nobilities was decisive. Their partnership with Europe's rulers was based on mutual interest: the central government secured decisive assistance in the task of ruling, while the élites obtained the opportunity of advancement and increased status and wealth, together with protection for their own interests.

This alliance was strengthened by two further considerations. King and nobility both expected that the élite would play a central rôle in government, as it had always done. Seventeenth- and eighteenth-century States were essentially traditional and hierarchical political structures. Their rulers were aware that their own authority ultimately rested on the same social and political hierarchy as that of the nobility. In other words, they could not seriously weaken noble power without simultaneously reducing their own authority. Crown and aristocracy might and did clash over the extent of the latter's influence, while one element in the assertion of monarchical authority in seventeenth-century Europe was an attempt by kings to emphasize that they were not simply *primus inter pares*, the greatest nobleman in the land, but ranked far above even the most powerful member of the aristocracy. Yet this is a very different matter from attributing to the monarch policies that were in any fundamental sense anti-noble. Cardinal Mazarin here spoke for all rulers in his celebrated death-bed advice in March 1661 to his royal pupil: 'The nobility (declared Louis XIV) was my right arm. I should support it and treat it with confidence and generosity in all respects.'[72] A century later, Frederick the Great reaffirmed the central rôle of the nobility in the Prussian State. In his first Political Testament, drawn up in 1752, he unequivocally declared that 'An object of policy of the Sovereign of this State is to preserve his noble class; for whatever

70. Here the main authority is H. G. Koenigsberger: see his numerous articles, conveniently assembled in *Estates and Revolutions: Essays in Early Modern European History* (Ithaca, N. Y., 1971) and *Politicians and Virtuosi*.

71. This was, for example, the case in the Habsburg Monarchy: see P. G. M. Dickson, *Finance and Government under Maria Theresia* (2 vols, Oxford, 1987).

72. Quoted in Richard Bonney, *Society and Government in France under Richelieu and Mazarin, 1624–61* (London, 1988), p. 76.

change may come about, he might perhaps have one which was richer, but never one more valorous and more loyal.[73]

Noble attitudes mirrored those of their sovereigns. The advance of State power, however limited in practice, threatened to impose new burdens on their tenants and even to challenge their own leadership of local communities. This threat, however, was always far less than the new opportunities presented by the expanded armies and administrations of the seventeenth and eighteenth centuries. Service to the ruler and to the dynasty remained a way of legitimating their own status as noblemen.[74] Such service, moreover, continued to be seen in terms of personal loyalty, rather than duty to an impersonal State. These obligations continued to rest on formal oaths of allegiance to a surprisingly late point. Eighteenth-century Prussia was the most military and bureaucratic State of the age. Yet when its most famous king, Frederick the Great, came to the throne in 1740, one of his first actions was to travel round all his territories receiving the personal fealty and homage of his noble subjects and the grievances and requests which accompanied this.[75] It exemplified the composite nature of even the eighteenth-century Hohenzollern State. It also underlined that nobilities and rulers both still saw their relationship primarily in personal terms. Nobles still expected to serve their king, whether on the battlefield or in the council chamber, and expected to be rewarded for loyal and meritorious service.

The final consideration, which weighed especially heavily on rulers in the eastern half of the continent, was the shortage of trained personnel to command royal armies and to staff central and local government. The expansion of government created an urgent need for more and more trained administrators, able to discharge tasks that were increasing both in number and in complexity. The seventeenth and eighteenth centuries saw the emergence of significant numbers of new officials. These men had already acquired an appropriate professional education or other training, and often came from social groups other than the nobility. Many of these officials themselves entered the nobility quite quickly, being rewarded with this status by a grateful ruler or, sometimes, actually purchasing it. Their numbers, however, everywhere fell short, and sometimes far short, of the totals required to staff the expanding State machines, especially in the crucial area of local government. These new men tended to fill the new administrative offices that were coming into existence, while the nobility continued to dominate the established agencies. This was exactly the situation in eighteenth-century Savoy, where the intendancies introduced under Victor Amadeus II were filled by commoners, while the higher nobility all but monopolized the provincial governorships.[76]

73. Translated in C. A. Macartney, ed., *The Habsburg and Hohenzollern Dynasties in the Seventeenth and Eighteenth Centuries* (New York, 1970), p. 332; the original is in Dietrich, ed., *Die politischen Testamente*, p. 310.
74. Atienza Hernández, *Aristocracia, Poder y Riqueza*, pp. 55–60.
75. Walther Hubatsch, *Frederick the Great: Absolutism and Administration* (London, 1975), pp. 41–55 *passim*. The King, of course, effectively ignored the nobility's pleas.
76. Nicolas, *La Savoie au XVIIIe siècle*, i. pp. 600–2.

The continued involvement of the nobility at all levels of government was thus essential; not that its permanent exclusion was ever seriously considered at this time. Public authority had traditionally been exercised by the Second Estate working in partnership with the Crown, and this continued to be the case throughout the seventeenth and eighteenth centuries. Rulers all over Europe expected to base their domestic régimes upon partnership with their nobilities, whose local power they continued to harness. Only occasionally did they encounter outright obstruction from the regional élites. One notable example of this came in seventeenth-century Brandenburg-Prussia where the 'Great Elector', meeting opposition to his policies from the particularist nobilities of the scattered Hohenzollern territories, built up and worked through an aristocratic élite that was largely recruited from outside his own lands. Confessional rivalry was here a factor: the new élite, like the ruling family, was Calvinist, while the lesser nobility were predominantly Lutheran. The Junkers found themselves, during the second half of the seventeenth century, temporarily excluded from much share in government, though they retained considerable influence at the local level. They retrieved their position spectacularly during the eighteenth century, joining in a partnership with the ruling family. The alliance was crucial for Prussia's emergence as a leading European power (Volume II, Chapter 4). This evolution, rather than the earlier exclusion, conformed to the wider European pattern. Almost everywhere, the expanded State structures of the seventeenth and eighteenth centuries provided careers, income and status for aristocracy and lesser nobility alike. This was most obviously the case where the rapidly expanding armies of the period were concerned.

Military service was the principal way in which Europe's élite served the State during the seventeenth and eighteenth centuries. This is at first sight surprising, since by the decades around 1600 the nobility's traditional military rôle and function had appeared to be threatened by the new scale and nature of land warfare. During the early modern period, armies and the battlefield came to be dominated by infantry and gunpowder weapons, rather than cavalry; modern-style defensive fortifications, better able to withstand the new field artillery, became widespread, at least in western Europe; while the military forces of most States grew rapidly in size, reaching a peak in the first decade of the eighteenth century. Measuring this increase is notoriously difficult, but the numbers maintained under arms by most European States multiplied at least six-fold during the early modern period and may have expanded even more rapidly. This was the key development in what has been labelled the 'Military Revolution'.[77] Campaigns also became longer and forces remained in existence at their conclusion.

77. The origin of the concept is Michael Robert's inaugural lecture at Queen's University, Belfast, in 1955: 'The Military Revolution, 1560–1660', reprinted in the author's *Essays in Swedish History* (London, 1967), pp. 195–225. The most persuasive recent views are those of Geoffrey Parker, *The Military Revolution: Military Innovation and the Rise of the West, 1500–1800* (Cambridge, 1988) and M. S. Anderson, *War and Society in Europe of the Old Regime, 1618–1789* (London, 1988).

The need to train these enlarged standing armies required more efficient military organization, and this was usually provided by the State, which alone could mobilise an entire society for war.[78]

These developments undoubtedly posed a considerable challenge to Europe's nobility. A central element was the rapid and final decline of heavy cavalry, which had consisted almost entirely of noblemen, and its replacement by a numerically far smaller group of light horse. This threatened the nobility's very *raison d'être* as the fighting class at a time when its near-monopoly of armed force was also being very rapidly undermined. The large-scale armies of the age of the Military Revolution consisted principally of infantry, overwhelmingly recruited and usually conscripted from the ranks of the common people. Simultaneously, the early modern period and especially, the seventeenth century saw a steady decline in the value and use of the noble feudal levy (principally the system of knight's service), as the heavily-armoured cavalry it largely produced became far less important.[79] In France, for example, the *ban* and *arrière-ban* seems to have been abandoned after the ending of the Nine Years War in 1697: occasional attempts to summon it during the preceding two generations had revealed its negligible military value. In Denmark the feudal levy was effectively abolished by the new absolute monarchy in 1661.[80]

The changes in warfare directly reduced the nobility's military potential, as the State slowly emerged as the monopoly provider of armed might and aspired to control all legitimate force. Government agents were replacing individual noblemen in the recruitment and control of armies, and the consequences were soon evident. The private forces that some great lords had maintained in earlier times became a thing of the past. They now survived principally in eastern Europe. In Poland-Lithuania some magnates long retained their own forces, but these increasingly had merely ceremonial functions. In seventeenth-century Hungary several aristocrats possessed their own armies, but these largely disappeared after the 1680s and 1690s when the Kingdom was reconquered from the Ottoman Empire and Habsburg control asserted (Volume II, Chapters 7 and 6). Elsewhere the nobility's military potential declined sharply. During the seventeenth century, private noble arsenals all but disappeared and private fortifications were destroyed: over 100 in the French province of Languedoc alone, after the government's defeat of the Montmorency rising in the early 1630s. This reduction in the nobility's military capacity was apparent in the way aristocratic uprisings were becoming a thing of the past. In Piedmont-Savoy, the final such rebellion was that of the marquis of Parella in 1682, while in France the last open insurrection by leading noblemen had taken place a generation earlier, the unsuccessful *Fronde* of the princes which

---

78. The experience of Spain in the decades around 1600 is an important exception to this generalization: see I. A. A. Thompson, *War and Government in Habsburg Spain 1560–1620* (London, 1976).

79. See C. Storrs and H. M. Scott, 'The Military Revolution and the European Nobility 1600–1800', *War in History* I (1994), on which the following paragraphs are largely based.

80. See Volume II, Chapter 3.

had ended in 1653. Almost everywhere aristocratic military power and the disruptive potential it contained were rapidly disappearing. The major exceptions to this general trend were the Highlands of Scotland, Hungary and Poland-Lithuania, where the nobility's private military power and even the feudal levy theoretically survived long into the eighteenth century and, very occasionally, beyond. This was due to the very traditional social structure of these regions, to the relative weakness of State control, and to the slow penetration of modern military technology.

The appearance of mass conscript armies, and the accompanying administrative and social changes, clearly challenged the exclusivity of the nobility's military function. In a period of increasingly organized land warfare, simple obedience seemed more important than the individual heroism and feats of valour in which the independent noble/knight had traditionally gloried. Yet the Military Revolution also created significant new opportunities for Europe's élite. The rapidly expanding armies of the seventeenth and eighteenth centuries might be based on mass conscription, but they still had to be officered. Indeed, one dimension of the growth of State control was an increase in the proportion of officers to rank-and-file, with the elaboration of a hierarchy of command, and this created further opportunities for noblemen in search of a military career. This period saw a remarkable and rapid increase in the size of the officer corps in every European State: that of Russia, for example, multiplied more than five-fold during the century after Peter the Great's death, rising from some 5,000 in 1725 to around 16,000 in 1796 and 27,000 in 1825.[81]

Noble propagandists always claimed that the qualities necessary for military leadership were to be found mainly and even exclusively in the Second Estate. Europe's rulers shared this preference and overwhelmingly employed noblemen to command their armies. This undoubtedly incorporated a realistic awareness that there was no other social group capable of providing officers in the numbers now required. But it proceeded primarily from a conviction that the nobility alone possessed an innate capacity for leadership and qualities particularly appropriate for the military vocation, and should therefore be given special preference when officers were being selected. It was assumed that a nobleman's overwhelming sense of honour, of family and of lineage would ensure that he would always do his duty. Military virtue was believed still to reside principally in the social élite, for whom army service long remained a defining characteristic and not simply a career choice.

The apotheosis of this attitude was in many ways the notorious Ségur Law of 1781, which sought to end the practice of selling commissions in the French army and instead restricted entry to the officer corps to those able to demonstrate four generations of nobility.[82] This initiative was for long interpreted as the victory of social privilege over military effectiveness. It has been demonstrated, however, that the advocates of this measure were inspired by the conviction

81. John P. LeDonne, *Absolutism and Ruling Class: the Formation of the Russian Political Order, 1700–1825* (New York and Oxford, 1991), p. 42.

82. David D. Bien, 'The army in the French enlightenment', *Past and Present* no. 85 (1979), 68–98.

that the older noble families, though generally poorer, were more likely to possess the correct military virtues and thus be moulded into good officers than the more recently elevated, who were not merely wealthier but also more independent (this volume, Chapter 5).

The attitude which these debates reveal was widely shared at the end of the *ancien régime*. The nobility continued to be viewed – and to view itself – as a military caste, whose privileged position within State and society principally derived from this enduring function. In every continental country, established families continued their traditions of army service during the seventeenth and eighteenth centuries. In France, the Saulx-Tavanes provided successive generations of soldiers, as did various branches of the Choiseul family, while the nobility's middle ranks contained many military dynasties, such as the Scépeaux clan which provided eighteen officers, nine of whom rose to be generals, between 1660 and 1789. In the Austrian Habsburg lands, successive generations of the Daun family served in the army, culminating in Maria Theresa's favourite commander, the notably cautious and ineffective Field Marshal. Spanish army dynasties included those of lesser nobles such as the Alos of Catalonia and the Gortazar of Vizcaya.

The nobility's grip on the officer corps of most continental armies tightened during this period. In France, for example, significant numbers of officers had been commoners at the beginning of the seventeenth century, but a hundred years later the nobility dominated the army command. This pattern was widely replicated. In Prussia, less than one-tenth of the total number of officers (695 out of 7–8,000) were non-nobles in 1806, while for Spain's army in 1800, the equivalent figure was around a quarter. The lesser, usually untitled, nobility filled the lower ranks of command, but everywhere the senior posts were the preserve of the titled, and often the Court, aristocracy. Louis XIV's generals, for example, were drawn overwhelmingly from this group and especially from the older families. No less than 93 per cent of France's aristocratic élite, the *ducs et pairs*, followed a military career, and 41 per cent became generals and 11 per cent marshals of France during the Sun King's reign.

Such service, moreover, involved battle action and a considerable risk of injury and even death, particularly for those noblemen serving in the lower ranks of the officer *corps*. The French nobility suffered considerable losses in Louis XIV's final war, that of the Spanish Succession (1702–13), while Sweden's élite was similarly weakened by the casualties it suffered during the Great Northern War (1700–21) (Volume II, Chapter 2). The losses suffered by Prussia's nobility during the wars of 1740–63 were far greater and due to Frederick the Great's desperate plight, especially during the Seven Years War, and they are an important reminder of the scale of noble blood-letting that could occur (Volume II, Chapter 4). Such losses were a significant element in the demographic problems of particular families and even of whole national élites, while the fact that some noble soldiers remained unmarried further weakened the biological continuity of the Second Estate.

One notable consequence of the Military Revolution, as Dr Thompson underlines (below, p. 206) was a sharp increase in the expenditure of money and time now demanded of the noble soldier. Equipment was expensive, while in those armies where commissions were sold, the costs of entry and, even more, of advancement were considerable. Many a family estate was burdened with substantial debts to launch and sustain a son's military career. Noblemen were also expected to advance their own money on those occasions when the State was unable to meet the regiment's costs. The commitment of time now demanded of a would-be soldier was an even more fundamental transformation. During the early modern period, a military career changed from being an occupation that was temporary and even occasional and sporadic to one that was more or less permanent. Standing armies were a scarcely less permanent vocation for the officers than for the rank-and-file. By the second half of the eighteenth century, a nobleman was expected to be with his regiment for most of the time. This in turn brought about an increased 'militarization' of noble life and culture by the closing decades of the eighteenth century.

The willingness of noblemen to serve in their State's armies in increasing numbers can be explained largely in terms of traditional duty and enhanced opportunity. The persistence and even intensification of the noble ethic of service to his monarch was crucial. The fact that a commission was usually sanctioned and sometimes personally bestowed by the ruler was especially valued by the élite, since it seemed to strengthen the bonds between nobleman and king. Military service, moreover, remained an important route – albeit a slow path – to promotion within the nobility and to ascent from the untitled majority into the titled élite. Army officers received around one-third of the titles (numbering almost 2,000) granted in the Habsburg Monarchy between 1711 and 1789, while in France over three-quarters of new creations between 1589 and 1723 were military in origin. There is some indication that, by the eighteenth century, military service was recovering its earlier pre-eminence.

The material rewards of such service were also important, especially for younger sons and for the middle and lower ranks of the nobility. The increasing prevalence of inheritance practices favouring the eldest male child placed additional pressure on younger sons to find a career or vocation that offered an appropriate lifestyle and income, but did not threaten noble status, as direct involvement in trade theoretically might do. One obvious target – and a traditional one – was the army. The financial rewards of a military career were not negligible though the costs could be equally high. The expenses involved in purchasing a command and supporting the expected lifestyle often exceeded salary, especially in the élite units stationed in the capital and near the Court. In the more obscure and isolated regiments, a careful officer of lesser means might just about make ends meet. Yet war remained potentially profitable for the nobility, as it had always been, though in a different way. One broad consequence of the Military Revolution was to transform the army officer from a freebooter into a salaried State official. Officers' salaries were not always high or paid promptly, but often they were all that separated a poor nobleman from the rest of the impoverished population and in this way enabled him to maintain his privileged status. Any promotion would bring an enhancement of financial rewards, while the spread of a broadly accepted hierarchy of ranks within most armies during the seventeenth and eighteenth centuries offered the possibility of a career path and with it increased income. The financial rewards of army service might be more apparent than real, but to the often-impoverished mass of the nobility, they were still a powerful lure.

Warfare in the age of the Military Revolution demanded higher professional standards of those who commanded, and the nobility exhibited some willingness to acquire this technical training. The decades immediately after 1600 saw the foundation of a series of noble academies intended primarily to prepare the aspiring officer for a military career. One of the earliest and most notable was that established at Sedan in 1606 by the duc de Bouillon, brother-in-law of the celebrated Prince Maurice of Orange. The next two decades saw a whole series of such foundations, including four in the Republic of Venice (1608–10) and the Colegio Imperial in Spain, set up in Madrid in 1625 by Olivares as a kind of military academy. The costs of the education provided by these institutions were far beyond the pockets of all bar the noble élite, and most soon closed their doors, or came to serve different purposes, such as preparing an aristocrat for life at Court. In the following century, however, such training came to be provided by the State which established and financed cadet corps, where sons of the nobility could be trained as soldiers before securing their first commissions. These corps were founded in Prussia (1717), Russia (1731), Bavaria (1756), Portugal (1757) and France (1776: the *cadets-gentilshommes*), while in Piedmont-Savoy (1737) and Spain (1738), cadet places reserved for young noblemen were established in each regiment. These initiatives were more enduring and successful than the earlier military academies, but even the significant increase in the number of places for cadets was far short of the demand for such training from the poorer lesser nobility for whom they were primarily intended.

Such initiatives underlined the State's belief that only the nobility could officer its armies. They also made clear that the élite itself was far from hostile towards change. On the contrary: noblemen great and small eagerly sought the modicum of technical education – and with it the patina of social polish – demanded of an officer in the age of the Military Revolution. These developments possess a much broader significance for the early modern nobility. By redefining themselves as a military service élite, the nobles and especially the lesser nobility were integrated to a greater and greater degree within the emerging absolutist State. The Second Estate was an agent and ultimately a beneficiary rather than a victim, of the Military Revolution: as of the administrative changes which had accompanied it.

A similar pattern is apparent in Europe's fledgling diplomatic services, though the number of noblemen involved was infinitely fewer and drawn almost entirely from the higher nobility. The seventeenth and eighteenth centuries saw an important expansion of resident diplomacy, with the ending of a long period of generalized warfare.[83] The Peace of Westphalia in 1648 brought to a close the Thirty Years War, while a decade later the settlement of the Pyrenees (1659) concluded a long-running Franco-Spanish conflict and that of Oliwa (1660) terminated half a century of intermittent fighting around the Baltic. The return of general peace – though this proved temporary – encouraged resident diplomacy, following the lead given by Louis XIV's France. By the end of the Sun King's long reign in 1715, Europe's capitals – with the single important exception of Constantinople – were linked by a reciprocal network of embassies and, in peacetime, all States usually maintained continuous political relations with each other.

This fundamental change in the nature of diplomacy had profound implications for the social standing of the men who transacted it. The earliest resident diplomats of the century after 1450 had been a very mixed group socially, but had contained relatively few members of Europe's élite. Noblemen had been sent on occasional and often formal missions of importance, to conclude a peace settlement or to arrange a dynastic marriage, but such embassies had always been short-lived and the aristocrat at its head had returned home once the negotiations had been concluded. During the second half of the seventeenth century, a new pattern evolved. The embassies which multiplied all across Europe were now more permanent and, though they contained a number of experts, often of relatively humble social origins, they tended to be headed by noblemen or, to a lesser extent, Churchmen and often by major aristocrats. Such men would increasingly have undertaken the continental Grand Tour with its mixture of travel, education and culture, and this would be an appropriate preparation for such an embassy. During the second half of the seventeenth century, diplomacy acquired the distinctly aristocratic tone that it long retained. The growing dominance of great noblemen resulted from the principle that an ambassador represented his sovereign: rulers would therefore send the men most capable of embodying their own majesty. The widespread employment of nobles also reflected a general desire not to offend a recipient by employing diplomats of lower social standing. It was reinforced by the expectation that – due to the belated and incomplete payment of expenses, which was universal – an aristocratic diplomat would have more of his own money to spend in the king's service.

The increasingly aristocratic tone of the new resident diplomacy was fully apparent to well-placed contemporaries. François de Callières, who served in the French foreign office and in the 1690s wrote the best-known guide to diplomatic practice, was quite clear on this point. The first requirements for a diplomat, he declared, were birth and lineage, together with an appropriate fortune to spend serving the monarch.[84] The extent of

83. An admirable recent survey is M. S. Anderson, *The Rise of Modern Diplomacy 1450–1919* (London, 1993), pp. 41–102.

84. *François de Callières: the Art of Diplomacy*, ed. H. M. A. Keens-Soper and Karl W. Schweizer (Leicester, 1983), p. 89.

aristocratic dominance has been underlined recently by a major study of the social origins of European diplomats in the period 1697–1715.[85] The results for Spain are especially striking: out of thirty-eight diplomats, no less than thirty-four were members of the titled élite (*titulos*) with three princes, five counts, twelve marquises and fourteen dukes.[86] The fact that most Spanish diplomatic missions during that period were sent to Paris undoubtedly increased the aristocratic tone, but these figures do highlight a general trend. The major posts in the diplomatic services of France and of the Habsburg Emperor were also dominated by the high nobility, while that of the Republic of Venice was overwhelmingly drawn from the noble urban patriciate. The only exceptions to this general trend were the Dutch Republic and, to some extent, England. Yet even members of the Republic's landed nobility were to be found in the Dutch diplomatic service, while that of the emerging British State contained a significant number of peers: out of thirty-eight diplomats during the years investigated, no less than sixteen were members of the House of Lords.[87]

The pattern apparent around 1700 persisted throughout the next century and beyond.[88] The embassies sent to the major capitals of Europe quickly became and long remained a near monopoly of Europe's élite, as the diplomatic hierarchy came to mirror the social hierarchy. Relatively few noblemen made an extended career in diplomacy, and those who did were drawn overwhelmingly from the lesser nobility. Members of leading families would seldom take more than one or two embassies, almost always to a major European capital: Paris, Madrid, or, increasingly, London and Vienna. *Ancien régime* diplomacy at its apex was not only aristocratic but also amateur: such professionalism as existed was provided by a cadre of experts who filled the lesser positions in an embassy and were usually men of much lower social standing. The fact that most ambassadorial appointments were limited in duration (most were for a few years), together with the attractions of spending time at a major foreign Court, explain why members of the high nobility were prepared to accept costly diplomatic appointments.

Embassies were, of course, integrated into established noble family strategies.[89] This was why members of the aristocracy were willing to accept posts where the income, in the form of an official salary and expenses, might well be inadequate and would often be paid very belatedly. Though far less plentiful than military commands or even posts in the civil administration, they were particularly prized for the glory they conferred and the opportunities they presented. Embassies were another form of service to the dynasty and a means thereby of elevating a family above its rivals. The

85. Lucien Bély, *Espions et ambassadeurs au temps de Louis XIV* (Paris, 1990), pp. 291–321.

86. *Ibid.*, pp. 294–5.

87. *Ibid.*, pp. 291–300, *passim*. For the enduring aristocratic element in Britain's foreign service, a minority but a very sizeable and significant one, see D. B. Horn, *The British Diplomatic Service 1689–1789* (Oxford, 1961).

88. This is immediately apparent, for example, from the lists of diplomats printed in the *Repertorium der diplomatischen Vertreter aller Länder 1648–1815,* 3 vols ed. L. Bittner et al. (Berlin, *etc.*, 1936–65).

89. See the comments of Bély, *Espions et ambassadeurs*, p. 307.

most important diplomatic posts tended to go to the most prominent families and, crucially, to those with regular access to the ruler. This was a further incentive for leading noblemen to spend an increasing proportion of their time at Court, where diplomatic appointments – like military and administrative posts – were normally to be secured. In the final decades of Louis XIV's reign, for example, the most important French embassies were monopolized by groups enjoying regular access to the King, above all the *noblesse de cour*, the *noblesse d'épée*, the *clergé de cour* and the leading *robe* families.[90]

This was part of a broader evolution, and one which has been seriously misunderstood. The presence of the noble élite at Court has often been viewed as part of the process by which the early modern State domesticated its aristocracy. The Court has been seen as the crucial link in a chain of developments which transformed the higher nobility all across Europe from local provincial power and even semi-independence to a dependent position in the king's entourage. It was viewed as a mechanism for cutting off the great nobles from their local power bases and the sources of their military strength, and in this way taming them. This was a central thesis of Norbert Elias, but after a period when his writings had considerable impact, there are now clear signs that his influence is waning.[91] This interpretation was based on a narrow range of sources, and principally the celebrated *Memoirs* of one disgruntled aristocrat at Louis XIV's Versailles, the duc de Saint-Simon. The framework advanced by Elias was simplistic and one-dimensional, rather than completely erroneous, as the revival of research on early modern Courts has demonstrated.

Recent research makes clear that the Court remained central in a political system within which patronage continued to be vital and the rôle of personalities of enduring significance. In many countries, the ruler's Court remained important in policy-making, and everywhere it provided an essential point of contact between the monarch and the political élite.[92] Once again a recognition that Crown and nobility were partners rather than antagonists was central to this reinterpretation. Though it was occasionally convenient for a ruler to be able to keep a close watch on the activities of one particular aristocrat or noble faction, the Court served many other purposes. It could, for example, actually be a stronghold of the higher nobility and the means by which it exerted its influence over the monarch or defended its position against non-noble élites. The presence of the aristocracy at Court was also crucial for the growing stratification of the Second Estate during the seventeenth and eighteenth centuries. It enabled key families and individuals to secure the lion's share of the available patronage

90. Bély, *Espions et ambassadeurs*, p. 292.

91. Norbert Elias, *The Court Society* (1969; Engl. trans., Oxford, 1983).

92. See in particular the collection edited by Ronald G. Asch and Adolf M. Birke, *Princes, Patronage and the Nobility: the Court at the Beginning of the Modern Age c. 1450–1650* (Oxford and London, 1991), the introduction to which (pp. 1–38) provides a valuable survey of trends in recent research; cf. also J. von Kruedener, *Die Rolle des Hofes im Absolutismus* (Stuttgart, 1973); J.-F. Solnon, *La cour de France* (Paris, 1987); and H. C. Ehalt, *Ausdrucksformen absolutistischer Herrschaft: Der Wiener Hof im 17. und 18. Jahrhundert* (Munich, 1980).

and in this way elevated the élite over the rest of the nobility. Here as elsewhere, the key was the regular access which the Court provided for fortunate individuals and groups.

Early modern Courts were significantly larger than their medieval and Renaissance predecessors and they came to be permanently located at one fixed point, rather than being peripatetic. These developments were obviously linked, and both influenced the noble élite in important ways. Royal and princely Courts expanded during the early modern period, though it is difficult to measure this increase with any precision. It can be illustrated by the example of the French Court, which grew dramatically in size, especially during the sixteenth century. There is a crucial distinction between the royal household (*maison du roi*) and the total Court population, which was much larger. Precise figures can only be given for the royal household, and even these are not completely reliable. A further complication is that most Court offices (which were dominated by the higher nobility) were held in rotation for periods as short as one month, but more often for three or six months: this practice was widespread at early modern Courts. Francis I's household in the 1530s contained slightly over six hundred people. The reign of the last Valois, Henry III (1574–89), saw an increase in size, to between 1500 and 2,000 at any one time. Allowing for the impact of office holding in rotation, this suggests a figure of around 6,000 as the overall size of the royal household. The personal rule of Louis XIV saw a further, though modest, increase in this total.

This was facilitated by the Court's move in May 1682 to Versailles, which proved to be permanent and where it would remain for over a century. During the decades after 1600, however, the Bourbon Court had become less peripatetic than its Valois predecessor. It seldom travelled outside Paris and the surrounding region of Ile-de-France, which contained a substantial number of royal residences. In the course of the seventeenth century, Paris and the royal Court became more important in the life of the great nobles, who spent a greater proportion of their time in the capital and built resplendent town houses there (this volume, Chapter IV). This development had its exact parallel in Spain (this volume, Chapter VI). Madrid had been the Spanish capital and the fixed location of the Court since 1561, but it was only in the early decades of the seventeenth century that the Castilian high nobility began to reside there for more extended periods and to build houses in the capital.

Developments in Spain and France had their parallels in central and eastern Europe. Vienna's position within the Habsburg Monarchy was particularly striking.[93] The political and cultural diversity of the Austrian Habsburg territories ensured that the Court and the ruling dynasty would

---

93. See R.J.W. Evans, 'The Austrian Habsburgs: the dynasty as a political institution', in A.G. Dickens, ed., *The Courts of Europe: Politics, Patronage and Royalty 1400–1800* (London, 1977), pp. 121–45, a fundamental survey; Volker Press, 'The Imperial Court of the Habsburgs', in Asch and Birke, eds, *Princes, Patronage and the Nobility*, pp. 289–312; and the recent study by John P. Spielman, *The City and the Crown: Vienna and the Imperial Court 1600–1740* (West Lafayette, Ind., 1993).

always be quite crucial: they alone unified the Monarchy's scattered and disparate possessions. Yet Vienna was too exposed to Ottoman attack, and too remote from the dynasty's lands and interests in the *Reich* for it easily to emerge as the political centre of the Habsburg realms. Though the seventeenth century saw an increasing identification between the city and the Habsburg dynasty, it was only after the relief of the second Turkish siege in 1683 that the city definitely became the capital and the permanent residence of the imperial Court. Throughout the seventeenth century, however, the Habsburg family had spent more of their time in Vienna which played an important rôle in the evolution of the Austro-Bohemian noble élite. In the decades that followed the second Turkish siege, the Monarchy's leading families – Austrian, Bohemian and even Hungarian – began to build the town houses and the suburban palaces which still adorn the city today (Volume II, Chapters 5 and 6). In Russia, too, noble residences came to be built in the leading city, where the élite would spend a larger proportion of their time. Peter the Great's thoroughgoing reform of all aspects of noble status involved forcing the élite to build residences in the new city of St Petersburg and to reside there (Volume II, Chapter 8).

The compulsion involved was unique to Russia, and because of the ruler's wish to create a new city, identified with himself, that would eclipse the traditional capital, Moscow. Elsewhere, the high nobility willingly flocked to Court. The reasons for this influx were overwhelmingly traditional: above all, the desire to serve the king or prince, the wish to be physically close to the ruler and to share the majesty of monarchy, the hope and expectation of reward, and the search for an appropriate education. Poland-Lithuania provides the principal exception (Volume II, Chapter 7). There, the Crown's chronic poverty militated against the establishment of a large royal household, and leading magnates maintained their own private Courts, often of a surprising size and splendour. In earlier times, this had been quite common, though by the seventeenth and eighteenth centuries it had become exceptional. A few great aristocrats continued to maintain their own Courts, sometimes with a thriving cultural life: most notably in the case of the Eszterházy princes in Hungary. But in most countries, noble Courts were a thing of the past. Royal Courts now occupied a dominant place in the life of the higher nobility than hitherto.

This was part of a wider process of social centralization, whose origins extended far back before 1600. Courts were important as marriage markets and cultural centres. The capitals in which – or near to which – they were located were often important financial centres and as such an obvious source of loans for hard-pressed aristocrats. It is impossible to draw up a balance sheet for the financial consequences of the aristocracy's presence at Court, though the expenditure involved clearly contributed to the growing indebtedness of many families at this time and this in turn reinforced the general trend. The capital also contained the principal law courts in the realm, and litigation was a frequent pastime for many noble families, who were likely to be involved simultaneously in several cases, usually involving disputes over property and inheritance.

All across Europe, the aristocracy's horizons were becoming more national, and even international. The growing numbers of noblemen making the Grand Tour and the spread of the French language, from the second half of the seventeenth century, among the élite of many continental countries advanced this process of integration. There is a sense, by the eighteenth century, in which national aristocracies were coming to be part of an international noble élite. Yet most great noblemen also remained in close touch with their own localities, both by regular correspondence and occasional – sometimes very occasional – visits and through their clients among the regional élites. This was facilitated by the widespread practice of holding Court posts in rotation, which ensured that noblemen could return from time to time to their own localities, in order to attend to their private concerns and to public affairs: which their continuing rôle in government at all levels made necessary. The migration was often seasonal: summers spent on their estates, the rest of the year in the capital and at Court. This system suited both the aristocrats and their rulers, who were able to draw on the advice and support of the élite both at Court and in the localities. During the two centuries covered by this collection, there may have been a tendency for leading noblemen to spend less time on their own estates. But this certainly did not destroy, and may not seriously have weakened, their provincial power.

The nobility's rôle at the heart of the State was to be important during the nineteenth century. It has become fashionable during recent years to point to the enduring nature of noble power and to emphasize its slow retreat in the face of the economic and political transformations of the later modern era. The chapters in this collection make this resilience more comprehensible. The second half of the eighteenth century had seen the origin of developments which would ultimately prove fatal to the Second Estate. The Enlightenment and the French Revolution represented a decisive philosophical and political challenge to Europe's élite, while the industrialization that began in Britain would create new sources of wealth and eventually lead to the emergence of a dominant middle class. Yet when old Europe was restored in 1815, at the end of a quarter-century of upheaval, the power of the aristocracy in many countries seemed as complete as ever. The consolidation of noble power – social, economic and political – during the preceding two centuries had paved the way for a further extended period of aristocratic influence and, at times, hegemony.

CHAPTER TWO

The British Nobility, 1660–1800

John Cannon

University of Newcastle upon Tyne

Let us start with a gentle paradox. 'Money confounds subordination,' wrote Samuel Johnson in 1775. It overpowers the distinctions of rank and birth, and 'weakens authority by supplying power of resistance, or expedients for escape'.[1] Johnson was commenting on the changing society he had found on his famous visit to the Western Isles of Scotland in 1773 and the authority being undermined was that of the Highland lairds. But in a later conversation with Boswell, he extended his remarks to include the whole of Britain:[2]

Subordination is sadly broken down in this age. No man, now, has the same authority which his father had – except a gaoler . . . I have explained in my Journey to the Hebrides how gold and silver destroy feudal subordination. But, besides, there is a general relaxation of reverence.

Even the Laird of Auchinleck, he told Boswell, to drive the point home, 'is not near so great a man as the Laird of Auchinleck was a hundred years ago'.

Though the decline of respect for authority is a constant complaint throughout the ages, few will dispute the truth of Johnson's observation, nor his correctness in identifying the cause of the changes taking place in Hanoverian Britain. In the course of the eighteenth century, the British replaced the Dutch as the leading commercial and trading nation. The commercial revolution was followed by a financial revolution and, in turn, by an industrial revolution. Among the European countries most affected by the Enlightenment, a notorious solvent of authority and stimulus to scepticism, was Britain. When Napoleon Bonaparte was engaged in his life and death struggle with Britain in the 1800s, he described it, not as a nation of aristocrats, but as a nation of shopkeepers. Yet landed aristocracy retained influence longer in Britain than in almost any European country and when, in the end, it fell back, its retreat was dignified, orderly and slow. As late as the 1860s, peers were in a majority in the cabinet. At the turn of the century, when Queen Victoria lay dying, Robert Arthur Talbot Gascoyne Cecil, the third marquis of Salisbury, was at No. 10. In 1963,

1. *A Journey to the Western Islands of Scotland*, Yale edition, ed. Mary Lascelles, p. 113.
2. *Life of Johnson*, ed. G. B. Hill, iii, pp. 262, 177.

the first minister of the Crown was a Scottish peer, the fourteenth earl of Home, though, in an egalitarian age, he had been obliged to give up his title in order to qualify. Power indeed followed wealth, but it followed at a respectful distance.

I

Unwelcome though it may be, it is hardly possible to start our survey of the British nobility without some discussion of methodology. We have to be sure which group of people we are talking about. The decision made on the size of that group, if it does not dictate our findings, must certainly influence them.

The first thing to note about the British peerage – that is, the titled nobility – is its small size by comparison with that of most continental countries. The granting of peerages remained firmly in the hands of the monarch, and although blandishments, intimidation or even bribery, were occasionally employed, there were severe limits to how many people could push past. By contrast, in a number of continental countries, nobility was attached to office, which could be purchased, or to service rank, which could be earned.

The English peerage took formal shape in the course of the fourteenth century, largely in response to the need to determine who was to be summoned to meetings of Parliament. Many of the spiritual peers vanished from the House of Lords at the Reformation and though twenty-six archbishops and bishops remained, the House became increasingly a secular body. The peerage retained its parliamentary character through subsequent vicissitudes. It therefore had an important institutional base from which to defend its privileges, and some degree of independence from the monarch, which it was jealous to maintain.

A further distinguishing characteristic of the English peerage was the practice of primogeniture, in both descent of titles and of estates. The fact that younger sons were technically commoners prevented the nobility from multiplying as elsewhere. Consequently, although there were always a few impoverished peers whose titles had been parted from their estates, we find nothing equivalent to the *hidalgos* of Spain, of whom it was said that they smiled more than they ate, or the *hobereaux* in France, scarcely distinguishable from peasants. Some of the provincial nobles who emerged in France in 1789 to claim privilege with the Second Estate were like scarecrows, and their embarrassed peers resorted to a whip-round to furnish them with a decent suit of clothes or respectable lodgings.[3]

At its lowest point, at the end of Henry VII's reign, the English peerage

---

3. G. Chaussinand-Nogaret, *The French Nobility in the Eighteenth Century: from Feudalism to Enlightenment*, trans. W. Doyle (Cambridge, 1985), pp. 62–3.

was no more than forty, and even after generous creations by the early Stuarts, the total had reached only 150 by the Glorious Revolution. On the continent, nobilities numbered tens or hundreds of thousands. The *szlachta* in Poland has been estimated as between six and seven and a half per cent of the population, giving a total which approached a million in the second half of the eighteenth century. After the reorganization of the Russian nobility by Peter's Table of Ranks in 1722, which added army officers and civil servants to the existing nobles, the numbers have been put at between 50,000 and half a million, many of whom were so poor that they ploughed their own lands. In France, the famous finance minister Necker calculated in 1785 that there were more than three thousand offices giving hereditary nobility.

This contrast has persuaded some historians that a sensible definition of the English aristocracy should include the gentry as a 'lesser nobility'. A 'gentry-peerage conjunction' has been suggested, and we are warned that we would otherwise create an 'implausible distinction' between the English nobility and that of the continent.[4]

It is true that in a number of seventeenth- and eighteenth-century writings, the gentry is referred to as minor nobility. But legal and technical definitions do not always catch social realities and the situation was constantly changing. The increasingly widespread use of the vague term 'gentleman' meant that the distinction between gentry and nobility became sharper, until by the nineteenth century, writers could doubt whether the peerage would any longer relish being described as gentlemen.[5]

We should pause before venturing down the road of a 'gentry-peerage conjunction'. It is unwise to adopt a definition in order to facilitate comparisons with the continent, since the definition adopted will not merely facilitate but, to a considerable extent, prompt the findings. Our first duty is to historical verisimilitude. If the gentry in England were not normally thought of as nobility, it is confusing to pretend that they were.

There is no doubt that some country gentlemen, particularly baronets, had larger estates and greater incomes than some poorer noblemen, and a number of them finished up in the peerage. But, as a group, the gentry was substantially less wealthy. The lifestyle of squire and average peer was quite different. The squire might exist on an income of £500–1,000 per annum, own a small manor-house, his park unimproved by Capability Brown, his aspiration to a place on the local bench. The peer could have estates in many counties, several large country houses, a London residence, an income of £30–40,000, and every opportunity, if he wished, for Court or public office at a high level. His ambitions were a Secretaryship of State, a Lordship of the Bedchamber, the Garter or the Thistle, and a Lord Lieutenancy of the county. In the 1790s, for example, when the income of the average gentleman was between £500 and £1,000 per

---

4. M. L. Bush, *The English Aristocracy: a Comparative Synthesis* (Manchester, 1984), pp. 1–2.

5. J. Lawrence, *On the Nobility of the British Gentry* (1824), quoted J. V. Beckett, *The Aristocracy in England, 1660–1914* (Oxford, 1986), p. 20.

annum, the earl of Derby was drawing nearly £50,000 per annum from 32 different estates. It is true that squire and peer formed part of the landed interest, but so did farmer and yeoman, bailiff and blacksmith.[6]

Running the gentry into the nobility may itself obscure, or render impossible, some of the questions we may wish to raise. It may be that the difference between gentry and peerage is a key to the understanding of English political and social development, which we should not throw away at the outset.

In the ranks of the English gentry, there were no formal definitions and no formal privileges. It was therefore a matter of opinion who was gentry and who was not, just as it was a matter of opinion who was a gentleman. Though a number of works have challenged the concept of an open élite, as far as the peerage was concerned, that merely disposes of the question in its more extreme form.[7] Clearly, it was much easier for families to slide into the gentry than into the peerage. If this made English society less rigid than continental, a 'gentry-peerage conjunction' could mask the point completely.

We must also bear in mind the extent to which the situation was fluid and changing. Let us take simple examples of a falling and a rising group. Sir Thomas Smith, in the 1580s, related knighthood to the possession of landed property, persons 'able to maintain that estate'. This was the basis of the attempts by the early Stuarts to extort money by forcing gentlemen to seek knighthoods. By the eighteenth century, the situation had changed completely, and knighthoods were given mainly to lawyers, admirals and city dignitaries. The link with land had gone. A rising group was the clergy, moving from medieval priest to graduate gentry. Their acceptance as gentlemen was demonstrated by a significant increase in the number of clerics put on the bench. But it would be idle to suggest that they should be regarded, or regarded themselves, as having risen into the ranks of the nobility, and their chances of receiving a peerage remained extremely poor.

The fact that at the bottom of the gentry there was a permeable membrane had important consequences. It undoubtedly allowed some families to move up in the world, but of equal importance was that it allowed unlucky or unsuccessful individuals to move down, and fall out of the category of gentry completely. The absence of any formal code of *dérogeance*, together with the effect of primogeniture, caused many younger sons of the gentry to be apprenticed to trade, or to enter the professions as lawyers, army officers, or clergy. The class of pauper nobility which helped on the continent to bring the noble order into disrepute, hardly

---

6. The gap between gentry and nobility is emphasized by G. E. Mingay, *The Gentry: The Rise and Fall of a Ruling Class* (London, 1976), p. 4 and by F. M. L. Thompson, *English Landed Society in the Nineteenth Century* (London, 1963), p. 20. A more recent enquiry, looking at the question in the early modern period, cast doubts on parallels with the continent and concluded that, in the rest of Europe, there was no group which quite corresponded with the English gentry. See *Gentry and Lesser Nobility in Late Medieval Europe*, ed. M. Jones (Gloucester, 1986), p. 11.

7. L. Stone and J. C. F. Stone, *An Open Elite? England, 1540–1880* (Oxford, 1984); J. A. Cannon, *Aristocratic Century: the Peerage of Eighteenth Century England* (Cambridge, 1984).

existed in England. There was a much smaller group of soured and embittered gentlemen, clinging to their rank because it was all they had left, and willing to embrace desperate and reactionary causes. That there were elements of this type among the backwoods Tories of Anne's reign, and possibly among Jacobite supporters, is undeniable, but they had nothing like the influence or the privileges of the Polish *szlachta*.

It has been suggested that not to include the gentry and the baronetage in the broader nobility places them in 'a social limbo, from which escape is possible only through promotion to the peerage or demotion to the commonalty'.[8]

This is rather a strange argument, for the 'social limbo' seems to exist only in the author's mind. It is something of a platitude to suggest that, socially, people must either move up or down, and I am not convinced that the middle classes felt perilously trapped between the aristocracy and the lower orders. The fact that the gentry was a group intermediate between the titled nobility and the mass of the people was a characteristic of which they were proud, rather than a predicament from which they were desperate to escape.

II

We should begin our survey by noting that, throughout the eighteenth century, there were three peerages in the British Isles.

Though the Welsh had had native princes and nobles, there had never been an independent Welsh peerage. Many families in the Hanoverian period held Welsh titles, but they did not necessarily possess any land in the principality, nor have any particular connection with it. The earls of Radnor, so created in 1765, were descended from a Huguenot refugee Jacob des Bouveries, and their main seat was at Longford Castle, south of Salisbury, in Wiltshire. Similarly the earls of Carnarvon lived at Highclere in Hampshire, the earls of Cardigan at Deene in Northamptonshire, and the marquesses of Carmarthen at Hornby Castle, near Bedale, in Yorkshire.

The English and Scottish peerages were separate until the Act of Union of 1707. Each was then closed and future creations made to the peerage of Great Britain. The Scots having lost their Parliament at Edinburgh, special arangements were made for their representation in the House of Lords at Westminster. Sixteen representative peers were chosen at every general election by their fellows. Since the practice soon developed of running a government list, they normally formed an augmentation to the ministers' majority in the upper house. The Scottish peerage lost nineteen of their number by attainder after the Jacobite rising of 1715 and a further

8. Bush, *The English Aristocracy*, p. 2.

seven after the 1745 rebellion. The number of Scottish peers fell from about 135 in 1700 to 68 a hundred years later.

Ireland retained its own Parliament at Dublin throughout the century, though until 1782 its powers were severely circumscribed. The Irish peerage remained open until the Act of Union in 1801, when it was replaced by the new peerage of the United Kingdom. Since Irish peers did not sit in the Lords at Westminster until 1801, they were eligible for election to the House of Commons, where they formed a significant addition to the powerful aristocratic group. English and British peers affected great disdain towards the Irish and waxed satirical at their expense: Irish peerages were certainly used as stepping stones to British ones or to fob off tedious aspirants. The terms of the Act of Union of 1801 were complex and represented a good deal of political compromise. Thirty-two representative peers were to be elected to the House of Lords, of whom four were to be archbishops or bishops. Those not selected retained their right to sit for a Commons seat, outside Ireland itself. The Crown was empowered to create one new Irish peerage for every three becoming extinct, until the number should fall to a hundred: after that, creations were to match extinctions.

Relations between the three peerages were not necessarily cordial. There were no problems about Scottish peers who held English titles created before the Act of Union. But when, in 1711, the fourth duke of Hamilton was created duke of Brandon in the new British peerage, the House of Lords refused to allow him to take his seat. This was in part suspicion that the royal prerogative might be used to subvert the House, though the formal argument was that Article 22 of the treaty had arranged for sixteen representative peers to sit and no more. Since the House had previously decided that Scottish peers with British titles had no vote for the representative peers, they were in the strange position of being almost completely disqualified, unless they were included in the chosen sixteen. By contrast, Irish peers seem over-indulged, since they could sit in the House of Lords at Dublin, be elected to the British House of Commons, and were also eligible for British peerages entitling them to a seat at Westminster. The second Earl Fitzwilliam in the Irish peerage was created Baron Fitzwilliam in the British peerage in 1742 and advanced to a British earldom in 1746: the second earl of Egmont, an Irish peer and an adviser to Frederick, Prince of Wales and George III in turn, was brought into the Lords at Westminster in 1762 as Baron Lovell. On the other hand, the English and British peers kept up a steady warfare against the Irish peers on matters of precedence, and in particular whether an Irish earl outranked an English baron. At the time of the marriage of the Princess Royal in 1734, the first Lord Egmont and his friends were greatly exercised over the issue, and a special cabinet had to be summoned to try to resolve it.[9]

9. *HMC Egmont*, I, particularly pp. 406–7, 409–11, 418–19, 428–9; II, 46–9, 54, 60–1.

The political situation of the three peerages varied considerably. The Scottish peerage was a declining one, the numbers falling decade by decade. The fact that most Scottish peers could sit neither in the House of Lords nor in the House of Commons placed them in the political wilderness. Little was done to rescue them. Sons of Scottish peers were eligible for the lower house and sixteen of them were returned at the general election of 1747. A few eldest sons of Scottish peers were summoned to the House of Lords in British baronies, as a means of getting round the resolution of 1711. Since the Scottish peers were, for the most part, much poorer than their English counterparts, they soon acquired a reputation, not wholly undeserved, for pertinacious rapacity.

The Irish peerage was potentially in a stronger position, since it had its own House of Lords in Dublin, and sent a number of its members to the Commons at Westminster. At the general election of 1727, twenty-two Irish peers were returned for British constituencies. These advantages were mitigated by two considerations. The Irish Parliament was, until 1782, a subordinate one, with severely prescribed powers: its appellate jurisdiction was specifically removed by a British Act of Parliament in 1719. The Irish peerage had little claim to speak for the Irish nation, north or south. Catholics and Presbyterians were disqualified by the operation of the Test Act. A number of those granted Irish titles had no interest in the country whatever, and never visited it or took their seats in the Irish House of Lords. The attempts to preserve in patents of peerage some fictitious decency led to such quaint geographical inventions as Milford in Ireland (Pembrokeshire), Slate in Ireland (Skye), and even Plassey in Ireland (Bengal).

We must remember therefore that remarks about the English and British peerages do not necessarily apply to the Scottish and Irish ones. In addition, we should note that, though it is easy to think of the nobility as a group very conscious of its own common interest, there were deep personal and party divisions within it. Noble families were often rivals for local supremacy and within the same family there could be much jockeying for position. Charles Francis Greville quarrelled with his brother Lord Warwick and defeated him in his own borough in 1784. Promotions within the peerage, from baron to viscount, earl, marquis and duke, took up much royal and ministerial time and were just as contentious as the creations of new peers: in 1802, when Baron Curzon was promoted to Viscount, it was his elder brother, Baron Scarsdale, who wrote to protest.

III

The English peerage which re-emerged in 1660 to claim its seats in the restored House of Lords numbered just under 150 persons. Our first task is to establish in what state they had survived the vicissitudes of the previous fifty years. These may conveniently be identified as economic, legal and political.

The historiographical controversy which raged over the condition of the nobility in the early Stuart period is too substantial to be investigated in depth here.[10] Lawrence Stone's suggestion that their position had deteriorated was vigorously counter-attacked, and it seems doubtful whether there was much significant change in their position relative to other groups by 1640. Hence, a massive restoration of their fortunes was not perhaps needed and a modest improvement might propel them into considerable prosperity.

The Civil Wars placed great strains on many noble families, through the assistance they gave to the royalist cause in loans or gifts, the destruction of property and the fines inflicted by their victorious parliamentary opponents. But though nine English peers were killed in battle and a further five executed, no peerage family failed to survive.[11] Individual families suffered greatly. Lord Brudenell witnessed his house at Deene plundered and his books and furniture removed, spent two years in the Tower, but survived to see the Restoration and to claim, at the age of eighty-two, the earldom of Cardigan. But the most authoritative survey of the position in 1660 concluded that most noblemen had found ways and means of staying afloat in the bad days, and their recovery after 1660 seems to have been vigorous.[12] Though there is some disagreement about the exact cause of the rise of the great estates in the late seventeenth and early eighteenth centuries, the general trend is not disputed. Conditions after the Glorious Revolution favoured the nobility and saw the foundation of great ducal houses by those who had placed their bets correctly. Until the Restoration, the title of Duke was reserved almost exclusively for members of the royal family or court favourites. There were no English dukes at all between 1572 and 1603, and between Norfolk (1553) and Albemarle (1660) the title was given to only one non-royal, Buckingham in 1623. After 1688, the flood gates opened. The dukedoms of Schomberg (1689), Bolton (1689), Bedford (1694), Devonshire (1694), Leeds (1694), Newcastle (1694), Shrewsbury (1694), Marlborough (1702), Rutland (1703), Buckingham (1703), Montagu (1705), Dover (1707), Kent (1710), Brandon (1711), Ancaster (1715), Kingston (1715), Portland (1716), Wharton (1718), Chandos (1719), Manchester (1719), Greenwich (1719), Bridgwater (1720) and Dorset (1720) followed each other in quick succession.

---

10. L. Stone, *Crisis of the Aristocracy, 1558–1641* (Oxford, 1965); reviewed E. Miller, *Historical Journal* 9 (1966), 133–6; D. C. Coleman, 'The "Gentry" Controversy and the Aristocracy in Crisis,' *History* 51 (1966), 165–78; J. H. Hexter, 'Lawrence Stone and the English Aristocracy', *On Historians*, Chapter 4; G. Aylmer, *Past and Present* no. 32 (1965), 113–25.

11. Strafford's earldom was lost by attainder in 1641 but recreated for his son six months later; the death of the second duke of Hamilton at Worcester in 1651 ended his English peerage of Cambridge, but the Scottish titles continued. All the other victims had heirs.

12. J. Thirsk, 'The Sale of Royalist Land During the Interregnum,' *Economic History Review*, 2nd series, 5 (1952) 188–207; 'The Restoration land settlement,' *Journal of Modern History*, 25 (1954), 315–28; H. J. Habakkuk, 'The Land Settlement and the Restoration of Charles II,' *Transactions Royal Historical Society*, 5th series, 28 (1978), 201–22.

One distinguished historian has written recently that 'who gained by the revolution of 1688 has yet to be decided, but it was not the House of Commons'.[13] One may modestly suggest that most peers, unless their judgement was very poor or they adhered to the Catholic religion, did not do badly. A family whose fortunes brightened dramatically after 1688 were the Russells. The origins of their wealth in the spoils of the monasteries in the reign of Henry VIII is well known: among dozens of estates, their haul included Covent Garden and the Cistercian abbey of Woburn. The fifth earl of Bedford was one of the few presbyterian peers and had fought for Parliament at Edgehill. His son, Lord Russell, was a fierce Whig, and was regarded by his party as a martyr when he was executed in 1683 for complicity in the Rye House plot. The Revolution changed everything. As early as March 1689 the attainder on Russell was reversed. The earl was appointed Lord Lieutenant of Bedfordshire and Cambridgeshire, and then Middlesex. In 1694, he was raised to a dukedom, the preamble to his grant declaring Lord Russell to have been 'the ornament of his age'. The following year, the duke's grandson and heir, at the age of fourteen, married the wealthy daughter of a London merchant, John Howland of Streatham, said to be worth £100,000. The duke was granted a further barony, of Howland of Streatham, to descend by special remainder to the heirs of the bride. On his succession to the dukedom in 1700, Wriothesley Russell was said to be the richest peer in the country. Not unnaturally, in the nineteenth century, Lord John Russell looked back at the Glorious Revolution with a good deal of affection.

An insidious threat to the authority and prestige of the peerage in the pre-Civil War period had been the vast increase in creations by the first two Stuart monarchs. Elizabeth had granted very few peerages, particularly in her later years, and there was a back-log of claimants: the financial straits of James I and Charles I meant that neither could be too fastidious.[14] As a consequence, a peerage which numbered no more than fifty-five or so at the accession of James I in 1603 had almost trebled by the Restoration. In 1621, thirty-three English peers protested to James I at the threat to their order posed by lavish creations and in 1626 it was mooted to prevent newly created peers taking part in the House.[15] Aristocracies usually use their influence to limit numbers and maintain quality, and the period of noble ascendancy after 1660 saw the brakes applied. The net increase in Charles II's reign was only eleven, despite debts of honour incurred during the Civil Wars and exile, and from 1685 to 1714 a further net increase of fifteen took place.

After a spate of Whig rewards at the accession of the new House of Hanover in 1714, creations slowed once more, and during the reign of George II, there was a slight decrease in overall numbers. One result was

13. J. P. Kenyon, *The Stuart Constitution* 2nd edition (Cambridge, 1986), p. 3.

14. Stone, *Crisis of the Aristocracy*, Chapter 3.

15. S. R. Gardiner, *History of England from the Accession of James I*, iv, pp. 37–8; C. H. Firth, *The House of Lords During the Civil War* (London, 1910), p. 45.

a greater sense of cohesion among the nobility. When from the 180 or so peers in the later years of George II's reign one subtracts peeresses (who could not sit in the Lords), Catholics (who were excluded from office), minors, peers who were too old or infirm to serve and those whose tastes did not much run to politics, the core of active political peers was no more than one hundred or so.[16] Although there was jealousy of new creations, there were not the divisions between a service and a traditional nobility, nor between robe and sword, which may have weakened noble solidarity in some continental countries.

The chief political difficulty with which the peerage had to contend after 1660 was the restoration of its own authority, since the House of Lords had been abolished in 1649 as useless and dangerous. The drift back towards authority began well before the Commonwealth came to an end. Though the House of Lords no longer existed, titles continued to be recognized. The Humble Petition and Advice in 1657 argued for a second chamber, which Cromwell accepted under the awkward and embarrassed name of 'the other House'. Only two rather obscure peers agreed to sit in it, but the summons was in traditional form, and ardent republicans noted disapprovingly that Cromwell addressed the members as 'lords'. An acknowledgement of the position due to the peers of the realm by their birth formed part of Charles II's declaration from Breda. The re-establishment of the House of Lords was unspectacular. Ten peers met in the chamber on 25 April 1660 and were reinforced over the next few days by others. Last to return were the lords spiritual, whose reinstatement demanded a special Act of Parliament in 1661.

IV

The hundred years between the Glorious Revolution and the summons of the Estates-General in France in 1788 were the golden days of the English aristocracy, its prestige and wealth at its height, its supremacy almost unchallenged. The Revolution itself has been described recently as an 'aristocratic coup . . . with the gentry – as was only proper – accepting the leadership of their seigneurial lords'.[17] Certainly there was no mass rising. The formulation is valid and helpful, provided that we recognize that it does not, as some historians seemed to believe, mean that the revolution was not of much consequence accordingly.[18] Nor does it imply that it was an unpopular action. On the contrary the Glorious Revolution was the

16. In 1758, for example, there were twelve papists, nine minors and seven peeresses.

17. Kenyon, *The Stuart Constitution*, p. 419.

18. See, for example, L. Pinkham, *William III and the Respectable Revolution* (Cambridge, Mass., 1954). For an excellent discussion of recent views on the Glorious Revolution, see *Liberty Secured? Britain Before and After 1688*, ed. J. R. Jones (Stanford, Ca., 1992).

foundation upon which aristocratic ascendancy was erected. The support of the great majority of subjects gave the peers a rôle and an identification with the perceived national interest which was crucial to them. Peers and people were united in their detestation of popery and despotism and James II rendered the nobility, by inadvertence, an invaluable service.

The most immediate outcome of the deposition of James and the substitution of William was the development of a balanced constitution, based upon the regular meetings of Parliament. Each consideration was of importance to the peerage.

The theory of the aristocracy as a balancing force between anarchy and despotism had a long and respectable pedigree. It was given more immediate publicity by the weight placed upon it in Charles I's *Answer to the Nineteen Propositions* in 1642. Subsequent events seemed to confirm the validity of the concept as the Republic, after 1649, lurched between the extremes of Leveller democracy and military dictatorship. John Thurloe, Cromwell's secretary, told the Commons in 1657 that if the constitution had one chamber only, 'we have anarchy or tyranny'.[19] After 1688, when the peers had stood up against the monarchy, the theory was given a new lease of life. This was of particular importance since the traditional rôle of the nobility as the fighting men and commanders was being undermined by the techniques of modern warfare, even if some identification with the army continued deep into the twentieth century. The new political rôle fitted well and could not but be flattering to their lordships. After 1688, and more especially after 1714, the constitution was vastly admired at home and abroad. It was gratifying that the peerage could claim to be, not a sectional interest, but the guardians of the constitution, a national heritage.

The position of the monarchy after 1714 could hardly have suited the nobility better. Relations between monarchs and their nobles were usually complex, a mixture of mutual dependence and mutual rivalry. With democracy effectively ruled out as a political possibility, political power became a tug-of-war between monarchs and their nobles. The limited British monarchy which emerged after 1688 retained enough power to prevent a slide once more into anarchy and confusion, yet it did not wield the kind of power which, on the continent, tempted many monarchs to challenge the privileges of their own nobility in the interests of efficiency and *raison d'état*. The English aristocracy did not have to face the kind of frontal attacks launched by Joseph II in the Habsburg Monarchy, Peter I in Russia or Gustav III in Sweden. The process of economical reform towards the end of the eighteenth century, which snipped away at pensions, perquisites and places, was a good deal more genteel and leisurely, and was carried out, in any case, under the auspices of nobles themselves.

The parliamentary régime which developed after 1688 also had manifest

19. P. Aubrey, *Mr Secretary Thurloe* (London, 1990) p. 153. A good discussion of Cromwell's 'other House' is in C. H. Firth, *The Last Years of the Protectorate* 2 vols (London, 1909), and *The House of Lords during the Civil War*.

advantages for the nobility. It was of consequence to have a regular constitutional platform and not to have to rely totally upon the precarious
and divisive politics of courts. Longer and annual meetings of Parliament
gave those peers who were interested in public life (we must not exaggerate
their numbers) an opportunity to meet regularly and a dignified place in
the government of their country. This did not go unnoticed. The Comte
de Ségur, a French observer, wrote of the invidious

. . . comparison between our present situation and that prevailing in England . . .
the brilliant but frivolous lifestyle of our nobility at the Versailles Court and in
Paris and other major towns, looks shallow when contrasted with the dignity, the
independence and the useful and important rôle played by a peer in England . . .[20]

No doubt this was too amiable an assessment of the activities of many
English peers, but their parliamentary duties offered some defence against
the kind of accusations put out in 1789 by Sieyès against the French nobility, that they were the enemies of the nation, a cancer devouring its
flesh, with neither function nor utility. Above all, the English peerage was
indentified with Parliament as a national institution at a time when its
prestige and its authority was probably at its height.

V

The eighteenth-century recovery of the nobility did not, however, rely
upon prestige or theory alone. There were more solid political, economic
and social factors underpinning their position.

There is a contrast between the limited formal privilege of peers as
individuals and the influence they wielded as men of wealth and as members of the corporate body.

Individual privileges were few and of modest importance. Peers could
claim freedom from arrest, save for certain crimes, and were not obliged
to take an oath. They could not be imprisoned for debt. In criminal cases,
they faced trial before the House of Lords. In the event of sentence of
death, they could claim decapitation. Dr Bush has commented on the 'impressive range of judicial rights' which peers possessed.[21] They were,
perhaps, more impressive in theory than in practice, unless a peer was
determined to lead a life of more than common crime and villainy. Lord
Ferrers, the only peer to be convicted of murder, was hanged in 1760,
not decapitated. The trial of the duchess of Kingston before the House
of Lords in 1776 on a charge of bigamy was more piquant than significant.

20. *Mémoires, souvenirs et anecdotes*, ed. F. Barrière, i. p. 89.
21. Bush, *The English Aristocracy*, p. 20.

In the 450 years between 1499 and 1948, there were no more than thirty-four trials before the Lords. Since in only nine of these cases was there an acquittal, it is difficult to argue with the conclusion that 'the results do not show that the procedure gave peers more lenient treatment than commoners'.[22]

Their corporate position in the House of Lords was different and was enhanced by the Restoration settlement. A rival source of authority was removed in 1660 when the Court of Wards was abolished. The royal prerogative of wardship, surviving from feudal times, had been a bone of contention for centuries, and, at times, a severe handicap to noble families. The demise of the Court of Star Chamber left the House of Lords as the undisputed highest legal authority in the land, through its appellate jurisdiction. It added considerably to the prestige of the House that it possessed this vital function and stood at the very pinnacle of the Law, at a time when the law received great admiration and respect. A further function was in cases of impeachment which, though of diminishing importance, did not atrophy until after 1806.[23]

Further assistance to many peerage families came through the increased use, after 1660, of the device of the *special remainder* in patents of creation. Until the Restoration, special remainders were uncommon, granted mainly to children of the royal blood or close Court favourites. But from 1660 onwards they were increasingly used to evade the consequences of there being no direct heirs male. We have already seen one example in the case of the duke of Bedford. During the reign of George I, more special remainders were granted than ever before. The effect was to improve considerably the chances of the title surviving and therefore to increase the cohesiveness of the peerage.[24]

With luck, royal favour and special remainders, strange and wonderful things could be accomplished. Jocelyn Percy, earl of Northumberland and Baron Percy died at Petworth in 1670, his honours becoming extinct. His daughter Elizabeth married the sixth duke of Somerset and died in 1722. Her son was then erroneously summoned to the House of Lords as Baron Percy. In 1748, at the age of sixty-four, he inherited the dukedom of Somerset from his father, the proud duke, who had died at the age of eighty-seven. Since the new duke had no surviving male heirs, he was, on 2 October 1749, granted the earldom of Northumberland, with a special remainder to his daughter's husband, Sir Hugh Smithson. For good measure, the following day he was created earl of Egremont, with another special remainder to his nephew, the son of his sister, Lady Katherine Wyndham. On his death in 1750, the dukedom of Somerset passed to a fifth cousin once

22. C. R. Lovell, 'The Trial of Peers in Great Britain,' *American Historical Review* (October, 1949) 69–81. The special parliamentary rights of peers – to vote by proxy, to enter formal protests and to be granted audiences with the monarch – were mainly of value in harassing and ambushing ministers.

23. The trial of Warren Hastings between 1787 and 1795 attracted great attention. The last impeachment was that of Henry Dundas, Lord Melville, acquitted in 1806 on all charges of peculation.

24. Discussed in J. A. Cannon, 'The Isthmus Repaired: the resurgence of the English Aristocracy, 1660–1760', *Proceedings of the British Academy*, lxviii (1982), 437–8.

removed, while the barony of Percy descended to his daughter. The old dukedom of Somerset had now sprouted three more titles. The new earl of Northumberland changed his name from Smithson to Percy and was created duke of Northumberland in 1766. In 1784, however, he was granted a further barony, Lovaine of Alnwick, with a special remainder to his second son, Lord Algernon Percy. Lord Algernon inherited in 1786 and a mere four years later was created earl of Beverley.

VI

The political and constitutional position of the peerage rested largely upon two platforms – its almost total monopoly of high office and its position in the House of Lords.

Control of the army, the national government and of local government meant that the commanding heights were firmly in the hands of the nobility. The commander-in-chief of the army was always a peer of the realm and frequently, as with Cumberland, York and Cambridge, a member of the royal family. Of the twenty soldiers who were made Field Marshal in the eighteenth century, fourteen were peers. Twenty of the twenty-six men who were first ministers of the Crown between 1714 and 1841 were peers or sons of peers. Their domination of the cabinet was equally complete. In the inner cabinet of 1763, George Grenville was the only commoner. But his own connections were far from humble. He was the second son of a peeress in her own right, his wife was the grand-daughter of a duke, and his two brothers-in-law were earls. The Lord Chancellor was the head of the law. Of eighteen Lords Chancellors between 1688 and 1832, only two were not peers. In the English shires, the supreme office was that of Lord Lieutenant. Of more than two hundred Lords Lieutenant appointed in the course of the century, only fourteen were not peers or peers' sons. In the higher reaches of government and administration in Hanoverian England, there was not much chance that the interests of the nobility would be overlooked.

The position of the House of Lords is more difficult to establish since it is the subject of some academic disagreement. In theory it was the senior house and most lords liked to think of it as such. The editors of the most recent study of the political rôle of the House of Lords assured us that it was the 'dominant partner' in the constitution in this period.[25] But at least one of their own contributors dissented from this opinion, remarking that the Lords was no longer the dominant House.[26] The proposition certainly

---

25. *A Pillar of the Constitution: the House of Lords in British Politics, 1640–1784*, ed. C. Jones (London, 1989): introduction by J. V. Beckett and C. Jones, p. 18.
26. J. Black, 'The House of Lords and British Foreign Policy, 1720–48', p. 135.

seems rather doubtful. The control of taxation, in a period of almost continuous warfare, gave the House of Commons an irresistible advantage. The most enduring first ministers – Walpole, Pelham, North and the Younger Pitt, who were in office collectively for 61 of the 85 years between 1721 and 1806 – remained in the Commons, and it is notable that each of them had a particular expertise in financial questions. There is also a good deal of contemporary testimony to the comparative unimportance of the House of Lords. When Lord Hervey was promoted to the upper house in 1734 to strengthen the government's debating team there, his father, the earl of Bristol, commiserated with him on having to accept promotion to 'so insignificant' a place.[27] It was said that when the two great parliamentary leaders, Walpole and Pulteney, met in the Lords in 1742 as Orford and Bath, the former remarked that they were now two of the most insignificant men in the kingdom. When George III as prince of Wales was set to write a constitutional survey in 1760 he concluded that the influence of the Lords was sadly diminished, mainly as a result of Queen Anne agreeing to the creation of the twelve peers in 1712 to swamp the anti-government majority.[28] It is not very likely that they were all mistaken.

As it happens, the question of the relative importance of the two Houses, though of interest, may not be of vital significance, since the peerage possessed very considerable influence in the House of Commons itself. First of all, many peers had interest or could nominate in a number of parliamentary boroughs. There is no doubt that this influence increased markedly in the course of the eighteenth century, despite pious Commons' resolutions denouncing it. Between 1702, when the number of seats under noble influence has been calculated at thirty-one, and 1786 for which it appears to be something like 210, it seems to have more than quadrupled.[29] Secondly, the number of peers' sons and Irish peers also increased greatly during the century. At the general election of 1702, seventy were returned: by 1796 it had risen to 120.[30] There were in addition many other members of the nobility in the Commons, who were neither peers' sons, nor Irish peers, nor sat for seats under noble influence, and who do not therefore come into either of the two previous categories. Sir John Bland, sixth baronet, sitting for Ludgershall in 1754, was a grandson of the first earl of Aylesford; Wenman Coke, member for Harwich, a Treasury borough, in 1754 was nephew of the first earl of Leicester, whose estates he inherited; John Albert Bentinck, a naval captain returned for Rye in 1761, was

27. *Memoirs*, ed. J. W. Croker, i.249.
28. Quoted in P. D. G. Thomas, ' "Thoughts on the British Constitution" by George III in 1760', *Bulletin of the Institute of Historical Research*, 60 (1987), 362.
29. J. A. Cannon, *Aristocratic Century*, pp. 104–15. It should be remembered that the House of Commons in 1702 was smaller, since 45 Scottish seats, making a total of 558, were added at the Union. 'Something like' is not carelessness but a reminder that influence is difficult to assess and that precise figures cannot be offered.
30. *Aristocratic Century*, pp. 104–15. There is of course considerable overlap between the computations since many peers' sons sat for the family borough.

son of a count of the Holy Roman Empire, and related to the dukes of Portland. Although disputes between the two Houses were sharp at times, they resembled family quarrels. To that extent, they helped to mask the basic unity of the governing class, rather as did the animosities of the party struggle. The very name, House of Commons, suggested a democratic element, which was scarcely borne out by the actual composition of the House. Even had the Lords possessed less influence in the Commons than they did, they were unlikely to be confronted by aggressive radicals, thrusting egalitarian legislation at them.

It may be argued that two of the more conspicuous defeats suffered by the House of Lords were blessings in disguise. Over taxation, the Lords lost ground after the Restoration until it was established that such matters were for the Commons only. Before the Civil War, the formula had been that money bills came from the Commons with the advice and consent of the Lords. A series of disputes after 1660 saw the Lords in full retreat. In 1671 and again in 1678 attempts by the Lords to amend money bills were defeated.[31]

In 1692, the Lords resolved that their power to assess their own taxes was 'an undoubted right from which their lordships can never depart', but they departed just the same.[32] Though some peers fought a hopeless rearguard action throughout the eighteenth century, it is not clear that they were wise to do so. The power to tax is important, but not always popular. The influence of the Lords over the Commons was sufficient to ensure that taxation policies inimical to the landed interest were unlikely to be adopted, and taxation of aristocratic assets was not savage. Above all, peers were not tempted to claim that most dangerous of all privileges, exemption from direct taxation, which provoked, on the continent and especially in France, so much popular criticism and helped to set the nobility apart from the rest of the nation. The British nobility paid the Land Tax, even if their assessments were often extremely kindly.

A second defeat was on the Peerage Bill of 1719. Though introduced by Sunderland, Stanhope and the Whig ministers, it gained a good deal of cross-party support, being, as Steele argued, 'a scheme which might hereafter set up some nobles above the Crown and commons both'.[33] Only six further peerages were to be permitted: after that, new creations were to be restricted to replacements for peerages becoming extinct. The proposal for Scotland, which aroused great indignation, was that the sixteen representative peers should be dropped, and twenty-five hereditary Scottish peers named. This, as was pointed out, would mean that those Scottish peers not of the twenty-five would have seats neither in the Lords nor Commons, nor would retain their vote for representative peers. They would therefore be totally deprived of parliamentary representation.

The scheme was baited with other reforms to make it more attractive.

31. Kenyon, *Stuart Constitution*, p. 417.
32. *Aristocratic Century*, pp. 93–4.
33. Steele attacked the proposal in *The Plebeian* and was answered by Addison in *The Old Whig*.

One clause forbade the use of special remainders, the generous employ-ment of which during George I's reign had provoked some resentment.[34] At one stage, the ministers seem to have contemplated offering the Com-mons repeal of the Septennial Act, whereby the lower house would continue in existence during the king's lifetime, as was the case in Ireland. This would have made both houses more oligarchical, but was dropped since, as Newcastle pointed out, it would look as if the ministry was afraid to face a general election.[35]

The motivation behind the proposal is still not completely clear.[36] Many peers disliked the arrangements under the Act of Union for elected Scottish peers, arguing that it was undignified, undermined the hereditary principle, and placed the representative peers under the influence of gov-ernment. Anne's use of her prerogative in 1712 to create the batch of twelve Tory peers to carry the Peace of Utrecht was still much resented and its dangers as an intimidatory tactic appreciated. Some of George I's creations had raised eyebrows as persons too much connected with the moneyed interest. Party advantage was certainly anticipated by some min-isters and the affair became caught up in the feud between George I and the Prince of Wales, who was said to have spent lavishly to defeat the measure. The king's attitude remains obscure. His public surrender of the prerogative in this matter was hailed by government pamphleteers as a remarkable gesture of trust and generosity by the new dynasty. But George I had already made many creations and would be able to make at least thirty-one more under the terms of the Peerage Bill, while his son, the future George II, would find his hands tied. The king was there-fore in the pleasant position of making sacrifices at someone else's expense.

The Bill was heavily defeated in the Commons and the House of Lords had a lucky escape. It has been suggested that the consequences of the measure would not have been great, since extinctions continued to run high and creations were so limited that the provisions of the Bill would not have begun to bite until the 1780s.[37] Numerically, of course, this is true. But the myth of open access to the peerage was a very valuable counter for the aristocracy and would have been destroyed. Had the mea-sure not been repealed in the meantime, it would have begun to narrow the peerage at precisely the moment when the volume of criticism of the aristocracy as a separate interest, apart from or even hostile to the rest of the nation, was reaching a crescendo. Walpole's opposition saved the peers

34. The effect of forbidding special remainders would have been, by pushing more titles into extinction, to speed up the process of renewal and meet, to some extent, the charge that the bill would create a narrow oligarchy. This was resolution No. 8 by the House of Lords.

35. Newcastle to Stanhope, 14 October 1719, quoted in J. F. Naylor, *The British Aristocracy and the Peerage Bill of 1719* (Wisconsin, 1968), pp. 243–5.

36. Naylor, *The British Aristocracy and the Peerage Bill of 1719* is a collection of documents, with a rather limited commentary. By far the best recent survey is Clyve Jones, 'The Political and Social Context of the Peerage Bill of 1719', in *A Pillar of the Constitution.*

37. Jones, 'The Political and Social Context of the Peerage Bill of 1719', p. 106.

from becoming, in his own words, 'a compact, impenetrable phalanx' and helped to ensure that they escaped the fate of the French aristocracy after 1789.[38]

VII

Though individual peers invested in the funds, developed ports and industries and, if they were fortunate, profited from court or public office, the basis of aristocratic supremacy remained, economically and politically, the landed estate. It was widely accepted that the ownership of land was an essential qualification for political influence: broad acres, as against moneyed wealth ensured stability, provided training in directing and organizing, and afforded the leisure necessary for public business. The principle was extended into government at all levels. The county voter was a freeholder, a man of independent means, and there was strong opposition to the extension of the franchise to copyholders. Property qualification Acts in 1711 and in 1732 insisted that members of Parliament, even sitting for the boroughs, should be possessed of landed property, and that justices of the peace should have a minimum income of £100 per annum from land.[39] Within the peerage, there was a rough correlation between rank and acreage, dukes having, by and large, more property than earls, and earls more than mere barons.

Aspirants for a peerage were well advised to acquire substantial landed property as quickly as possible. This was not easily done. Families in difficulties sold off minor properties or outlying estates before parting with their core inheritance and large estates, ready made, did not come on the market very often. With luck, it was easier to marry into landed wealth than to set about acquiring it piecemeal. Charles Anderson was born in 1749, the son of a Lincolnshire gentleman. He succeeded his father in 1758, and in 1763 inherited from his great-uncle, Charles Pelham, whose surname he added. In 1770 he married the daughter and heiress of George René Aufrère, himself the grandson of a French Huguenot marquis. In 1794, Charles Anderson Pelham was duly raised to the peerage as Baron Yarborough. His son married another heiress and was created earl. National heroes elevated to the peerage had to be kitted out with appropriate landed estates. A grateful nation gave Blenheim to the duke of Marlborough, Trafalgar House to Nelson's descendants, and Stratfieldsaye to the duke of Wellington. George III had originally objected to Nelson's peerage on the grounds that he had no

38. *Parliamentary History*, vii, 623.
39. 9 Anne cap. 5 and 5 George II, cap. 18. In each case, peers and peers' eldest sons were exempt, on the amiable understanding that they would have far more than the minimum qualification.

landed property: it was, wrote the king, 'quite out of the question'. He was persuaded to change his mind.[40]

There were, of course, vicissitudes and exceptions. The dukes of St Albans, Grafton and Manchester were not as well off as their colleagues. The great Chandos empire disintegrated almost as quickly as it had been acquired. The fortunes of the Paston family went into decline almost as soon as they acquired their earldom of Yarmouth in Charles II's reign, partly for political reasons. Some of the more remote descents produced strange results. The fourteenth Lord Willoughby de Parham from Lancashire was variously described as a carpenter and a weaver and existed on only £150 per annum. A number of impoverished peers had to be given small royal pensions to keep up appearances.[41]

But the great majority of noblemen in the eighteenth century prospered. The limited powers of the monarch, together with the acceptance of the principle of hereditary descent, for both title and land, gave Hanoverian noblemen a security of tenure greater than in many other countries. Royal disfavour remained unpleasant and closed off many avenues of honour and advancement, but peers could be dispossessed only by bills of attainder or by due process of law. They were not totally dependent upon the monarch. The Russian nobility, on the other hand, struggled hard to get the principle of hereditary descent acknowledged.

Since land was of such consequence, particular means were taken to retain it in the family. Primogeniture, considered unfair by many younger sons, was regarded by the nobility as bedrock, and comparisons were made with France, where the Code Napoléon insisted upon equal inheritance. Among the punitive measures designed to weaken the Catholic interest in Ireland was an act of Anne's reign imposing partible inheritance. In Britain, by contrast, any attempt to tinker with primogeniture met uncompromising resistance. As late as 1859, Lord Palmerston offered total opposition to the Real Estate Intestacy Bill on the grounds that it would damage great estates.[42]

[He] objected on every possible ground . . . constitutional monarchy required the existence of a landed aristocracy – in other countries, where the equal division of land prevailed, the landed aristocracy, the landed gentry, had sunk into comparative insignificance.

The effect of primogeniture was enhanced by the increased use made after the Restoration of the legal device of the strict settlement, whereby the greater part of the family estate was under entail and could not be alienated.

---

40. *The Later Correspondence of George III*, ed. A. Aspinall, iii, No. 1844. In No. 1846, the King remarked, with mordant humour, 'As the new peer has unfortunately no estate, he could not with much propriety to the title of Nelson add so proper an appendix as of the Nile.'

41. See E. Gregg and C. Jones, 'Hanover, Pensions and the Poor Lords, 1712–13', in *Peers, Politics and Power: the House of Lords, 1603–1911*, ed. C. Jones and D. L. Jones (London, 1986).

42. *Parliamentary History*, clii, 1155. The Bill was defeated by 271 votes to seventy-six.

Though the efficacy of this as a safeguard has been disputed, and under exceptional circumstances the entail could be broken, strict settlements helped to hold together family estates, and thereby made it harder for newcomers to push into landed society.[43]

VIII

Since the Glorious Revolution had effectively ruled out the possibility of royal absolutism and the Hanoverian nobility was hardly likely to be confronted by mass democratical movements, it follows that the crucial relationship was with the commercial and professional middle classes, some of whose incomes in the course of the century began to rival or even outstrip those of all but the greater nobility. When we are talking about social and political attitudes, it is not easy to be precise. Some noblemen were snobbish, others not; some businessmen aspired to nobility or gentry, others were well content with their lot. We are still far from an agreed verdict, and two historians who do not often disagree, have offered very different summaries. To one, the nobility was 'made the tool of an increasingly dictatorial bourgeoisie': to the other, the remarkable thing about the bourgeoisie was 'not their assertiveness but . . . their strange submissiveness, their acquiescence in aristocratic rule'.[44]

We have already seen, in the enthusiasm of the House of Lords for the Peerage Bill of 1719, some indication of the nobility's dislike of the early effects of the financial and commercial revolutions, and a feeling that the old order was in danger of going down before the new moneyed interest. Several of Harley's dozen peers in 1712 were thought to be slight men or tainted by trade. Jonathan Swift struck the same chord when, with taxation biting hard, he demanded to know in his *Conduct of the Allies* in 1711 what the war was about: 'what have we been fighting for all this while? . . . We have been fighting to raise the wealth and grandeur of a particular family; to enrich usurers and stock-jobbers; and to cultivate the pernicious designs of a faction, by destroying the landed interest.' Fresh sounds of indignation and dismay came at the end of the century, also in the midst of a great war, and were provoked by Pitt's lavish creations of peers. But for most of the eighteenth century, a *modus vivendi* was reached, and the threatened breach between landed and commercial wealth did not develop.

A number of reasons may help to account for this. Though the landed nobility held preponderant power, commercial and business interests were neither excluded nor disregarded. In the Polish diet, towns were not represented

43. *Aristocratic Century*, pp. 132–7.
44. P. Langford, *Public Life and the Propertied Englishman, 1689–1798* (Oxford, 1991), p. 510; Cannon, *Aristocratic Century*, p. ix.

until the reforms of 1791. In the British House of Commons, the burgesses for London, Bristol, Hull, Liverpool, Newcastle, Norwich, Nottingham and Southampton were present to express their town's interests. Bankers, brewers, merchants and industrialists took an increasing number of parliamentary seats, either sitting for their local boroughs or using their wealth to buy seats in boroughs which had escaped aristocratic control.[45] The policies followed by most Hanoverian governments – colonial development, low taxation and a minimum of government interference – were ones which were acceptable to landowners and businessmen alike. Though there were occasional clashes of interest and disagreements, particularly over war and military strategy, there were few large-scale confrontations, such as occurred over the Corn Laws in 1845 when Peel was afraid that the dispute had got on to dangerous ground – 'a war between the manufacturers, the hungry and the poor, against the landed proprietors, the aristocracy, which can only end in the ruin of the latter'.[46]

It did not take the nobility long to perceive, in the new developments of Anne's reign, opportunities for their own profit. Though there was no formal rule of *dérogeance*, there was a marked distaste for direct participation in trade or business: Thomas Harley, younger brother of Lord Oxford, was unusual in setting up in the 1750s as a wine-merchant, though he made enough money to build an extremely elegant house at Berrington, just outside Leominster. But the same objections did not apply to investment, and from an early period peers speculated in the funds, exploited the mineral resources of their estates, promoted new harbours or spas, or developed their urban properties. The Cavendishes sponsored Buxton as a spa, the Stuarts invested heavily in Cardiff and South Wales, the Grosvenors helped to develop Belgravia.[47]

A rather different form of investment was marriage with the daughter of a wealthy commoner. This was to be avoided if possible, but if circumstances were sufficiently desperate and the dowry good enough, matters could be arranged. We must not exaggerate the scale of such intermarriage at the highest level: peers married overwhelmingly within their own circle. But there were enough examples of exogamous marriages to raise hopes and to blur the edges. John Bristow and Peter Burrell were fellow directors of the South Sea Company and held government contracts for supply during the Seven Years War. Three of Bristow's daughters married the son of an English earl, the son of a Scottish baron, and a future Irish peer. The advance of Burrell's family was even more spectacular. Two granddaughters married dukes and a third married an earl. Burrell's grandson married the daughter of the third duke of Ancaster. She succeeded in 1779 to the estates, to a barony of Willoughby de Eresby in her

---

45. Or, of course, from noblemen who were obliged to sell the seats which they controlled.

46. Prince Albert's memorandum, 25 December 1845, *Letters of Queen Victoria*, 2 vols, ed. A. C. Benson and Lord Esher (London, 1907), ii, p. 66.

47. The contribution of the nobility to economic development is dealt with very fully in Beckett, *The Aristocracy in England, 1660–1914*, part two.

own right, and to the hereditary court office of Lord Great Chamberlain. She appointed her husband as deputy. In 1787 he succeeded to his great-uncle's baronetcy under a special remainder and in 1796 was raised to the peerage as Lord Gwydir, taking his title from one of his wife's estates. In 1787 an acquaintance wrote, 'Sir Peter Burrell's good luck is never failing'.

Adam Smith was among many commentators to suggest that the ambition of most men in business was to retire early and set up as country gentlemen. There are, of course, many examples. Sir Joseph Mawbey, erstwhile vinegar manufacturer, succeeded in becoming knight of the shire for Surrey, even if supercilious members of Parliament never allowed him to forget his humble origins or the fact that he fed his pigs on the barley husks from the distillery. But the scale of the tendency has recently been questioned. Many businessmen enjoyed work, relished city life, found the country dull, and did not fancy the delights of setting a mettlesome horse at a gate. Henry Thrale preferred a handsome villa in Streatham, with a modest park, while keeping on his brewery at Southwark.

The rôle of the gentry in assimilating and absorbing new wealth was clearly of much greater importance than that of the nobility. But repeated attempts to quantify the process have run into severe difficulties of definition, variations over time, and different rates in different counties. The Stones inclined to regard the interchange of personnel as something of a myth. F. M. L. Thompson and Paul Langford found the process of renewal and replacement much more vigorous.[48]

In a recent article, Henry Horwitz has attempted to illuminate the question by investigating a number of London businessmen in the period 1694–1714, while the commercial and financial revolutions were under way.[49] The findings suggested a considerable amount of reciprocal movement between the gentry and the London business establishment. Of 128 citizens of London, seventeen were from landed families, all of them younger sons. Two hundred and forty citizens in turn produced 148 eldest sons, of whom nearly one-third purchased landed estates. The figures are not conclusive and may be interpreted either way. But one figure, not stressed in the article, seems highly significant. No less than 68 per cent of the daughters of Aldermen married into landed families. This was certainly a vigorous interchange and helps to suggest why the threatened divorce between trade and land did not take place.

Valuable though this evidence is, we must not generalize too readily from London, which was not England. At the end of the seventeenth century, the degree of urban development was unremarkable. London, indeed, had a population of half a million, but it dwarfed all other towns,

---

48. L. and J. C. F. Stone, *An Open Elite?* (Oxford, 1984), pp. 421–4; Thompson, *English Landed Society in the Nineteenth Century*, pp. 21–2; Langford, *Public Life and the Propertied Englishman, 1689–1798*, pp. 39–40. There is a lively discussion of the controversy with the conclusion 'tradition happens to be right about the openness of the English landed élite', in D. and E. Spring, 'Social Mobility and the English Landed Elite', *Canadian Journal of History*, 26 (1986), pp. 333–51.

49. Henry Horwitz, ' "The Mess of the Middle Class" Revisited', *Continuity and Change*, vol. 2, part 2, (1987), 263–96.

accounting for more city dwellers than all the rest put together. Norwich and Bristol, the two next largest towns, had no more than 30,000 and 20,000 inhabitants each. The proportion of people living in towns has been estimated for 1700 at 17 per cent, rising to 27 per cent by the end of the century. In many of the provincial towns there was an active municipal life, socially and politically, but there is not much evidence of wider horizons or of any national bourgeois leadership. In a society still dependent upon the speed and strength of horses, interests were limited mainly to the town or the shire. What, for convenience, historians like to call the bourgeoisie displayed in practice a multitude of fissures and gradations. Businessmen were just as likely to see each other as rivals than as allies in a common cause against the nobility. Towns in the same region were often competitors in trade and commerce. Although wealthy bankers and city aldermen might rub shoulders with noblemen, admiring or condemning them according to taste, one doubts whether most shopkeepers, attorneys, doctors or printers saw many of them, or thought a great deal about them. If the bourgeoisie had a political objective, it would have been to seek improved parliamentary representation as a means of extending their influence. Yet the lack of interest in the growing towns of Manchester, Birmingham and Leeds in the 1780s was obvious enough for opponents to taunt reformers on the small size of their stage army. Above all, though contemporaries referred often to the 'middling classes', in the largely agricultural communities of Hanoverian England, this category included many farmers and tradesmen, living in small market towns and villages, and likely to identify with gentry and aristocracy as part of the landed interest.

It follows that, for the eighteenth century at least, the existence of a bourgeoisie as a self-conscious and cohesive class, capable of challenging the nobility, seems doubtful. Nor is it obvious, had it existed, what it would have been increasingly dictatorial about. The prosperity of many merchants, bankers, industrialists and professional men was proof that the policies of governments, though aristocratic, were not hostile to the great commercial interest. Statesmen from Walpole to Pitt prided themselves on their concern for trade. Businessmen had a share in government which was increasing. If they wished to move into the ranks of the gentry, it could be done: there was no prohibition on the purchase of estates, as existed in some continental countries. If they aspired, grandly, to found a noble family, it was not totally out of the question.

The suggestion that from 1780 onwards, the nobility was fighting a continuous rearguard action until 1914 against an embittered and aggressive middle class seems difficult to sustain. The nobility was not overthrown but, in the end, was squeezed out, by a number of coinciding factors: the growing complexity of public business, which rendered the ideal of the amateur untenable; the relentless search for more revenue which caused chancellors of the exchequer to cast an eye on large aristocratic fortunes, much as some eighteenth-century continental rulers had done; the renewed growth of religious dissent, which threatened Anglican supremacy, and produced a number of politicians from Bright to Lloyd George, who had little reverence for the aristocracy; the growth of large industrial towns, where aristocratic ideals seemed remote and irrelevant; the spread of education, which rendered deference towards leisured rank a less reliable commodity; the decline in the importance of agriculture in the national economy, which left the aristocracy looking less like the great landed interest and more like a mere agricultural lobby.

IX

These were distant and insidious considerations. At the end of the eighteenth century came a grand shake, which convinced many people, some of them aristocrats, that the days of the nobility were numbered.

The first shots were fired, not outside the Bastille in July 1789, but on 14 April 1775 at the village of Lexington, where the American militia had the better of the exchanges with British regulars, commanded, appropriately enough, by Lord Hugh Percy, future duke of Northumberland. Commonwealth and levelling notions, suppressed if not eradicated in eighteenth-century England, had transplanted well to America, where titles had never been recognized. Americans, wrote Thomas Jefferson later, 'of distinction by birth or badge . . . had no more idea than they had of the mode of existence in the moon or planets'.[50] The Declaration of Independence in 1776 concentrated on the misdeeds of the monarch, but in his pamphlet *Common Sense*, Tom Paine identified one of the two bases of the English constitution as 'the remains of aristocratic tyranny in the person of the peers'. The draft Articles of Confederation in 1777 stipulated that the new American government could create no titles, and this was repeated in Article 1 of the Constitution.[51] The new states also abolished aristocratic adjuncts, such as entail and primogeniture.

The challenge to aristocracy posed by the American revolt did not produce severe repercussions in Britain. America was distant and had never known nobility. Very different was the French Revolution. On 19 June 1790, the National Assembly declared all titles abolished, and the revolutionaries took pains in the following years to spread the glad tidings throughout Europe. This time, many in Britain did respond. The Society for Constitutional Information reactivated itself to distribute radical and reform literature. Paine's *The Rights of Man* in 1791 included a sustained and contemptuous onslaught on the very concept of nobility:[52]

50. *Democracy by Jefferson*, ed. S. K. Padover (New York, 1939), p. 125; Governor Francis Bernard was among many loyalists who had argued that, to provide stability, an American peerage should have been created, with life tenure if not hereditary descent.
51. Articles, VI; Constitution, Article 1, section 9.
52. *The Rights of Man*, ed. H. Collins, p. 102.

The thing is perfectly harmless in itself, but it marks a sort of foppery in the human character which degrades it . . . It talks about its fine *blue ribbon* like a girl, and shews its new *garter* like a child . . . It is properly from the elevated mind of France, that the folly of titles has fallen. It has outgrown the baby clothes of *Count* and *Duke* and breeched itself into manhood. France has not levelled: it has put down the dwarf, to set up the man.

That the work of the Society struck some chords can be inferred from the question posed by the Stockport Society of the Friends of Universal Peace: 'can the grievances arising from the aristocracy be redressed while the House of Lords retains its present authority in the legislature?'[53]

Under these attacks, the aristocracy looked to its defences, legal and ideological. John Reeves and his Association for the Preservation of Liberty and Property against Republicans and Levellers undertook to parry the literary arguments and to root out 'domestic traitors', and there was a massive campaign to bring Paine into ridicule and dislike. Edmund Burke was not impressed by the elevated mind of France. He devoted part of his *Reflections on the Revolution in France* to a threnody for the nobility, which he wrote with tears falling on the page in front of him:[54]

But the age of chivalry is gone. That of sophisters, economists and calculators has succeeded; and the glory of Europe is extinguished for ever . . . All is to be changed. All the pleasing illusions which made power gentle and obedience liberal . . . are to be dissolved by this new conquering empire of light and reason . . . On this scheme of things, a king is but a man; a queen is but a woman; a woman is but an animal, and an animal not of the highest order.

The aristocracy which emerged in 1815 from its revolutionary ordeal was very different from that of Charles II's reign. More of its income came from non-landed sources. It was much larger, the creations from 1776 onwards having doubled it compared with 1660. In some respects it was a more cohesive body. The influence of Lord Bute, tutor to George III and, as he was never allowed to forget, a Stuart, was soon felt after the accession in 1760. He was warned off his first attempt to secure a British peerage for himself and advised not to risk a direct confrontation with the Lords. But within five months, his wife had been created a baroness

---

53. *State Trials*, ed. T. B. Howell, pp. xxiv, 388.
54. *Reflections*, ed. C. C. O'Brien, pp. 170–1. The exchange between Burke and Sir Philip Francis over the draft version of this passage can be followed in *The Correspondence of Edmund Burke*, vol. vi, ed. A. Cobban and R. A. Smith, pp. 85–92.
Francis objected that 'all that you say of the Queen is pure foppery.' Burke replied:

What, are not high rank great splendour of descent, great personal elegance and outward accomplishments ingredients of moment in forming the interest we take in the misfortunes of men? The minds of those who do not feel thus are not even dramatically right. 'What's Hecuba to him or he to Hecuba that he should weep for her?' . . . You do not believe this fact, or that these are my real feelings, but that the whole is affected, or as you express it, 'downright foppery.' My friend, I tell you it is truth – and that it is true, and will be true, when you and I are no more.

in her own right, with a special remainder to Bute's children, and in 1776 his eldest son was created Baron Cardiff, taking his seat without objection. The Campbells, to whom Bute was closely related, were also advanced two steps: first, the heir to the dukedom of Argyll was granted a British barony as Lord Sundridge in 1766; then, in 1776 his wife, a lady of the bedchamber to Queen Charlotte, was made Baroness Hamilton, with another special remainder. At the same time the eldest son of Lord Marchmont was created Baron Hume of Berwick.

Clearly, the defences against the Scots were going down and in 1782 the House of Lords reversed its decision of 1711, allowing the eighth duke of Hamilton to take his seat as duke of Brandon. After this the trickle became a flood. The dukes of Roxburgh already had a British earldom with the title Ker and the dukes of Montrose another earldom as Graham of Belford. In the next fifty years many of the remaining Scottish families obtained British titles: Gordon (1784), Queensberry (1786), Atholl (1786), Abercorn (1786), Fife (1790), Morton (1791), Galloway (1796), Moray (1796), Perth (1797), Seaforth (1797), Eglington (1806), Breadalbane (1806), Cassilis (1806), Cathcart (1807), Hopetoun (1809), Dalhousie (1815), Wemyss (1821), Rosebery (1828) and Sutherland (1833). The effect of this, together with the creation of a new United Kingdom peerage after the Act of Union with Ireland in 1801, was to bring about the creation of a much more united British peerage in the nineteenth century.[55]

Something of a counter-weight to this tendency towards cohesion was that the social composition of the peerage was becoming more diverse in character. As early as 1812, Sir Egerton Brydges had referred to the nobility as 'more blended with the people . . . the power and the distance of a stately and reserved aristocracy are lost'.[56] Whether the people themselves noticed much blending is another matter, but the gesture towards democracy and affability was in itself significant. There was less talk of noble blood and more talk of service to the community.

There had always been a number of lawyers, soldiers and diplomats promoted on merit, who might not be of noble birth and broad acres. To these were added, in the course of the nineteenth century, historians like Macaulay and Acton (1857 and 1869), bankers like Overstone (1860), engineers like Armstrong (1887), poets like Tennyson (1884), scientists like Kelvin (1892), and even a painter, Leighton, in 1896.

Yet we should be cautious before concluding that utility had triumphed and that the House of Lords had become the repository of all the talents. Few of the peers mentioned above took much part in the routine public

---

55. Since Irish peers had always been eligible for British titles, there was not quite the same pressure. Moreover, after 1801, the Irish representative peers were elected for life, which put them in a stronger position than the Scottish representative peers after 1707. In 1777, the *Court and City Register* listed 156 Irish peers (including eighteen created in July and August 1776 which had caused some opprobious comment). Of the 156, sixteen also had seats at Westminster in the Lords. Over the next twenty-three years, up to the Act of Union, a further twenty-eight Irish peers were given British titles. They included such important families as Donegal, Drogheda, Ormonde, Shannon and Tyrone.

56. Preface to 1812 edition of Collins' *The Peerage of England*.

business of the House. Tennyson was 75 and Armstrong 77 when ennobled: Macaulay was a peer for only two years and Leighton for no more
than one day. Few of them founded peerage families: if they had done,
there was no guarantee that the son of a distinguished poet would also
be a distinguished poet, whereas the son of a landed magnate, all things
being equal, would be a landed magnate. Throughout most of the nineteenth century the peerage remained, as it has always been, the bastion of
the landed interest. Fundamental change to its character depended upon
life peerages, against which the decision in the Wensleydale case in 1856
locked the door for a hundred years.[57]

Although a slow alteration can be discerned in the composition of the
peerage, which was becoming more of a service nobility, it seems excessive
to suggest that 'a new political élite' was emerging in the period 1801–30.[58]
Professor McCahill has drawn attention to forty-seven peers, created between 1750 and 1830, who possessed less than 3,000 acres of land,
pointing out that this represented nearly 20 per cent of total creations in
that period.[59] It is, of course, true that by the end of the eighteenth century
most of the great landowners had already been ennobled and new claims
depended, for the most part, on vicissitudes of inheritance. But the list is
not totally convincing. First, it implies that more than 80 per cent of those
given peerages still had more than 3,000 acres of land. The precise figure
of 'landless' peers should be forty-six, since the list is one short. Some of
the peers should perhaps not have been included. It seems curious to count
Lord Niddry, ennobled in 1814 for gallant military conduct, as a landless
man, without mentioning that he was heir-presumptive to the earldom of
Hopetoun, which he inherited some two years later, together with
Hopetoun House and fifty thousand Scottish acres. Lord Stewart, ennobled
in 1823, was brother of Lord Castlereagh, whom he succeeded: the family
estates were estimated in 1883 at fifty thousand acres. Lord Manners, given
a barony in 1807, was for twenty years Lord Chancellor of Ireland. He
was a great-grandson of the third duke of Rutland, brother of the archbishop of Canterbury, and uncle to the Speaker of the House of
Commons. Rather than being a new type of peer, he was very much an
establishment figure, whose relatives, the dukes of Rutland, owned some
70,000 acres. Lord Grenville, the future prime minister was, as a younger
son, relatively landless; Dropmore was a mere 600 acres, though large
enough to accommodate a gift of 7,000 beech saplings from Stowe.[60] But
his brother was the first marquis of Buckingham and his nephew was
raised to a dukedom: his wife was heir to her brother, Lord Camelford,

---

57. David Hume had suggested life peerages in his *Idea of a Perfect Commonwealth*, published in 1742, in
his *Essays, Moral, Political and Literary*.

58. M. W. McCahill, 'Peerage Creations and the Changing Character of the British Nobility, 1750–
1850', in *Peers, Politics and Power*, p. 419. For a recent discussion of the question, see P. J. Jupp, 'The Landed
Elite and Political Authority in Britain, c. 1760–1850', *Journal of British Studies*, 29 (1990), pp. 53–79.

59. McCahill, 'Peerage Creations and the Changing Character of the British Nobility', p. 422, note 3.

60. *VCH. Bucks*, iii, 167; *HMC. Fortescue*, iii, 390. There is much valuable information on Grenville's
finances and properties in P. Jupp, *Lord Grenville, 1759–1834* (Oxford, 1985).

whose Cornish estates she inherited. Lord Granville, given a viscountcy in 1815, was brother of the second marquis of Stafford, created a duke in 1833, with far more land than any other nobleman: his wife was a daughter of the duke of Devonshire. There is little reason to believe that the elevation of Lords Niddry, Stewart, Manners, Grenville and Granville posed much of a threat to the traditional character of the nobility.

Nor does the fate of the remaining forty-one peers suggest that the aristocracy was in danger. The titles of twelve of them expired with the grantee, leaving no families to threaten anybody. Six more became extinct before 1883, when Bateman's survey of the great landowners was published. Of the remaining twenty-three, by 1883 the family of Wellington had acquired 19,000 acres, Hill 16,000 acres, Abercromby 15,000 acres, Camperdown 14,000 acres, Amherst 7,600 acres, Nelson 7,000 acres, Sidmouth 6,000 acres, and eight others over 2,000 acres. Eight families on the original list seem to have kept less than 2,000 acres. But we must not necessarily presume that they were doomed to lives of pitiful poverty. Lord Seaford, one of the eight, was created baron in 1826 for diplomatic services. His son already held the barony of Howard de Walden and married a daughter of the fourth duke of Portland: he was ambassador at Brussels for more than twenty years and died in 1868 in his chateau near Namur. His descendants scraped up enough money to lease from their relatives the Braybrookes their pleasant little house at Audley End.

There is no doubt that twenty years of gruelling warfare between 1793 and 1815 speeded up the process of replacement. The descendants of some of the landless peers certainly had distinguished public careers: Canning's son and Ellenborough's son each became Governor-general of India. But there is not much evidence that, for most of the nineteenth century, the older landed families were elbowed aside. A random list makes the point that well-established county families continued to play their part in the government of empire: Aberdeen (prime minister); Carlisle (Lord Privy Seal); Clarendon (foreign secretary); Dalhousie (Governor-general); Devonshire (secretary for war); Derby (prime minister); Granville (foreign secretary); Grey (prime minister); Lansdowne (foreign secretary); Malmesbury (foreign secretary); Marlborough (Viceroy of Ireland); Melbourne (prime minister); Newcastle (secretary at war); Northumberland (Viceroy of Ireland); Portland (Lord President of the Council); Richmond (Lord President of the Council); Rosebery (prime minister); Russell (prime minister); Rutland (Chancellor of the Duchy of Lancaster); Salisbury (prime minister); Spencer (Viceroy of Ireland). The concept of public service was not an invention of the bourgeoisie.

Though the French Revolution did not revolutionize the British nobility, it did it some service. It brought patriotism to the rescue of the peerage by identifying egalitarianism with the national enemy, the alien creed of a giddy and godless nation. Atrocity and Terror appeared to confirm what political philosophers had asserted for centuries – that democracy must lead to anarchy, spoliation and military dictatorship. The monarchy and the nobility found refreshed rôles as leaders of the nation in its desperate struggle.

The Revolutionary and Napoleonic Wars nudged Britain, like many continental countries, towards meritocracy and the career open to talents, even if the careers were mainly in killing and the pace of advance faltered as soon as peace returned. They provided a stream of heroes to be recruited into the peerage, bringing with them their glory and their prestige. At least ten naval and thirteen army officers were given peerages for distinguished conduct, not counting people like the Hood brothers, promoted from Irish barons to British viscounts, or Lord Uxbridge, one of the heroes of Waterloo, created marquis of Anglesey. The peerage was reinforced by Howe, victor of the Glorious First of June; Duncan of Camperdown; Jervis, in command at Cape St Vincent; Collingwood who took over command at Trafalgar; Graham, who led the British into France in 1813 and was ennobled as Lynedoch; above all, Horatio, Lord Nelson and the Duke himself, statues to whom occupied pride of place in cities and towns throughout the United Kingdom. The Duke's remark that Waterloo was won on the playing fields of Eton can be played backwards: Eton was saved on the field of Waterloo.

CHAPTER THREE

The Dutch Nobility in the Seventeenth and Eighteenth Centuries

J. L. Price
University of Hull

Until very recently historians of the Dutch Republic have not given the nobility a great deal of attention, and there was little or no systematic discussion of their rôle in politics, society or the economy. This absence, or only incidental appearance, of the nobility was especially true of writing in English, but works in Dutch also tended to assign to the nobles a rather insignificant part in the life of the Republic. In the standard texts, the political importance of the nobles in many provinces was mentioned, but otherwise they tended to be treated almost as picturesque survivals of a former age. One reason for this low profile of the nobility has been the prevailing tendency to concentrate on Holland at the expense of the other six provinces of the Republic. This was, and is, justifiable, given the political and economic dominance of this province, but as the political power and social influence of the nobles was minimal – or appeared to be so – in Holland, this has led to a underestimation of their importance in the Republic as a whole. The dominant image of Dutch society took Holland as the norm and has thus been urban, mercantile and perhaps even bourgeois or capitalist; there has been little place for the nobility in this schema.

Yet even for Holland such a view of the Republican period may be misleading. One important theme of recent research has been whether the regents, the ruling oligarchs of the towns, underwent a process of aristocratization in the course of the late seventeenth and early eighteenth century. A related question might also be the degree to which they already constituted something like a nobility at the beginning of the seventeenth century, that is whether the regents were a separate order in Dutch society and, if so, whether this could usefully be regarded as noble. Another intriguing aspect of the history of the nobility in this period is their suspiciously sudden disappearance from a leading rôle in the transition from the Revolt to the first years of the Republic. In most recent studies of the Dutch Revolt, the nobles have been assigned an important – perhaps even an exaggerated – rôle, yet already by the 1580s they virtually disappear from history, leaving only the House of Orange to represent a seemingly vanished, or at best marginalized, class. There was always something inherently implausible about this violent change of perspective: the division between North and South in the course of the Revolt meant that the great southern nobles were excluded from the new state, but that still left the lesser nobility of the northern provinces who had also played a significant part in the outbreak and progress of the Revolt. It seemed unlikely that the nobles of the North would lose all their power and influence within a matter of decades.

The Dutch nobility did not disappear or lose most of its power in the course of the Revolt of the Netherlands, and it continued to play an important rôle in the political, economic and social life of the new state. The nobles were not unaffected by the dramatic political changes stemming from the Revolt, nor by the even more revolutionary economic and social changes of the late sixteenth and early seventeenth century; but neither they nor the values they represented were swept away. The persistence of traditional forms in politics, society and even economy in the apparently transformed Dutch Republic should not be underestimated. Recent research has begun to shed some light on the nobilities of the various Dutch provinces in the Republican period. This has mostly concentrated on the politically less influential and economically less advanced provinces, but the apparently insignificant nobility in Holland itself has also enjoyed a reappraisal. This work is in its early stages as yet and there are still disturbing gaps in our knowledge, but it is already clear that the Dutch nobility was much more important in the life of the Republic as a whole than was once assumed.

It is also necessary to take another look at the Dutch regents in this context, and consider whether this privileged stratum of Dutch society should be seen as a species of nobility rather than of burgher – perhaps somewhat reminiscent of the recent transformation of historians' interpretations of the nature of the French *noblesse de robe*. Whatever the final judgement on this issue, the regents deserve at least a brief mention in any consideration of the Dutch nobility.

To begin with, it is necessary to make a distinction between Holland (and perhaps Zeeland as well) and the rest of the Republic. Whatever the behind-the-scenes influence of the nobles in Holland, their formal political power was very slight, whereas in most of the other provinces the nobles' public rôle was much more important. This division is not entirely clear cut, as the political influence in practice of the nobles in Friesland is uncertain, but in general the distinction holds: outside Holland the nobility had an important, if not dominant, part to play in provincial government whereas in Holland its position was relatively insignificant.

The social position of the nobles outside Holland was also considerably more prominent in a number of important ways, as the social and political structure of the lesser provinces showed more similarities with the rest of western and central Europe than did that of the dominant province. To this extent there are two stories to be told: the ways in which the nobility in Holland reacted to the political and social changes which took place in this economically advanced area of the Republic, and the persistence of noble power in the more traditional areas.

Yet there is another, and perhaps even more important aspect to the question, and that is the degree to which the noble values and culture which were still dominant in the rest of Europe also maintained their hegemony in the Dutch Republic, not only in the more traditional provinces but in Holland as well. Even in the leading province with its dominant towns, powerful regents and mercantile economy the superior status of the nobility went almost unchallenged until the second half of the eighteenth century. The attack on noble privilege did not come, as might have been expected, in the course of the economic transformation of the sixteenth and seventeenth centuries, and not primarily in Holland. It came chiefly in the later eighteenth century and in the land provinces where the nobility was most privileged and powerful. For most of the period with which this essay is concerned the Dutch Republic shared the social and cultural values of the rest of Europe to a significant degree. Even in Holland, the cultural challenge to the nobles remained implicit in the economic and social changes of the time, and there was very little explicit opposition to the complex of ideas and attitudes which helped to underpin the privileges and superior status of the nobility.

AN ANATOMY OF THE DUTCH NOBILITY

It is not easy to give a clear and comprehensive description of who was entitled to noble status in the various provinces of the Republic, but this seems to be a problem for historians rather than for contemporaries. With the exception of the lowest levels of the nobility, where there were various social groups and individuals with some claim to noble status but enjoying very few powers and practically no privileges, there seems to have been very little doubt concerning who was noble and who was not; later historians may find it difficult to pin down with any precision the criteria used, but there seem to have been remarkably few problems at the time. Although the town regents were a powerful, and even privileged, social group, they were clearly distinct from the nobles proper and both sides recognized the difference. It may well be that they constituted a new form of nobility, and this matter will be considered below (see pp. 107–13), but it was clear to contemporaries thay they were not nobles in the traditional sense.

A basic problem which affected the nobility throughout the Dutch Republic was the lack of a sovereign authority which was able to create new nobles to compensate for demographic erosion. While it was theoretically possible for the republican political authorities to create new nobles, such action was never taken, nor does it seem ever to have been seriously contemplated, either because the power to create nobles was seen as an attribute of monarchy alone, or because of the vested interests of the existing nobles who did not wish to share their privileged position with newcomers. In any event, there was no significant influx of new families into the nobility in this period, and as a consequence there was a general tendency for noble numbers throughout the Republic to decrease until something like a crisis seemed to be imminent by the end of the eighteenth century.

In terms of numbers of nobles the situation was healthy at the beginning of the seventeenth century, but the demographic weaknesses common to élite groups in this period led quite quickly to a general decline, though the tempo varied from province to province. This development was particularly clear in Holland, where the decisive fall in noble numbers took place in the second half of the seventeenth century: there was already cause for concern by about 1650 with only twenty-one noble families left in the province, and by 1730 there were only six. Similarly, in Friesland the number of noble families declined, partly at least as a consequence of determined endogamy, from fifty-eight in 1600 to thirty-four in 1700 and only sixteen by the end of the eighteenth century. In Groningen the decline in numbers of the old *jonker* families was offset to some extent before about 1650 by the admission of new families into the ranks of the recognized nobility, but from this point onwards closure was enforced and numbers began to fall. While there had been forty-five noble families in the province in 1600, by the end of the eighteenth century only ten were left. A very similar pattern can be observed in Drente. The evidence for the province of Utrecht is less clear but points in the same direction; here too there were already signs of numerical decline by the middle of the seventeenth century.

Gelderland was, along with Overijssel, the archetypically noble-dominated province but did not escape the seemingly unavoidable fate of nobilities in the Republic, although the reckoning does seem to have been deferred rather longer. At least in the Veluwe (one of the three political divisions, *kwartieren*, of the province), the number of noble families fell in the same way as in the rest of the Republic, but the number of actual *ambtsjonkers* (the nobles who controlled local administration in the region) remained little affected, remaining between thirty and forty throughout most of the period. Rapid decline in this respect only came after about 1785. At present little is known about the size of the nobility in Overijssel and Zeeland, but there is no indication that they escaped the general trend.

Another development which seems to have been common among the nobilities of every province was the pressure towards the creation of élites within the élites, particularly in terms of the monopolizing of political power. This move towards the creation of a privileged group within the nobility centred on the creation, or increasingly exclusive nature, of the *ridderschappen*. These were the representative orders of the nobility in the provincial States of Holland, Gelderland, Overijssel, Utrecht and Drente, and membership became limited to select groups within the nobilities of these provinces in the course of the seventeenth century. In some cases this exclusion was achieved by restricting eligibility to those possessing particular types of landed property or houses: *havezaten* (Drente, Overijssel) or *ridderhofsteden* (Utrecht). The effect of such restrictions was to concentrate the political power of the nobility, and particularly the access to influential and lucrative offices, in the hands of a select group of families. However, as the size of the various nobilities shrank, so the significance of such exclusivism became less important. Certainly by the later part of the eighteenth century, far from there being too many nobles for the available posts there were rather too few.

Although the tendency to concentrate power and the profits of office in ever fewer hands was not absent in Friesland and Groningen, *ridderschappen* were never formed; in the former province the nobles had few privileges and had to work within its peculiar system on more or less the same terms as non-nobles, and the *landdag* of the Ommelanden of Groningen (the countryside of the province not under the jurisdiction of the town of Groningen) remained open, at least nominally, to both noble and non-noble landowners. In Zeeland, the only political representation of the nobility in the provincial States was the so-called First Noble, a position which was in the hands of the House of Orange throughout this period. This might be seen as an extreme case of the concentration of power into the hands of a privileged inner group, though the origins of the situation date back to before the Revolt and are thus not the consequence of the supposed tendency of the Republican régime to encourage oligarchic processes.

In general, the formal distinctions within the nobility were few: there was no complex hierarchy of noble titles, with most nobles being called lords of their manors (*heerlijkheden*) or, in the land provinces and Groningen, *jonkers*. There were a handful of more impressive titles, either surviving from the Burgundian and Spanish periods, or granted by foreign sovereigns, but they seem to have cut little ice, and during the Republic no new noble ranks could be created. The higher levels of the nobility were distinguished by greater political influence and privilege not by titles or other outward marks of distinction.

It will be becoming evident that the Dutch nobility were not a homogeneous group and that there were considerable differences between the various provinces. A clearer overall pattern can be obtained, however, by putting these provincial nobilities into three broad regional groupings, though it is possible that the superficial differences between them only disguise a basically similar historical development. In Holland and Zeeland, the nobles had been eclipsed politically, had very little economic power, and very limited social influence. Also, in these provinces they had no significant legal privileges. While they may, in fact, have retained rather more political power and social influence in Holland than was once thought, this can in no way compare to the constitutionally entrenched political power of the nobility in the second region: Utrecht, Gelderland

and Overijssel. This was the region of the Republic with the strongest feudal traditions, and here the nobles dominated the countryside and had at least parity with the towns at the provincial level. Here we see the obvious characteristics of a traditional European nobility: large landowners with very great judicial, administrative and political power. The third region consists of Friesland and Groningen, where feudalism had hardly taken a hold and where, although noble influence was important at all levels of society, it had to make itself felt in rather different ways than in the previous region. Here this period saw the development of oligarchies of landowners, partly noble partly not, with the nobles being distinguished by a higher status in the estimation of the surrounding society rather than by any considerable degree of special powers or privileges.

Although these three regional nobilities are somewhat different on the surface, it needs to be noted that there was intermarriage between them, and noble families were able to move – partly through such marriages – from region to region. In the end, despite these sharp regional differences, it can be argued that certain common characteristics unite the historical experience of the nobilities during the Republican period. In the end it might be asked whether, by the end of the eighteenth century, the dilemmas facing the nobles of the Veluwe were so very different from those which the nobility in Friesland had to confront.

As has already been indicated, recruitment to the Dutch nobility was a major problem, and by the end of the eighteenth century threatened to be a fatal one. First, the Republic lacked the normal means of élite renewal, most importantly creation by a recognized authority such as a monarch. However, the problem was exacerbated by the progressive closure of the regional élites to the possibility of renewal from below. Whereas in the sixteenth and even in the early seventeenth century it was still possible for new families to gain recognition as noble in at least some of the provinces, this avenue of recruitment was closing up in this period. This closure had already taken place in Holland by the beginning of the sixteenth century, and in the Veluwe it was determined at the end of the sixteenth century that only nobles from families recognized as such before 1500 could become *ambtsjonkers*. Similarly, in Friesland the nobility had already become a closed order by about 1500. In Groningen, however, as late as the first half of the seventeenth century a number of families from the town of Groningen were able to gain entry to the nobility of the Ommelanden, probably because of pre-existing family connections with local nobles, and also a few of the leading landowners were able to achieve recognition as nobles. This situation was exceptional, and in any case seems to have ended by about the middle of the seventeenth century.

With no new creations and an increasingly effective closure to recruitment from below by more or less spontaneous means, few possibilities were left. Some men were ennobled by foreign princes but the numbers involved were not great enough to counteract the demographic erosion, nor, it would appear, were such creations generally recognized as far as admission to privileged bodies such as *ridderschappen* were concerned. There was a certain amount of internal movement from one province to another. William III, for example, brought his close collaborator, Bentinck, from Gelderland into the Holland *ridderschap* in 1676 – he had bought a suitable manor (*heerlijkheid*) within the province to qualify – and in 1619 his predecessor Maurice had done the same for his ally François van Aerssen and another 'foreign' noble; the object in both these cases was political, however, and not designed to deal with a shortage of native nobles. Friesland and Groningen also absorbed nobles from other provinces, but such internal movements could not solve the overall problem that the fall in the number of nobles affected the Republic as a whole, and not just a few provinces. In fact, a solution to the problem was not found until after the end of the Republic. The Orange Monarchy created a new nobility in the early nineteenth century by a policy of wholesale ennoblement of leading landowners and established regent families, but that was not an option available before this time.

SOCIAL AND ECONOMIC POSITION

The relatively advanced economy of the Republic meant that the economic position of the nobility in the country as a whole was markedly less powerful than in most of the rest of Europe. This was most clearly the case in Holland, where the development of commercial capitalism and urbanization had made most progress, but it was true to a significant extent of the other provinces as well. Even in those provinces – Gelderland, Overijssel – where the nobles were traditionally strongest, their economic position was less than predominant. Even in the poorest and most economically backward of the provinces the economic grip of the nobility was relatively weak.

As was the case in the rest of Europe, the Dutch nobility were landowners, but they were not the only landowners, and ownership of land was not the key to economic power that it was in most other areas of the continent. Thus the economic position of the nobility was undermined in two ways: their control of the land was challenged by other social groups, and the trade and manufactures of the towns were serious rivals to the land as a source of wealth and power in most of the Dutch provinces, and in some they overshadowed it altogether. Perhaps even more importantly, throughout the Republic agriculture was integrated into the market economy, even the farming system of the proverbially backward Drente was fundamentally affected by the pull of the powerful Holland market. It is possible that the irresistible development of commercial agriculture in changing the economic structures of the Dutch countryside also brought a parallel transformation in social and cultural terms. Neither the social domination of the nobility, nor the value system which upheld this supremacy could go unchallenged by the triumph of the market in the agrarian sector, but the process was a slow one and, as elsewhere in Europe at a rather later period, the prestige of the nobility and its cultural ideals outlived the economic system which had produced both. So to argue for the relative economic weakness of the nobility is not to argue either that its social prestige had been eclipsed or its cultural values replaced. As we shall see, the political power of the nobles was still considerable in many provinces; whether this was a result of the continuing strength of their social influence, it was certainly an important factor in maintaining that influence.

Land ownership is obviously a central issue: the nobles were a land-owning class, but nowhere in the Republic were they in control of the greater part of the land. Nobles owned land almost by definition, but everywhere in the Republic freeholders and other non-nobles held more land than they did. As might be expected this was most clearly the case in Holland, where it is estimated that the nobility owned less than 10 per cent of the farmland in the seventeenth century, with most land being held by farmers and townspeople. What is perhaps more surprising is that the situation was not so very different elsewhere in the Republic. In Gelderland during the same period less than 15 per cent of the land was in noble ownership in most parts of the Veluwe, and it seems unlikely that the position would have been very different in the other two quarters of the province. On the other hand, there seems to have been no significant decline in noble landownership up to the middle of the eighteenth century, and only a slight fall before 1800. In Groningen, the province itself – having taken over the landholdings of the monasteries after the Reformation – was the greatest landowner, and in the course of the eighteenth century its tenant farmers achieved a position equivalent in most respects to that of freeholders. The nobility here held about 20 per cent of the land at the beginning of the eighteenth century – twice as much as in Holland, and rather more than in the Veluwe but still quite modest. The percentage of noble land-holding was somewhat less than 20 per cent in Drente, and here again the position of the freeholders (*eigenerfden*) was notably strong. In Overijssel the situation varied from quarter to quarter: by the middle of the eighteenth century, 20 per cent of the land in Salland and Twente was still in noble hands, but only about 11 per cent in Vollenhoven.

In the other provinces the situation is less clear. In Friesland a large proportion of the land was rented out, and the percentage of land owned by nobles and regents tended to increase, especially in the late seventeenth century (particularly for political reasons), but given the sharply falling numbers of the nobles in this province it seems likely that the lion's share of this increase went to the urban regents and other non-nobles. The situation in Utrecht was probably not dissimilar to that in Overijssel, but the position with regard to noble land ownership in Zeeland is unclear.

However, nobles were primarily landowners and drew most of their income from the exploitation of their estates. Given their relatively small, and falling, numbers, their individual holdings could be considerable. Overall, rents seem to have been more important economically than direct exploitation or seigneurial rights, though income from the latter was often quite considerable. In this respect, provincial differences do not seem to have been very great, though in some provinces there were seigneurial rights not directly attached to land ownership which could be important for noble influence and income.

In Holland the nobles rented out most of their land on five- or six-year leases and thus were able to respond fairly flexibly to changes in agricultural prices. Here around 60–70 per cent of the income from estates came from rents, but this still leaves a substantial amount in many cases to be drawn from seigneurial rights, tithes and the like. Noble income from land was thus largely, but not exclusively, dependent on the movement of agricultural prices. In Overijssel some nobles appear to have been dependent on fixed rents, which meant that they began to suffer as a result of rising costs in the eighteenth century, but this does not seem to have been typical of the Dutch nobility who largely held their own as far as personal wealth was concerned, though their declining numbers undermined their economic influence as a class.

The economic, and even more the social, position of the nobles was affected by their possession of lordships of the manor and similar rights associated with the administration of justice in the broadest sense. The social status and local political power which such lordships conferred on their owners was probably more important than the monetary income they brought in. The buying-up of packages of such rights (but not manors as such), associated with justice and drainage administration especially, was a typical investment of nobles in Groningen by the eighteenth century, but it has been argued that these were investments in prestige rather than in the expectation of getting a particularly high return in terms of income. In Holland a lordship gave at least nominal control over local government in rural districts and included other rights, often the advowson of the village church. Here over 80 per cent of such lordships had been held by nobles in the sixteenth century and even by 1650 this figure was still around 60 per cent. By this time, however, competition for lordships was coming not only from urban regents in search, perhaps, of prestige, but also from town governments wanting to extend their political control over the adjacent countryside. This political and judicial aspect of manorial lordships was separate from landownership and thus allowed the nobles initially a greater share of control over the countryside than their landholdings might seem to warrant, but later brought competition from the dominant towns of the province. Elsewhere such lordships combined with other judicial and administrative rights to form the basis of the political power of the nobles.

It is hard to make useful generalizations about noble wealth, except that the relative importance of the wealth of the nobility as a whole was much greater in some of the land provinces than in the more economically developed regions of the Republic, and specifically Holland. In the latter, though individual nobles may have been very wealthy, the enormous expansion of the urban economy together with the importance of commercial farming in the province (where the greater part of the cultivated land was in non-noble hands) meant that the noble share of total wealth was almost insignificant. In contrast, in Overijssel and Gelderland, where the urban sector had failed to match the explosive growth of Holland, the agrarian sector had been less profitable, and the proportion of land in noble hands was distinctly higher, noble wealth was much more important though probably not predominant. In all of the provinces, nobles can be found among the richest of the inhabitants, but nowhere were the nobility as a group economically dominant.

There is some evidence pointing to an overall decline in noble wealth during this period, though the evidence presents serious difficulties of interpretation. In particular records of assessment for taxation must be treated with caution, as in at least some areas the apparent fall in noble wealth seems to have been the result of nobles using their political influence to secure systematic under-assessments for tax purposes. It has been argued, for example, for Overijssel that noble income was caught between fixed rents and rising prices after about 1675. The result in Salland and Twente was an apparent fall of about a third in the wealth of nobles with session in the *landdag*. However, the evidence for continued noble prosperity in the Veluwe of Gelderland, despite the effects of the agricultural depression, casts some doubt on such figures. On the other hand, it may well be that in Twente at least the rise of the rural textile industry plus the improved position of the freeholders (*eigenerfden*) decisively undermined the social dominance of the nobility, whatever may have been the case in the rest of Overijssel.

A further reason to be suspicious of tax records, particularly when they seem to indicate a fall in noble wealth, is given by the case of Groningen. The records of the tax on wealth when it was first introduced in the province in 1672, give an impression of noble fortunes which fits in well with evidence drawn from other sources, but subsequently the tax returns apparently show the nobility of the Ommelanden to be declining in wealth, whereas in fact average fortunes seem to have increased considerably. One calculation gives the average wealth of noble families in the seventeenth century as f.86,600 and in the eighteenth century as f.142,455. The nobles appear to have been able to weather the agricultural depression of the late seventeenth and early eighteenth century successfully, and indeed may have been able to increase their holdings at the expense of small farmers who failed to keep their heads above water. Similarly, in Drente the evidence points to the nobility surviving the depression with undiminished if not increased fortunes. Here fortunes were generally rather smaller than in the Ommelanden, rarely passing f.100,000–the f.750,000 of Carel de Vos van

Steenwijk stands out, but was derived largely from inheritances from outside this relatively poor province. It is evident that in both these provinces the nobility were not totally dependent on land economically. In the Ommelanden, only about half of noble wealth was represented by land, the other half being invested in seigneurial rights, mortgages, and especially the provincial debt. There was little investment here in the Dutch East India Company, rather more in the West India Company: there was a regional chamber of the latter in Groningen and possession of a certain amount of stock opened up the attractive possibility of becoming one of its directors. In Drente the pattern was similar, though there were no seigneurial rights to buy, and investments in provincial bonds doubled in the eighteenth as compared to the seventeenth century. In Holland, Johan van Mathenesse's wealth was assessed at f.160,000 in 1602, which is unlikely to have been an overestimate, and this seems to have been far from exceptional for the nobility of this province.

Although such fortunes are on the face of it impressive, and in Groningen and the land provinces (not to mention Drente) sufficient to put these families among the richest of their provinces, nevertheless they did not overshadow the sort of wealth which could be accumulated by the most successful of the merchants and manufacturers of Holland. For example, in Amsterdam in 1674 over two hundred people were assessed for tax purposes at a wealth of f.100,000 or more, and nearly seventy at over f.200,000. Even allowing for the exceptional prosperity of Amsterdam, such fortunes compare well with those of the nobility in general, and the evidence suggests that at least the leading citizens of the other Holland towns did not fall far behind such levels of wealth.

In general it may be said that the nobility in the Republic, with some possible regional exceptions, was not declining in wealth as far as the fortunes of individual families were concerned. On the other hand, their falling numbers meant that, however great the wealth of the average noble was, the group as a whole did not command overwhelming economic power even in those regions where it was strongest. Also, it seems clear that the rapid growth of the trading and manufacturing economy in the Republic during the sixteenth and seventeenth centuries, primarily but not exclusively in Holland, completely overshadowed the collective wealth of the nobility. Economic power lay with the towns of Holland, together with the market-orientated farmers of the more developed regions of the country. Even in the early seventeenth century the economic strength of the nobility had nowhere been unchallenged, and by the later eighteenth century the remnants of noble economic power were being successfully undermined by the rise of freeholders and tenant farmers even in Gelderland and Overijssel.

The Dutch nobility was a provincial nobility, or rather, a series of provincial nobilities. This is true in a trivial and in a more significant sense. First, the highly decentralized nature of the Republic meant that there was very little of a centre to which the nobles could relate; all the Dutch were provincials in this sense, the nobles perhaps rather less than other sections of the population as they were rather more inclined than most to look to the court of the princes of Orange as a unifying symbol for the Republic as a whole. The Dutch nobles were also provincial in the rather more significant sense that they lived in their provinces, on their estates, and centred their economic, social and political activities on their provinces. There were, of course, exceptions. It could be argued that the members of the *ridderschap* of Holland, for example, were national figures in a sense, because of their central, albeit largely decorative, rôle in Holland's political life. This is, however, not because they had moved beyond the affairs of their province, but because Holland's provincial politics were of national significance in themselves, and in this respect quite unlike those of any other province. Also, the structure of politics allowed a small minority of nobles from the lesser provinces to play a prominent part in the political life of the Republic. The provinces were, of course, not hermetically sealed off from one another, and nobles from Overijssel, say, intermarried with their like in other provinces, and nobles from one province bought land and invested in other ways in provinces outside their own as well. However, the nobility as a whole was primarily provincially orientated – where, that is, this primary orientation was not even more localized, such as within the quarters of Overijssel or Gelderland.

The main residence of most nobles was on their estates in the countryside, often in castles or fortified houses rebuilt in more comfortable styles if not in the seventeenth then certainly in the eighteenth century. As far as economic interests were concerned, they were primarily landowners, and their political and social interests also drew them into the country. However, in most cases this did not mean turning their backs on the towns: in a small country with good communications, towns were easily accessible from almost anywhere in the Republic, and the chief towns of the provinces drew the nobles in for political reasons. The Hague was a special case, because of the presence of the prince of Orange's Court for at least part of the year, and as the seat of both the States General and the States of Holland, and it had a more aristocratic air than most Dutch towns. Its attractive power for the mass of the nobility was limited, however: their political interests were provincial if not local. The relationship between the nobles and the towns is better illustrated, perhaps, by the situation in Gelderland where a high proportion of nobles lived in the area between Arnhem and Deventer, thus in the countryside but within easy reach of the major towns of the province.

One of the reasons for the primarily regional orientation was the importance of office-holding for the political influence, social status and even economic well-being of the nobility. Such judicial and administrative posts were fundamental to the position of the nobility and were to be found, in the main, within the provinces. In particular, control of various local offices was a lynchpin of noble influence, as well as strengthening their financial position, not only through the emoluments attached to these posts, but often in other ways as well.

A perhaps extreme example of the fundamental importance of local office for the Dutch nobility is the case of the *ambtsjonkers* in Gelderland, who effectively controlled the countryside of the province. This position was as much a status as an office: the *ambtsjonkers* were in effective control of the administrative subdivisions of the quarters of Gelderland, the *schoutambten*, and had to be from recognized noble families, and also satisfy quite high wealth requirements. In the Veluwe particularly, the *ambtsjonkers* were able to draw considerable economic advantages from their control over tax assessments and collection in their *schoutambten*. Although this formal noble monopoly of local office was perhaps unusual, effective control of such positions by the nobility was not. Even in the notoriously 'non-feudal' Friesland the *grietmannen* (the chief officials of the *grietenijen*, the subdivisions of the quarters of the province) were predominantly noble throughout this period, despite the declining numbers of the nobility here. Similarly, in Groningen by the middle of the eighteenth century two-thirds of the *rechtstoelen* – the basic local administrative cum judicial units – were under noble control.

The provincial orientation of the nobility was further encouraged by the availability of offices of power and profit for the nobility at provincial level and, through the province, positions in the Generality, that is the central institutions of the Dutch State, though these were only within the reach of the most influential. The political power of the nobility in the separate provinces will be considered in the next section; here provincial and Generality office-holding will be considered as lucrative and prestigious career openings for nobles. It is important to note that normally Generality office came through the province, that is nobles gained such positions either as the representatives of their province, or as its nominees.

The apparatus of central government in the Republic was very small in size, however, as befitted its very limited powers and restricted scope; consequently the number of desirable posts was also strictly limited, and in effect only open to the élite of the provincial nobility. There were far more places to share out in the government of the provinces, though there was also a strong tendency for the most powerful and financially rewarding positions to be monopolized by a limited number of leading families. To some extent this tendency towards the concentration of power and of the profits of office in the hands of an inner group within the nobility as a whole was counteracted by shrinking numbers – as with the *ridderschappen* in some provinces there were hardly enough nobles to fill the places available by the end of the eighteenth century. The fall in the number of *ambtsjonkers* in the Veluwe towards the end of the eighteenth century, for example, seems to have been the consequence of both a restrictive recruitment policy, and of a fall in the number of suitably qualified candidates.

A particularly well-documented example of both noble control of provincial office and the concentration of the most desirable of these into relatively few hands is given by the Ommelanden of Groningen. Here all the provincial posts in the gift of the Ommelanden (as opposed to those controlled by the town of Groningen) went to nobles, at first through the power of 'leagues' of nobles and then, after their introduction in 1659, through noble political control of the *onderkwartieren*. In this province such offices circulated from quite an early date according to fixed rotas, set for years in advance. The profits of office here were not enormous, but neither were they negligible: for example, in the first half of the eighteenth century a deputy to the States General or to the Generality exchequer received about f.2,000 per annum, which was the equivalent of a very respectable middle-class income. Although the *onderkwartieren* were abolished in 1749 and the *stadhouder* (provincial governor, in this case the prince of Orange) gained considerable influence over such appointments, the system of noble control remained essentially unchanged. Some individuals suffered, but not the nobility as a whole.

Besides this concentration on local and provincial office, the Dutch nobility, especially in the land provinces, also saw military careers as suitable to their status and needs. This was notably the case in Drente, but appears to have been true in less impoverished provinces as well. The reduced size of the army after the Treaty of Utrecht (1713) meant that such careers were less readily available in the eighteenth century, and may have had some effect on the finances of the nobility as a whole. More clearly, the appetite among the nobility for military commissions together with the great influence which the princes of Orange wielded over military appointments (with the important exceptions of the two stadhouderless periods, 1650–72 and 1702–47) strengthened the patronage links between the nobles and Orange. Indeed, in general the influence which the princes could exercise, formally or informally, over civil as well as military appointments, was one of the ways in which they drew the nobles into their patronage system. Politically this was very advantageous for the princes because in most of the provinces the power of the nobles was considerable.

POLITICAL POWER

With regard to the political rôle of the nobility, there are again very sharp contrasts to be noted between the different provinces of the Republic. At one extreme stands Holland where the nobles had very little political power in comparison to the all-powerful towns. Although the political eclipse of the nobility of Holland has been questioned recently, this has served to introduce nuances rather than to suggest any significant shift in the location of political power. Zeeland is to some extent in the same camp, though the peculiar influence of the princes of Orange in this province is an important qualification. In the rest of the Republic, however, the nobility either shared power with the towns or were in effect dominant, though the ways in which noble power manifested itself differed between, on the one hand, Friesland and Groningen, and, on the other, Utrecht, Gelderland and Overijssel with their more markedly feudal past.

The very restricted political power of the nobility in Holland is expressed clearly by their position in the States of Holland, where the *ridderschap* as a body had one vote as opposed to the eighteen of the towns. In contrast to some of the other provinces, the nobles had very little or no influence on the towns and very few were members of the urban oligarchies and so this route to greater influence was effectively closed to them. However, the formal system offered the nobles certain advantages. The important committees of the States, most significantly the standing committee (*gecommitteerde raden*), always had a noble as member, as did Holland's delegation to the States General. Thus individual nobles could find themselves in a position to play a not inconsiderable political rôle within the province. The social prestige of the nobles, perhaps surprisingly, appears to have been as high in Holland as in the rest of the Republic, despite the fact that they were economically and politically overshadowed by the towns. It would thus be a mistake to write off the nobles as a force in Holland politics, particularly when there was a *stadhouder* in office.

Such revisionist considerations, however, should not be allowed to obscure the fundamental fact of the power of the towns within Holland. The eighteen towns represented in the States of Holland ran the politics of the province, and their only effective rival – besides each other – was the *stadhouder*, not the nobility. The nobles may have played a more significant part individually than has been recognized in the past, but as a body they remained clearly subordinate to the voting towns.

What the nobility lacked in Holland was an independent power base: when there was a powerful *stadhouder* in the province the nobles acted as his clients, and during the stadhouderless periods they stood in a structurally similar position to the *raadpensionaris* (grand pensionary) as the representative of the power of the States. In the early seventeenth century, they may have controlled the greater part of the *heerlijkheden* in the province, but this gave them no extra political clout because it brought no increase in their representation in the provincial States, and in any case during the later seventeenth and eighteenth centuries they were facing competition from the towns and from town regents over control of such rights. In brief, the nobles in Holland were already in a weak position *vis-à-vis* the towns before the Revolt, and the increase from six to eighteen in the number of towns represented in the provincial States – perhaps the most significant constitutional change to take place during the Revolt – definitively relegated the nobility to a subordinate political rôle. What saved them from complete political eclipse was partly the influence of the princes of Orange as *stadhouders* of the province for much of this period, but mostly the ingrained traditionalism of the political system: apart from the increase in the number of towns represented in the States of Holland, the province was governed as far as possible in the same way as it had been before the Revolt, which meant that the nobles retained their traditional offices and powers. The nobility still spoke first in the deliberations of the States, for example, but usually were in effect the mouthpiece of the *stadhouder* or *raadpensionaris*; they retained the chairmanships of many committees, even of the powerful standing committee of the States, but were unable as a group to pursue, or perhaps even formulate, a distinctive policy of their own.

In Zeeland, the position of the nobles was even weaker, though here the beneficiary of the decline of noble power was the House of Orange even more than the towns. The representation of the nobility in the States of Zeeland had shrunk in the course of the Revolt to the First Noble alone – with one vote in the States as against the six of the towns – and this position was held by the princes of Orange throughout this period to the exclusion of the rest of the nobles of the province. As lord of Vlissingen and marquis of Vere, as well as holding the post of *stadhouder* when it was in existence, the princes had very great influence within the province, but whether this can legitimately be counted as part of the power of the Dutch nobility as a whole is very doubtful. The position of the princes of Orange in the Dutch Republic will be discussed subsequently (see below, pp. 102–3) but clearly they were rather in the position of constitutional rulers than leading nobles – at least after 1618. So it can be said that Zeeland was unique in the Republic as it was here alone that the nobility had been totally squeezed out of the political system.

In sharp contrast to the subordinate position of the nobles in Holland and their eclipse in Zeeland was their power in the group of land provinces with a feudal past – Utrecht, Overijssel and Gelderland. Here the nobility had a formal parity with the towns in terms of political power, but in fact were probably the dominant element in the political system. This dominance was achieved through a combination of their formal powers within the various governmental structures with their social prestige and their influence over the urban oligarchies of their provinces. Whereas in Holland it was the towns who paid the piper and thus called the tune as far as politics was concerned, in these land provinces it was the nobles who, in the main, were able to dictate to the town regents.

The States of Utrecht had three members: the *ridderschap*, the town of Utrecht together with the smaller towns, and the *geëligeerde* (the representatives of the secularized chapters of the chief churches of the town of Utrecht). The members of the chapters were chosen turn and turn about by the nobles and the towns, and so in principle there was an even balance between nobles and townsmen in the *geëligeerde*, and thus parity between nobility and towns in the government of the province as a whole. An important change in the political balance within the province came in 1674 with the granting of greatly increased powers to the prince of Orange as *stadhouder*. These powers lapsed on the death of William III but were renewed in 1747. The enhanced powers of appointment for the *stadhouder* under this system may have strengthened the position of the nobility within the province, but only as clients of the House of Orange. Throughout the period of the Republic, Gelderland was divided into three quarters, (the fourth quarter having been separated from the rest in the course of the Revolt), each with their own States or *landdag*, and in each of these there was formal parity between noble and town influence. This parity was carried through to the provincial *landdag*, composed of representatives from the quarters. Despite this formal parity, Gelderland had the reputation of being dominated by the nobility, partly because the divide between nobles and urban oligarchs was less complete than, for example, in Holland. The nobility had considerable influence in the towns: nobles sat in town governments, had family connections with other regents, and in general were able to build up a considerable clientèle in the towns. Although there were already complaints in the 1620s that the nobility were losing power to the towns, and these have misled some historians into exaggerating the power of the towns in this period, it is the eighteenth century before there is any sign of a serious challenge to the dominance of the nobility in Gelderland, and the evidence is far from conclusive even at this time. Indeed, it could be argued that the most direct challenge to the power of the nobility in the eighteenth century came not from the towns but from the leading freeholders (*geërfden*). The latter had little immediate success, but in retrospect can be seen as having paved the way for the defeat of the old nobility, not only in the Batavian period, but also definitively in the early nineteenth century. Here also the picture is complicated by the greatly increased powers gained by the princes of Orange as *stadhouder*, first in 1675 and again in 1748.

The situation was similar in Overijssel with regard to the careful, formal balance in power between towns and nobles. The *ridderschap* as a body, though its members voted individually, had as much weight as the three towns represented in the *landdag*, Deventer, Zwolle and Kampen, taken together. Also in the standing committee of the provincial States (*gedeputeerde staten*) the precise balance between nobles and towns was maintained. The division between towns and nobles went even further here than in most of the other provinces (though Groningen was somewhat similar in this respect), in that the unity of the province was rather fragile, with the three great towns tending to look to their past as free imperial cities while the nobles could claim separate authority over the countryside. Thus there was a sense in which the province was a union between the three towns and the nobles, with each side having a claim to a sort of sovereignty.

In practice matters rarely went to such an extreme – though there were serious splits in response to the French invasion of 1672 – but internal disputes could be bitter and particularly difficult to resolve because of the pretensions to independence of both sides. This potential impasse between towns and nobles was by-passed after 1674 by means of the *regeringsreglement* (regulation of government) imposed by William III. As in Utrecht and Gelderland this gave the prince, as *stadhouder* of the province, far-reaching

98

powers of appointment in government and administration, and thus decisive political influence. This system was swept aside on the prince's death but restored again in 1748 in the course of the Orange restoration.

Drente was not represented in the States General but was formally autonomous, though not entirely so in practice. In the States of the province, the *ridderschap* (formed only as late as 1600) had one vote against the two of the representatives of the freeholders (*eigenerfden*), this separate session having been won in the course of the Revolt. This constitutional arrangement, with the nobles having to share power, not with the towns but with the leading freeholders in the countryside, makes this small province comparable to Friesland and Groningen rather than the other land provinces with their balance between towns and nobles to the complete exclusion of the non-noble rural population.

The feudal system had touched the northern provinces, Friesland and Groningen, only slightly if at all, and thus the basis of noble power here was significantly different from the previous group of provinces where the feudal past was still influential. However, despite the very different ways in which noble power had to express itself, the result was perhaps in the end not so very different from the situation in those provinces where noble political power was entrenched in the formal system of government. Conversely, also, the effective challenge to noble power in the eighteenth century was probably no greater in these provinces than in Gelderland or Overijssel. Even in Friesland, where the political system was so different on the surface, the reality of noble and regent power had already overtaken the peasant democracy of the Middle Ages by the beginning of the seventeenth century, and only grew stronger subsequently. In Groningen, likewise, despite their lack of a formally privileged position, the nobles were able to exploit the political system so as to achieve dominance in the Ommelanden, and considerable power in the province as a whole.

The States of Groningen had two members, the town and the representatives of the Ommelanden. The degree of integration between the two elements was limited; indeed, the province was usually termed *Stad en Lande* (Town and Country). Although the nobility were not without connections in the magistracy of the town of Groningen, their primary source of political influence was their control over the assembly of the Ommelanden. Here they were able to use their wealth and land to manipulate the electoral system. A minimum landholding was required for eligibility for the *landdag* of the Ommelanden, and the nobles made what amounted to fictitious sales of parcels of land of the appropriate size in order to create qualified *eigenerfden* who were in fact under their control. Similarly through their control of local government, they were able to keep a firm hold on appointments to positions of power and profit within the Ommelanden, and also on those provincial posts in the gift of the Ommelanden. The balance of power between the nobility and Groningen seems, however, to have favoured the town, as the regents were able to move into the Ommelanden by land purchases and marriage alliances. For much of this period the influence of the *stadhouder* was distinctly limited, but in 1749 his powers were greatly increased especially as regards influence over appointments both at provincial level and in the Ommelanden. As in the other provinces where the Orange restoration brought significantly enhanced powers, this change went far towards making the nobility a dependent clientèle of the princes of Orange, while leaving more or less intact the deformations of the system it had been intended to cure.

The situation in Friesland was complicated by a political system very different from that in most of the rest of the Republic. The provincial states had four members: the eleven towns and the three quarters into which Friesland was divided. The quarters were subdivided into *grietenijen* – thirty in all – each of which returned two representatives to the *landdag*, one of which had to be a noble. The right to vote in the country districts was attached to particular pieces of landed property, and the degree of popular participation was nominally very high – there were roughly 10,000 votes in a population which probably remained less than 150,000 throughout this period.

However, to a large extent this apparent peasant democracy was controlled – and increasingly so in the course of the seventeenth century – by an oligarchy of nobles, non-noble landowners and urban regents, who bought up vote-conferring properties and in general exercised considerable ingenuity in manipulating the peculiarities of the system. Thus the nobility were able to attain considerable political power as part of the dominant oligarchy of the province, despite their lack of a formally privileged position within the governmental system. It remains difficult to assess, however, just how important a part of this oligarchy they were. They held a high proportion of the positions of *grietman* until the very end of this period, and demographic problems seem to have been more of a threat to their political influence than any other factor. Here also the revival of Orange power in the mid-eighteenth century strengthened the position of the *stadhouder* from 1748 onwards, but as elsewhere in so far as this was intended as an attack on the numerous and notorious malpractices it was ineffective.

So, if we look at the political power of the nobles in the Republic as a whole, their eclipse in Zeeland and their very restricted rôle in Holland can be set against their much stronger position elsewhere, with at least parity in Utrecht, Gelderland and Overijssel, and with comparable influence in effect in Friesland and Groningen. In the course of the seventeenth and eighteenth centuries, the picture underwent significant changes. In general it can be suggested that the seventeenth century was a period of oligarchic consolidation in which the nobles played their full share. In Groningen and Drente, at least, by the middle of the century the nobility had closed itself off from renewal from outside, and in Friesland the oligarchic exploitation of the voting system was only fully established by the second half of the century. Similarly, in Gelderland there is evidence that the seventeenth century was a period of consolidation of noble power, particularly as regards control of local government.

In the eighteenth century, in contrast, noble power began to come under challenge from various directions. Most obviously, after the high summer of oligarchy in the early eighteenth century during the second stadhouderless period, the restoration of the House of Orange to real power in the Republic brought distinct limitations to noble autonomy in its train. In Holland and Zeeland the situation of the nobility changed little, though there is some evidence of resentment at Orange power in the *ridderschap* of Holland, in the rest of the Republic the increase in the influence of the *stadhouders* meant that the nobles became politically much more dependent on the princes of Orange. One aspect of the Patriot movement in the 1780s was resentment by republican nobles and other notables at the tutelage which had been imposed on them by Orange since the middle of the century.

There were also challenges from below surfacing as the *plooierijen* (popular attacks on the power of some local oligarchies) immediately after William III's death, the popular movement in support of Orange in the 1740s, and finally in the more radical wing of the Patriots. The gains were not spectacular: the *plooierijen* were politically inchoate and gained nothing, the restoration of Orange merely moved corruption around, and even the Patriot movement achieved less, and some would argue much less, than seemed at one point to be likely. The power of the established oligarchy in the Republic was only broken after the French conquest of 1795 – if then. However, it can be argued that in retrospect it was already clear by the middle of the century that the political hegemony of the nobility over much of the Dutch countryside was doomed. Outside the urbanized west of the country, this challenge to the position of the nobles came not so much from the towns as from the freeholding farmers. Even in the Veluwe where noble domination was most notoriously entrenched, it has recently been argued that the *geërfden* were capable of mounting as serious a challenge to the local power of the nobility as the traditionally much freer farmers of Friesland. Similarly, in Overijssel and Groningen, the more prosperous farmers were strengthening their economic position and preparing the ground for a political offensive against the established oligarchy. Little was achieved in practice, however; the oligarchy, of which the nobility was an integral part, maintained its political dominance until the upheavals following the French conquest.

Throughout the Republic, however, the most obvious – and perhaps, in the short term at least, the most important – threat to the political power of the nobility was demographic. In Friesland as well as Holland, in Gelderland as well as Groningen, the decline in the number of noble families was beginning to have a serious effect by the second half of the eighteenth century if not before. This demographic failure affected the political sphere rather belatedly, as for a considerable period the nobility could live very happily with the concentration of the available offices, positions and profits into fewer and fewer hands. By the last decades of the eighteenth century, however, the situation had been reached where noble numbers in many provinces were simply too small to support the political power and privileges to which the surviving nobles still clung.

In this discussion of the political power of the Dutch nobility, the princes of Orange have only appeared incidentally up to this point. This omission has been deliberate: the peculiar position of the princes within the political system of the Republic puts them clearly above and outside the ranks of the Dutch nobility as a social group or class, however much this elevation was resented by some nobles of ancient lineage who regarded the Nassaus as relative upstarts. For a significant part of the seventeenth and eighteenth centuries the princes of Orange were only a little less than rulers of the Republic, and their relationship with the rest of the Dutch nobility was not so much *primus inter pares* as universal patron. Even during the stadhouderless periods, their position was rather that of monarchs in (internal) exile waiting for a restoration, than that of ordinary nobles. The House of Orange had great landed wealth, a considerable accumulation of *heerlijkheden* and similar rights throughout the Republic; the head of the House was a member of the *ridderschap* of Holland and was First Noble of Zeeland; but it was neither the great land holdings nor these privileges which gave the princes their power within the Republic, but a combination of reputation, tradition and such an accumulation of offices as to make them more an integral part of the Dutch State than an overmighty subject.

This was in part a cumulative development, but decisive moments can also be seen. The leading rôle played by William of Orange during the Revolt set the stage, but at the beginning of the seventeenth century his son, Maurice, although leader of the army and *stadhouder* in a majority of provinces, had not yet learnt the potential of his position and was clearly subordinate to Oldenbarnevelt and the States of Holland. Only with Maurice's victory over Oldenbarnevelt in the internal crisis of 1618–19, did the princes of Orange become the effective political leaders of the Republic. From this point on they were successively able to exploit their political and military positions and through a combination of formal powers and informal, but very extensive, patronage to make themselves the other pole of power in the Republic to the States of Holland. Indeed, for the rest of these two centuries, with the exception of the two stadhouderless periods (1650–72, 1702–47), they acted more like constitutional rulers than the subordinate officals that they in strict constitutional terms were. This position was significantly strengthened after the Orange restoration of 1672 and the recovery of the land provinces from French occupation: the stadhoudership of Holland was made hereditary, and the *regerings-reglementen* greatly increased the prince's powers as *stadhouder* in Utrecht, Overijssel and Groningen. After the hiatus in the first half of the eighteenth century the princes returned to effective rule with even greater powers, though they were always weakest where it mattered most – in Holland. In brief, the remarkable record of this one noble family, while showing the effects of wealth, privilege and the accumulation of office typical of the nobility, exaggerates these to such a degree as to make them clearly distinct from the Dutch nobility as a whole.

THE IMAGE OF NOBILITY

The nobility in the Dutch Republic were able to maintain their superior social prestige to a considerable extent despite the changes in the Dutch economy and society which were taking place, particularly in Holland and the maritime regions. Culturally, the noble ideal was far from being completely displaced by a new ideology arising from the booming urban economy, and not even in Holland were what might be called bourgeois values totally triumphant. On the other hand, there is evidence to suggest that the noble ethos, even in the provinces where noble political and economic power was greatest, was being modified by the cultural influences spreading out from Holland. Where should the emphasis lie: on the surprising resilience of traditional values, or on the forces for cultural change?

These are complex matters and much remains unclear, but it would appear to be the case that not even in Holland was there any strong direct challenge to the conventional image of social hierarchy before the late eighteenth century. In the Republic as a whole the political and, where they existed, the social privileges of the nobility were accepted as an integral part of the existing social and political system, and thus were largely unquestioned until the whole *ancien régime* came under attack in the last decades of the period. The nobles benefited from a general political and social conservatism, but also from being only a part of a much larger and more powerful oligarchy.

One of the reasons for the survival of noble power was that the Revolt had been a reassertion of the traditional political system against what was seen as Spanish usurpation. Thus what was right was what had existed before the Spanish innovations, and the privileged constitutional position of the nobles was clearly part of that traditional system. To this extent, the acceptance of noble superiority can be understood as part of a much more general acceptance of the Dutch version of the ancient constitution, rather than any specific recognition of noble claims or acquiescence in the value system of the nobility. Admittedly, the position of the nobles in a number of provinces was strengthened in the seventeenth and even early eighteenth century, but again this process should be seen as part of a more general consolidation of oligarchy in the Republic rather than a triumph for noble values as such.

For the political power and privileges of the nobility were only part, though an important part, of the domination of oligarchy throughout the Republic, and indeed of its growing strength up to about the middle of the eighteenth century. Seen in this perspective, the closing up of the nobility to recruitment from the outside looks rather more like an example of growing oligarchic exclusivity than an expression of noble class consciousness. The social and political values which became dominant at this time were oligarchic rather than noble; and the sense of a more specifically noble identity may in fact have been weakened in the process.

There were certain characteristics of the Republic, both politically and socially, which encouraged the survival of the idea of nobility. Most obviously, the success of the princes of Orange in becoming almost rulers of the Republic after 1618 favoured the nobility in a variety of ways. The princes from Frederick Henry onwards gathered a semi-monarchical Court round them, and in this princely entourage nobles played a major rôle; the education of the princes together with their social conditioning predisposed them to find in nobles the most congenial companions for their leisure hours, but also to prefer them as their advisers and agents also. It would not do to exaggerate this tendency, as the princes had to and did work through regent politicians as well, but it is unmistakeable that nobles played a more prominent rôle in the central government of the Republic when the princes of Orange were the moving force in Dutch political life than during the stadhouderless periods, when the grand pensionary of Holland was the centre of activity. The princes and their Court provided a weak version of the royal Courts of the *ancien régime*, and encouraged the persistence of a rather anaemic version of the noble ethos dominant in the monarchies of the time.

This suggestion of a diluted rather than a full-blooded version of the noble culture which was dominant elsewhere in Europe has, however, to be balanced by the perhaps surprising absence of a self-confident burgher consciousness challenging such noble values. Perhaps the chief reason for this lack, quite apart from the difficulty of working against the grain of the common European culture which the Dutch shared, was the narrowness of the social base of the oligarchy. The Dutch political system was run, not by the bourgeoisie as a whole, but by a very small élite to the exclusion from all participation in political life of even the best qualified, especially by property, of those outside it. Within such a system too much of a stress on bourgeois values might well have led to a questioning of the ideological underpinnings of the régime, and to a call for a significant broadening of the political élite, as indeed it did in the works of radical republicans from the middle of the seventeenth century onwards. The attack on the *ancien régime*, when it came, would be focused as much on the regents of the towns as on the nobles in the countryside.

Nevertheless, the dynamic economic development of Holland in the sixteenth and seventeenth centuries could not be entirely gainsaid, nor could the effects of this remarkable expansion be confined to Holland itself. The growth of urban wealth and capitalist farming went further towards making the nobles economically insignificant in Holland – even as far as landowning was concerned they were already relatively weak by the begining of the seventeenth century as we have seen — than in any other province, but nowhere in the Republic were the nobles the dominant landowners, and everywhere the rural economy was deeply affected by the spread of commercial capitalism driven on by the power of the Holland market. In such a changing world, behaviour and ideas also changed, and the nobles were affected along with the rest of the Dutch population.

In the early eighteenth century, one of the leading members of the Holland *ridderschap* described his official reception at the English Court as 'regt apenspel', which is almost untranslatable but pungently indicates contempt for empty ceremony, and may indicate that at least something of the matter-of-fact attitude of the Dutch burgher had rubbed off on even a leading noble. Even if the attitude was affected rather than genuine, it is significant that he found the pretence worthwhile. Be that as it may, the lifestyle of the Dutch noble was not dissimilar to that of other landowners, or even of the urban regents. There is not a great deal of information available for the education of the Dutch nobility, but what there is points to there being few significant differences from that of the other wealthy strata of Dutch society. There is no discernible cultural gap between the nobles and the regents or indeed the wealthy in general. It may be going too far to talk of the development of a bourgeois nobility, but in some ways, not least as regards economic behaviour, there was a progressive narrowing of the gap between noble and non-noble in the course of this period. The movement was not only one way: the upper bourgeoisie, and particularly the regents in Holland, were distancing themselves to some extent from the rest of the urban population and emulating the social habits of the nobility. There seems to have been something like fusion of the privileged groups in town and countryside into a more or less homogeneous class of notables by the later years of the eighteenth century, who shared similar life styles as well as political power.

At present much of this remains speculation, and must be balanced by the evidence for a continuing sense of social distance and superiority among the nobility as a whole. The clearest evidence for this is the degree to which endogamy was maintained by the nobles of most provinces. Indeed the demographic crisis experienced by the nobilities of almost every province has been largely ascribed to such restrictive marriage strategies. With some exceptions, Dutch nobles chose to marry other nobles, very largely to the exclusion of the regent group. To this extent there was still a distinct social distance between noble and even the most privileged non-noble even at the end of our period.

The sense of family and pride of descent was, of course, strong among the nobility, and they placed great importance on long and elaborate genealogies where the demonstration of impeccable pedigrees was more important than precise historical accuracy. From the perspective of the nobles this awareness of family was intended to express the unbridgeable social gap between them and the rest of Dutch society, but it also encouraged non-nobles, and regents in particular, to provide themselves with comparable family histories, often seeking to prove links with indisputable noble lines.

In their economic behaviour, however, the nobles adjusted to the changing circumstances without too many problems, but without being too ostentatious in their acceptance of commercial values. In Groningen, over the period as a whole roughly half of noble wealth was invested in land, and various seigneurial rights and provincial loans took care of much of the rest. In contrast it has been argued that the nobles in the Veluwe were markedly open to the economic possibilities of the time, being prepared, among other innovations to invest in the growing of tobacco and in paper-milling. There seem to have been few economic links with Holland, but some readiness to invest in the modernization of the local rural economy.

The economic interests of the majority of the nobility appear to have been limited to their own provinces, and the provinces where the nobles were most plentiful were also those where economic development was least evident, and thus where the opportunities for investment in trade or manufactures were most restricted.

In the eighteenth century, the position and privileges of the nobility came under attack, but more as part of a general challenge to the established power structures in politics and society than against the existence of a nobility as such. After the death of William III, various movements arose to attack the local oligarchies which had been closely associated with the somewhat authoritarian leadership of the prince. These were particularly strong in the land provinces where William's political influence had been greatest. In so far as they were intended to change the system, rather than simply its beneficiaries, they failed. In any case they were perhaps as much the last stirrings of a tradition of popular participation in government as a harbinger of any significant change in political attitudes. Similarly, the popular movements in favour of the prince of Orange in 1747/48 may have been an expression of resentment at oligarchic and noble control, but apart from strengthening the prince's hand they achieved little.

It was only with the Patriot movement in the last decades of the century that an unmistakeable new direction could be seen in Dutch political life, with a general attack on the power and privileges of the entrenched élites in town and countryside. Although the movement was not specifically directed against the nobility as such, it is perhaps significant that it seems to have had its most powerful appeal in some of the provinces where noble power was still a real force, such as Overijssel. It made little impact on Gelderland, however, so here at least the nobility was still able to defend its position effectively. Indeed, in general the Patriots can be said to have failed to overthrow the power of the oligarchy, but they were clearly the representatives of a new set of political and social values which rejected the *ancien régime* and all its works – the privileged position of the nobility along with the rest.

It is otherwise notable that the tone of the Dutch Enlightenment, however rational, was socially conservative, and considerably less critical of the establishment than elsewhere in Europe. By the late seventeenth century, Dutch society was relatively tolerant and enlightened, in many ways approximating to the ideal of moderate reformers in the rest of Europe. The political élite in the Republic were opponents of monarchical absolutism and clerical obscurantism, and were far from being the most reactionary element in Dutch life. In such circumstances, the oligarchy could still rely on considerable intellectual support from the champions of reason, until its failure to live up to its own ideals became all too obvious in the last decades of the century.

The nobility in the Dutch Republic lived and died politically with the oligarchy as a whole: as long as the oligarchy, based especially on the urban regents of Holland, was strong, the nobles were safe from everything but demographic failure, but when the regents began to weaken so did the position of the Dutch nobility.

THE REGENTS

Although the regents – the oligarchs who were the political masters of the towns in every province of the Republic – were not nobles in the normal sense, nevertheless there are good reasons for giving them more than a passing mention. First, they were politically the most important social group outside the nobility: they were overwhelmingly powerful in Holland, the dominant province, and this helped them to set the tone for the Republic as a whole. Perhaps more significant in this context is that they were a privileged group, and that their privileges were of the same sort as those enjoyed by the nobles in this polity. The Dutch Republic was ruled essentially by a combination of two social groups, the regents and the nobles, with the rest of society having little say. The position of this dual oligarchy strengthened in the course of the seventeenth century, and its dominance remained unshaken if not unchallenged until the last decades of the eighteenth century and, according to one interpretation at least, continued long into the following century. Given the shared power and privileges of these two groups, it is worth considering whether the regents should be seen as a species of nobility, and if not why not.

The regents were defined essentially by their political rôle as rulers of the towns, and through the towns, as a powerful force in the government of the provinces and in the institutions of central government. The social composition and particularly the wealth of the regents varied greatly both within provinces and between them. At the one extreme were the rulers of the larger towns of Holland, with their great wealth derived, at least originally, from trade and manufactures; and at the other the much more modest wealth and less commercial orientation of the regents of even the leading towns of Gelderland or Overijssel. In Holland itself, the difference between the regents of Amsterdam and those of the smaller towns, such as Edam, Purmerend or Monnikendam, was at least as great. Indeed, it is tempting to put the regents of Amsterdam and a handful of other Holland towns – Rotterdam, Leiden, Haarlem and perhaps Delft and Dordrecht – into a different league from those of the other towns in Holland and elsewhere, but the peculiar nature of the Dutch political system meant that, at least as far as political influence was concerned, these differences were less significant than might have been expected. Each of the eighteen towns represented in the States of Holland had one vote, irrespective of size or wealth. Formally at least, tiny Edam with a population of little more than 5,000 was the political equal of Amsterdam with around 200,000 inhabitants by the late seventeenth century, and with a wealth that was proportionally probably even greater. The six 'great' towns plus Rotterdam had some formal advantages, and in practice the larger towns had considerably more say in political decision-making, but the formal equality built into the system gave the regents of the smaller towns a significant rôle in the politics of Holland. Similar considerations worked in Zeeland and Friesland to even up the differences between the towns represented in the provincial States, which were in any case less marked than in Holland. The actual number of towns represented in the provincial assemblies was smaller in most of the other provinces. Only the town of Groningen itself had a place in the States of *Stad en Lande*, and only Deventer, Kampen and Zwolle were represented in Overijssel. In Gelderland rather more towns had session in the States, but the chief towns of the three quarters, Nijmegen, Zutphen and Arnhem, each had equal weight to the smaller towns of their regions combined. Similarly, in Utrecht the town of Utrecht dominated the four smaller towns which were also represented in the States.

Although the political élite in all the towns in the Republic shared some characteristics, it would seem that a distinction should be made between the regents proper, in towns with representation in the States of their province and thus with a significant voice in its political life and by extension in that of the Republic as a whole, and the political élites of the unrepresented towns, whose power was restricted to the local level, and even here was less secure from interference from outside. The regents of the minor towns represented in the States of Utrecht and Gelderland can be seen as a marginal category, with some influence on provincial policy but largely restricted to a local rôle. Even with these definitions in mind, it is not easy to give an estimate of how many regents there were. In many towns the line between regent and non-regent was not always as clear as tidy-minded historians would like, but the existence of uncertain categories does not, in all probability, affect overall numbers very greatly. The following figures refer to individual members of town councils, and their immediate families should certainly be included in any assessment of the size of the oligarchy as a social group. Regents proper were most numerous in Holland at *c*.500, with the much smaller Zeeland having about a third of this number and Friesland roughly a half. If the smaller towns are included, Gelderland fits into this first group, with numbers almost approaching those of Holland, but if only the three most important towns are included, then it moves into the group of those provinces where regents proper were rather thinner on the ground. In Utrecht, probably only the regents of the capital and, at a pinch, Amersfoort, should be included, but even if the three smallest voting towns are counted the numbers would still hardly reach a quarter of those of Holland. At the lower end of the scale the three voting towns of Overijssel and the single one of Groningen produce only a comparative handful of regents. At a very rough calculation this produces an overall total of less than 2,000 regents for the Republic as a whole (or, rather for the seven provinces: the Generality Lands have been excluded as they had neither representation in the States General nor provincial autonomy, and thus their regents were restricted to local importance only).

Such numbers are not impressive, particularly in the land provinces and Groningen, but they compare favourably with those of the nobility, even before the demographic attrition of the late seventeenth and eighteenth centuries. In Holland, of course, the nobles were massively outnumbered from the very beginning of this period, but even in the land provinces the regents could more or less match the nobles in numbers, and the single town of Groningen produced almost as many regents as the Ommelanden did nobles in the early seventeenth century, and more by the late eighteenth. For, in contrast to the nobles, the number of regents was more or less stable throughout this period, with demographic failures being compensated for by the recruitment of new families into the regent élite. The fixed number of places within the town oligarchies, for example the size of the town councils, was clearly a powerful force in keeping up overall numbers, and encouraged the admission of suitable outsiders to the local élites to fill the available places. There was probably some decline in the total size of the regent group in the course of these two centuries – some of the smaller towns of Holland, for example, reduced the size of their councils in the course of the seventeenth century – but such changes were not large enough to make a significant difference overall, especially when compared to the drastic decline in the size of the nobility. The regents kept up their numbers at the cost of a certain loss of exclusivity; the nobles maintained their social distance at the price of near extinction.

The regents differed from the nobles in another respect – their membership could be affected by outside interference, specifically by the intervention of the princes of Orange in their capacity as *stadhouders*. In every province the *stadhouder* had some influence over the appointment of magistrates and sometimes even of regents, but this normally amounted, in form at least, to little more than selection from a shortlist presented to them, though their effective influence may well have been greater, even in Holland. More drastic interventions by the *stadhouder* to change the membership of the local oligarchies in Holland came only at times of political crisis such as 1618, 1672, and again in 1747–8, but in the land provinces the *stadhouders'* standing powers in such matters were greatly increased in 1674 and renewed in 1747–8. A similar situation also obtained in Groningen in the second half of the eighteenth century. Thus, whereas the princes of Orange could not create new nobles, they could create new regents and demote existing ones, and this ability to influence the careers of local regents became a major part of their political influence in the Republic as a whole.

What the regents of the voting towns (i.e. those represented in the provincial States) all had in common, whatever their differences in wealth, was a combination of almost absolute power within their own towns with considerable influence on politics at the provincial level, and through that even on the central governing institutions of the Republic. At the local level there could be little effective interference with what the regents did either from above or from below. The traditions of medieval urban democracy seem to have been weak if not non-existent in the Republic, and in any case seem to have atrophied by the seventeenth century. This was particularly true of Holland, where even those few towns with some traditions of broader citizen participation in government had suppressed such remnants in practice by the beginning of the seventeenth century. Elsewhere, notably in Utrecht, burgher democracy had stronger roots, but the upshot was the same: the triumph of effectively untrammelled oligarchy in the course of the seventeenth century, if not before.

There were considerable differences in detail in the composition of town governments, with marked provincial variations, but what all had in common was the control of political power by a small group of families. Membership of these oligarchies was usually for life, and recruitment was by means of open or covert cooption. In Holland, the core of the town government was formed by a council (*vroedschap* or *raad*) of between about sixteen and forty men, chosen by cooption and holding office for life. The *burgemeesters* and other magistrates would be chosen by and usually from these councils, or by a more select group within the regent body. Outside Holland the names were different and the institutions varied, but the essence of control by closed oligarchies was the same.

One of the obvious characteristics of the regent group was wealth, though this also varied between towns and between provinces. The wealthiest oligarchy was that of Amsterdam, but the regents of the other towns in Holland were also notably prosperous. Assessments for the eighteenth century give an average wealth for the regents of Hoorn, a town in serious economic decline by this time, of no less than f.200,000 (but the figures are distorted by the members of one extremely rich family, and the median is a more plausible f.140,000), for those of Leiden the average was f.154,000, and even in Gouda it reached nearly f.70,000. Most of the regents in the rest of the Republic were probably less well off than those in Holland, but were still among the most prosperous of their own towns with very respectable fortunes.

The regents were a distinct political élite with almost absolute powers in their own sphere. The decentralized nature of the Dutch political system meant that not only were the provinces largely autonomous, but that within the provinces the towns also enjoyed a very large degree of autonomy in practice, being sharers of sovereignty as much as subject to it. As controllers of town politics, the regents wielded the powers of the towns at provincial level, though this power varied greatly from province to province. In Holland the eighteen towns represented in the States of Holland were almost all-powerful, having to contend only with the single vote of the nobles, whereas the towns had to share power on at best an equal basis with the nobility in Utrecht, Gelderland and Overijssel. In Zeeland the influence of the towns was only checked by that of the princes of Orange as First Noble and *stadhouder*, while in Friesland and Groningen the position was more complicated but still allowed the urban oligarchs a considerable if not predominant share of power.

It is, thus, not surprising that the regents have been seen as a sort of aristocracy, increasingly more closed to entry from outside its ranks, and with a style of life and thought progressively different from those of the rest of the population of the Dutch towns, even the more wealthy. The chronology which has been suggested for this development is that at the beginning of the seventeenth century the regents were relatively well integrated into the upper ranks of urban society, but that in the course of the century they became increasingly specialized politicians and administrators, largely withdrawing from active involvement in trade or manufactures and becoming rentiers (and also increasingly dependent on the profits of office). They also became notably endogamous, and in effect began to form an urban aristocracy by the eighteenth century. This interpretation of the development of the regent group makes them seem very like the nobility, at least by the beginning of the eighteenth century: a privileged, hereditary and largely endogamous social group with a marked sense of superiority with regard to their fellow citizens. This was supposedly accompanied by the pursuit of a consciously aristocratic lifestyle, including the purchase of country estates and of manors which allowed them to sport a pseudo-noble title.

However, this picture is not entirely convincing. It is undoubtedly true that the regents were a political élite, who clung tenaciously to their monopoly of power, but it is questionable to what extent they ever formed a separate social group. Although established regent groups tended towards endogamy, there were always some factors encouraging marriage alliances with outsiders. For example, close blood relatives could usually not be members of the town councils at the same time, but such restrictions did not apply to relatives by marriage, so family political strategy could also include bringing outsiders into the oligarchy through marriage alliances. Even more important were demographic factors: like the nobility, regent families tended to die out, but unlike the nobility the regent group maintained its numbers by recruiting new families to its ranks. In this if nothing else the contrast with the nobles was marked. The nobles were dying out through demographic failure but the regents had no such inhibitions against recruiting from their richer fellow citizens. Similarly, the nobles refused to marry into regent families, but there was no such sharp and clear social divide between regent families and the rest of the upper bourgeoisie of the towns.

In addition, it would seem that the differences in lifestyle between the regents and at least the upper ranks of urban society have been exaggerated. The regents did buy country houses, but as summer retreats and there were rarely large estates attached, and in any case in this they did not differ from the habits of the wealthy in general. Similarly, like non-regents as well as nobles, the regents bought manors as investments, but not on a large scale and titles from such manors were not commonly used. In their economic behaviour also, the regents were not markedly different in the pattern of their investments from the rest of the upper classes. Perhaps the chief difference in this respect was that profits of office and other perquisites provided a cushion to regent income which was particularly welcome during the relative decline of the Dutch economy in the eighteenth century, when neither trade nor manufactures were as profitable as in the previous century. It also seems to have been the case that studying law at university became more and more a necessary part of the education of young men from regent families, and was almost universal by the eighteenth century. A university education was less common even for the wealthy outside the regent group, but it can perhaps be seen rather as a form of professional training than as marking a clear-cut distinction in status. In general it would be fair to say that it is doubtful whether the regents developed into a distinct urban aristocracy in the course of this period even in the larger towns of Holland, and in the smaller towns of this province and in the rest of the Republic the regents' lifestyle was distinctly more modest.

Given the peculiarly powerful position of the regents in Holland, it might have been expected that here the social distance between them and the nobles would have been the slightest, but this does not seem to have been the case. On the contrary, there was very little intermarriage between nobles and regents in Holland, though the occasional noble still appeared in the town councils in the seventeenth century. Also in Friesland there was an apparently sharp social divide between regents and nobles. Yet in Groningen there was a much greater degree of interpenetration between nobles and the regents of the town of Groningen, while nobles were much more involved with the weaker towns of Gelderland and Overijssel, both through noble membership of town governments and through clientage, but with regents as the junior partners.

If we judge by the standards of the time, the regents were not nobles, although they falsified their genealogies and flaunted their coats of arms as enthusiastically as if they were. The distinction between the two privileged groups was clear. However, the nobles were dying out by the late eighteenth century and the regents were finding their grip on political power under threat for the first time since the Revolt. The stage was set for the leading regent families to move out of the contested ground of local and provincial politics, and seek confirmation of their privileged status by promotion to the new nobility which was created under the Orange Monarchy in the early decades of the following century.

CHAPTER FOUR

The French Nobility, 1610–1715

Roger Mettam
Queen Mary and Westfield College, University of London

If historians are generally agreed that the population of the French kingdom numbered some twenty million souls in the closing decade of the seventeenth century, there is no consensus as to how many of them belonged to the nobility. The ministers and advisers of Louis XIV were more concerned than their predecessors to compile precise statistics about all aspects of life in the realm, and some of their inquests suggest that there were approximately 260,000 nobles in 1700. The French historian Roland Mousnier suspects that this figure is an underestimate, and prefers to apply to this period the calculation made some fifty years later by the abbé Coyer, who claimed that 400,000 was a truer total. As it is impossible to know for certain which estimate is correct, it seems prudent to accept the lower figure for the 1690s, because it was based on contemporary assessments and was confirmed by the precise statistical mind of the military engineer and fiscal reformer, the maréchal de Vauban.

For the earlier seventeenth century there are no reliable estimates, making it impracticable for modern scholars to debate the extent to which there was a dramatic increase in the number of ennobling offices in the bureaucracy at the expense of the traditional nobility. Some historians have confidently asserted that the *noblesse d'épée*, the military houses, declined as the bureaucratic *noblesse de robe* increased in size and influence, but their case remains un-proven and there is much evidence to suggest that they are mistaken. It is true that the *épée*, appalled at the claims of the *robe* to be included in their ranks, used every form of public statement to defend the exclusive nature of their order, but it should not be inferred from these diatribes against 'parvenus' that the *nobles d'épée* believed their own power to be under threat.

THE MILITARY ARISTOCRACY AND THE CHALLENGE OF THE ROBE

The definition of nobility was undeniably the most contentious issue in early seventeenth-century France. Within the ranks of the *noblesse d'épée* there were always disputes about precedence between individual families or between different strata of the hierarchy. Yet these were as nothing when compared with the new challenge to aristocratic values posed by the nobility of office-holders. The literary world and the salons of the capital were dominated by the debate about the true nature of *noblesse*, and whether military valour was the only criterion for ennoblement. At the same time members of the *épée* mounted a vigorous campaign, at Court and in the provinces, to exclude *robins* from those areas of influence which they regarded as their own. Once the turbulence of the sixteenth-century civil wars had subsided, it was evident that the *robe* was not staging a mass invasion of *épée* preserves, and the passionate debate in the salons was therefore more about social values and precedence than about the practical exercise of authority.

The sale of ennobling offices had been increasing throughout the sixteenth century. It was not part of an organized plan by the Crown to involve more of its subjects in the administration of the kingdom and to reduce the rôle of the traditional noble élites. The motive was financial, as the ministers of impoverished monarchs discovered that it was a way of extracting money from socially ambitious men, who were prepared to pay handsomely for a post which would ennoble their families, either immediately or in the future. The *noblesse d'épée* could not deny that the sovereign had the right to create nobles, but the ferocity of its complaints about the unsuitability of these 'parvenus' prompted a number of kings to temporize. Louis XII went so far as to proscribe venal offices in 1493, although he continued to create them. François Ier expanded the system so dramatically, and came to rely on the income from this lucrative practice, that proscription was no longer an option. There was an increasing number of wealthy purchasers who were prepared to defend the system, and *vénalité* thus became a contentious issue at meetings of the *états-généraux*. Monarchs tried to appease the *épée* without alienating the *robe*.

Aristocratic hostility intensified as it became clear that a venal office was not merely being sold to an individual, but to his heirs or to someone else who might subsequently wish to purchase it. In the sixteenth century the Crown could never afford to buy back these posts, and so it was for the office-holder to dispose of his *charge* as he wished, by bequest or by sale. This development meant that the king was no longer able to choose his servants, and yet some of these men were participating in that most important function of monarchy, the administration of justice. The monarch, said pamphleteers at the time, was selling, not giving justice – 'vendre', not 'rendre'. For the king the system of venality had advantages to compensate for his sale of part of his authority to men whose successors he could not designate. Not only was there the money from the initial creation of the office, but these judicial and financial office-holders performed many of the duties assigned to them, and with enthusiasm. This is not surprising as it was from judicial fees or from a percentage of the taxes they collected that they reimbursed themselves for the cost of acquiring their post, and then went on to make a good living. It was these rewards as well as the guarantee of ennoblement which caused office values to rise steadily, and there was soon a profitable trade in these posts which further incensed the old military nobility.

Although the *robe* did not invade the traditional spheres of *épée* influence to any extent, there were frequent conflicts between the two élites, often giving rise to lengthy litigation. The most common reason was that the jurisdictions of royal officials appeared to encroach upon aristocratic privileges. Ironically, the only way in which the *épée* noble could obtain justice was to take his case to court, that is to say to a tribunal presided over by members of the *robe*. When two *nobles d'épée* were in dispute, about a serious matter of precedence, privilege or honour, they could decide the matter by using the sword, the *épée* which they carried as a symbol of their status. It was impossible to challenge a *robin* to a duel, because the basis of aristocratic hostility to the administrative nobles was that they lacked military valour. There could be no question of chivalrous nobles throwing down the gauntlet before such unworthy opponents, and yet the alternative was to have recourse to a system of justice dominated by those same men.

If the tension between *épée* and *robe* was a recurrent theme in social theory and in everyday life, it did not prevent the two groups from reaching a pragmatic alliance in the daily running of the provinces. The military power of the nobility and the judicial authority of the courts were both important in the maintenance of order and stability in the localities. The two élites could cooperate especially in controlling a troublesome peasantry or the urban poor and in resisting the attempts of monarchs to impose increasing fiscal burdens on their area.

There was also cooperation, if of a different kind, between the uppermost strata of the *épée* and the *robe*. At the top of the judicial system, immediately below the king, were the *parlements*, based in Paris and in some great provincial capitals. These law courts had a distinguished history and were held in high esteem. The Parisian court was also the *cour des pairs*, the only tribunal in which a peer, a *pair*, could be tried. The peers, the most prestigious members of the aristocracy, therefore greatly valued the Paris *parlement*, having recourse to its judgement in their disputes with each other and with their sovereign. The *parlementaires* in return were accommodating towards the peers, because their court gained added prestige from being the *cour des pairs*, although there were occasions, of course, when the peerage and the *parlement* were in dispute.

No noble would have denied that a senior judge, like the *premier président* of the Paris *parlement*, should be accorded great respect and be given a prominent place in processions and ceremonial. Difficulties arose when these leading judges also made great claims for the *noblesse* of their families and not just for the prestige of their office. As the decades went by, some of these men could boast that they and their ancestors had been members of this judicial élite for generations. They claimed that both the length of time since the original ennoblement of their family and the period during which they had held such high positions enhanced their noble status. They regarded themselves as equal to the uppermost levels of the *épée*, and might make their claims palpable. They did so by living in a style suitable for the greatest of aristocrats; they built palatial houses and might even move to a *quartier* of a city which was normally the preserve of the old aristocracy.

THE ARISTOCRATIC LIFESTYLE AND THE DEFINITION OF NOBILITY

Although the *noblesse d'épée* would never accept the most prestigious judge as a social equal, there was a slow change in the values of the old aristocracy which made it easier for the *robe* to acquire the trappings of nobility. In the seventeenth century the royal Court ceased to travel outside Paris and the Ile-de-France, save for rare special occasions. The increasingly elaborate ceremonial around the monarch required the participation of larger numbers of the *épée*, and therefore more leading nobles spent longer periods of the year in their town houses, their *hôtels particuliers*, in Paris. They rebuilt and extended them, made their own household organization more elaborate, and invited guests to attend *soirées* and salons. They patronized the finest artists, architects and sculptors, and their salons became places where high society listened to music, saw the latest plays and discussed intellectual topics. Many of the literary works presented and debated there were concerned with the ideas of *noblesse* and honour, including that most controversial of issues, the possible conflict between the duty of the noble to preserve his own honour and his obligations towards his sovereign.

The senior families of the *noblesse de robe*, who could never compete with the *épée* when it came to reciting the deeds of brave ancestors in battle, were able to build great houses, patronize the finest artists and hold civilized salons. In a society where no one ever attended an event hosted by a social inferior, it was impossible for members of the *épée* to be present, but the reputation of a few *robin* salons became impressive. That of the *premier président* of the Paris *parlement*, Lamoignon, and held in his *hôtel* built in the middle of the aristocratic *quartier* of the Marais, became a centre for philosophy, and renowned writers like Boileau attended it. If the *nobles d'épée* felt unable to be there, they learnt the details of its debates and continued them in more socially acceptable surroundings. This was easily achieved because cultured *robins* were regularly present at the leading aristocratic salons, such as the hôtel de Nevers. There *épée* nobles, judges, royal ministers, churchmen, playwrights, poets and philosophers mingled with each other and discussed the burning social and philosophical issues. The historians who have described a rising *robe* and a declining *épée* have made a further mistake when they have dismissed the *épée* as ill-educated.

117

Many great nobles were undoubtedly well versed in the arts of war, but they were knowledgeable on literature, philosophy and the visual arts.

On the most pressing issue of the day, the definition of *noblesse*, there were many opinions. All parties agreed that nobility was associated with *honneur*, but how to define 'honour' and what other criteria had to be satisfied before a man was truly noble were matters of contention. The *épée* nobles had widened their definition beyond the narrowly military. They insisted that valour in battle had been the reason for every ennoblement in the past and must remain so in the present. Beyond that the noble should be honourable in all his actions and not just on the battlefield. He should be noble in spirit, able to put aside human desires in his pursuit of a greater good. The *robins* wished further to widen the qualifications for ennoblement, in order to include service to the king in his administration and particularly in the dispensing of justice, a most honourable profession. Such a definition was unacceptable to the *épée*, because it meant that nobility was being granted for professional work. A true aristocrat had no profession and nor did he earn his living through work. Payment for professional services savoured too much of the bourgeois world from which, as *épée* nobles were quick to point out, many *robin* families had emerged, some in the not too distant past. The nobles of the *robe* rejected these charges, and indeed their adoption of an aristocratic lifestyle, not only in their urban *hôtels* but in the rural châteaux they built on their landed estates, was a deliberate attempt to distance themselves from the milieu of the bourgeoisie.

Commerce and industry were forbidden by law to the nobility, and no noble would have been seen to participate in them. The legal penalty for such involvements was *dérogeance*, loss of *noblesse*. Ambitious judicial families, still commoners but seeking ennobling office, would already have detached themselves from the commercial world long before they gained nobility and were required to do so by law. They began 'vivant noblement', living nobly, and invested in urban property and country estates, although to the *épée* they were still bourgeois. Nevertheless, *robe* and *épée* could agree that wealth was never a criterion for nobility, and nor was poverty a reason for forfeiting it. 'Pauvreté n'est point vice, et ne désanoblit point', said Antoine L'Oisel in his *Institutes coutumières* of 1607.

The *épée* nobles could not agree among themselves about the precise rules for evaluating noble status within the hierarchy. They could reject *robin* claims without difficulty, but their own family histories differed in significant ways and required selective interpretation. For example some Houses could trace back their ennoblement to a distant century, and cite many instances of valour and honourable service to the king, although they had never been granted the highest title of *duc et pair*. Others, *ducs et pairs*, might have been ennobled more recently, perhaps less than two hundred years ago, and yet they had reached the uppermost stratum of the aristocracy. The former group therefore stressed the importance of a long lineage, while the latter preferred to emphasize the prestige of the titles they currently held. The important point was that, whether *épée, robe* or a member of a lesser élite, a family never ceased to publicise its own claims to social status, even though it was unlikely to persuade its rivals to accept them.

The Crown and its publicists kept a watchful eye on the discussions in the salons about nobility, because some of them had implications for monarchical power. The insistence on noble *honneur* and the right to resolve disputes by the sword implied that there was an aristocratic justice independent of the royal courts. Kings accordingly issued a series of prohibitions on duelling which, although they could not be enforced, reiterated the claim of the monarch to be the supreme judge in the realm. Royal ministers were quick to respond when nobles claimed that *honneur* was paramount, because it suggested that they might disobey a command of their sovereign if they felt that it compromised their honour. In 1637 the tragedy of *Le Cid*, by Pierre Corneille, seemed to put honour above obedience, and the chief minister, Richelieu, ensured that a riposte, *Roxane* by Desmarets de Saint-Sorlin, stressed duty to the sovereign above all other considerations. *Robin* claims too caused disquiet at Court, because their defence of justice similarly implied that the law courts could overrule royal commands if they were deemed to be illegal. As there had been disputes between the Crown and the courts in the past, there was again a need for the king to remind the *noblesse de robe* that his power was supreme and that they held judicial office by his wish.

The debates about the definition of nobility declined in passion as the seventeenth century progressed, although the *épée* never accepted the *robe* as equals. The *noblesse d'épée* continued to dominate those spheres of influence which were precious to it – the officer corps of the army, the great offices of the Crown, posts in the royal household, senior positions in the Church and governorships of provinces – and *robins* very rarely encroached upon these preserves. Louis XIV was more determined than his predecessors that such upward mobility should not be countenanced. *Épée* and *robe* also worked together on many occasions, during the reign of Louis XIII and the minority of Louis XIV, resisting attempts by the royal government to increase fiscal burdens and undermine local privileges. The two kinds of noble were therefore often in alliance, and were not competing for the same posts. Only the rapid success of men who became royal ministers remained a source of irritation, although once again Louis XIV was more careful than his predecessors in avoiding unnecessary offence to the nobility, and did not bestow high aristocratic titles upon ministerial houses.

Ministers always had a precarious hold on power, as they were entirely dependent upon royal favour. Fall from grace meant a drastic decline in their social status, whereas a great noble House or a senior *parlementaire* family did not lose its standing in society just because one of its relatives had incurred the displeasure of the king. A major reason for this difference in fortunes was that the adherents of a minister, some of them too high ranking to be called his clients, would abandon him the moment that his loss of royal favour made him useless as a channel for obtaining patronage. When a member of an established *épée* or *robe* House offended the king, the extended family would be sustained by its reputation, its wealth, its local power base and usually by its patrons and clients until the king forgave the offender. Moreover, it was never the practice of the sovereign to punish the whole of a distinguished family for the misdemeanours of one of its members.

In the seventeenth century membership of the nobility for most men had been determined by birth, because their family had been ennobled already, whether for valour, for outstanding royal service, or by purchasing an ennobling office. For the same reasons others joined the nobility during the reigns of Louis XIII and his son. Both kings also granted higher titles to deserving members of existing *épée* Houses, and raised a few ministerial families from the *robe* to the *épée*. On rare occasions in the past, and very rarely in this century, men were ennobled for a financial payment, at a time when the royal treasury was impoverished. The numbers elevated in this way were usually small, the *noblesse* was personal to them and only occasionally was it made hereditary on payment of a further sum. During the reign of Louis XIV the only edicts permitting the sale of nobility were issued, apart from one in 1643 to celebrate his accession, in 1696 and during the War of the Spanish Succession, in those two final wars when Louis had to condone any means of raising revenue. Even so, the 1696 edict was precise in stating that only men of proven merit, virtue and good qualities need apply. Significantly an edict of 1664 revoked all such creations made since 1630, and a further decree of 1715 annulled those made since 1689. Sale of *noblesse* was a last resort in a financial crisis, but it was never allowed to become a route to permanent membership of the French nobility.

In defining nobility, the emphasis was always on men, because *noblesse*, like the Crown itself, could pass only through the male line. Sometimes, when a noble House had no male heir, the king might transfer the defunct title to the husband of the eldest daughter, also for exclusively male transmission thereafter. Exceptionally a woman might be honoured in her own right. The childless niece of Richelieu became a *duchesse et pair* and had the authority to choose her own successor of either sex, before the male principle came into force after that. This departure from tradition was occasioned by the wish of the king to bestow a further favour on a devoted minister who, because he was a cleric, had no direct heirs, and to honour the *duchesse* for her own long service to the Crown. A few royal mistresses were also allowed to hold titles, but basically noble titles in France were in the hands of men. It is ironic therefore that within the *noblesse* some of the most skilful politicians and shrewd family strategists were women, often dowagers who ruled their family with unquestioned authority.

PATRONAGE AND CLIENTAGE

Scholars have written at length in recent years about the importance of clientage and patronage in explaining the political and social mechanisms of Bourbon France. Many of them were inspired to do so to counter a group of administrative historians who, while sensibly discarding notions of absolutism, had proposed an alternative power structure based on a rising *robe* and a declining *épée*. Those historians, relying too heavily on the theoretical writings of seventeenth-century jurists, had become obsessed with the growing power of the hereditary, venal bureaucracy, to the point that they even suggested a 'bureaucratic monarchy' where many royal powers had in reality passed into the hands of the administrative hierarchy.

A number of injudicious assumptions and a selective use of the archival evidence led them to this conclusion. As with their views on absolutism, their starting point was a sensible one. They criticized earlier scholars for focusing too exclusively on the Court and the royal ministers. They believed that an understanding of the power structure would be reached only by studying the workings of institutions, and turned instead to the wider world of the judicial and financial administration, unfortunately to the exclusion of other power groups. As they often concentrated on well-documented occasions when institutions had been at odds with the royal government or had simply disregarded its orders, they concluded that it was the bureaucracy, and the vested interests of the *robe*, which dictated the path to be followed. They failed to stress the considerable extent to which the bureaucrats and the Crown cooperated, had common aims and were mutually dependent.

A more serious error was their failure to recognise that the influence of the *noblesse d'épée* remained undiminished, at Court and in the provinces. By concentrating on institutional and bureaucratic mechanisms, they were ignoring the channels through which the *épée* nobles exerted their influence and transacted their business. It is this omission which the historians of patronage have sought to remedy, some of them becoming equally guilty of excess in their own enthusiastic revisionism. The reality is that the two systems coexisted in parallel. Beside the formal institutional structure there was the informal network of relationships which was cemented by patronage and clientage.

For the more extreme patronage historians the system was simple. At the summit of the network was the king, who had at his disposal many curial, military, religious and senior administrative posts which were eagerly sought by the nobility. He could also distribute pensions and financial rewards which would supplement or restore the resources of noble Houses. Leading members of the aristocracy petitioned the Crown in order to obtain the most prestigious positions for their own family and lesser ones for their clients. The provincial nobles therefore gathered round a great aristocrat in the hope that this patron would speak successfully on their behalf to the king or to a minister. In return for obtaining favours for those below him, the patron could demand their support in his own causes.

This idealized account needs considerable modification before it corresponds to clientage and patronage as they functioned in seventeenth-century France. One important question concerns the durability of patron and client relationships, and the extent to which traditional loyalties were merely a veneer while personal advantage was the driving force. Loyalty and self-advancement were always intertwined in Bourbon France and no one would have been surprised or shocked that this was so. Even the king, although he insisted that all subjects owed unqualified obedience to his divine and dynastic power, knew that he had to reward good service. The process was a cyclical one. Service merited rewards, which in turn fostered a continued willingness to serve in the knowledge that there would be further rewards. The same assumptions could be found at all levels of the clientage system.

In dispensing patronage the monarch was not always a totally free agent. For many sensitive posts a list of possible candidates emerged through circumstances beyond his control. For example the appointment of a provincial governor was constrained by two factors. First the king was restricted by the need to select either a royal prince or, more usually, a *duc et pair*, because the governor had to be socially equal or superior to all those whom he would encounter in carrying out his provincial duties. Secondly, if he were to be really effective, his family should already have lands, important offices, clients and *crédit* in the area. It was his influence in the province which the king wished to harness to the royal authority. Because a governorship would enhance the status of the family, both at Court and in the province, the governor would try simultaneously to serve the king and to further the interests of the local élites. The two tasks were not always compatible, especially in times of war and high taxation. It was usual for a governorship to pass from father to son, unless a family caused excessive offence to the king or had no suitable heir. There were many offices held by the *épée* which were *de facto* hereditary within a noble House, and for the king to give them to other families would have been a slight upon the reputation of a whole kinship network.

Many examples can be found of clients whose families had served the same aristocratic house for generations, largely because it continued to provide provincial governors or bishops who were often successful in petitioning the king for patronage. It should not be inferred from these enduring ties that the client was in a totally servile position. A great aristocrat needed the support of the lesser nobility as much as they needed his good offices in the quest for royal patronage, and he had to satisfy their aspirations if he was to retain their loyalty. At times when the royal authority was unstable, especially during periods of regency when patronage might be dominated by certain factions at Court, a great noble who was not in favour would be even more dependent on his provincial power base. Then his clients might strike some hard bargains with him in return for their continued support. If he was unable to restore his influence at the centre of power, they might switch their allegiance to a more effective champion.

It was possible to be a client of more than one patron at the same time. A provincial noble family might look to the governor for military and civil posts and to the archbishop for ecclesiastical preferment. A great magnate would therefore seek to instal himself in the governorship and a member of his kin in the archbishopric, as the Villeroy family did for many years in Lyon. The king, in contrast, was normally reluctant to put all the reins of provincial patronage into the hands of one aristocratic House. Competition among the suitors for royal largesse was healthy. All were likely to give good service as long as they were in search of further favours, and rivalry among the petitioners made them even more eager to please the king. As Louis XIV noted in his memoirs for his son, it was also incumbent upon the monarch to be seen to be distributing his favours evenhandedly. No family should feel that its claims were being disregarded and that a less worthy House was being favoured. Favouritism caused instability. Those who received an excess of patronage became arrogant and demanding, while those who felt that they had been denied their rightful rewards might waver in their loyalty and become disaffected. It was a fine balance to maintain. The recent history of late Valois France provided some examples of great nobles who, on falling from favour at Court, had lost their provincial power base, and others where local loyalty had remained firm and the provinces had supported an aristocratic leader in an insurrection against the Crown.

PATRONAGE AND CLIENTAGE: PERIODS OF STABILITY AND INSTABILITY

If a stable and balanced system of patronage was desirable for patrons and clients, it was not always possible. In the year 1610 instability seemed to be in the ascendant. The assassination of Henry IV by an ultra-catholic fanatic threatened to bring to an end the process of healing the rifts in French society which had been caused by some forty years of civil and religious strife. During those civil wars the system of royal patronage had ceased to function in large parts of the realm, while in other areas it had been distributed by factional interests at Court rather than by the king himself. Many great magnates found themselves excluded from royal beneficence and accordingly sought to make themselves supreme in the provinces where they had influence. Although their prime purpose was to advance the power of their families, they also used religious issues as a means of gathering further supporters and instilling fervour into them.

In the late 1580s, the three branches of the House of Lorraine – the Guise, the d'Elbeuf and the d'Aumale – had consolidated their hold over a swathe of provinces from upper Normandy, through Picardy and into Champagne, claiming in addition that these lands were the bastions of ultra-catholicism. Much of the south, where protestantism was the dominant creed, was loyal to Henri de Navarre, the future Henri IV. At Court the Montmorency family had ousted the Guise, but there was another group which had been favoured by Henri III, the much satirized *mignons*, the most powerful of whom were the duc de Joyeuse, who died in 1587, and the duc d'Epernon, who lived on until 1642.

It took Henri de Navarre four years, from his accession in 1589, to gain recognition from all parts of his realm as the legitimate king and the man most likely to restore calm. Henri IV restored a system of royal patronage which reached every part of the kingdom, and all families could resume their strategic search for advancement in the knowledge that no single aristocratic faction controlled the distribution of royal largesse. The king, knowing that conciliation was the only realistic course of action, rewarded his supporters and made generous offers to his former enemies. In doing so, he could not please everyone, and at his death in 1610 there were some leading aristocrats who hoped that a period of regency might give them an opportunity for revenge.

One of the most aggrieved was the duc d'Epernon, the royal *mignon* who had played a major rôle in organizing a rapprochement between Henri III and Henri de Navarre, leading to the king formally designating Navarre as his successor. D'Epernon felt that he deserved a substantial reward and requested the governorship of Provence, only to learn that Henri IV was offering it to his former enemies, the Guise. That princely House, with its Italian links, willingly accepted the post. Henri was pleased that the Guise would be further away from Paris than they had been in their dangerously close provinces of Normandy and Champagne, where there remained many strongholds of the ultra-catholic League. The change was not so dramatic as Henri may have hoped, because the extensive Guise clientage network in Normandy was taken over by their relatives, the d'Elbeuf and the d'Aumale, who remained in the northern provinces. Another possible cause of instability in 1610 was religion. Few catholics and protestants had been reassured by the tolerant Edict of Nantes in 1598, and expected further religious strife. That seemed more likely as the power of Henri IV passed into the hands of his widow, an Italian queen-regent who was thought to be both pro-Spanish and ultra-catholic.

Periods of regency were always disruptive in a society where the effective use of royal patronage was vital to stability. The regents for Louis XIII and Louis XIV were both foreign queens who, on the death of their royal husband, lost their only power base within the kingdom. They therefore had to rely heavily upon some of the great French aristocratic Houses. If some of these indigenous magnates were prepared to provide support, they would also use this opportunity to extract considerable patronage for their families. Other Houses who were excluded from this circle would become aggrieved, accusing the regent of falling prey to evil counsellors.

Sometimes a regent might accede to pressure from a rival group of families, and use their support to oust advisers who had become excessive in their demands. Therefore ambitious aristocrats, whether currently in or out of favour, could hope for great rewards from their careful plotting. If they continued to be ostracized, they might raise the standard of revolt, still claiming that they were fighting for the king and against his ministers. Only when the king came of age could he disown or approve the patronage dispensed by his mother, and, as with Louis XIII in 1617, it was often convenient for a young monarch to dissociate himself from families who had played a major, and unpopular, rôle during his minority. Then he might turn to great nobles who had carefully infiltrated themselves into his affections as a child, often by providing one of their younger relatives as his playmate and teenage companion. These aristocrats knew that a regency was finite and could feel ever more confident as the monarch passed through adolescence, increasingly impatient at having the title of king but not the authority.

The years 1610–17 were therefore times of fierce aristocratic rivalry, although with only one serious revolt, under the leadership of the prince de Condé. During his adult reign, Louis XIII was able to restore some order to the patronage system but there were still difficulties. As always once a king had reached his majority, it was impossible for nobles openly to denounce his decisions, however much they disapproved of them and of the men who advised him. No longer could they say, as under a regency, that they were defending the Crown against evil counsellors, for now the king himself had spoken. As these were difficult years for Louis XIII, with internal campaigns against rebellious protestants who were prepared to enlist the help of foreign rulers, and then with the entry of France into the Thirty Years War, the king often preferred to allow his minister, the cardinal de Richelieu, to appear as the author of unpopular policies. He could take the blame and, if they turned out to be particularly disastrous, be made a scapegoat and dismissed. On more than one occasion Richelieu feared that his dismissal was imminent.

There were two further reasons why royal patronage could not be stabilized during the ministry of Richelieu. First there was one man who was a natural focus for discontent within the kingdom, and yet could not be treated too harshly. Gaston d'Orléans, the brother of Louis XIII, was the heir to the throne of the childless king for twenty-one years of his adult rule. He never planned to remove Louis XIII, but he laboured ceaselessly to obtain great power for himself and his followers at Court and in the provinces. Increasingly Richelieu seemed to be the main obstacle to the realization of these plans, and every attempt was made to persuade the king that the Cardinal should be sacrificed. Some of the conspirators who supported Gaston were apprehended, and executed or exiled, but the heir presumptive had to be tolerated. Also Richelieu had no wish to meet an unpleasant fate, should Louis die and his brother succeed him.

There were other conspiracies at Court against the minister, some of them nearly succeeding as the king wavered and only belatedly decided to retain the services of the Cardinal. During the years 1610–40 there were few large-scale rebellions, where a great noble inflamed an entire province into an attack on the royal government. There were many local revolts against fiscal burdens, and there was religious strife as the king whittled away the military strength of his Huguenot subjects, but there was also a reluctance to take up arms merely to support a great princely family in its ambitions. A return to the faction fighting of the later sixteenth century was unattractive to many Frenchmen. Accordingly, the magnates turned from provincial revolt to Court conspiracy as the means of gaining the power they sought. Many lesser nobles voiced concern about these attempted *coups* against Richelieu, fearing that some of these ambitious aristocrats would be no more evenhanded than the Cardinal in distributing patronage, and might be less competent than he was in administering a kingdom ever more deeply involved in European war.

A second reason for continuing instability in the patronage system resulted from the powerful but precarious position of the Cardinal. Many aristocrats believed, with good reason, that Richelieu was channelling too many rewards towards some families and denying advancement to others. The minister never felt secure in the affections of the king. He knew that Louis XIII, during the regency of Marie de Médicis, had distrusted and disliked him, and that, although he had become the dominant voice on the royal council after 1624, there were aristocratic conspirators and provincial opponents of his fiscal policies who might cause his downfall. He therefore used his influence as *premier ministre* to shower himself, his family and a group of powerful aristocrats, some of them too high in rank to be called clients, with titles, offices, pensions and revenues. He thus hoped to create a power base which would sustain him against his enemies, both by enlisting the support of great nobles who would defend him at Court and by creating a territorial stronghold in western France where he had appointed his adherents to all the principal civil and military offices. If he were to lose the struggle for pre-eminence at the centre, he would have a secure provincial haven to which he could retreat. In pursuing this policy he offended many families who also had claims upon the positions he allocated to members of his own faction, and the death of Richelieu in 1642 was the signal for them to begin their revenge. A series of legal suits ensued, in which many of them succeeded in wresting from the family and clients of the Cardinal some of the wealth and offices he had procured for them.

The death of Louis XIII in 1643 ushered in another period of regency under a foreign queen, his widow Anne of Austria. Her minister, Mazarin, tried to placate some of the aristocrats who had been alienated by Richelieu, but before he could bring any long-term stability to the distribution of patronage the kingdom was plunged into the civil wars of the Frondes. Once again aristocrats from various factions could claim that they were fighting to preserve the young king and his Crown by rescuing him from evil counsellors. Only with the declaration of Louis XIV in 1661 that he would rule personally did the patronage system become once again an effective method for inspiring nobles to give good service to the Crown. He achieved this transformation by distributing rewards evenhandedly and by discouraging rapid social mobility. He created few peerages, refused to promote faithful ministers to the highest ranks of the nobility, and ensured that *robe* families did not acquire the kinds of office which were traditionally the preserve of the *épée*. Only in the last years of the reign did he reverse this policy when, seeing his dynasty in difficulties because he had outlived his son and grandson and knew that a long regency for his infant great-grandson was inevitable, he tried to buy support for his heir by giving peerages and other patronage to some of the most powerful Houses in the realm.

THE ARISTOCRATIC HIERARCHY: PRECEDENCE AND RANK

It is easier to list the categories of French nobles than to determine exactly which families should be placed within each of them. Some claimed that they were being denied their rightful position in a higher stratum, while others were accused by rivals of occupying a position in the hierarchy which they did not merit. Even among members of a single category there were disputes about precedence. For example when a *duc et pair* had no male heir and the king was persuaded to allow the title to pass to a son-in-law, the question arose as to whether this was or was not a new peerage. The difference was important, because peers were ranked according to the dates when their title was created and registered at the *parlements*. There would always be opponents and supporters of the family who were prepared to defend these respective interpretations. An appeal to the king might not resolve the dispute, especially under Louis XIV who became renowned for his skill at avoiding socially sensitive decisions. He would either announce that he would consider the matter or would refer it to the *parlement* of Paris, where a lengthy and probably inconclusive legal wrangle would almost certainly ensue.

The order of precedence was governed, not only by noble rank, but by the offices in the possession of a family. Indeed the king might sometimes appease an aggrieved family by granting it a prestigious office when he felt unable to accept its claim to a higher rank. The one constraint upon him was that it was never wise to favour a noble House to such an extent that many other nobles would become enraged. Only in his wish to honour his illegitimate sons and his mistresses was Louis XIV prepared to abandon his cautious approach, and the outcry was loud and immediate. There was fortunately no dispute about the rank and precedence of most noble families, and the king could grant them offices commensurate with their status, taking into account only their record of loyalty and service.

At the top of the hierarchy of rank was the royal family, although its precise membership was also a matter of some contention. The official list, the *Etat de la France*, for 1676 gives an example of one such disputed claim. Its first, and uncontroversial, chapter lists the *princes du sang* ('princes of the blood') alive in that year, namely the direct and legitimate descendants of Louis XIV and Louis XIII, followed by the other branches of the House of Bourbon – the Condé, the Conti and the Bourbon-Soissons. In the second chapter, and not classed as *princes du sang*, were the legitimized natural children of Louis XIV and Henri IV. It is the third chapter which bears witness to a disputed claim. It contains only one family, the d'Orléans-Longueville whose royal blood through direct male descent came from a Valois bastard line, although they had subsequently arranged princely marriages and had an impressive list of relatives. In 1653 Louis XIV promised the duc de Longueville, who had played a seditious rôle in the *fronde des princes*, that he would make them princes of the blood if the *duc* would effectively abandon his dangerous power base in Normandy of which he was the provincial governor. The family was given a separate chapter in the 1676 list to show that the king no longer regarded them as *princes étrangers* ('foreign princes') and was raising them to a level immediately below the *princes du sang* and the royal *légitimés*, with the implication that he was still intending to honour his promise of 1653. Yet he never took any steps to present the Longueville case to the *parlement* of Paris. He had successfully lured them away from Normandy and he did not wish to annoy other princes by a controversial elevation of the House to the summit of the social hierarchy. This skilful use of patronage is in marked contrast with his desperate and rash decision during his last years, when his direct line was weakened by premature deaths, to include his already legitimized natural sons, the comte de Toulouse and the duc du Maine, among both the *princes du sang* and those eligible to succeed to the throne. Princes, peers and the *parlement* of Paris were horrified at this change in the royal succession, which offended against the morality of the Church and the fundamental laws of the realm. The king could not alter the laws of God and man which had governed his own accession to the throne.

Immediately below the royal family were two groups whose allegiance to the French king was less than wholehearted. First came the cardinals, who had to balance their duty to the sovereign against their obligation to the pope, a difficult task in an age when relations between the French Crown and Rome were often strained. Many of them owed their nomination to the king, but their position in the hierarchy was dependent upon their membership of a Roman institution, the Sacred College. Many ambitious families sought the cardinal's red hat for one or more of their relatives, in order to gain a higher position in the social structure than their inherited titles qualified them to occupy, and to have influence over the allocation of the many ecclesiastical offices which conferred both power and wealth on their holders. Even the *princes étrangers*, who ranked immediately below the cardinals in the hierarchy, still sought the red hat as an added mark of status. Thus in the later sixteenth century the House of Lorraine could boast two members of the Sacred College, the cardinal de Lorraine and the cardinal de Guise. The La Rochefoucauld, whose claim to be *princes étrangers* had not been recognised, had its cardinal, who therefore took precedence over the princes whose ranks the family could not enter. A number of royal ministers also used this office to elevate themselves above the nobility and to gain greater access to ecclesiastical patronage. They included Richelieu, Mazarin, Dubois and Fleury, while the cardinal de Retz regarded his own red hat as a vital part of his strategy to succeed Mazarin as *premier ministre*, a goal he did not achieve.

The next stratum, the *princes étrangers*, also had divided loyalties. They held French titles but came from sovereign princely Houses, which either still ruled elsewhere in Europe or had once exercised sovereignty over lands which were now part of the kingdom of France. The extensive lands of these international Houses might lie within the dominions of two or more rulers, and their marriage alliances might involve them in the affairs of other states as well. Given the frequent French participation in European warfare during the seventeenth century, the *princes étrangers* often found that they had family lands and relatives within territories whose sovereign was at war with the king of France. In the 1676 *Etat de la France* six families were recognized as *princes étrangers*, five of them because their families exercised sovereign power outside the kingdom. They were the Lorraine, the Savoie, the La Tour d'Auvergne, the Grimaldi de Mourgues and the La Trémoïlle. The sixth, the Rohan, was a House which had formerly ruled a part of the present kingdom of France, the province of Bretagne. Most of the titles stemming from the sovereign Houses which had governed French provinces in the days when they were independent but had now been united by carefully planned marriages to the Crown. They included the ducs de Bourgogne, the comtes de Toulouse and the ducs de Bretagne. The last of these three had been the rulers of Bretagne after Rohan sovereignty had ended but it was nevertheless proper to recognize the Rohan as *princes étrangers*, because they were direct descendants of a Breton king, no matter how far back in the past.

The claim of the La Rochefoucauld that they too should be accorded princely status rested on their having been sovereign princes of Marsillac before it was incorporated into the French kingdom. Louis XIV was as unwilling as his predecessors to accede to their wishes, but he was prepared to compensate them by giving them Court offices of such prestige that they would normally be appropriate only for princes of the blood or *princes étrangers*. One was the established post of *grand veneur*. The other, the *grand maître de la garderobe*, was created for the duc de La Rochefoucauld, and it was to be regarded as so prestigious that it was listed, in the *Etat de la France* for 1676, as fourth in the Court hierarchy, immediately after the *grand chambellan*.

After the royal family, the cardinals and the sovereign Houses came the French nobility, led by the peers. All peerages were hereditary in families save for the most senior group of all, the six ecclesiastical peers, where the title of peer was inseparable from the episcopal office. Of these six prelates, the first three – the archbishop of Reims, the bishop of Laon and the bishop of Langres – were *ducs et pairs*, and the remainder – the bishops of Beauvais, Châlons and Noyon – were *comtes et pairs*. Apart from the prestige of their peerages, they played a crucial rôle in the *sacre*, the anointing, of each new monarch. Their supremacy did not go unchallenged because some of them had ecclesiastical superiors who were not peers. The most striking example was in Lyon, where the archbishop was 'primat des Gaules', the senior prelate in the realm, and yet the *duc et pair* of Langres was a bishop under his jurisdiction. Saint-Simon, himself a *duc et pair*, said that it was 'indécent' for Langres to be a suffragan to an archbishop who held no peerage, and the *primat* in turn took every opportunity to demonstrate that his was the superior authority. Despite such disputes the prestige of the six *pairs ecclésiastiques* remained high, as was shown when Louis XIV wished to create a peerage for the archbishops of Paris. He did create one, but it was the secular *pairie* of Saint-Cloud, because he deemed it imprudent to add a seventh to the six prelates without whom he could not have been anointed as king.

In theory the six prelates should have been followed by the six secular peers who were similarly charged with an important rôle in the anointing of the monarch. Those titles had by now been acquired by the royal family as part of the patrimony of the Crown, and were either vacant or were held by princes of the blood who were to be found higher up the list of precedence. The six prelates were therefore followed by the *ducs et pairs* and the *ducs non pairs*. Save in the royal family and among the ecclesiastical peers, there were no longer any *comtés-pairies*. They had either died out or had been raised to *duché-pairies*, perhaps to avoid precedence disputes between *comtes* who were peers and those *ducs* who were not.

The crucial moment in the establishment of a peerage was when the royal letters under the great seal, which announced its creation, were registered by the *parlement* of Paris, the law court which was also the *cour des pairs*. Precedence in the hierarchy was determined by that date. Thus the *ducs et pairs*, in order of registration, were followed by *ducs non pairs* ranked by the same criterion, for *duchés non pairies* had also to be approved by the Paris court. After them came *ducs et pairs*, and then *ducs non pairs*, who had obtained registration only in a provincial *parlement*, and at the end came the ducal peers and non-peers whose letters remained unregistered. Therefore a *duc non pair*, registered in Paris, took precedence over a *duc et pair* whose letters had been registered elsewhere or not at all. Clearly the approval of the Paris court was vital, but some families encountered great difficulties when the Parisian *parlementaires* found reasons for refusing registration or merely made no decision. For example the *duché* of Villars-Brancas, created in 1652, was registered at the *parlement* of Aix in 1657, but not until 1716 could the Paris judges be persuaded to inscribe it in their own registers.

The *ducs et pairs*, but not the *ducs non pairs*, were allowed some of the honours otherwise reserved for princes of the blood and *princes étrangers*. They were addressed by the king as 'mon cousin'; they were allowed to enter the courtyard of a royal palace in a carriage or sedan chair; they could dance with the queen and the royal princesses; and their wives, but not their daughters, were permitted to be seated on a *tabouret* in the presence of the queen. More practically, they held many of the important curial, military and provincial offices. If they were involved in litigation they could insist that the Paris *parlement*, as *cour des pairs*, was the only tribunal in the kingdom competent to hear their case, and they were all members of that court as of right.

Below the *ducs*, whether peers or not, came the *marquis, comtes, vicomtes* and *barons*, followed by the lowest level of the *épée*, the *seigneurs*. The *noblesse de robe* were not listed here, save where its members had managed to obtain titles of *épée* rank. The *robe* therefore, although it had been recognized by the Crown as noble for service in the bureaucracy, was not included within the Second Estate. This was a source of grievance at the rare meetings of the *états-généraux* and the regular sessions of the provincial *états*, when the *robe* could not sit among the members of the noble Estate. Their only place was among the Third Estate, the commoners, which seemed to them to be socially demeaning, although *nobles d'épée* would have confirmed that this was where such 'parvenus' should be seated.

The order of precedence as determined by rank was complicated by the hierarchy of offices in the gift of the king, whether at Court or in the wider realm. There was fierce competition for these posts because they could raise the prestige of a family even if they did not change its rank. Moreover, many of them brought substantial financial benefits as well. In order that the maximum number of noble families might be associated with the royal entourage, many of the Court offices were held in rotation – half-yearly, quarterly and even monthly. This system had a number of advantages. Families would welcome the opportunity for a senior member to be at Court where it would be easier to solicit patronage, but would not want him to be in attendance upon the king for the entire year. In the case of a trusted *duc et pair*, it suited the king to have him as a close companion for some months and to ask for his advice on many matters of State, but it was then essential for him to return to the province where he was governor and work to implement royal policies.

The ceremonial structure gives only a general indication of the influence exerted upon the king by individual courtiers. The most senior of them had numerous opportunities to speak to the king privately, but whether they were soliciting patronage or were being asked for their advice on matters of importance was impossible to ascertain. Nevertheless, shrewd observers were expert in identifying the men on whose counsel the king seemed to rely. The task was difficult because the immediate circle around the monarch included some trusted advisers, some men he wished to honour for past services but did not choose as confidants, and a few whom he positively distrusted to the point that he wished to monitor their every movement. In the last category was the duc de La Rochefoucauld, suspected of having been a *frondeur* and a Jansenist. His post of *grand maître de la garderobe*, which could not be refused because it implied that the king was sympathetic towards the princely claims of the family, was one of the few where the holder had to attend upon the sovereign for the entire year. He was therefore under constant royal surveillance.

Despite the strict hierarchy of rank and office, some peers, bishops and, of course, ministers were therefore treated with more deference than their social position demanded, because it was known that they had the ear of the king. The small group of clerics who advised him on the distribution of benefices was a particular focus for sustained lobbying, because of the wealth, as well as the power, which those posts might confer upon their holder. Yet these clerical advisers, in common with the aristocratic counsellors, were concerned to maintain their own reputation and integrity in the eyes of the king, and would not support every request for favours which was brought to them. Petitioners knew that the more effective a patron was likely to be in obtaining royal patronage, the more rigorously would he assess the suitability of the applicant before deciding whether to mention his name to the king.

THE WEALTH AND ECONOMIC INTERESTS OF THE NOBILITY

In a kingdom where nobility was incompatible in law with commercial and industrial activities and where the *épée* despised venal office as a route to *noblesse*, it was inevitable that land would be the most socially desirable form of investment. Moreover, the titles of *épée* nobles were tied to specific estates, and the *robin* with an ennobling office would also seek to purchase a fief in order to acquire the respectability afforded by a landed title. In the definition of nobility wealth was not one of the criteria, and money matters were never an appropriate topic of conversation in polite society. Yet the lifestyle of an aristocrat was an expensive one, because the expression of his status in visual terms – in art, architecture, dress and hospitality – was a necessary part of living in a hierarchical world. The *nobles de robe*, although they had entered the nobility through a bureaucratic rather than a military route, felt equally obliged to display themselves ostentatiously in the traditional aristocratic manner. The cost of maintaining both country houses and urban *hôtels particuliers* was very great, and the latest fashions in building demanded ever increasing expenditure as families sought to outdo each other in fashionable splendour. A great aristocrat would need to keep up his château in his native province and an *hôtel* in its principal city, as well as another palatial house in Paris where he could participate in the social life of the capital and be accessible to the royal Court. A family which became impoverished, whether temporarily or in the longer term, had no alternative but to retire from society until it had once again acquired the means to sustain the public lifestyle appropriate to its rank.

Kings and ministers were concerned at the proportion of noble wealth which was expended on display, when it might have been invested in royal enterprises such as the colonial companies. Yet it was impossible to alter this fundamental characteristic of an hierarchical society, especially as the lavishness and ceremonial of the royal Court set a bad example and encouraged courtiers to outdo each other in their own splendour. Colbert tried to restrict the import of foreign luxury goods, but with only partial success, and Louis XIV confined his detailed strictures to the behaviour of the highest nobles, particularly the *princes étrangers*, whose ostentation sometimes seemed more suitable for a monarch rather than for a subject. Then his displeasure, with its implied withdrawal of future patronage, would be made known to the offender in unmistakable terms.

There was therefore neither an economic nor a political decline of the *noblesse d'épée* during the seventeenth century. Family fortunes fluctuated, and within every stratum of the nobility it was possible to find the very rich, the very poor and every degree of prosperity between those extremes. For the *épée* expenditure rose drastically in wartime, when commanders had to pay to their regiments the sums which the royal treasury was too impoverished to provide. At times of civil disaffection troops again had to be paid, and only those on the side of the government could hope for reimbursement from the king in due course. Even in peacetime the *noble d'épée* would seek to supplement the income from his estates by seeking royal patronage and perhaps by borrowing money. In time of war borrowing was almost inevitable. There were always wealthy men, often members of the *noblesse de robe* and sometimes rich *épée* nobles, who would advance money to an aristocratic House or lend directly to the royal treasury.

The lenders of these sums were often motivated by political and social, as well as financial, considerations. A group of *robins* could hope that its provision of urgently needed funds would be rewarded, not just by the repayment with interest of the money, but by a royal confirmation or enhancement of institutional privileges, fiscal exemptions, rights of precedence and other signs of social status. This could be achieved by lending to a grateful monarch, or to a great aristocrat – who would then ask that his creditors be rewarded by the king. At times of civil war or provincial rebellion wealthy men would finance an aristocratic campaign, the more so if they thought it likely to succeed. Thus rich Normans had given generously to the Guise onslaught on the forces of Henri III, and many in the south had sustained the cause of Henri de Navarre. If the campaign were to be successful and its leaders were able to achieve a dominant position at Court, royal patronage would undoubtedly flow towards those who had financed it. A further reason why *robins* were so willing to lend money was that their social status precluded some other forms of investment. A bourgeois could invest in trade, but the office-holding nobility, eager to be seen to be 'vivant noblement', regarded commerce as socially demeaning. The *noblesse de robe*, once it had satisfied its need for lands, splendid houses and further offices, had to invest its surplus resources in the world of finance and credit.

For the *noblesse d'épée* there were a number of ways in which to supplement family funds. Kings were prepared to grant pensions and to assign portions of their revenues to aristocrats who had served them well, although it was not always easy to collect the taxes which the Crown had assigned. Most lucrative were some of the offices in the royal gift, especially ecclesiastical benefices. Bishoprics and rich abbeys brought large sums into the coffers of leading aristocratic Houses. Some senior secular posts also brought opportunities for making extra money. For example provincial élites and especially the *états* often made regular and generous gifts to a governor who continued to defend the interests and privileges of the province.

A number of royal ministers tried to remove the stigma associated with colonial and wholesale trade, and changed the law so that nobles could participate in it without *dérogeance*. Yet the aristocratic disdain for commerce, and the *robin* fear of being considered bourgeois, meant that few responded to these ministerial initiatives. Some of the greatest nobles and most senior office-holders did invest in the colonial companies during the reign of Louis XIV, but often because such pressure was put upon them that a refusal would have incurred royal displeasure. In contrast, it is known that some wealthy *épée* and *robe* did invest from choice in commerce and industry, but as they used middle-men or hid behind assumed names the full extent of their involvement is impossible to quantify.

Land remained the principal source of income for the *épée*, and both land and office for the *robe*. Purchase of a bureaucratic office was regarded as an investment in property, exactly as if it were an estate. It usually increased in value over the years, and it could be bequeathed to heirs or sold like any other property, save only for the annual payment to the Crown under the *paulette* legislation of 1604 which guaranteed the right of the office-holder to dispose of his post as he pleased. The military offices held by the *épée* were not subject to the *paulette* and therefore were not able to be made hereditary by the payment of an annual fee. Yet the holder of such an office was usually able to purchase the 'survivance' to the post for his son many years before he himself intended to retire.

Robin office-holders recouped the purchase price of their post from two sources – partly from the royal salary to which they became entitled and largely from the administrative tasks they performed. Judges received fees from litigants and fiscal officials retained a percentage of the taxes they collected. At times of financial crisis in the royal treasury, which included the entire period from 1634 to 1659, the stability of the system could break down. The Crown might create more offices for sale, but the income from collecting taxes or hearing law cases did not increase. A larger number of officials wanted a share of a static amount of administrative profits. A judge who learnt that a second judgeship was being created in the jurisdiction which had hitherto been his alone had two courses of action open to him. He could do nothing, in which case he would have to share with the new judge the income that he had been accustomed to keep for himself, or he could purchase the new office, paying yet again for the sole right to the fruits of a piece of 'property' which he thought he had acquired already. Royal salaries went unpaid in years of crisis, and the Crown offered rises in the future level of salaries on the condition that office-holders made immediate loans to the treasury. When Mazarin even threatened not to renew the *paulette*, thus ending the hereditary transmission of these 'properties' the office-holders rose in revolt in the first Fronde of 1648–9, and forced the regency government to confirm their rights in the peace signed at Rueil in 1649.

The rules of landholding in France permit no simple generalizations. Feudal tenure had been common in the north, but rare in the southern provinces where much of the Roman legal system had survived. There was a further difference between the *pays d'élections* and the *pays d'états*, regardless of whether they were northern or southern. In the *pays d'élections* the noble paid no land tax because the *taille* was *personnelle*, and if a man was 'personally' noble he was exempted from paying it on all his lands. In the *pays d'états* the *taille* was *réelle*, and was levied on estates designated as commoner land without reference to the social rank of the owner. Most *épée* nobles owned no commoner land and paid no tax under either system, but many *robe* nobles had to purchase it in their desire to have country estates and landed respectability. *Robins* in areas of *taille personnelle* paid no land tax, but elsewhere they would be subject to the *taille réelle* on their common lands. That did not dissuade the *noblesse de robe* in *pays d'états* such as Bretagne and Bourgogne from enlarging its rural patrimony, although it may have been a deterrent in Languedoc and Provence. In those two southern provinces the nobles, *épée* and *robe*, had always spent a larger part of the year in their urban *hôtels* than was customary elsewhere in the kingdom. They also expended more energy and money on adorning their town houses and less on their rural châteaux. A southern *noble de robe* would acquire a country estate in order to be 'vivant noblement', and would hope to purchase one of the fiefs, rare in that part of the realm, which carried with it a landed title. Beyond the achievement of those ambitions, he would have no further interest in rural property. Moreover those *robin* châteaux were often very close to the provincial capital on which power and social life was centred. (It should be noted that a commoner who purchased a fief did not become noble in consequence.)

The management of family wealth and the acquisition of new lands and offices, whether by purchase or by marriage, were major preoccupations of *robe* and *épée* alike. They required careful and strategic planning, which is why a council of the extended family would be summoned to decide on the course to be followed. Money was a factor in these decisions, whether it was to come from a lucrative office or from a bride who would bring a substantial dowry and a large future inheritance, but it was socially improper to examine the details of financial advantage when an aristocratic family council was in session. The overt, and equally important, reasons for discussing a new office or a marriage alliance were questions of increased influence, rank, status and prestige.

A noble House was always careful to ensure that it had members who were suitably qualified for every kind of desirable office. Among the *épée*, some sons were prepared for the army, others for the Church, and at least one for the administrative post, such as provincial governor or *lieutenant-général*, currently held by the head of the House. *Robe* families educated their sons in the law so that they could take on the offices that their elders already possessed and acquire new ones. Some of the leading *épée* Houses consolidated their political and economic power in a spectacular way. Thus in 1617 the Villeroy governors of Lyon intermarried with the Lesdiguières, who were governors of neighbouring Dauphiné and owned lands in Switzerland, Provence and Languedoc, all of them regions important to the long distance trade which was the basis of Lyonnais prosperity. Similarly, the Noailles married into the Gramont, so that the two families now governed the Pyrenean frontier provinces and Languedoc, a huge swathe of southern France from the Bay of Biscay to the Rhône. The Noailles also obtained a red hat and the archbishopric of Paris for one of their relatives.

A final difference between northern and southern France, and one which affected these family strategies, concerned the laws of inheritance. In the north the principle of primogeniture was accepted, the eldest son taking most of the family patrimony although some provision was made for other brothers and for sisters. Under the Roman legal tradition of the south there was no such principle, and accordingly much greater weight was placed upon the testament of the property owner. It was his task to keep most of the patrimony intact by choosing one son, not necessarily the eldest, as his chief legatee, but with the proviso that all his other offspring had the legal right to an equal share of one quarter, or in some areas one third, of the total fortune. A father, eager to preserve the territorial integrity of the family estates, usually fulfilled his obligation to his other children in cash, rather than in grants of land. Sometimes he would claim that the dowry of a daughter, or the cost of paying for a child of either sex to enter the Church, was an advance payment towards the sum which would be due at his death. Those members of the family who were childless, usually because they had taken holy orders, would bequeath most of their resources to their relatives because the preservation of the collective patrimony of the lineage was the prime consideration. Dowries were subject to legal rules which ensured that they never passed out of the family. The dowry of a bride could be used by her husband but it did not belong to him, and he was legally required to pass it on, undiminished, to the children of the marriage. When a man married twice, the dowry of each bride went only to her own children and not to the progeny of the two marriages. If a wife died without offspring, her dowry had to be repaid to her own family.

The economic improvement of a family was intimately linked with its quest for office and status because, while money was necessary for social advancement, social success brought financial rewards. Surprisingly in view of the claims made by historians for eighteenth-century nobles, the nobility in the France of Louis XIII and Louis XIV showed no interest in exploiting the land, the economic resource which was an essential characteristic of 'vivant noblement'. Nor was the Crown concerned to promote agriculture, save for its efforts to find better horses for the cavalry. Ministers were preoccupied with the expansion of trade and industry, activities which were not suitable for nobles.

THE POWER OF THE NOBILITY IN THE KINGDOM

At Court and throughout the provinces an informal structure of government coexisted with the formal institutional framework. To study the latter in isolation, as some historians have done, is to ignore some of the links which held together the society of the *ancien régime*. Despite the increase in size of the *robe* bureaucracy, the *noblesse d'épée* retained its dominance over most areas of the administration. That was undoubtedly true in the army where all positions of command were in *épée* hands. There had been some symbolic changes, in order to enhance the image of the monarchy, but in reality almost everything remained as before.

At the summit of the military hierarchy, the post of *connétable* was not filled when the duc de Lesdiguières died in 1627. Historians of absolutism have seen this decision as a determined step by the king to gain personal control of his forces and of the immense powers of patronage and justice which had been the prerogative of the *connétable*. Yet the king did not personally assume these powers. Instead he entrusted them intact to the senior *maréchal de France*, a seniority determined by the date of appointment. Even when the two war ministers of Louis XIV, Le Tellier and Louvois, increased their control over the routine of army organization and expanded the civil bureaucracy which serviced the armed forces, they left discipline and military justice entirely in the hands of the *maréchaux de France*. In an age where sons normally inherited the army commands of their father, the point had been made in 1627 that the post of *connétable* was too important to be treated in this way. Yet there could be no question of transferring its powers from the aristocratic, military hierarchy into the domain of civilian ministers of *robin* origin. Noble officers would not have tolerated such a step.

Lower down the army establishment, the nobility continued to have a monopoly of command. The posts of *colonel* and *capitaine* were venal, but, unlike the offices of the civil bureaucracy, they did not automatically pass from father to son and could not be sold at the whim of the holder. Royal approval was required, although in fact the succession almost always passed to the relative preferred by the officer or, if he had been killed in battle, by his family. Two practical reasons made this outcome likely. First, the father would have carefully trained his son in the necessary skills; secondly, the continuation of a command in a family was important in recruiting troops. Regiments were recruited in the localities and, although they knew that they served a remote monarch, felt that their real loyalty was to their noble commander who came from a respected local family. It was he who inspired them to serve, often in distant lands and for causes which had no apparent relevance to their native area. At a time of civil war or revolt, it was he who would rally them either to support the Crown or to oppose it in defence of provincial liberties. Moreover, it was the noble commander who paid his regiment when the money due to it from the royal treasury was in arrears, a common occurrence in wartime. Therefore, although the Crown used every kind of propaganda to assert that this was the army of the king, fighting for his glory, the effective bonds within the military were those between soldier and local commander, and between lesser officers and their superiors.

Another preserve of the *noblesse d'épée* was diplomacy. Here too, under Louis XIV, there was an increase in the number of professional bureaucrats. They assisted with foreign policy and accompanied ambassadors, but the royal envoys themselves had to be drawn from the great nobles. Not only had they been educated to play this rôle, but they had to be of sufficient rank to be socially accepted at the foreign Courts to which they were accredited. Many *ducs et pairs* had great success at mastering the power networks of other princely Courts, and showed considerable skill as negotiators. The king trusted these ambassadors, as he did his generals and provincial governors, to make decisions when there was no time to refer a difficult problem to him and his council.

Generals and ambassadors had to work extremely hard, as their lengthy and frequent reports, as well as their voluminous correspondence, clearly demonstrate. Yet war and diplomacy were not without periods of respite, between spells of intense activity. More demanding therefore, because there were always tasks to perform, were senior positions in the French provinces. The problems were different, according to whether the province was a *pays d'élections* or a *pays d'états*. In the former the royal officials played a larger rôle in the administration, and the judicial machinery was ultimately accountable to the *parlement* of Paris. The leading nobles in the *pays d'élections*, who might be governors, *lieutenants-généraux*, bishops or simply great aristocrats with lands and influence in the province, were key figures in the informal processes of government which complemented the administrative mechanisms. They acted as brokers for royal patronage, identified men upon whom the Crown could rely, and used their influence to persuade the local élites that they should carry out the policies and wishes of the royal government. They also made representations to the king on behalf of the province, explaining its problems and asking for assistance. Governors and prelates who were held in particularly high regard by the king were not afraid to be outspoken. They might recommend that it would be counter-productive to insist on implementing a very unpopular royal policy, or even that the policy was misconceived. The king and his ministers were always willing to consider advice from these reliable sources, for there was no other means by which the Crown could obtain such objective on-the-spot reports, although they did not feel that they could accept it on every occasion. A governor or bishop often had to steer a difficult course between the demands of the Crown and the opposition, often justified, of the province. If he totally alienated the local élites, he would lose the influence over his area which made him so valuable to the Crown, an outcome which the king was also eager to avoid.

In the *pays d'états* the tasks of governors, bishops and great aristocrats were even more complex, because much of the provincial administration was in the hands, not of royal office-holders, but of local officials under the supervision of the elected *états*. These provinces, many of them very large, were mostly recent additions to the kingdom of France and were fiercely proud of their separatist origins. In addition to electing their own *états*, they each had their own *parlement*, and so the king could not use the effective legal weapon of the *parlement* of Paris as he could in the rest of the kingdom. A group of trusted nobles was essential to the Crown in its attempts to influence the institutions of the *pays d'états*, peripheral provinces which bordered foreign, and often enemy, territories. Noble assistance was particularly vital in fiscal matters because, whereas in the *pays d'élections* the king could announce the sums he required in direct taxes, in the *pays d'états* the Crown had to negotiate with the *états* about the amount they were prepared to authorise. Also the *états* and provincial *parlements* might obstruct or oppose new indirect taxes. The royal government was normally reluctant to become involved in the details of local administration, preferring to leave them to duly constituted provincial and municipal bodies. It was only when royal revenues were at stake that the Crown and the provinces became involved in negotiations, which were often prolonged, sometimes acrimonious and occasionally so bitter that the provincial citizenry was prompted to take up arms.

The provincial governor, assisted by one or more *lieutenants-généraux*, all of them high aristocrats selected because they were held in high esteem by the province, had the task of liaising between the Crown and the provincial institutions, and guiding the negotiations. They were assisted by the *intendants*, drawn from the *robe* and in theory from outside the province, although in these proud *pays d'états* the *intendants* were often local men from leading *robin* families. Other great nobles played a guiding rôle as well. Where the three Estates met as a single chamber, which was the practice in Languedoc, the president of the assembly was a crucial figure. In that province the presidency was held *ex officio* by the archbishop of Narbonne. In Bretagne the three Estates assembled separately, and the king and the governor sought to identify suitable presidents for each of them. Many other leading nobles could exert their influence during the course of the debates on the level of taxation. Bishops put pressure on the members of the Third Estate who came from their diocese, great aristocrats wooed lesser nobles, and the governor tried to win over some groups by promising them his support in their disputes with other local élites. At the end of the session of the *états*, the governor and senior bishops would send the king a list of the men who had been particularly assiduous in advancing the royal cause, and ask for patronage .to be granted tò them. Such rewards, well publicised, would hopefully encourage others to be similarly cooperative at future meetings of the *états*. Of course the governors and bishops also hoped that they too might be rewarded for their skilful management of the assembly.

The provincial *noblesse d'épée* were eager suitors for the offices, both military and ecclesiastical, the revenues and the pensions which were in the royal gift. It is less obvious why senior members of the *robe* rallied to governors and bishops. These *robins* were socially ineligible for the offices and benefices that the king could bestow. They constituted a closed élite, advancing the status and influence of their families by purchasing further offices and by arranging marriages within their own stratum. For example, *parlementaire* families seldom married into the *épée* and almost never into the lesser *robe*. It was therefore not personal or family advancement which led the *noblesse de robe* to enlist the help of governors, bishops and great aristocrats, but the need to preserve the collective privileges of the institutions and social groups to which they belonged. Sometimes they felt themselves under threat because of an attempt by the Crown to undermine their liberties, but more often they needed aristocratic support at Court to help them to resist the claims of a rival provincial institution or élite. The situation in Languedoc demonstrates this point clearly. The *parlement* in Toulouse and the permanent officials of the *états* in Montpellier were often at odds. The former might appeal for assistance to the archbishop of Toulouse, the latter to the president of the *états*, the archbishop of Narbonne, thus involving two prelates who were themselves rivals. Alternatively or in addition, both sides might seek to enlist the aid of the governor. Intervention in these rivalries could earn for governors and prelates the gratitude of an important élite, which might be persuaded in return to show greater compliance towards royal fiscal demands. Yet no great noble wished to be too closely associated with any single interest group, because the next conflict might be between two provincial bodies which had both received his support in earlier disputes.

Whatever their links with aristocratic patrons, the *nobles de robe* dominated much of provincial life through their own offices and prestige. *Parlements*, other courts and royal fiscal mechanisms were controlled by them and their clients. They frequently dispensed justice or collected revenues in the manner prescribed by the Crown, but they delayed or resisted royal orders when their own interests, or those of their province, were threatened. As with the *noblesse d'épée* it was important for the robe to retain the respect of their locality as well as to serve the king.

Most strata of the *noblesse de robe* were composed of a small group of families, rivalling each other for a greater share of offices and income but united in seeking to prevent new entrants from penetrating their closed world. Registers of the men serving in provincial institutions reveal a continuity of family names over many decades. If it was the *robe* which ran the judiciary and the fiscal system, the powerful city councils were often composed of a wider variety of nobles. Moreover, in some privileged cities election to the council conferred nobility automatically on those who did not already possess it. That was true for the *capitoulat*, the civic rulers of Toulouse. Yet an examination of the pedigrees of *capitouls* over many decades reveals that these elected councillors always included some who had been ennobled by election, but many who came from leading families of the *robe* and the *épée*.

Nobles therefore played a major rôle in all aspects of the administration of the kingdom, whether ecclesiastical, military, judicial, financial or municipal. On their own estates most of them had further rights, because they had the power to dispense justice. Louis XIV, who was always concerned to reduce the numerous disputes between local jurisdictions, whether secular or ecclesiastical, and never ceased to emphasize the supremacy of royal justice, did not attempt to abolish these seigneurial courts. He contented himself with regulations forbidding them to impinge upon other jurisdictions.

As the seventy-two-year reign of Louis XIV drew to a close in 1715, most nobles would have agreed that the king had been a rigorous defender of aristocratic values and of an hierarchical society. He had impoverished his kingdom through his wars, and everyone longed for a period of peace, but the rules and the fabric of society were intact. Only a clairvoyant could have foreseen the extent to which these fundamental social assumptions would have been challenged before the eighteenth century had run its course.

CHAPTER FIVE

The French Nobility, 1715–1789

Julian Swann
Birkbeck College, University of London

Studies of the eighteenth-century *noblesse* were long distorted by the powerful and enduring influence of the social interpretation of the French Revolution. According to traditional wisdom, the events of 1789 marked the triumph of a new class of bourgeois entrepreneurs over an aristocracy whose political power was based upon outmoded social and economic foundations.[1] The Revolution was, therefore, seen as a decisive and necessary step in the transition of French society from a feudal to a modern capitalist form. Convinced of the inevitability of these changes, historians proceeded to impose a whole series of value judgements upon a class that was, by 1789, reactionary, selfish and anachronistic by definition. Tied to the land, incapable of adapting to changing circumstances or seizing the opportunities offered by the eighteenth-century expansion of the economy, the *noblesse* allegedly turned in upon itself. The result was a deliberate attempt to prevent new members from entering its ranks, a fierce and highly effective defence of its fiscal privileges and desperate efforts to maintain its economic position through the ruthless exploitation of the seigneurial rights imposed upon the peasantry. These were the principal ingredients of what was known as the feudal, or aristocratic, reaction, during the half century before the Revolution.

During the last forty years, historians have gradually revised their ideas about both the Revolution's origins and the *noblesse's* rôle in *ancien régime* society. Few would now subscribe to a purely class based analysis, or claim that 1789 was the direct result of the capitalist bourgeoisie sweeping aside the remnants of a feudal social order. Instead, there has been a growing awareness of the social, cultural and economic ties that bound the *noblesse* and members of the wealthier bourgeoisie together.[2] Doubt has also been cast upon the traditional view that the élite was engaged in a reactionary defence of either its privileges or economic position. It has even been claimed that the *noblesse* represented the most progressive social group in

---

1. The social interpretation has a long and distinguished history but its finest exponent was Georges Lefebvre, *La révolution française*, 7th edn (Paris, 1989). Another good example is the work of Albert Soboul, *The French Revolution, 1787–1799. From the Storming of the Bastille to Napoleon* (London, 1989).

2. For example, see: G. V. Taylor, 'Noncapitalist Wealth and the Origins of the French Revolution', *American Historical Review* 79 (1966–67), 469–96; C. Lucas, 'Nobles, Bourgeois and the Origins of the French Revolution', *Past and Present*, no. 60, (1973) 84–126; and G. Richard, *La noblesse d'affaires* (Paris, 1975).

the kingdom, open not only to the liberal intellectual currents of the Enlightenment, but also able and willing to use its position in order to act as the vanguard of industrial development in pre-revolutionary France.[3] That such a dramatic shift in historical thinking has been possible reflects both the amount of new research that has been concentrated upon this important social group and the continuing arguments that surround the French Revolution. It is, therefore, necessary to treat some of the more extravagant claims made on behalf of the *noblesse* with caution.

I

Before 1789, French society was still officially composed of the three medieval orders of clergy, nobility and Third Estate. Membership of the Second Estate or *noblesse* was, at least superficially, easily defined because it depended upon a simple system of judicial proofs. When called upon to do so, a noble was expected to produce some form of legal document, such as a testament, royal *arrêt* or *brevet* of office, which confirmed that he, or one of his ancestors, was of recognized noble stock. During the reign of Louis XIV (1643–1715), his finance minister, Colbert, had attempted to carry out a census of the *noblesse* as part of his fiscal reform programme. His efforts failed to produce a comprehensive list and thereafter the scheme was abandoned. Colbert's failure has been a source of disappointment to historians ever since. Put simply, we have absolutely no way of knowing how many individuals belonged to the Second Estate at any given point in the eighteenth century. A number of contemporary writers did, however, offer some wildly conflicting estimates. In 1707, Louis XIV's principal military architect, Vauban, claimed that the kingdom contained 260,000 nobles. Later, in 1756, abbé Coyer calculated that there were approaching 400,000 nobles, and in his famous pamphlet, 'What is the Third Estate', written in 1789, abbé Sieyès quoted a figure of 110,000.

More than two centuries later, historians are still no nearer providing a generally acceptable estimate. Using a different method of calculation, Jean Meyer has come close to the figure of Coyer and suggests that at the end of the *ancien régime* there were approximately 350,000 members of the Second Estate.[4] He arrives at this total by estimating the number of nobles in key categories such as the army, court and judiciary and multiplying by a coefficient of 4 in order to include their family or dependants. There are difficulties with such estimates, however, not least because it was common

---

3. This argument has been expressed with great flair by G. Chaussinand-Nogaret, *The French Nobility in the Eighteenth Century. From Feudalism to Enlightenment* (Cambridge, 1985). His work has been crucial in shaping the arguments of revisionist historians such as W. Doyle, *The Origins of the French Revolution*, 2nd edn (Oxford, 1988), and S. Schama, *Citizens* (London, 1989).

4. J. Meyer, *La noblesse française à l'époque moderne (XVI–XVIIIe siècles)* (Paris, 1991), pp. 98–103.

for one family to have several members serving in different offices. Moreover, the cadets, who filled the lower ranks of both the army and navy, rarely married. Guy Chaussinand-Nogaret, on the other hand, has offered a total of 120,000 which corresponds closely to that of Sieyès.[5] His calculation is based upon an analysis of the lists of noble electors to the Estates General of 1789 and the *capitation*, or poll tax, rolls. Unfortunately, these lists are not exhaustive, and confronted by these discrepancies, it is tempting to fall back on the earlier calculation of Henri Carré who posited the figure of 230,000, which at least has the virtue of falling between the two extremes.[6] Whatever the exact total may have been, the *noblesse* represented no more than a tiny fraction of the French population which, after expanding throughout the eighteenth century, had reached around twenty-eight million by 1789. Depending upon the estimate used, the *noblesse* therefore made up between 0.75 per cent and 1.25 per cent of the overall population, or approximately 1 per cent as a round figure. A lack of information makes it difficult to be precise about whether or not the *noblesse* was increasing or decreasing in size relative to the population as a whole, but it is clear that it was continuing to welcome new members into its ranks.

For a wealthy bourgeois, who had made the necessary fortune and wished to join the Second Estate a variety of options were available. The most obvious strategy was to invest in an ennobling office. It was, for example, possible to buy the office of councillor or judge in one of the thirteen *parlements* that dominated the major cities of the kingdom. To purchase such a position required a massive investment, approximately 50,000 *livres* for that of Paris in 1750, although prices in the provinces were usually lower. Such an office conferred social prestige, fiscal privileges and career and financial opportunities, but what made the office especially attractive was its ennobling qualities. Twenty years of continuous service, or death while in charge, and the owner, or his heirs, could petition for letters of hereditary *noblesse*. It has been argued that in the course of the eighteenth century, entrance into the *parlements* became increasingly difficult, and there is some evidence to support this assertion. Between 1749 and 1789 the number of offices in the *parlement* of Paris fell by over a hundred from 248 to just 144, a fact of some importance if one considers that at any given point only about 10 per cent of the available offices were in the hands of those in the process of becoming ennobled.[7] The provincial *parlements* were, if anything, more restrictive. That of Rennes was a notorious example, allowing only those with a proven noble pedigree of at least 100 years to sit on its benches. By 1789, the judges in Toulouse

5. Chaussinand-Nogaret, *The French Nobility*, pp. 28–31. François Bluche, *La vie quotidienne de la noblesse française au XVIIIe siècle* (Paris, 1973), p. 12, also quotes this figure.

6. H. Carré, *La noblesse française devant l'opinion publique au XVIIIe siècle* (Paris, 1920), pp. 14–18.

7. Included in this figure are the first president, *présidents à mortier*, presidents and councillors of the *enquêtes* and *requêtes* and the principal members of the *parquet*. Honorary members, *greffiers*, substitutes and other officers have been deliberately excluded.

were almost exclusively noble, and it is probable that this represented a more general pattern.[8] For certain provinces, the result was to block the paths to social advancement. Bretagne was one such case. The exclusivity of the *parlement* of Rennes made it impossible for successful lawyers to buy an ennobling office, which may account for the bitter antagonism displayed towards the *noblesse* by the local bourgeoisie in 1789.[9] Similar tensions could arise in comparatively isolated provinces like Béarn. The *parlement* of Pau again represented the only direct route into the *noblesse* for the legal bourgeoisie, and it was no coincidence that when Louis XV (1715–74) reformed the troublesome court in 1765, he was able to recruit new judges with surprising ease.

Elsewhere in the kingdom, there was no shortage of alternative law courts which were generally less exclusive than the *parlements*, including the thirteen *Cour des Aides*, twelve *Chambre des Comptes* and twenty-nine *Bureaux des Finances*, all of which contained ennobling offices. Other popular routes to the Second Estate passed through the royal administration, notably the 900 offices of *secrétaires du roi*, which were the most significant source of new nobles by 1789.[10] Advancement was also possible through what was known as the *noblesse de cloche*. This was the title given to the various municipal offices that conferred hereditary *noblesse*. These included the prestigious Capitouls of Toulouse and the Consuls of Lyons, but similar offices were to be found in towns such as Angers, La Rochelle, Niort and Tours. Although the government ceased to create new ennobling offices after 1715, there were still approximately 4,000 of these posts at the end of the *ancien régime*. Admittedly, only a fraction were available for purchase at any given time, but the market in offices continued to function representing one of the principal means of social ascension.

There were, however, a number of innovations during the reign of Louis XV. In 1750, comte d'Argenson, minister of war, introduced an edict which conferred hereditary *noblesse* on all army officers who had risen to the rank of *officier général*, or from whose families three successive generations had won the coveted Order of Saint Louis.[11] From mid-century, reward of merit was increasingly apparent in the letters of *noblesse* granted by the Crown to deserving subjects. Thus, the intendant of Bretagne, Bertrand de Molleville, secured letters for his *subdélégue*, Robert de La Mennais, who had acted on his own initiative, using his personal wealth, to provision the town of Saint-Malo during the dearth of 1786. In an extension of Colbert's efforts to prevent the flight of capital into land or offices, the Crown also awarded letters of *noblesse* to successful merchants. Though such letters had always existed, under Louis XIV they had occasionally been sold as a fiscal expedient. Yet, the numbers that were

8. R. Forster, *The Nobility of Toulouse in the Eighteenth Century* (Baltimore, Md., 1960), pp. 103–5.

9. J. Meyer, 'Noblesse des bocages: essai de typologie d'une noblesse provinciale' in B. Köpeczi and E. Balàzs, eds, *Noblesse française, noblesse hongroise (XVI–XIXe siècles)* (Budapest and Paris, 1981), pp. 38–41.

10. D. D. Bien, 'Manufacturing Nobles: the chancelleries in France to 1789', *Journal of Modern History*, 61 (1989), 445–86.

11. Carré, *Noblesse française*, pp. 11–12.

honoured in this fashion were very small, and it did not mark a fundamental shift in either royal thinking or noble mentality. The same government that was dispensing letters of merit to worthy commoners was also demanding proofs dating back to 1400 before allowing candidates to receive the honour of presentation to the king and the royal family at Court. Too much importance should not be attributed to a policy that promised more in theory than it delivered in practice.

Taken as a whole, therefore, the avenues to social advancement were by no means closed before 1789. Since the sixteenth century, the French *noblesse* had been constantly renewing itself through the various channels outlined above, and during the eighteenth century new blood continued to join its ranks. To enter was expensive, but feasible, and there is no convincing evidence of a general desire to exclude newcomers. Even the infamous Ségur ordinance of 1781, which required all prospective members of the officer corp to provide genealogical proofs of four quarters, or about 100 years, of unbroken *noblesse*, merely brought the army into line with the regulations of the *Ecole Militaire*.[12] Rather than being part of an aristocratic reaction against the Third Estate, the measure was conceived as a reform that would professionalise the army by preventing wealthy *parvenu*, whether noble or not, from buying their way into a military career. While there are still disputes about the exact number of noble families, it is now generally agreed that the majority were of comparatively recent extraction, having acquired their titles since 1500. However, the *noblesse* was in no sense a class defined by socio-economic criteria, and an almost limitless number of methods can be employed to identify distinct noble groups, or the hierarchies that existed between them. The Second Estate was a matrix criss-crossed by lines of wealth, profession, birth and provincial custom, and a purely class based analysis is certain to produce distorted results. Indeed, it can even be argued that the idea of a French *noblesse* is a misnomer, for there was not one but several nobilities.

II

Throughout the eighteenth century, the most commonly cited distinction was that separating *épée* and *robe*, although as the century progressed a third category, that of *finance*, became increasingly current. Put simply, these were professional demarcations denoting nobles who pursued the profession of arms (the *épée*), those who served in the royal courts or administration (the *robe*), or those who managed the tax farms or acted as bankers (*finance*). There is no doubt that contemporaries placed the *épée* at the top and *finance* at the bottom of the

12. D. D. Bien, 'The Army in the French Enlightenment: reform, reaction and revolution', *Past and Present*, no. 85 (1979), 68–98.

hierarchy within the *noblesse*, but, without ever being entirely eradicated, these barriers gradually blurred as the century progressed. Money was the most potent solvent of ancient distinctions, whether social or professional, and by the reign of Louis XVI (1774–92) Versailles and Paris were dominated by an élite composed of the wealthiest members of the three groups. Without money, a noble with an impeccable pedigree could be obliged either to pass his life in genteel obscurity, or serve with little hope of preferment in a lowly military or ecclesiastical post. Alternatively, a member of the Third Estate with a sufficiently abundant fortune could aspire to rapid social promotion. Bourgeois de Boynes rose through the ranks of the royal administration and in 1771 became naval minister. Yet he was the son of a banker who had bought an ennobling office after making a fortune through investment in John Law's notorious banking system – one of the great speculative follies of the eighteenth century, which saw millions won and lost before the final crash in 1720. Among the many finance ministers employed by the Crown were Boullongne, Moreau de Séchelles, Peyrenc de Moras and Terray, all from recently ennobled families and all very rich. Shared wealth gave cohesion to the élite of noble society centred upon the Court and the capital, where traditional distinctions of *épée*, *robe* and *finance* became increasingly meaningless. United by common bonds of culture, lifestyle and, often, family, this élite monopolized the political and institutional life of the *ancien régime*. By 1789, the real distinction within the *noblesse* was, therefore, between those with access to positions of power at Court or in government, and their less wealthy cousins who, while often distinguished in the context of their own neighbourhoods, could rarely surmount the obstacles that relative poverty had placed in their path.

Marriage patterns provide a valuable indicator of changing attitudes within the *noblesse*. During the seventeenth century, matches between *robe* and *épée*, or worse still *épée* and *finance*, were described as a 'misalliance' and were a source of gossip if not dishonour. At the top of noble society, this form of social exclusivism, or snobbery, had largely disappeared by 1789, and *épée*, *robe* and *finance* happily intermarried. Thus, René Nicolas Charles Augustin de Maupeou, the future chancellor, married into the Roncherolles, an *épée* family of ancient extraction, while the duc d'Ayen – an aristocratic Noailles – married into the distinguished *robe* family of d'Aguesseau. *Robe* and *épée* stood on increasingly level ground when it came to choosing partners, and both competed in the élite marriage market for wealthy heiresses, especially the daughters of financiers. For example, the fabulously wealthy banker Samuel Bernard married his daughter to president Molé, one grand-daughter to president Lamoignon, both among the élite of the Paris *parlement*, and another to the aristocratic marquis de Mirepoix.[13] Dowries of 800,000 *livres* went to each new son-in law, and the marquis d'Argenson was surely not alone in lamenting that his parents had failed to find him a similar match.

13. Y. Durand, *Finance et mécénat: les fermiers géneraux au XVIIIe siècle* (Paris, 1976), p. 152.

If wealth was the great leveller in noble society, there were other distinctions which, depending on circumstances, could facilitate a career, offer the opportunity for an advantageous marriage, or simply command the respect of society. One of the most important was that of pedigree. Those who could prove four degrees, or about a century of unbroken *noblesse* in the male line were said to belong to the *noblesse de race*. Even more distinguished were nobles of ancient extraction, whose family trees could be traced back beyond 1400. Included in this category were some of the most illustrious in the kingdom, such as La Rochechouart, Montmorency and Tessé. In a society that honoured the collective, whether a family or an institution, rather than the individual, this was of crucial importance in affirming rank against peer groups and, above all, social inferiors, principally the newly ennobled. Despite the claims of aristocratic writers such as the duc de Saint-Simon or the comte de Boulainvilliers, who equated the *noblesse* with the military vocation and sought to establish a link between the aristocratic *épée* and the knights of the Hundred Years War, the crusades or, in the case of Boulainvilliers, the Frankish conquerers of Gaul, it would be wrong to assume that every courtier, or *noble d'épée*, was descended from a family of ancient extraction. Under Louis XV, few enjoyed such a glamorous or successful career as the maréchal de Belle-Isle. During the War of the Austrian Succession (1740–48), he commanded the royal armies at the siege of Prague, and he was later minister of war. Belle-Isle's status as what contemporaries called a *grand seigneur* was beyond question, yet he was the grandson of Louis XIV's notorious finance minister, Fouquet.

Paying too much attention to the idea of pedigree can distort the true picture of noble society. Louis XV discovered this to his cost in 1760, when he agreed to an edict restricting the honours of the Court to those who could trace their ancestry back at least to 1400. This embarrassed several important courtiers, including the maréchal d'Estrées, a member of the royal council, who had to be given a special dispensation. Nor should we believe the malicious pen of Saint-Simon, who wrote contemptuously about *robins* and described Louis XIV's ministers as the 'vile bourgeoisie', by which he meant they were of *robe* origin. Not every member of the *parlements* or the royal administration was of recent noble vintage. The *noblesse de robe*, so-named because of the robes worn by the judges who were its most conspicuous members, also contained its own *noblesse de race*, and the families of Le Febvre de Laubrière, Longueil and La Bourdonnaye could trace their roots back at least as far as Saint-Simon's own. Moreover, *robe* dynasties such as the Pasquier, Molé or Séguier had been conspicuous in royal service since the sixteenth century. Like the *épée*, the *robe* derived immense pride from its corporate identity and professional reputation. Robert de Saint-Vincent, a long-serving member of the Paris *parlement*, began his memoirs with a firm refusal to invent a false genealogy tracing his family back into the Gothic mists. Instead, he wrote that honesty, virtue, education and talents were the source of his family's reputation and that he bequeathed these traditions to his successors. The marquis de

148

Maniban, on the other hand, threatened to disinherit his son if he refused to follow family tradition by entering the *parlement* of Toulouse.[14] Not that young men had to be forced into service in the *robe* because it was potentially a route to promotion and favour. Royal ministers such as Machault d'Arnouville, Calonne and Turgot had all served in the *parlements* at an earlier stage in their careers.

These distinct definitions of *robe* and *épée* continued to have a resonance throughout the eighteenth century, but they were professional demarcations which carried no legal, and diminishing social, meaning.[15] Among the *robe* families, it was extremely common for one son to serve in a law court, while another pursued a military career, and families such as the Chauvelin, Maupeou or Saint-Vincent had representatives in both branches. Nor was this a purely Parisian phenomenon, and provincial families followed the same pattern of placing their sons in both the law courts and the army. If the *robe* regularly joined the *épée*, it is true that the reverse was less often the case. The old prejudices certainly continued to hold sway for the most prestigious court families, but it was possible to see a member of the *épée* sitting as a judge. A good example was Michel de Ferrand, who had lost a leg fighting the English at Fontenoy in 1745. No longer able to continue his chosen career, he bought an office in the *parlement* where he soon became a great favourite due to his colourful and far from judicial language. Ferrand demonstrated how service was central to the noble mentality and that army and law were equally honourable vocations.

Professional frictions could, however, occasionally rise to the surface. Eminent *robins* like Louis XV's controller general of finance, L'Averdy, and Hue de Miromesnil, Louis XVI's keeper of the seals, were not averse to insulting 'militaires' in their private correspondence. There were also frequent disputes involving young men on both sides, sometimes resulting in violence. Dupré de Saint Maur, a young judge exiled to Bourges in 1753, quarrelled with an officer from the local garrison and was wounded in a duel. His colleague, Jonville, was more successful, killing an officer in a combat at Angoulême. Disputes and struggles for precedence between *robe* and *finance* were, according to contemporary observers, even more bitter than those involving the *épée*. When the *parlements* were reformed and their judges exiled by chancellor de Maupeou, the financiers were among the few to rejoice.[16] The *coup* of 1771 also struck a favourable chord amongst a section of the poorer *noblesse*. Great hope was invested in the duc d'Aiguillon, named minister of foreign affairs in June of that year, who was inundated by letters from provincial gentlemen denouncing the *parlementaires* with all the vehemence, if not the prose, of Saint-Simon.

14. Forster, *Nobility of Toulouse*, p. 165.

15. For an alternative view, see B. Stone, 'Robe Against Sword: the parlement of Paris and the French aristocracy, 1774–1789', *French Historical Studies*, 9 (1975), 278–303, who claims that disputes between the two groups were more serious.

16. Durand, *Finance et mécénat*, p. 100.

Frustration and envy lay behind these outpourings, which associated the *parlements* with the power and wealth of recently ennobled families. It was the ability of new money to buy itself not only into the courts, but also very rapidly into plum posts in the army and bureaucracy that fuelled this resentment. Given the nature of the system of *vénalité* there was nothing very novel or surprising about these complaints, but they do indicate the increasing importance of wealth in shaping eighteenth-century society.

III

The French *noblesse* was, therefore, a legally constituted order and not a class defined by common socio-economic characteristics. It contained sharp contrasts in income and wealth. The wealthiest groups were congregated at Court and were headed by members of the extended royal family. Louis XV's cousin, the duc d'Orléans, had an income estimated at 2,000,000 *livres* in 1740, while just prior to the revolution the prince de Conti had an estimated annual revenue of 3,700,000 *livres*.[17] *Grands seigneurs* such as the ducs de Bouillon and de Mortemart both received in the region of 500,000 *livres* annually. Among the high *robe* and financial circles of Paris, there were many with capital sums that ran into millions and similar, although far fewer, fortunes could be found in the provincial capitals. In order to put these figures into perspective, it is worth remembering that an annual income of a few hundred *livres* was a considerable sum for the majority of the population. These were the privileged minority, however, and there were many nobles who counted themselves fortunate with incomes of 10,000 *livres*. Gentlemen farmers in the Lauragais, one of the agriculturally more fertile regions of Languedoc, earned considerably less. An income of 5–8000 *livres* was a good annual return. For many nobles even this comparatively modest figure represented an unattainable degree of luxury, but stories of poverty, including the notorious case from Poitou, where seven nobles dressed as peasants arrived to take part in the elections to the Estates General without swords or money to pay for their upkeep, were quite exceptional. Noble indigence certainly existed, but it was relative rather than absolute because a title often raised expectations that could not be fulfilled.

Given the great diversity of fortunes, it is clear that there was no such thing as an average noble, or of a typical noble income, and stereotypes of impoverished provincials or fabulously wealthy courtiers should be avoided. Instead, there were various noble types often with recognizable income structures composed of one or more of a whole variety of sources, including landowning, *rentes*, offices, pensions and even commercial or

17. Carré, *Noblesse française*, p. 58.

industrial ventures. Professional or regional considerations could have a significant impact. Nobles in a booming maritime city like Bordeaux or Nantes would have neither the same outlook nor income as their peers in economically less precocious areas such as the Auvergne or Périgord. The presence of natural resources, ministerial patronage or favourable customary law could also play a part. Quantification of income and its sources is therefore extremely problematic and any general conclusions can always be undermined by a specific regional or individual example. However, the very heterogeneity of noble revenues demonstrates the foolishness of any attempt to resurrect the old *clichés* about a declining class tied irrevocably to the land. Much of the disparagement of investment in landholding was the result of the misguided belief among historians that late-eighteenth century France was experiencing something approaching an industrial revolution. In fact, economic change was, in general, slow and traditional attitudes, combined with the influence of physiocratic propaganda, ensured that contemporaries continued to see land as an attractive investment in terms of both social esteem and financial return.

Although the *noblesse* only constituted around 1 per cent of the total population, it owned between a quarter and one-third of the land in the kingdom, and in some regions, notably around Paris and Versailles, this proportion was much higher. In addition to this impressive patrimony, it is worth remembering that much of the land which belonged to the Church (between 5 and 10 per cent) was also under noble control because of the *noblesse*'s near monopoly of key ecclesiastical offices. For the vast majority of nobles, landownership was the principal source of income and it therefore required careful husbanding. The importance of land in simple financial terms can be gauged by looking at a number of examples. An aristocratic family such as La Tremoïlle had an estimated income of 278,847 *livres* in 1788–9 of which 191,978 *livres* (over two-thirds) was derived from land.[18] As a general rule, the land owned by these great Houses was scattered across several provinces and could contain many tiny plots. For example, prince de Montbarey, a career soldier and courtier, had lands in Franche-Comté, Rousillon, Languedoc and Bretagne.[19]

Many nobles proved to be effective and conscientious in the management of their estates. Among the Court aristocracy were renowned agronomes like the duc de Chaulnes, president of the agricultural society of Laon, and the duc de La Rochefoucauld-Liancourt, who even impressed Arthur Young, generally so critical of French agricultural endeavours. It is true that the vast majority of *grands seigneurs* relied heavily on their stewards, but the impression of a comparatively efficient and informed management is reinforced by the accounts kept by families such as the Saulx-Tavanes or La Tremoïlle, who recorded income and expenditure

18. Bluche, *La vie quotidienne*, pp. 103–4.
19. Prince de Montbarey, *Mémoires du prince de Montbarey, ministre, secrétaire d'état sous Louis XVI*, 3 vols, (Paris, 1826–7), I, pp. 98–9.

down to the last *centime*.[20] Both the duc de Saulx and his fellow courtier the duc de Luynes employed a professional intendant, Jean Godard, a lawyer in the Paris *parlement*, to oversee their administration, while the duc de La Tremoïlle and his wife had weekly meetings with their intendant to discuss business affairs. A similar interest in financial rectitude can be detected amongst the *robe*, and provincial magistrates such as président de Chifflet or councillor Damay of Besançon scrupulously recorded their annual expenses.[21] An aristocratic disdain for responsible expenditure was by no means universal, and nobles could, if they chose, exercise all the virtues of thrift and economy that are often said to be typical of the bourgeoisie.

The principal source of income from land was farming, either directly or by peasant leaseholders, but these revenues could be boosted through the exercise of the various seigneurial rights which belonged to the landowner. These rights were not a monopoly of the Second Estate, and could be owned by commoners or even institutions, usually the Church, but they made an important contribution to the income of the *noblesse*. Potentially the most lucrative of these dues were those levied on the produce of the peasantry, known variously as the *cens, terrage* or *champart*.[22] These allowed the *seigneur*, or his agent, to collect a proportion of the peasant's annual harvest which he could then consume or market as he saw fit. Peasants were also subject to a variety of dues levied on transfers of property, which in some areas, such as upper Languedoc, were more lucrative than those on the harvest. A *seigneur* could also enforce a number of monopolies, known as *banalités*, which obliged the local peasantry to use the lord's ovens, mill or wine press and to pay for the privilege. The *banalités* were often leased out, providing the *seigneur* with a steady income, while passing the disagreeable job of enforcement on to a third party interested only in their strict application. The landlord also possessed exclusive rights to hunting and fishing as well as control over the collection of firewood, wild fruits and mushrooms from the forests on the estate. Apart from a few isolated pockets, notably in Franche-Comté, serfdom had long since disappeared from the French countryside. However, the *corvée*, a system by which the peasantry was required to provide a fixed number of days of unpaid work on the seigneurial domain, or pay for exemption, was still widely practised. Although bitterly resented by the peasantry, the opportunity for the *noblesse* to command free labour at key times such as the harvest was not to be scorned.

The monetary value of seigneurial rights not only varied from one province to another, but even from one village, or field, to the next. In some cases the return could be substantial. *Seigneurs* in the Rouergue received as

---

20. Forster, *The House of Saulx-Tavanes: Versailles and Burgundy, 1700–1830* (Baltimore, Md., 1971), pp. 61–3.

21. M. Gresset, *Le monde judiciaire à Besançon de la Conquête par Louis XIV à la révolution française*, (2 vols, Paris, 1975), II, pp. 634–40.

22. P. M. Jones, *The Peasantry in the French Revolution* (Cambridge, 1988), pp. 42–59

much as 70 per cent of their income from this source and in parts of the Auvergne and Bourgogne as much as one third. Elsewhere the weight of these impositions was much lower, amounting for example to only 8 per cent in the Lauragais, but even these sums were far from negligible and they formed a respectable portion of total noble income. However, it was long argued that in the course of the eighteenth century the *noblesse* sought not only to defend these rights, but even to extend them in order to bolster their incomes, supposedly declining relative to the bourgeoisie. To do so, they ransacked their barns and attics in search of ancient parchments (or *terriers*) recording their rights. They were then able to force the peasantry to pay dues that had either fallen into arrears or lapsed altogether. A branch of the legal profession (*feudistes*) specialized in these cases and countless handbooks were written offering helpful hints about how to update a *terrier*.[23]

The notion of a feudal reaction in the countryside has nevertheless been criticized.[24] Without seeking to deny that the *noblesse* was active and interested in conserving the privileges of landownership, it has been argued that there was nothing new about the process of updating, or modifying, *terriers*, which was a normal response to changing tenancies. Attention has also been focused upon the *cahiers de doléances* (lists of grievances) sent by the peasantry to the Estates General of 1789, and these texts used to justify the argument that social conflict was largely absent from the French countryside on the eve of the Revolution. It is unlikely that the peasantry would have shared this idyllic view of social relations, and there is no doubt that the principal target of rural anger between 1788 and 1793 was the seigneurial system. That does not necessarily mean that the burden had in real terms increased, although it is possible that the efficiency which the eighteenth-century *noblesse* had demonstrated in managing its estates was being reflected in this area too. What it does seem to confirm, however, is the growing resentment felt by the peasantry towards the Second Estate. In the seventeenth century, the privileges and social preeminence of the *noblesse* had gone largely unchallenged, and during the troubled years before 1660 there were many examples of communal solidarity against outside interference, most notably from royal tax collectors. By the eighteenth century this was no longer the case, and in many regions the *noblesse* had abrogated its rôle as both protector of the community and arbiter of its disputes. If not inevitable, some sort of explosion in the countryside was certainly likely by 1788–9, with, or without, the collapse of Louis XVI's political authority. Where seigneurial rights were heaviest the violence was at its most intense, and it was those *seigneurs* who were either known for their rigour in imposing their rights, or who sought to defend them, that were most

23. J. Q. C. Mackrell, *The Attack on Feudalism in Eighteenth-century France* (London, 1973), pp. 61–6.
24. See the key articles by W. Doyle, 'Was there an aristocratic reaction in pre-revolutionary France?', *Past and Present*, no. 57 (1972), 97–122, and G. V. Taylor, 'Revolutionary and non-revolutionary content in the cahiers of 1789: an interim report', *French Historical Studies*, 7 (1972), 479–502.

roughly treated.[25] For the peasantry, the destruction of these anachronistic and often humiliating impositions was the Revolution's single most important and lasting achievement.

Landowning and its benefits were far from being the only source of income for the *noblesse*. Amongst the more familiar investments were *rentes*, or stock which paid a fixed annual return usually about 5 per cent. Investing in loans floated by the government was clearly one possibility, but the shrewd investor was more likely to be tempted by the *rentes* offered by, among others, provincial Estates, municipalities or the clergy, all of which had a reputation for prompt payment. *Rentes* were favoured by groups such as the magistrates of the *parlement* of Paris, many of whom invested heavily in the government and the *Hôtel de Ville* of the capital.[26] Nicolas IV Doublet de Persan had 84.9 per cent of his fortune invested in *rentes*, Le Febvre de Malmaison 76.4 per cent and Jean Jacques Nouët 64.5 per cent, and they were not alone. Yet, if the Parisian magistrates were the *rentiers par excellence*, there were few families among the *noblesse* that did not have at least part of its fortune invested in this fashion.

The lucky few were able to supplement their revenues by the acquisition of a royal gift or pension. The Court was, at one level, a vast honey-pot and the plunder of immense sums from the royal treasury makes it easy to see why the aristocratic bees aroused such envy from among the rest of the *noblesse* and the population at large. It also explains why the courtiers, many of whom could afford to live like princes in their own right, continued to tolerate the tedious etiquette, cramped conditions and frequent boredom of Versailles. By serving in Court offices, it was possible to petition for the favours needed to sustain an already opulent lifestyle. Louis XV, who was notoriously generous to his intimate circle, gave 200,000 *livres* to his war minister, the comte d'Argenson, in order to complete the purchase of his château at Paulmy.[27] Maréchal de Belle-Isle, another royal favourite, received 133,000 *livres* annually from the treasury. Nor were ministers the only beneficiaries. A family such as the Fitz-James received a quarter of its annual income of 200,000 *livres* from this source. As for Marie-Antoinette's favourites, the notorious Polignac, it has been estimated that they amassed more than 2,500,000 *livres* in cash, offices, pensions and preferments during Louis XVI's reign.[28]

Large sums were also awarded to royal servants in ministerial, judicial and administrative office. On their appointment in 1774, Vergennes and Maurepas received 100,000 and 60,000 *livres* respectively from their royal master, while the outgoing duc d'Aiguillon was paid a staggering 500,000 *livres* to cover the expenses he had incurred. Key officers such as the first president or *procureur général* of a *parlement*, the president of a provincial Estates or a meeting of the French clergy, also received substantial grants

25. Jones, *Peasantry in the French Revolution*, pp. 70–1.
26. F. Bluche, *Les magistrats du parlement de Paris au XVIIIe siècle* (Paris, 1960), pp. 143–59.
27. Carré, *Noblesse française*, p. 85.
28. Chaussinand-Nogaret, *The French Nobility*, pp. 54–6.

from the treasury in order to help them with the ruinous entertainment costs incurred on government business. Substantial payments for loyal service were equally common. The Parisian magistrate, Pasquier, received 50,000 *livres* in 1766 for his rôle in the rigged trial of Lally-Tollendal, while a year later his colleague, president de Saint-Fargeau, was paid 100,000 *livres* for his cooperation in securing the *parlement*'s approval for royal taxation. For an invalid, or retired, army officer, a royal pension could be the only hope of escaping genuine financial distress. In 1781, the war minister, Ségur, accorded a pension to an infantry captain who had only 400 *livres* annually with which to support himself and his aged parents.

With the notable exceptions of those positions which provided regular access to the monarch or a member of his intimate circle, serving the Crown was less rewarding than might have been expected. To buy a regiment could be phenomenally expensive. In 1769, the duc d'Aiguillon paid 1,200,000 *livres* for the prestigious position of *capitaine-lieutenant* of the *Chevaux-Légers*. Other élite regiments were equally expensive, but none were cheap, rarely less than 20,000 *livres*, and six-figure sums were not unusual. In return for these enormous investments, the purchaser received a *gage* (in effect an interest payment) of between 5 and 8 per cent of his capital, although during moments of serious crisis such as the Seven Years War (1756–63) payment could cease altogether. Magistrates in the sovereign courts also received a *gage*, and, in addition, certain other gratifications such as the *épices* paid by litigants to the judge before whom their case was pleaded. Judges in Rouen received, on average, 3,000 *livres* annually from this source, those in Dijon 1,500–2,000 *livres* and their colleagues in Besançon less than 1,000 *livres*. Although these sums were not negligible, they did not represent a very impressive return on the capital invested, and made up only a fraction of the total revenues of the individuals concerned. Whether in the *épée* or the *robe* it was upholding family honour by serving in a prestigious capacity, rather than the hope of making a fortune, that made the expense worthwhile.

IV

A genteel lifestyle based upon landowning, allied with offices, pensions and *rentes*, make up the classic image of the eighteenth-century *noblesse*. Prevented by the laws of *dérogeance* from practicing forms of economic activity considered incompatible with his rank, notably retail trade, the noble could hardly be further removed from another familiar stereotype, that of the innovative capitalist entrepreneur, taking risks in order to corner new commercial or industrial markets. However, concerned by the tendency of the wealthiest members of the Third Estate to abandon commerce in order to live nobly, the Crown had regularly issued edicts designed to reverse the flow of capital into unproductive sectors of the economy by allowing the *noblesse* to engage in wholesale trade. In the long-term, noble prejudice proved stronger than the law, and before 1750 these efforts produced very few tangible results. It is true that during the Regency (1715–23), John Law's financial schemes had tempted the *noblesse*, along with other social groups, into an orgy of speculation and fortunes were dramatically won and lost. However, the participation of nobles such as the duc de Bourbon, who won millions as a result, was more an extension of the aristocratic mania for gambling than anything else. When the duc de La Force sought to take advantage of the relaxed atmosphere of the times by engaging covertly in retail trade, his exposure resulted in a famous trial before the *parlement* of Paris. Although he escaped serious punishment, the dishonour was sufficient for his brother to consider changing his name. Trade, when it was undertaken, was conducted through a system of *prête-noms* (straw men), and was largely confined to colonial ventures where the risk could be high, but little entrepreneurial skill was involved. Yet, in the second half of the eighteenth century, the *noblesse* cast off many of the taboos that had surrounded economic activity and undoubtedly profited from the wealth that new industrial and commercial ventures generated. It was the already powerful and affluent élite that was most likely to ignore the laws of *dérogeance* on a grand scale, but noble attitudes were, once again, conditioned by a host of factors including geographical location, local customary law and access to capital.

Bretagne, as so often, provides a perfect illustration of *ancien régime* diversity. Through local customary law, it was possible for a Breton to suspend his *noblesse* temporarily, while he engaged in activities that elsewhere would have carried the penalty of *dérogeance*. For those who had fallen on hard times, or for the many impoverished cadets, the prospect of enriching themselves by engaging in maritime or colonial trade beckoned. A classic example of this phenomenon was Châteaubriand's father who went to sea at the age of fifteen and proceeded to make a fortune. Equipped with the necessary funds, he bought the old family château of Combourg and settled back into life as a respected provincial *seigneur*. Such spectacular success was no doubt rare, but the route he had taken was by no means an isolated one. Bretagne was particularly fortunate, but other provinces such as Artois enjoyed similar privileges; elsewhere the bulk of noble economic activity consisted of the exploitation of the domain. In addition to the monopolies of mill, oven and wine press, many landed proprietors also had exclusive ownership of mineral rights. This privilege was especially attractive in areas such as Franche-Comté, Alsace or Lorraine where there were substantial and easily accessible deposits of coal or iron ore. For the unadventurous, these rights could be leased, or worked on a small scale to provide for the estate or local economy. However, to extract coal or produce iron in a genuinely industrial sense required a substantial capital investment, technical expertise and marketing skills, none of which are traditionally associated with the *noblesse*.

There is now no doubt that some nobles were engaged in just these kinds of enterprises, and that this behaviour was not simply confined to the élite of Versailles and Paris. In 1789, Franche-Comté, the second most important iron producing province in the kingdom, had seventy-two major enterprises, of which forty-one were owned by nobles.[29] Amongst the wealthiest members of the *parlement* of Besançon were Pourcheresse d'Etrabonne, whose fortune was estimated at 1,600,000 *livres* in 1746, and Maréchal de Vezet, with a capital of 900,000 *livres* in 1787: both had been enriched by iron. Not that every member of the Second Estate in the province had followed their example. Of the 187 families who were represented in the *parlement* between 1676–1790 as few as 19 (around 10 per cent) had established an industrial enterprise. Franche-Comté was by no means exceptional. In the region of Alençon in Normandy, noble proprietors were responsible for over 80 per cent of iron production by 1780.[30] In Bretagne *seigneurs* were also to the fore, although production was monopolized by a handful of great Houses including those of the governor, the duc de Penthièvre, and the ducs de Rohan-Chabot and Bethune-Charost.

The *noblesse* were also involved in developing numerous other industrial enterprises. In 1751, the chevalier de Solages opened what was to become his hugely successful enterprise in Carmaux, and in 1757 the duc de Cröy founded the Anzin company to exploit his mines in Fresnes and Bruay; finally, in 1766, the duc de Bethune-Charost began to exploit the mines of Roche-la-Molière in Le Forez. When the marquis de Mirabeau, admittedly using his secretary as a front, organized a joint stock company to work his lead mines in the Limousin, he was joined by prestigious courtiers, including the ducs de Nivernais, d'Aumont and Duras.[31] In booming *entrepôts* such as Bordeaux, *robe* families such as Dupaty, Saige and Féger were all involved in the colonial trade.[32] The reign of Louis XVI saw a genuine proliferation of such enterprise and the enthusiasm for industrial projects even succeeded in penetrating the ranks of the royal family. The duc d'Orléans owned glass making factories at Villers-Cotterets and Bagneux, and the comte d'Artois, through his treasurer, bought the forge of Ruelle and was instrumental in the establishment of the Javel chemical works.

The link between the *noblesse* and early French industrial development is, therefore, established, but it is legitimate to question how far these examples denote a general change in either mentality or sources of revenue. For many *seigneurs*, exploiting resources of coal or iron was simply an extension of an established ability to maximize the profits from their estates, or a response to favourable customary law. Others had been ennobled because of their success in trade or commerce, and could hardly

29. Gresset, *Besançon*, II, pp. 755–66.
30. Richard, *Noblesse d'affaires*, p. 93.
31. Carré, *Noblesse française*, pp. 146–7.
32. W. Doyle, *The Parlement of Bordeaux and the End of the Old Regime, 1771–1790* (London, 1974), p. 102.

be considered representative of anything more than the continuing social mobility within *ancien régime* society. Finally, it is necessary to be wary of the motives of an already opulent and fantastically privileged aristocratic élite when it became involved in industrial ventures. Princely fops such as the comte d'Artois had little interest in the management of an industrial concern, and his funds found their way into such schemes because of decisions taken by his financial advisers. In the booming 1770s and 1780s these enterprises were increasingly seen as a route to rapid and substantial returns and, with their capital and contacts, the aristocracy was ideally placed to profit from these new opportunities. Finally, only a tiny minority were actively engaged in the productive process, though their willingness to invest in industrial ventures confounds the traditional stereotype of a reactionary, feudal, aristocracy.

V

Diversity is, therefore, the key word when assessing the sources of noble income. To understand how fortunes were consolidated, it is necessary to examine the structure of the family and the flexibility and skill exercised in the management of patrimonies, which in some cases equalled those of small states. Louis XVI's brothers, Provence and Artois, the dauphin and the princes of the blood had households that duplicated, in microcosm, the king's own, employing intendants and treasurers to oversee financial and administrative affairs. Unfortunately, social eminence and fiscal responsibility rarely went hand-in-hand and the princes indulged themselves with an opulent lifestyle. The result was sadly predictable. Louis XIV's bastard sons, the duc de Maine and the comte de Toulouse, had left debts of 3.5 and 9 million *livres* respectively, and the comte d'Artois had accumulated an impressive 21 million *livres* of debt at the comparatively tender age of 24. Parasitic though their lifestyle appears, it is important not to plunge into anachronistic condemnations of individuals who saw themselves, with good reason, as on a par with any crowned head in Europe. Eighteenth-century monarchs believed in ostentatious display, and so did French princes.

Their casual approach to financial affairs was imitated by many among the Court *noblesse*, the financiers, and even some members of the *robe* who generally had a reputation for strict social mores. Spending on a lavish scale and a cult of luxury pushed to its limits could produce absurdities such as the 25,000 *livres* spent by the marquis de Stainville on a doublet of silver and gold worn for the festivities held to mark the Dauphin's wedding in 1745.[33] This was equivalent to the annual expenditure of

33. Carré, *Noblesse française*, p. 56.

président de Chifflet, a wealthy provincial *parlementaire*, and four times that of a rich noble in the countryside around Toulouse. Stainville's behaviour illustrates the significance attached to display, but the sums invested on sartorial elegance were dwarfed by those devoted to entertainment. Prince de Robecq spent 58,000 *livres* on the expenses of his table in 1787, and 2,054 *livres* to hire boxes at the theatre and opera.[34] Entertaining the female stars of the stage was more costly than the performance itself, and the vogue for choosing mistresses from among the dancers of the opera could lead to some amazing expenditure. President de Rieux, son of the banker Samuel Bernard, paid a staggering 80,000 *livres* annually to mademoiselle Leduc during the 1730s, and when prince de Conti and comte de Lauraguais disputed the favours of Mademoiselle Hingre, the laurels of victory cost Lauraguais 60,000 *livres*. Embellishing the family château was potentially even more hazardous. The maréchal de Belle-Isle spent vast sums on his country house at Bizy, and even the duc de Cröy, who was a shrewd manager of his vast estates, could not resist spending 450,000 *livres* on his folly, l'Hermitage, near Condé. However, nothing could compare with the vice of gambling when it came to separating the *noblesse* from its money. In one memorable evening, vicomte de Tavanes lost 300,000 *livres* in a game of Faro.[35] More ominously, in view of the perennially parlous state of the royal treasury, the *intendant des finances*, Orry de Fulvy, lost 400,000 in a game of Pharaon. Conspicuous consumption was a daily reality, and for those who were either unable or unwilling to exercise restraint bankruptcy was the result. By far the most spectacular crash was that of the Rohan-Guéménée, who fell owing 32 million *livres* in 1782. Other notorious spendthrifts included the duc de Choiseul who, despite marrying the daughter of the banker Crozat and receiving enormous sums from Louis XV, died owing several million *livres* in 1785.

Not every noble family took such a *blasé* attitude towards the administration of its patrimony, and if gambling and extravagant living were avoided, the greatest threat to the preservation of a patrimony was posed by the natural rhythms of birth, marriage and death. A particularly sad example was that of maréchal de Belle-Isle, who, after a long career, had accumulated offices, wealth and power in abundance. All of his dynastic hopes were placed upon the shoulders of his only son, the comte de Gisors, who was widely acknowledged as one of the most impressive young men of his generation. Gisors died a hero at the battle of Créfeld on 23 June 1758, and all of Belle-Isle's ambitions fell with him. When tragedy had been averted, however, inheritance patterns followed local laws and customs. For the great aristocratic Houses, with land scattered around the kingdom, this was not only a serious complication, but also a significant cause of the endless litigation provoked by inheritance disputes. In Alsace, for example, the *noblesse* divided its inheritances into equal portions, resulting

34. Chaussinand-Nogaret, *The French Nobility*, pp. 57–8.
35. Forster, *House of Saulx-Tavanes*, p. 32.

in the proliferation of small and relatively poor estates. Elsewhere, the Second Estate demonstrated a firm commitment to the preservation of the principal family holdings. With the important exceptions of Provence and parts of Languedoc, the laws of inheritance generally followed a recognizable pattern. The eldest son inherited two-thirds of the estate, and the remainder was then split into equal portions upon which he and his brothers and sisters had a share (although in the case of married women the portion was usually assumed to have been paid as part of her dowry). In the event of the family having five or more children, the proportion of the estate liable to division was increased to one half of the total. In the event of the direct male line failing, the principal succession passed to the cadet branches, but if they too had no male heir then the eldest daughter in the direct line would inherit. Given the importance of these arrangements, it was common for the eldest son's marriage to mark the point at which the inheritance and its obligations were fixed. The eldest son retained the landed estates, while younger sons and daughters often received their portions in the form of *rentes*. Not only did this provide a regular revenue, but a modest portion was often insufficient to provide for the dowry or lifestyle required to contract an honourable marriage, and the extinction of cadet branches had the advantage of reuniting lost capital with the family domain. The best a male cadet could hope for was a sufficiently large sum with which to buy a commission, but for his unmarried sisters the picture was often bleak. They had little alternative but to eke out an existence independently, or accept the limitations of remaining within the family home.

High mortality rates ensured that restricting the number of marriages was an effective, if risky, method of protecting the patrimony from division. However, it was the dowry that was central to the family strategies of the *noblesse*, representing the point at which substantial capital sums were lost or gained. Ideally they aimed to strike a positive balance, receiving more from incoming dowries than they in turn dispensed, although before committing itself to an alliance a family was obliged to consider a whole variety of factors, including the pedigree, offices, wealth and prestige of its prospective partners. Although families of roughly comparable profession, rank and regional backgrounds tended to intermarry, dowries well in excess of total annual income were common. As a general rule, those wishing to marry a daughter into a higher social circle paid for the privilege and delusions of grandeur could lead to punishing financial consequences. Clearly no more than a handful of families had the resources or credit of a Crozat or Bernard to assist them in finding the money to pay for a dowry, and a variety of techniques were used to deflect the financial blow. These included passing a dowry from mother to daughter in the form of *rentes*, collecting contributions from uncles, aunts and other close relatives, amortizing out of current income, delaying payment and taking out loans. Borrowing was generally organized on a small scale with comparatively low sums drawn from a wide group of professional colleagues, friends and neighbours. The risk of a sudden liquidity crisis was thus substantially reduced. Yet, whether a noble had an income of 5,000 or 500,000 *livres*, the problems of finding a good match at an affordable price were the same.

With so much at stake, marriages were far too important to be left to the whims or passing fancy of the individuals concerned. At best a young woman might hope for the chance to say no to a prospective suitor. This was a prerogative exercised on more than one occasion by the rich heiress Lucy Dillon, niece of the powerful archbishop of Narbonne. Eventually she agreed to a match which pleased her, but she could never have taken the initiative herself. Marriages were generally arranged by the immediate family. A good example was provided by the duc des Cars. Writing in his memoirs, he explained how he was pressed to wed after his elder brother's marriage failed to produce an heir. Attached to the bachelor lifestyle, he objected on the grounds that as a cadet he would be unable to attract a decent dowry. But, to placate his sister he accepted his fate on the condition that she arranged a match with Pauline de La Borde, daughter of a wealthy court banker. By this rather cunning manoeuvre, Cars was convinced that he had eluded both marriage and the wrath of his family. He had overlooked the resourcefulness of his sister, who within forty-eight hours had secured the match by whirlwind diplomacy involving Marie-Antoinette, influential courtiers such as the duc and duchesse de Choiseul and, finally, La Borde himself. Although few could expect the financial windfall of a dowry from La Borde, the speed with which matters had been arranged, the fact that the couple had never met, and the rôle played by family members was typical.

With social prestige and money, rather than affection, providing the basis for matrimony, the consequences could frequently be damaging. After having been educated in Paris, comtesse de Lostange was married into a respectable *Périgourdine* family. To her horror, she discovered that her future lay not amidst the bright lights of Paris or Versailles, but in the quiet domesticity of a provincial château. The *comtesse* proceeded to rebel by adopting a nocturnal lifestyle, eating and paying visits in the middle of the night, associating with unsuitable company, and amusing herself with endless lawsuits against her mother who she held responsible for her fate. Problems of another sort faced Mlle de Mailly, who, on leaving the convent, was married at thirteen years of age to the much older prince de Montbarey. Within three years she had produced two children, but, as her husband confided cheerfully in his memoirs, he had soon tired of his wife's youthful charms and returned to his libertine ways. Despite this inauspicious beginning, the pair were still together over forty years later. Working as a team on matters concerning the future or honour of their House, they nevertheless lived separate lives. It was a pattern that held good for a large proportion of the élite. Once the continuation of the male line was assured both partners were free to pursue independent personal lives. Occasional scandals could, nevertheless, erupt. One memorable example came to light in 1748 when the financier, La Poupelinière, discovered that his wife was conducting an affair with the infamous maréchal de Richelieu.[36] A false chimney had been constructed to connect the house of La Poupelinière with that of his neighbour, and it was via this unlikely route that the two lovers had made their *rendez-vous*. Through motives of either shame or jealousy, La Poupelinière separated from his wife. Such touchy manners were by and large rare, and both sexes enjoyed a fair amount of liberty as long as a suitable degree of decorum was maintained.

It is unlikely that the élite attitude to marriage altered much before 1789, but it would be wrong to assume that the *mores* of the Court and Paris were typical of the *noblesse* as a whole. The letters and memoirs of, among others, Malesherbes, Robert de Saint-Vincent, the Joly de Fleury and Belle-Isle bear eloquent, and overwhelming, witness to the bonds of love and affection which could unite spouses, or parents with their children. It is a warning not to take the generalizations of sociologists about aristocratic or bourgeois family values too literally. Just as there was more than one definition of *noblesse*, there was more than one way of living nobly.

The education of young nobles was determined by sex and family background. For the sons of the wealthy élite, one of the great colleges such as that of Clermont, Harcourt or Louis le Grand beckoned, where future military officers, such as the prince de Soubise, mingled with young *robins*, including Lefebvre d'Amécourt his lifelong friend, or the sons of bankers like Gabriel de Rieux. A classical education followed, with a heavy diet of Latin and rhetoric interspersed with instruction in the courtly arts of dance and fencing. For those unable to afford the substantial fees required to enter these colleges, there were plenty of smaller, less expensive, schools run by either the Jesuits, until 1764, or one of the other teaching orders such as the Oratorians. A possible alternative was offered by the *Ecole Militaire*, established in 1751 to educate 500 boys from among the poorer *noblesse* at the king's expense. Finally, there was also the option of a private tutor, and many an impoverished cleric or noble cadet earned his upkeep in this capacity.

At around the age of the first communion (12–15 years), it was common for career choices to be finalized. Wealth and station were crucial, but the number of children in the family was also important. As the future head of the family, it was natural that the eldest son's career prospects took precedence, which usually meant following the course charted by his father. As the only child in an *épée* family, the prince de Montbarey was destined to serve alongside his father and uncle in the regiment of Lorraine. His father's enthusiasm knew no bounds, and the boy served, and was wounded, in his first campaign at the age of twelve.[37] Similar patterns were apparent even in ministerial offices, and the comte de Saint-Florentin, minister of the *maison du roi* (1725–74) and the comte de Maurepas, the Naval minister (1723–49), both members of the Phélypeaux clan, had inherited

36. Durand, *Finance et mécénat*, p. 143.
37. Montbarey, *Mémoires*, I, p. 11.

their positions while very young. A similar pattern was also apparent among the magistrature, where generations of Titon, Pasquier, Séguier and Joly de Fleury sat upon the benches of the sovereign courts. An extreme example were the Anjorrant, who had served in the *parlement* of Paris almost since its foundation without ever having achieved anything of distinction. When one of their number made a speech in March 1755, his colleagues joked that it was the first time a member of his family had done something useful since the time of Saint Louis.

When there were several children to be placed money was vital, and in the early eighteenth century the Saulx-Tavanes provided a good example of how three sons could be established to good advantage.[38] The eldest, Henri-Charles, inherited the regiment, lands and offices of his father and pursued a long career as commandant of Bourgogne. The second son, Charles-Nicolas, entered the Church at an early age and was taken under the wing of archbishop Fénelon. He subsequently pursued a brilliant career as a courtly prelate, was on intimate terms with the royal family, finishing as cardinal archbishop of Rouen and grand almoner of France. The third brother, Charles-Henri, had an honourable, if undistinguished, military career. There were countless variations on this theme with cadets entering the navy or *robe* as well as the army or Church, and a large successful clan would have one or more in each. Some aristocratic Houses would even place sons in service at foreign Courts in order to further their own interests. For families from Lorraine, such as the Choiseul, it was common to have representatives at both Vienna and Versailles. Thus, the duc de Choiseul was obliged to withdraw his brother from the Austrian Court after his own rapid rise to power in France.

The educational and career opportunities of noblewomen were by comparison very restricted. For the daughters of the wealthy, places in prestigious convents such as that of Fontevrault or Pentemont were especially sought after. In general their reputation for learning was not high. A curriculum of saints' lives and the catechism was hardly stimulating, although a young woman intended to shine at Court or in society would, in addition, receive expensive lessons in music, singing and dance. For the daughters of the less well off, on the other hand, a personal tutor or instruction from the local clergy was the norm. Career choices did not exist in any meaningful sense, and the alternatives scarcely stretched beyond marriage, spinsterhood or the convent. It is not difficult to find cases of unfortunate young women such as Catherine Dillon, who was confined in a Benedictine convent from the age of seven. Overall the numbers suffering such a fate probably declined in the course of the eighteenth century, but the threat was still used to frighten young girls into obedience. Spinsterhood was nevertheless common. Dowries were expensive and the two sisters of the Parisian magistrate Robert de Saint-Vincent cannot have been the only ones obliged to renounce their marriage prospects to facilitate a brother's career.

38. Forster, *House of Saulx-Tavanes*, pp. 1–54.

Superficially attractive by comparison, marriage might come very early, with cases of girls being betrothed to much older men at 12 or 13 and having several children in quick succession. However, on average noblewomen married between the age of 18 and 22, and, if they avoided the perils of childbirth, could expect to have a long series of pregnancies. The case of Lucy de La Tour du Pin who had seven children, only one of whom survived her, was not exceptional. Despite the fashion for maternal breastfeeding apparent under Louis XVI, most noble children were sent into the countryside to a wet-nurse, which ought to have increased the fecundity of their mothers. In fact, there is some evidence that the high aristocracy was practicing contraception, especially once the all-important male succession had been secured, but it is unlikely that such behaviour extended far beyond the Court and capital.

Yet, if the career opportunities for noblewomen were limited, the importance of their contribution to the consolidation and advancement of the family should never be underestimated. Undoubtedly the most powerful women were those widowed with sufficient time and money to enjoy the fact. Astride many an aristocratic House stood an imposing matriarch such as the dowager duchesse des Cars or comtesse D'Aguesseau-Tavanes.[39] Responsible for the administration of the patrimony, and with the power to decide the careers and marriage prospects of their children, grand-children, nieces and nephews, they controlled the destiny of their families. Nor should the often decisive contribution of aristocratic women to the political world of the Court, or even the government, be neglected. While the men were away from Versailles, on military, diplomatic or administrative service, it was the women who were expected to protect, and if possible, advance the interests of the House. At the end of Louis XV's reign, Versailles was split between the feuding cabals of the ducs de Choiseul and d'Aiguillon. The duchesse de Gramont, sister of Choiseul, threw herself enthusiastically into battle on behalf of her brother, frequently insulting the king's mistress, Mme du Barry, who supported his rival, in the process. She caused so much disturbance that many held her personally responsible for Choiseul's fall. When d'Aiguillon replaced him, his reputation had been severely damaged by the feud. His mother, known variously as the invincible or fat duchess, used her considerable popularity at Court to bolster his position with lavish entertainment and appearances at official functions. Celebrated for her translations of Ossian and Pope, on intimate terms with the luminaries of Enlightened salon society and helping to control the interests of her House, the duchesse d'Aiguillon displayed many of the talents demanded of an aristocrat.

The French *noblesse* was, therefore, adept at protecting and building-up its patrimonies and in doing so displayed a sense of family that put the collective above the individual. At difficult moments, the House could actually be

39. Duc des Cars, *Mémoires du duc des Cars. Colonel du régiment de dragons-artois, brigadier de cavalerie premier maître d'hôtel du roi* (2 vols, Paris, 1890), I, pp. 5–19, 97–8, and Forster, *House of Saulx-Tavanes*, pp. 41–6.

divided better to protect its interests. It was claimed that the Noailles did so well out of royal patronage because they always had at least one member in each of the major Court factions. For some their success was one of the 'great crimes of the monarchy', while for others it was a source of inspiration. It was once joked that when the king asked one of his subjects 'what can I do for you?', he received the reply 'Sire, make me a Noailles'. During the Revolution these strategies were still employed, and one intrepid Breton family, the Talhouet, had a son serving as the revolutionary mayor of Rennes, another remained neutral, while a third was a leading royalist.[40] Serving the best interests of the family could lead to acts of self-abnegation when it came to career or marriage prospects, but at the very least it demanded that an individual use any influence or patronage at his or her disposal to advance their relatives. The pious magistrate, L'Averdy, who was unexpectedly catapulted into the post of controller-general in 1763, was at first thoroughly lost at Versailles, where, as he justly noted, 'people had no religion'. Amused courtiers were, however, soon able to remark that he had learnt the trick of promoting his family to positions of influence. Even the most superficial glance through the personal papers of ministers or the diaries of courtiers reveals the immense amount of time devoted to the task of securing a pension, office or promotion for relatives. That the French *noblesse* was highly privileged is beyond doubt, but to succeed in a fiercely competitive environment required considerable resources of time and energy, and in this respect the family was vital.

VI

Until comparatively recently much of the literature discussing the political and administrative life of eighteenth-century France was based upon the mistaken assumption that the *noblesse* was threatened by the State. It is true that the monarchy and its servants produced many reform programmes that were designed to reduce the privileges of the Second Estate, and especially those of a fiscal nature. Yet it is a myth that nobles did not pay taxes: they had always been subject to indirect taxation and in certain regions even paid the *taille réelle*. In the course of the eighteenth century, they became subject to an increasing number of direct impositions, including the *capitation* (poll tax) and, after 1749, the *vingtième*. Nevertheless, the Second Estate was grossly undertaxed when either its wealth or the fiscal burden upon the rest of French society is considered.[41] A brief look at

40. Meyer, 'Noblesse des bocages', p. 52.

41. For a discussion of the *noblesse* and taxation see C. B. A. Behrens, 'Nobles, Privileges and Taxes in France at the end of the ancien régime', *Economic History Review*, 2nd series 15 (1963), 451–75. The criticisms of G. J. Cavanaugh, 'Nobles, privileges and Taxes in France. A revision reviewed', *French Historical Studies*, 8 (1974), 681–92, and a reply from Behrens published in the same journal in 9 (1976), 521–7, should also be consulted.

the sums set aside to meet fiscal demands makes it clear just how privileged the *noblesse* actually was. As the monarchy tottered towards bankruptcy in 1788–9, the duc de La Tremoïlle paid only 7058 *livres*, or 2.53 per cent of an income estimated at 278,874 *livres* in direct taxation to the treasury.[42] This was six times less than the 44,859 *livres* spent on his table expenses, and not much more than the 4147 *livres* devoted to his horses and carriages. Another courtier, the duc de Saulx, was paying an estimated 6 per cent of his gross income in direct taxation during the 1780s.[43] Finally, the comte d'Escouloubre, with an income of 6–8000 livres, paid approximately 8 per cent of the total to the exchequer in the 1750s.[44] Although it has been said that most of the king's subjects were privileged in one sense or another, the *noblesse* was particularly favoured.

It was long argued that the *parlements* defended the privileges of the *noblesse* and prevented reform of the iniquitous fiscal system as part of a more general aristocratic reaction against the State. Such an interpretation overlooks the central paradox that the *noblesse* was in many ways the State. Seduced by the myth that Louis XIV had broken the power of the *noblesse*, historians have too often forgotten that before 1789 a member of the Second Estate held the levers of power in every important civil, religious, military and judicial post in the kingdom. The success of absolutism had been to harness the *noblesse* to the emerging State structure and, despite its evident drawbacks, the system of *vénalité* had provided an opening for the most successful members of the Third Estate to join its ranks.

This is confirmed by a brief examination of the key government offices and their incumbents. Of the ministers (*secrétaires d'état*) and controllers general employed by the French monarchy between 1715 and 1789, all but a tiny handful were from the *noblesse*. The exceptions were the two foreign adventurers, John Law and Jacques Necker, and the cardinal Dubois. A much larger number were from recently ennobled families, or were in the process of becoming so, such as Silhouette, Sartine, Bertin, Boullongne, L'Averdy and Calonne. However, the majority of non-nobles not surprisingly held the post of controller-general, which because of a mixture of aristocratic disdain and the need for contacts in banking and financial circles constituted a special case. The vast majority of royal ministers and members of the king's councils were instead drawn from ministerial dynasties such as the Phélypeaux, leading *robe* families like the d'Argenson or d'Aguesseau, or from among the military élite at court, for example, maréchals de Noailles, D'Estrées and Villars. The praetorian guard of absolutism, the intendants, were by the eighteenth century, drawn almost exclusively from the *noblesse*, and overwhelmingly from *robe* families, as were the *conseillers d'état*, *maîtres des requêtes* and even large numbers of the *commis*, who worked in the offices of the finance minister. As we have already seen, the judiciary was also dominated by the Second Estate and the numbers

42. Bluche, *Vie quotidienne*, pp. 103–5.
43. Forster, *House of Saulx-Tavanes*, pp. 140–1.
44. Forster, *Nobility of Toulouse*, p. 34.

of non-nobles entering the most prestigious courts, the *parlements*, had by 1789 slowed to a trickle.

The highest commands in the military hierarchy were the exclusive preserve of the *noblesse*. French victories were won by maréchal de Villars, prince de Conti and the maréchal duc de Richelieu, as well as by adopted noble champions such as the duc de Berwick and maréchal de Saxe, respectively the illegitimate sons of 'James III' of England (the Old Pretender) and Augustus the Strong, Elector of Saxony and king of Poland. Defeats were also reserved for aristocratic commanders such as the inept prince de Soubise. By 1789, all 136 members of the French episcopate were from the *noblesse*, and the majority of lucrative benefices and places in cathedral chapters were in its hands. Despite the generally high moral and intellectual standard of the eighteenth-century clergy, faith was not a prerequisite for success as the sparkling careers of courtly prelates such as cardinals Dubois, Bernis and Brienne testified. Indeed, the dominance of the Court aristocracy was sufficient to allow families to hold several bishoprics simultaneously.[45] In 1700 a Colbert was to be found in the bishoprics of Rouen, Auxerre and Montpellier, while in 1789 the La Rochefoucauld had representatives in Rouen, Beauvais and Saintes. Others maintained control of a particular see over several generations, a good example was provided by the Rohan who were bishops of Strasbourg continuously from 1704–1803. It was the Revolution rather than the Council of Trent which would break this aristocratic stranglehold upon the power and wealth of the French Church.

However defined, it seems difficult to escape the conclusion that in the eighteenth century the French State, or its principal means of administration, coercion and even routes to salvation, was in the hands of the *noblesse*. The beneficiaries of the system were the rich élite of the Court, high-*robe* and *finance* of Versailles and Paris. It was the *grands seigneurs* who monopolised the principal positions in the Church and armed forces, while the great *robe* families of Paris and the wealthiest of their cousins in the provinces dominated the royal administration and judiciary. The losers were those individuals, noble or not, who lacked the means or contacts to break into this charmed circle. An estimate of 1,000 families, perhaps 5,000 individuals, had access to these positions and to the glittering careers, financial rewards and social honours that success could bring. That left nearly 28 million people whose ambitions were unlikely to be fulfilled. Membership of this élite within an élite always remained open but it constituted a tiny fraction of the *noblesse* as a whole. While the Revolution did not destroy the power of this élite, it certainly guaranteed that after 1789 talent played a more conspicuous part in the recruitment of the country's rulers.

The Court played a key part in reinforcing the bonds of exclusivism already cast by the accident of birth. Access to Versailles offered the

45. J. Delumeau, *Le catholicisme entre Luther et Voltaire* (Paris, 1971), pp. 75–6.

opportunity to petition for favour, and the better a courtier's credentials the more likely his chances of success. By the end of the *ancien régime*, it was easier for a military officer to win promotion by besieging a minister than a town, and the maxim held good for pensions and patronage generally. The marquis de Valfons, a career soldier who lived on the fringes of Court society, provided a splendid example of how the system worked. Tired of being passed over for promotion by younger, and often untested, scions of aristocratic houses, he pestered Dubois, *premier commis* of the minister of war, for an explanation.[46] He was informed that the only route to success was to acquire the good graces of a Court lady with the ear of the minister. Although it wounded his military pride, Valfons eventually complied and his promotion followed with alarming speed. For many more, the Court was a necessary evil to be endured in the furtherance of personal or family interests. The duc des Cars expressed this attitude neatly when he wrote that the Court 'was for me, and for most of the French *noblesse*, less a goal than a means of facilitating a military career'.[47] Yet, for every Valfons or Cars, there were countless other officers, noble or otherwise, who could never hope to have access to the Court and were obliged to suffer their indignity in silence. That a financial crisis was the catalyst of the Revolution is beyond doubt, but there was no shortage of grievances to explain the violent reaction against the aristocracy once the monarchical house of cards collapsed.

The grip exerted by the courtiers upon the levers of power in the French State strengthened after 1715. It is true that the system of conciliar government, known as the *polysynodie*, in which aristocratic thinkers such as Fénelon, Chevreuse and Saint-Simon had invested so much hope, came to naught, largely because of the Regent's political acumen. However, from the middle of the century, the courtiers began to enter and, ultimately, control the governmental mechanisms bequeathed by Louis XIV. During the 1750s and 1760s, the vital ministerial offices of war, navy and foreign affairs fell into the hands of the *grands seigneurs*. As the duchesse de Praslin, wife of the minister, haughtily remarked, 'It's done, these places are now in our hands, these petit bourgeois [the *robe*] will meddle no more'.[48] The duc de Choiseul even toyed with the idea of adding the finance ministry to his already lengthy list of offices in 1763, before eventually choosing instead to insert one of his creatures.

By allowing the Court families to establish themselves within the ministry, Louis XV unwittingly signed the death warrant of French absolutism. Placing military men in the high-spending service ministries was bad enough, but as courtiers partly dependent either for themselves or their families upon the pensions that flowed from the royal treasury, they had no interest in reforming abuse or trimming expenditure. Moreover, the advantage of knowing the Court, while being surrounded by friends and

46. Marquis de Valfons, *Souvenirs du marquis de Valfons, 1710–86* (Paris, 1860), p. 351.
47. Cars, *Mémoires*, p. 115.
48. C. Collé, *Journal et mémoires de Charles Collé*, 3 vols (Paris, 1868), III, pp. 516–17.

family, meant that genuine reformers from *robe* backgrounds, such as Turgot or Calonne, were extremely vulnerable. Intrigue had always been a fundamental feature of Court life, but by allowing aristocrats such as Belle-Isle, Choiseul or d'Aiguillon into ministerial positions, the king, if anything, made matters worse. *Grands seigneurs* could not be rewarded on the same scale as mere *robins*, and, for example, the duc de Choiseul received offices and pensions with an estimated annual value of 800,000 *livres*. In addition, he was elevated to the coveted rank of *duc et pair*, an honour shared by his cousin and ministerial *protégé*, Praslin. Nor could such ministers be dismissed lightly. Choiseul's exile in 1770 sparked a mini *Fronde*, and the king was obliged to watch as a procession of over 200 of his most powerful subjects made the pilgrimage to the duke's château of Chanteloup. With the reins of government in the hands of those who profited from its abuses, and with France ruled consecutively by two weak kings, serious change could only occur by accident as was the case in 1771.[49] The Court was, therefore, instrumental not only in blocking any change that might have revived the monarchy, but also in fuelling the resentment against the aristocracy that exploded in 1789.

It has also long been assumed that in the provinces the political power of both the court aristocracy and the local *noblesse* had been eroded by the intendants. It would certainly be foolish to underrate their importance to the smooth-running of the royal administration and in the *pays d'élections* the power of the intendants was immense, but in the *pays d'états* matters were more complicated and required the careful handling of still-powerful local Estates. The model of a successful eighteenth-century intendant was Guignard de Saint-Priest, who was sent to Languedoc in 1756.[50] He had the good sense to establish harmonious relations with the local élite, and undisturbed by any scandal accumulated both fortune and respect. His son was named as his deputy and future successor in 1764, and a younger son was accorded the distinguished title of colonel-in-second to the Estates of the province in 1784. In neighbouring Provence, the intendant, Galois de La Tour, did not even need to acquaint himself with the *mores* of the Midi. He was the son of the previous intendant, and at the same time first president of the *parlement* of Aix. In Bourgogne, between 1749 and 1761, the intendant was Jean François Joly de Fleury. Although now dominating the *parquet* of the Paris *parlement*, the Joly de Fleury were originally from Beaune in the heart of the province, and clearly had no trouble maintaining local links. A knowledge of regional habits and customs made the task of coaxing taxes or concessions out of the *pays d'états* easier, but the relationship was inevitably founded upon a certain amount of reciprocity, and the intendant served as a conduit through which individuals or institutions could petition the Crown for special favour or patronage.

The Court aristocrats, however, were not cut off completely from affairs

---

49. W. Doyle, 'The Parlements of France and the Breakdown of the Old Regime, 1771–1788', *French Historical Studies*, 6 (1970), 415–58.
50. Forster, *Nobility of Toulouse*, p. 28.

in the provinces. Throughout the eighteenth century both the provincial governors and the military commandants exercised an important rôle, especially in the *pays d'états*. An energetic commandant, such as the duc de Randan in Franche-Comté or the duc d'Aiguillon in Bretagne, could, on occasions, even dominate the intendant, who became little more than an adjunct. Such examples were probably exceptional, but with their links to ministers and even the royal family, both governors and commandants were used by provincial institutions to negotiate informally with the Crown. Another means of preserving provincial ties was the family regiment. When the marquis de Belleval, a native of Abbeville, was old enough to begin his military career, his mother contacted the duc de Chaulnes, governor of Picardy and Artois and lieutenant-general of the *Chevaux-Légers* and reminded him of the services of the boy's uncle in the same colours.[51] His entry was thus assured, and Belleval recorded in his memoirs an occasion when on parade Louis XV asked him his name and province. When Belleval had replied, the king declared that 'the duc de Chaulnes is right to put the gentlemen of his province in my *Chevaux-Légers*, they are loyal and serve me well'. Exiled to the isolated town of Maur in the Auvergne during the particularly bitter winter of 1771, the Parisian magistrate, Robert de Saint-Vincent, was overwhelmed by the kindness and consideration of the local *noblesse* during the difficult journey between Clermont-Ferrand and his place of exile. Clearly, few of the *Auvergnats* had heard of Louis XV's quarrels with the *parlements*. They had, however, received a message from the Noailles, the principal landowners in the region, telling them to accord every honour to the visitor. One final example was provided by the comte de Cars who, despite being crippled at Versailles by gout, was nevertheless elected a representative to the Estates General of 1789 by the dutiful *noblesse* of the Limousin, where the majority of his estates were located. These examples serve as a warning not to underestimate the continuing influence of the courtiers on the lives of the provincial *noblesse*.

When examining *ancien régime* government, it is necessary to avoid falling into the trap of seeing nothing but a nascent bureaucracy. Before 1789, power was in the hands of a tiny number of individuals, and the tendency of this élite to intermarry and to live in the same social and cultural milieu meant that policies often were formed, and conflicts resolved, through unofficial channels. Yet, one of the great ironies of the eighteenth century was that a State run by, and for, a section of the *noblesse* died, to a large extent, by its own hand. From around the middle of the century, divisions began to appear among the ruling élite about the precise nature of the French constitution. The influence of Montesquieu's *L'Esprit des Lois* (1748) and a more general fascination for all things English gave an initial fillip to the idea of a monarchy tempered by some form of institutional check, which for many meant the *parlements*. Admittedly, under Louis XIV, there had been no shortage of complaints about ministerial despotism, but

---

51. L-R. de Belleval, *Souvenirs d'un Chevaux-Leger* (Paris, 1865), pp. 29, 121.

after 1750 the religious and financial quarrels between the Crown and the judiciary began to change the nature of the debate. Yet, this was not a battle between the State and the *noblesse*, but rather an internecine feud within the Second Estate about the legitimate exercise of power.

The reforms of chancellor de Maupeou, implemented in 1771, brought these problems into the open. Ordered to present edicts dissolving the old *parlements*, some provincial commandants and even the intendant of Bretagne, Dupleix de Bacquencourt, refused. Their resistance was matched by that of several hundred judges and most of the princes of the blood, all of whom were exiled for their disobedience. These divisions cut across noble professional boundaries and members of the *épée*, *robe* and *finance* were to be found in both camps. Maupeou's reforms were possible because a sufficient number of the *noblesse* in both civil and military posts were prepared to obey Louis XV, but the monarchy paid a high price for its triumph. Many of the *noblesse* and much of literate opinion remained convinced that the Crown had slipped into the murky waters of despotism, and Louis XVI's decision to re-establish the old courts after his accession in 1774 was perfectly understandable. His decision sent a clear message to those who had obeyed Louis XV, namely that the Crown could not be relied upon to finish what it started. After Maupeou, the *parlements* were not especially troublesome, but their recall had demonstrated that government without them was impossible. Yet, the judges were neither willing nor able to sanction change on the scale required to save the State from financial ruin. While it may be true that nothing is inevitable, in 1774 it did not require a crystal ball to predict that another expensive war would oblige the king to call either the Estates General, or some other form of representative body.

That moment came at the end of 1786 when Louis XVI agreed to summon an Assembly of Notables. Two years of noble opposition to successive royal ministers and their policies followed before the king finally agreed to the meeting of the Estates General, which began on 1st May 1789. Confusion still surrounds the true aspirations of the *noblesse* at the very end of the *ancien régime*, but again the explanation lies in the heterogeneity of the Second Estate. There was undoubtedly a strong liberal presence, reflecting the significant rôle played by the *noblesse* in the French Enlightenment. The Second Estate had produced *philosophes* like Condorcet and Holbach, scientists such as Lavoisier and even historians, notably président de Hénault. Mme de Lambert and the marquise du Deffand had been the driving force behind the Parisian salons, and at the head of the provincial academies that flourished throughout the kingdom were nobles such as président de Montesquieu in Bordeaux, président de Brosses at Dijon and duc de Tallard in Besançon. After 1750, the spread of freemasonry also owed much to noble participation and patronage. The aristocratic seal of approval was applied by the duc d'Orléans, grand master of the Grand Orient, and among over 3,000 noble freemasons were the prince de Broglie and the duc d'Aumont. They were accompanied by the *parlementaires*, Richard de Ruffey, Maréchal de Vezet and La Briffe, and financiers among whom featured the names of La Borde and Megret de Sérilly.

It has been suggested that participation in learned academies and masonic lodges helped to break down the barriers separating different social classes, and to broaden noble horizons. While this should not be totally discounted, evidence for the general applicability of such theories remains elusive. More compelling is the evidence of the wide dissemination of enlightened literature among the *noblesse*. Thus, a cleric such as the abbé Nigon de Berty, councillor in the *parlement* of Paris, could declare himself charmed by Montesquieu's *L'Esprit des Lois* which, confirms 'so many of my own ideas'.[52] Meanwhile, in the depths of the Auvergne, the marquis de Nancaze, an elderly provincial *seigneur*, had by 1771 a library containing the works of Bayle, Voltaire and Rousseau. In 1781, the duc des Cars claimed that he was obliged to discipline two of his officers for insubordination after their 'heads had been turned by reading the works of Rousseau'.[53] Finally, the taciturn M. de Châteaubriand, living in the apparently splendid isolation of his Breton fortress, nevertheless subscribed to such periodicals as the *Gazette de Leyde*, the *Journal de Francfort* and the *Mercure de France*.

Having produced, or contributed, to many of the great works of the Enlightenment, the *noblesse* did not feel unduly threatened by its principles before 1789. Given the élitist tone of much enlightened opinion and the self-confidence of the governing élite, that attitude was perfectly understandable, and many in the Second Estate were undoubtedly prepared to contemplate wholesale reform of the State. In their lists of grievances sent to the Estates General, there was a strong demand for certain basic liberal freedoms, notably religious toleration, a free press and legal safeguards against arbitrary arrest or punishment.[54] More remarkably, many nobles, perhaps the majority, were prepared to renounce their fiscal privileges for the good of the State, and, in keeping with the mood of the times, declared themselves in favour of regular meetings of the Estates General to act as a permanent constitutional check on the Crown.

Yet, the enthusiasm of one half of the *noblesse* was mirrored by the rapid disillusion and fear of the other. Cracks began to develop during the furore surrounding the composition and organization of the Estates General. In September 1788, the *parlement* of Paris issued its much misunderstood *arrêté* calling for the observation of the regulations followed at the last meeting of the Estates in 1614. Rather than signalling a determination to defend the interests of the *noblesse* against the Third Estate, it was a typical act of a court of law obsessed by legal forms and historical precedent. The decision nevertheless symbolized the growing unease of a section of the *noblesse* which was confirmed by the protest delivered to

---

52. B. Lacombe, *La résistance janséniste et parlementaire au temps de Louis XV: l'abbé Nigon de Berty* (Paris, 1948), p. 223.
53. Cars, *Mémoires*, I, p. 220.
54. Chaussinand-Nogaret, *The French Nobility*, pp. 145–65.

Louis XVI by the princes of the blood in December 1788. When the Estates General finally met in May 1789, the noble deputies showed themselves to be badly split about whether or not to vote in common with the other orders. These problems were exacerbated by the political vacuum at Versailles, and led to the fatal stalemate which preceded the declaration of a National Assembly of 17 June. Yet, despite the legitimate fear that once the unique constitution of each order was lost, the *noblesse* would be swamped by the numerically stronger Third Estate, the noble deputies obeyed Louis XVI's order of 27 June to join the National Assembly.

Thereafter, the *noblesse* never threatened to form an independent political programme and its members fragmented. As the Revolution gathered momentum, it was liberal nobles such as Mirabeau, Lafayette and Lally-Tollendal who directed the reforms of the Constituent Assembly (1789–91). Indeed, it was a noble, Mathieu de Montmorency, who made a speech in June 1790 that would lead to the decree abolishing the Second Estate. Even after the fall of the monarchy in 1792 there were former nobles such as the duc d'Orléans and Hérault de Séchelles who sat in the republican convention. There were also republican martyrs, notably Le Peletier de Saint-Fargeau, scion of a powerful *parlementaire* family, who was assassinated in January 1793 after voting for the execution of Louis XVI. More typical were the many noble officers or administrators who continued to serve successive revolutionary regimes either out of necessity or principle. Napoleon provided the ultimate example of how the Revolution could open doors for the ambitious, but he was not alone. Others either fled the country or sought to escape the revolutionary turmoil by living quietly on their estates. Finally, many thousands were executed or murdered, often in the most horrific circumstances, by the republican regime or those who acted in its name. As for those who opposed the Revolution, there was no one issue which pushed them into the counterrevolutionary camp. There was surprisingly little resistance to the upheavals of 14 July or 4 August 1789, but noble opposition was stirred by the attacks on the Catholic Church and, above all, the person of the king. Yet, even the execution of Louis XVI could not unite the second order, and the Revolution's wounds cut across the *noblesse* as they did the rest of nineteenth-century French society. Admittedly, under Napoleon and subsequent regimes, the *noblesse* re-established its powerful position within society and government, but the hegemony that had characterized the last two centuries of the *ancien régime* had been lost for ever.

CHAPTER SIX

The Nobility in Spain, 1600–1800

I. A. A. Thompson
University of Keele

There is no nation that boasts more of being noble, nor that puts more value on being honoured than the Spaniards (Moreno de Vargas, 1622).

NOBILITY: CONCEPT, COMPOSITION AND 'CLOSURE'

Hidalguía, the generic term for nobility in Spain, was defined in the Middle Ages as 'the nobility which descends to men through their lineage'. It was a privileged, legal status shared by the entire noble hierarchy from simple *hidalgo* to *caballero*, *título* and grandee. *Hidalguía* was the common base of all nobility – 'the first rank of nobility from which one rises to all the rest' (Count-Duke of Olivares, 1624). 'Such is the excellence of this word *hidalgo*,' wrote Benito de Peñalosa y Mondragón, in 1629, 'that it includes within it the gentlemen, counts, marquises and grandees of the Kingdom'.

The different kingdoms and provinces of the Spanish monarchy had their own polities, constitutions and laws which existed alongside the central institutions of the Court and the monarchy until some measure of uniformity was imposed by the new Bourbon regime between 1707 and 1716. However, not all internal legal, political and social institutions were affected, and in both the seventeenth and the eighteenth centuries the nobilities of the provinces of the Crown of Aragon, in particular, Catalonia, Valencia and Aragon itself, retained nomenclatures and peculiarities of their own: *ricos hombres*, *caballeros* and *infanzones* in Aragon; *nobles* and *cavallers* in Catalonia and Valencia. They were also distinguished by an intermediate, pre-noble grade of *ciudadanos*, *ciutadans honrats* in Catalonia, *ciutadans* or *ciudadanos del inmemorial* in Valencia, which was lacking in Castile and which permitted a less abrupt transition from commoner to noble status, until legislation in 1724 equated the *ciudadanos del inmemorial* and the *ciutadans honrats* of the major cities with the Castilian *hidalguía de sangre*, thus separating them from the remaining *ciutadans* and contributing to a broader, long-term Hispanization of nobility in Spain.[1]

---

1. In addition to the titles on the Crown of Aragon in the Guide to Further Reading, see P. Molas Ribalta, 'Títulos de hidalguía en el setecientos valenciano', in M. Lambert-Gorges, et al., *Hidalgos et hidalguía dans l'Espagne des XVIe–XVIIIe siècles* (Paris, 1989), 189–205.

Spain at the end of the sixteenth century would seem to have been in a category similar to Poland, or Hungary, with a nobility proportionately four or five times that of other western European countries, such as France. Although we have no figures for Spain as a whole, Castile, by far the largest unit of the Peninsula, had 134,223 households, some 10 per cent of its population, classified as *hidalgo* in 1591. That global figure is, however, misleading. The distribution of *hidalgos* was geographically very skewed. The great bulk of *hidalgos* lived in Spain north of the Duero and the Ebro. Sixty-two per cent of all Castile's *hidalgos* were in the administrative provinces of Burgos with Trasmiera (Cantabria) and Leon with Asturias. Seventy-five per cent of the population of Trasmiera was *hidalgo*, 85 per cent of that of Asturias, and the entirety of that of Vizcaya and Guipúzcoa. These were the mountainous redoubts which had held out against the invading Moors in the eighth century and where the ancient and noble blood of the Visigoths had been preserved unsullied to spread southwards as the Christian Reconquest advanced. But south of the Guadarramas, and in twenty-six of the forty fiscal districts of Castile, *hidalgos* made up less than 5 per cent of the population, and in eleven of them less than 3 per cent. In the 1570s, in five provinces of New Castile there were only 2,548 *hidalgo* households (*vecinos*) in a population of over half a million (124,000 *vecinos*), some 2 per cent; and in Cordoba province in 1591 a mere 518 in 46,209 *vecinos*, just over 1 per cent, a figure very close to the estimates for Catalonia and Valencia, and to the 2 per cent of the Aragonese population that was *caballero* in 1702.[2]

This meant that the *hidalgo* was sociologically very different in some areas than in others. In northern Spain, his very numbers naturally meant that there was little that distinguished him from the rest of a largely peasant and artisan population. Although the 'lumpen-*hidalguía*' was a characteristic of the extreme north, even in other parts of Old Castile there was quite a numerous *hidalgo* proletariat. In the city of Soria, of 800 households in 1642 there were sixty households of *hidalgos*, yet 'the other householders are wealthier than the *hijosdalgo*', for, except for four or six *caballero* households, 'the rest are extremely poor'.[3] But further south, the *hidalgo* was, in general, a relatively wealthy and, in contrast to the north, a predominantly urban creature. In Jaén they were practically all in towns of over 2,000 households; in Cordoba four out of five were resident in six centres; and in the districts of Murcia, Ciudad Real, Madrid and Toledo more than 90 per cent were in the capital city. In many villages in central and southern Spain there might be no *hidalgos* at all; that was the case, for

2. E. García España and A. Molinié-Bertrand, *Censo de Castilla de 1591. Estudio Analítico* (Madrid, 1986), pp. 79–93; A. Molinié-Bertrand, 'Les "Hidalgos" dans le Royaume de Castille à la fin du XVIe siècle: Approche cartographique', *Revue d'Histoire Economique et Sociale* 52 (1974), 51–82; N. Salomon, *La campagne de Nouvelle Castille à la fin du XVIe siècle d'après les 'Relaciones topográficas'* (Paris, 1964), pp. 288–300. For Aragon, G. Colás Latorre and J. A. Salas Ausens, *Aragón bajo los Austrias* (Zaragoza, 1977), p. 48; L. González Antón, *Las Cortes de Aragón* (Zaragoza, 1978), p. 168.
3. AM [Archivo Municipal de] Soria, Libro de Acuerdos 11[2], f.83v, 12.7.1642.

example, in 256 villages in Guadalajara province, in five out of six villages of the province of Avila, and in 80 per cent of places in Extremadura with less than 500 households. There were poor *hidalgos* in the south but they were not particularly common. In New Castile in 1575 only about a dozen are noted among 2,500 *hidalgos*.

Nobility, therefore, was a vertical slice, not a horizontal stratum. It was not a class; it shared no uniformity of wealth, occupation, or common relationship to the means of production, or to the market. The 188 members of the 'estado noble' listed in Logroño in 1752 (12 per cent of households) spanned a social divide from the marquis of Santa Cruz, Grandee of Spain, at one end, to Domingo Gutiérrez, aged 90, lacemaker by trade, but now living off his wife's work as hosier, at the other, and included a tailor, a carpenter, a spinner, a bricklayer, a muleteer, a chocolate-maker, merchants, tanners, lawyers, a surgeon, tax officials, a royal councillor, military officers, vine-growers, sheep-owners and farmers. Even in Ciudad Real, where the forty nobles comprised only 2.3 per cent of the population in 1752, the noble estate included a small-holder, two servants looking after livestock, and two day-labourers.[4]

Hidalguía was a privileged status, passed on in the male line to all children, legitimate or illegitimate. The quintessential privilege, that which above all distinguished the nobleman from the commoner, was exemption from taxes on the person. But the nobility also enjoyed a range of other privileges and exemptions. They were exempt from billeting, forced levies and conscription, nor could they be compelled to serve public or municipal office; they were not to be subjected to torture or other degrading punishments, and were not to be held in the common gaol; they were not liable to imprisonment for debt, nor could their homes, horses or arms be distrained. They were permitted to have coats of arms and to display their escutcheons on portals, tombs and chapels; they had the right in many towns to half of all offices of justice and government, and many city councils, collegiate and cathedral chapters had statutes restricting membership to nobles of the blood; proof of nobility was required for knighthood of the Order of St John and of the great Spanish military orders of Santiago, Calatrava, Alcántara and Montesa, as well as for membership of a large number of local religious, social and charitable fraternities. The nobilities of Catalonia, Valencia, Aragon and Navarre also had representation as Estates in their respective Cortes, or parliaments; in the case of Aragon the upper and the lower nobility were represented separately. The Castilian Cortes had no noble estate after 1539, but in practice the great majority of the proctors representing the cities were nobles, *caballeros* of their ruling oligarchies, and included from Philip III's reign a substantial number of individual grandees, titled nobles and *señores*. The difference between the Cortes of Castile and those of the Crown of

---

4. F. Abad León, *Radiografía histórica de Logroño a la luz del Catastro del Marqués de la Ensenada* (Logroño, 1978), pp. 418 ff.; C. R. Phillips, *Ciudad Real 1500–1750. Growth, Crisis and Readjustment in the Spanish Economy* (Cambridge, Mass., 1979), p. 107 and n. 28.

Aragon, therefore, was not the absence of the nobility from the former, but the absence of clergy and commoners, and the much more direct involvement of Castile's nobility in the politics of the cities.

Though much complained of by contemporary critics, the material value of these privileges and exemptions was probably a good deal less than was imagined. Exemption from direct, personal taxation was, in general terms, of little financial importance. There were many places, and even entire regions, where either everybody was exempt from the heaviest of these personal taxes, the *servicios*, or where everybody paid, nobles included. Moreover, by the second half of the sixteenth century it was a diminishing asset, as the *servicios* declined rapidly in comparison with indirect taxes from which the nobleman was by and large not exempt. One exceptionally rich *hidalgo* in a provincial town near Toledo, who supposedly had more property than all the other 309 families put together, may have saved himself 300 *reales* a year, half a year's wages of a working man, but only a tenth of the investment value of what he was prepared to pay for the privilege, which often was acquired for other reasons entirely – to give entry to municipal office, for example. More normally, thirty *reales* may not have been a low figure. By the eighteenth century fiscal privilege, undermined in the reign of Philip IV by sales taxes on luxuries, compulsory donatives and levies on the interest from government bonds which fell most heavily on the privileged classes, was of little practical importance to the *hidalgo* and of diminishing concern to the *pechero*, the tax-paying commoner.[5] Nobility, of course, also meant service, particularly military service, or its equivalent, and the costs, inconvenience and dangers of that, though requested only sporadically, and even more erratically complied with, not least in the mid seventeenth century when it was most needed, have to be set against the material benefits of its exemptions.

More important than the privileges themselves were the deep-rooted assumptions of a society of orders that believed in the practical and moral necessity of hierarchy, and that attributed particular functions, talents and virtues to each order of society. Nobility meant honour, a presumption of virtue, and a divine right to command. Not only was the nobleman to be preferred in office, all other things being equal, and rewarded commensurately with his status, but there were duties with which only he could be entrusted. Only a nobleman could give or receive the oath of fealty required from the castellans of royal fortresses, for example, and only nobles could be allowed employment in the royal household, even in the most menial of posts. Even in the high Enlightenment of the later eighteenth century, the most progressive ministers of the Crown could still feel that the 'exceptional qualities required by the highest offices' were more easily to be found 'amongst

---

5. The value of fiscal privilege is discussed in I. A. A. Thompson, 'The Purchase of Nobility in Castile, 1552–1700', *Journal of European Economic History* 8 (1979), 313–60, at 329–32; see, *Actas de las Cortes de Castilla*, vol. 13, p. 72 (4.11.1593); J. Fayard, *Les membres du Conseil de Castille à l'époque moderne (1621–1746)* (Geneva-Paris, 1979), p. 188. On the unimportance of fiscal exemption in the eighteenth century, Phillips, *Ciudad Real*, p. 106; A. Domínguez Ortiz, *La sociedad española en el siglo XVIII* (Madrid, 1955), p. 326.

those families whose abundant means, splendour and attitudes accustom them to put honour before interest and to seek their fortunes only in reputation or glory', than among men 'with a poor and obscure background'.[6]

What constituted nobility was very much an open question that was the subject of a prolonged polemic, already running in the mid-fifteenth century and continuing, sometimes in exactly the same words, two hundred years later. There were in essence two opposing views: first, the 'vulgar' opinion which saw nobility as 'natural', that is, genetic, a quality of the blood and of lineage (*nobleza del linaje*). Its classic expression was the famous sentence of the late thirteenth-century Partidas of Alfonso X, 'fidalguia es nobleza que viene a los omes por manera de linaje' (*'hidalguía* is the nobility that comes to men through their lineage'); secondly, 'moral' nobility, (*nobleza de costumbres*): a nobility manifested in arms, letters and 'good deeds' ('buenas costumbres'), in other words a nobility of personal merit and service. It was a learned, Bartolist, 'absolutist' view of nobility as an honour bestowed by the prince.[7]

The debate about the nature of nobility was, therefore, not only a conflict between the group and the individual, or between social stasis and social change, a dimension of the *arbitrismo* that sought a revitalization of the Spanish economy through the encouragement of individual talent and initiative, an attempt to incorporate new professions into the canon of honour, but also a conflict between different views of political authority. If in the seventeenth century the weight of the learned, formal treatises of nobility was heavily 'absolutist', the 'vulgar' view, reflected in the theatre, the novel and in the justifications of the claimants to nobility themselves, was stubbornly traditional. 'The rude, unlettered mass of the people have a common saying, which is that the king can make knights, but not gentlemen' (Diego de Valera, 1441). Nobility was thus part of a natural order outside the scope of royal authority. As Benito de Peñalosa y Mondragón put it in 1629, 'Being an *hidalgo* is sufficient to say that one owes nothing to the king.'

One of the key differences between Castile and Aragon was in the way that nobility could be acquired. In Castile *hidalguía* could be established by the grant (or purchase) of a patent of nobility (*privilegio*) from the king, by a declaration of the courts (*executoria*), or by the uninterrupted exercise of the privileges of nobility for three generations. Nobility was established preferably by reputation ('por notoriedad'), by the unchallenged acceptance of the local community, or if challenged, by a sentence of the courts sitting in judgement on the *evidence* put before them.

For the upwardly mobile commoner, therefore, the key to ennoblement

6. Jovellanos, quoted by M. García Pelayo, 'El estamento de la nobleza en el despotismo ilustrado español', *Moneda y Crédito* 17 (1946), 37–59, at p. 51.

7. Diego de Valera (*c*.1441), following the much-quoted early fourteenth-century jurist, Bartolus of Sassoferrato: 'nobleza es una calidad dada por el príncipe', in 'Espejo de verdadera nobleza', *Biblioteca de Autores Españoles*, vol. 116, 89–116, at 92; and Fray Juan Benito Guardiola, *Tratado de nobleza* (Madrid, 1591), f. 3v; Bernabé Moreno de Vargas, *Discursos de la Nobleza de España* (1622: Madrid, 1659 edition), ff. 5v, 31v, 6; Benito de Peñalosa, *Libro de las Cinco Excelencias del Español* (Pamplona, 1629), f. 86; J. A. Maravall, *Poder, honor y élites en el siglo XVII* (Madrid, 1979), p. 58; on the opinion of the *vulgo*, Valera, pp. 91, 100, Moreno de Vargas, f. 31.

was not the purchase of an expensive *privilegio de hidalguía* which gained the respect of no one, but the ability to intervene in the drawing up of the community's tax rolls (*padrones*) and to influence its litigation. That was most successfully achieved by securing a place on a town's governing council. However, if a claim to be enrolled as noble in the *padrones* was rejected by a municipal council, acting ostensibly in defence of the common interest of the *pecheros*, the claimant could appeal to the tribunal of the *alcalde de hijosdalgo* of the appropriate regional high court (*chancillería*) in Valladolid or Granada. He would then attempt to prove his *hidalguía* by presenting genealogical evidence of his affiliation to some family of known noble descent, and oral and written testimony to his acceptance as noble by his peers and compatriots, adducing his inclusion in the rolls of those exempt from personal taxes, the holding of offices reserved to the nobility, membership of noble guilds and fraternities, marriage relations with and participation in the social life of the nobility, together with an appropriate lifestyle, with house, arms, servants and horses. A whole series of social and political institutions, from meetings of *hidalgos* in local churches for the election of officers, to the numerous socially selective charitable and religious confraternities, associations of noble Houses, like the 'Casas de los linajes' of Reoyo and Tovar in Valladolid, or the 'Doce Linajes Troncales' of Soria, the *maestranzas* (noble riding clubs) of Andalusia and Valencia, even the great Military Orders of Santiago, Calatrava, Alcántara and Montesa, existed substantially, if not entirely, as means for the validation of status and for the fomentation of corporate consciousness. If the appeal to the tribunal was upheld, the court would issue a *carta executoria* declaring its sentence in his favour, which would then, bound in leather and decorated with miniatures and gilt, be his certificate of nobility.

Despite much that has been written, the sale or grant of *privilegios* was of very little importance in Castile after the ending of the Granadan Wars in the reign of the Catholic kings, probably not more than two a year on average between 1550 and 1700. In contrast, some 30,000 lawsuits (*pleitos*) were instituted in the *Chancillería* of Valladolid between the late-fifteenth century and 1834, and in the other *Chancillería* in Granada, between 1490 and 1610, there was an average of 20 a year from the single region of Extremadura alone. Those figures are expression enough of the balance of view about what nobility was and how it was created.[8]

The courts did not, however, *make* a man noble, and their sentences were in no way definitive. Their judgements merely gave legal confirmation to a nobility that they found proved already to exist. The same evidence might satisfy the judges in the case of one brother, for example, but not

---

8. Thompson, 'Purchase of Nobility'; A. Basanta de la Riva, *Archivo de la Real Chancillería de Valladolid. Sala de los Hijosdalgo: catálogo de todos sus pleitos, expedientes y probanzas*, 4 vols (Valladolid, 1920), vol. 1, p. 5; J. Fayard and M-C. Gerbet, 'Fermeture de la noblesse et pureté de sang en Castille à travers les procès de *hidalguía* au XVIème siècle', *Histoire, Economie et Société* I (1982), 51–75. In 1602 there were more than sixty *pleitos de hidalguía* being defended by Alfaro, a town with a population of not much more than 900 households, AGS [Archivo General de Simancas] Cámara de Castilla: Oficios, leg. 1 (Agreda).

in that of another. Although nobility was manifested in lifestyle and in the enjoyment of fiscal exemptions and other privileges, it did not consist of lifestyle or privileges, for they could also be enjoyed by non-nobles, sometimes on a temporary basis, by royal grant. Nobility inhered in the lineage and each individual had to demonstrate his relationship to that lineage as often as it was challenged. Without the acceptance of the community, he and his successors could be forced to defend their nobility in the courts over and over again. Nobility was therefore a matter of common repute; the most respected *hidalgo* was the 'hidalgo notorio de sangre y solar conocido' ('recognized noble of known blood-line and family home'). Perhaps more so than anywhere else in western Europe, including the Crown of Aragon where nobility was not proved in the courts either, it depended not solely on acceptance by one's peers into a shared lifestyle, but on acceptance also by the commons, whose representatives participated in the drawing up of the *padrones* of exemptions. As Don Francisco de Amaya observed in 1639, 'It is evident that purity and nobility is not something essential, corporeal, actual and palpable, but something that exists in the opinion of men, in the opinion of the common people.'[9]

In Aragon, by contrast, nobility was not determined from below by a plea in the courts, but 'descended', preferably by acceptance by the corps of nobles themselves, though increasingly commonly by grant from the Crown. In Catalonia, for example, there were clear public tests for nobility (summons to the Corts, membership of the noble Estate, the *estament militar*, enrolment for the noble *diputació*, or standing committee), as well as a register of *ciutadans honrats* inclusion in which required the approval of three-quarters of the quorum. Each grade was a formal and distinct status. Not only, therefore, was the very notion of promotion (from commoner to *ciutadan*, to *cavaller*, to *noble*) built into the system, but the dominant values were élite rather than popular. It is perhaps for this reason that wealth, culture and civility displaced innate racial characteristics in the self-definition of the Catalan nobility at least a century earlier than in Castile.[10]

In Castile, on the other hand, qualification for nobility was locked into conservative values, designed primarily to prevent upward mobility and thus the escape of the wealthy from the obligations of the *pechero*, by a rigid insistence on traditional concepts of lineage, selflessness and sacrifice associated with the historic military function of the nobility as *bellatores* and *defensores*. Yet with the ending of the wars of the Reconquest it was ceasing to be generally possible to move into the nobility through urban knight service (*caballería villana*). Ennoblement in the sixteenth century was overwhelmingly a civilian process effected through the courts and the phoney militarism of the Military Orders. More and more, nobility was

---

9. A. Domínguez Ortiz, *La clase social de los conversos en Castilla en la edad moderna* (Madrid, 1951), p. 193; Moreno de Vargas, f. 29v, comments that it was easier to be accepted as *hidalgo* where no fiscal exemptions were involved.

10. J. S. Amelang, *Honored Citizens of Barcelona. Patrician Culture and Class Relations, 1490–1714* (Princeton, N. J., 1986), pp. 86, 145.

being acquired by financiers, lawyers, administrators, and men for whom war was remote and foreign. Yet a functional view of nobility as the order of *defensores* persisted. The 'path of letters' ('el camino del saber'), though much written about, was not an open road to nobility. Graduates of the great universities of Salamanca, Valladolid, Alcalá and Bologna were not automatically ennobled, as is often imagined; they were merely accorded the privileges of nobility, which might in due course become nobility by custom. The *parvenu* noble, therefore, compensated for his personal military deficiencies by an exaggerated adherence to a feudal-military ethos, translating his own administrative or financial services into the language of war and vassalage, and conjuring up deeds of valour by his family and forebears. More than four out of five of the justifications adduced for the grants of nobility sold in the seventy years after 1580 represented military services of one kind or other.[11]

The opposition of *linaje* and *costumbres* raised a number of issues concerning the relationship between blood and virtue, and the material prerequisites of 'living nobly'. The mass *hidalguía* of northern Spain and the Basque notion that the nobility of the 'Patria' necessarily ennobled all its sons meant that neither in theory nor in practice could nobility be confined to the rich and the leisured, nor so defined as to exclude tradesmen and labourers. Contrary to what is often believed, trade and menial occupations did not by themselves derogate from *hidalguía*,[12] though they might be bars to membership of other noble institutions; and poverty was regarded in practice as neither shameful nor a barrier to nobility. Though poverty might be a reason for being unable to maintain one's status, nobility itself was not lost through poverty, merely 'obscured'. An individual might lose the *privileges* of nobility by treason or some other shameful act, or by neglect, or by the inability to vindicate them, but the noble line itself remained unbroken.

The other side of the coin, the necessity for wealth, remained nevertheless a question of some ambivalence. Wealth was an 'accident', fortuitous; it facilitated generosity, promoted independence and dampened the urge to vice, but was it merely an aid to the preservation of nobility, or a *necessary* adjunct?[13] And was it only inherited wealth that was licit? New wealth of course raised the further question of the compatibility of acquisitiveness with nobility, and the threat to the entire noble ethos from the pretensions of *parvenus* and *arrivistes*. Even in the

---

11. I. A. A. Thompson, 'Neo-noble Nobility: concepts of *hidalguía* in early modern Castile', *European History Quarterly* 15 (1985), 379–406, at 388.

12. Juan García de Saavedra, *Tractatus de hispanarum nobilitate et exemptione* (Alcalá de Henares, 1597), 'Nobilis nobilitate sanguinis per exercitium oficii vilioris nihil sibi nocet': cited by the Marqués del Saltillo, 'La nobleza española en el siglo XVIII', *Revista de Archivos Bibliotecas y Museos* 60 (1954), 417–49, at 417; see also Moreno de Vargas, ff. 49v–51v.

13. F. Albía de Castro, *Memorial de Logroño* [1633], (Logroño, 1953), p. 143, defines wealth as 'nobleza fortuita', 'But it should be noticed that, although wealth is an aspect of nobility, in that it enables one's behaviour to be ostentatious, it is not nobility itself, since, as Horace said, wealth does not change the essence, it merely illumines the exterior.'

sixteenth century many writers thought that nobility was impossible without wealth, and historians have argued that there was at the same time an accentuated emphasis on wealth and on the importance of living nobly in the justifications of appellants in the courts. In Castile, however, in contrast to the Crown of Aragon, where a specific level of wealth was a prerequisite of nobility, there was prior to the middle of the eighteenth century a less than wholehearted acceptance of wealth as a *sine qua non* of nobility. The language of the justifications concerning lifestyle was very formulistic, and the references to wealth vague and imprecise, even coy, one might say. Only in fifteen of the 255 cases analysed in Fayard and Gerbet's examination of Extremaduran *pleitos* was there any direct stress on wealth as such. In the Crown of Aragon, where there was no mass noble proletariat and where fiscal exemption was virtually an irrelevance, the association of nobility and wealth was more explicit and the sensitivity to ignoble occupations more pronounced. Social promotion could be accepted much more overtly as a reward for worldly achievement in Catalonia and Valencia than it could be allowed to be seen to be in Castile, whatever the social reality.[14]

The obverse of this was the degree, exceptional in western society it has been argued, to which in Spain honour values were attributed to the non-noble. A crucial and unique element in that attribution was the concept of *limpieza de sangre*, or purity of blood, clean of taint of Moorish or Jewish race. The distinction between the 'limpio' and the 'notado', the tainted, was perhaps as fundamental a division of Spanish society as that between the noble and the commoner. The neat simplicity of Ferrand Mexia's, 'Since the beginning of the world there have always been some good and noble, and others evil and base',[15] was picked apart by *limpieza*, for *nobleza de sangre* and *limpieza de sangre* did not necessarily overlap. In the eyes of some, they seemed hardly even to intersect, for the *hidalgo* of the south whose family connections could be traced in the records and whose urban residence inevitably seemed to associate him with the wealthy Jewish financier and businessman, could not avoid suspicion of impurity. There were thus said to be two types of nobility, *hidalguía* which it was more honourable to possess, and *limpieza* which it was more shameful to lack, 'for in Spain we esteem a commoner who is pure of blood more than an *hidalgo* who is not'.[16] *Limpieza de sangre* can, therefore, be seen as a sort of 'counter-*hidalguía*', the defiance of the peasant *labrador* to the urban, rich, ruling-classes of the cities which dominated the countryside. Thus, despite an initial acceptance of the validity of the Moorish nobility of pre-Reconquest Spain and of the Indian élite of pre-Conquest America, *limpieza* imposed itself

14. For examples see, BL [British Library] Additional Ms. 28383, ff. 98, 158; C. Riba y García, *El Consejo Supremo de Aragón en el reinado de Felipe II* (Valencia, 1914), p. 242; H. Kamen, *Spain in the Later Seventeenth Century, 1665–1700* (London, 1980), pp. 267–9.

15. *Nobiliario Vero* (1485), lib. I, cap.xl.

16. 'Porque en España más estimamos a un hombre pechero y limpio que a un hidalgo que no es limpio', quoted in Domínguez Ortiz, *Clase social de los conversos*, p. 229.

as a prerequisite for nobility during the course of the sixteenth century, if only to blunt the edge of what some historians have seen as its inherent 'anti-hidalguismo'.[17]

The sixteenth century, particularly the middle decades, seems to have been a period of accelerated growth in noble numbers. Two-thirds of the nearly 1,800 Extremaduran lawsuits in Granada between 1490 and 1610 were initiated in 1550–69. The process appears to have been a natural one, facilitated no doubt by a phase of economic and territorial expansion, generally conducive to social mobility.[18] It was probably made up of two main components: the upward mobility of administrators, lawyers, businessmen and successful farmers; and an increased concern with social definition related to new legal and documentary means for legitimating status. The establishment of tribunals of *hidalguía* in the high courts of Valladolid and Granada at the end of the fifteenth century provided the institutional means by which nobility could be proved and authenticated, and the bureaucratic and archival revolutions of the sixteenth century created a permanent record of noble status that compelled families to have their nobility put on record lest the absence of the record imply the absence of the status.

In the Crown of Aragon, although the mechanisms of social promotion were different, the upward movement was the same. The number of *nobles* and *cavallers* in Catalonia rose from 488 in 1518, to 780 in 1626, and continued to climb thereafter, with 555 creations under Philip IV and Charles II; only 120 of the 410 families represented in 1626 went back to 1518. In Valencia, the number of eligible members of the *Braç Militar* grew from 508 at the time of the 1626 Corts to 550 in 1645.[19]

In Castile the proliferation of *hidalgos* seems to have been checked at the end of the sixteenth century. There was a serious attempt made late in Philip II's reign to control the laxity and evident abuses of the tribunals in nobility litigation, and it may be that the 1591 figure was somewhere near the peak. We have no reliable evidence for the number of *hidalgos* in the population as a whole between the 1591 census and those of the 1750s. In the years between, the Crown sold only a few hundred patents of nobility in Castile, and prior to the 1660s some two or three thousand *regimientos* which also perhaps facilitated the informal processes of ennoblement. In the mid eighteenth century the proportion of *hidalgos* was not very different from 1591, and subsequent censuses showed a rapid decline in numbers

---

17. In addition to the classic study of *limpieza de sangre*, A. A. Sicroff, *Les controverses des statuts de 'pureté de sang' en Espagne du XVe au XVIIe siècle* (Paris, 1960), see J. I. Gutiérrez Nieto's 'La estructura castizo-estamental de la sociedad castellana del siglo XVI', *Hispania* 33 (1973), 519–63, and 'Limpieza de sangre y antihidalguismo hacia 1600', in *Homenaje al Dr D. Juan Reglá Campistol* (Valencia, 1975), 497–514.

18. In Cuenca *hidalgos* increased from 7 per cent of the population in 1537, to 11.4 per cent in 1597, mainly by enlargement of the top thirty-odd families, R. Carrasco, 'Les *hidalgos* de Cuenca à l'époque moderne (1537–1642)', in Lambert-Gorges, *Hidalgos et hidalguía*, 167–88, at 171.

19. Amelang, *Honored Citizens*, pp. 66–7; J. H. Elliott, 'A Provincial Aristocracy: The Catalan Ruling Class in the Sixteenth and Seventeenth Centuries', *Homenaje a Jaime Vicens Vives* (Barcelona, 1967), 2, 125–41, at p. 129; J. Casey, *The Kingdom of Valencia in the Seventeenth Century* (Cambridge, 1979), p. 239, n. 4.

to a figure in 1797 less than 4 per cent of the population.[20] However, the decline seems too abrupt to be accepted at face value, and may reflect changes in the treatment of the near universal *hidalguía* of the north, but not necessarily a decline in the more élite *hidalguía* of the south. By the end of the century, instead of three in four, only one Asturian in six was *hidalgo*; yet, at the other end of the country, reliable evidence from the Andalusian city of Cordoba shows a 70 per cent increase in the number of registered *hidalgos* between the end of the sixteenth century and 1715, and no significant decline by 1775.[21]

In contrast to the check to the *hidalgo*, there was a spectacular increase in the number of Dons, *caballeros* of the Military Orders, *títulos* and grandees. Whereas in the sixteenth century, even in its last third, no more than one-fifth or one-third of the *regidores* (aldermen) of the great cities of Castile would have used the title Don, by the second half of the next century practically all of them were Dons, as was anyone of any social pretension whatsoever.[22] During the course of the seventeenth century no less than 14,000 Habits (*hábitos*) of the Military Orders were applied for, and 9,000 issued;[23] whilst the number of titled noblemen increased more than fourfold, from 120 or so to over 500. In Catalonia twice as many *nobles* and *cavallers* were created by Philip IV and Charles II as by Philip II and Philip III (555 to 279), even before this final wave the proportion of *nobles* in the *estament militar* increasing from 7.6 per cent in 1518 to 32.6 per cent in 1626. In Valencia, the privileged groups in Castellón more than doubled in number between 1608 and 1702 and became three and a half times richer, and royal grants of nobility (giving the right to use the Don), being sold for the first time in the 1630s, peaked in the 1640s and in the 1680s and 1690s.[24] Everywhere Spain was becoming a more aristocratic and a more status-conscious society in the seventeenth century.

The fact that *hidalguía* was a legal status, a juridical rather than a social reality, separated nobility from eliteness. *Hidalguía* was socially prescriptive, a necessary though not sufficient condition for social esteem; but it was not necessarily related to any other criteria of eliteness – power, wealth, or even respect. The stereotype of the impoverished *hidalgo* was a figure of ridicule in the literature. Divorced from arms, merit, service, wealth, even, in the popular view, from purity of blood, *hidalguía* was merely an arbitrary division of persons between those with certain privileges and those without. In places where the *hidalgo/pechero* distinction was of no

20. 722,794 in 1768; 480,592 in a population of 10,270,000, in 1787 (*c.*4.7 per cent); 402,059 in 10,540,000, in 1797 (*c.*3.8 per cent): G. Anes, *El Antiguo Régimen: Los Borbones* (Madrid, 1975), p. 48.

21. M. del C. Pérez de Guinea, *Estudio sobre la sociedad soriana en el siglo XVIII* (Valladolid, 1982), p. 73 for Asturias, pp. 69, 72, 128 for Soria; J. Aranda Doncel, *Historia de Córdoba, 3 La época moderna (1517–1808)* (Córdoba, 1984), pp. 36, 213.

22. In Cuenca, Dons were 4.6 per cent of *exentos* in 1558, 61.7 per cent in 1628–42, Carrasco, 'Cuenca', p. 174.

23. E. Postigo Castellanos, *Honor y Privilegio en la Corona de Castilla. El Consejo de las Ordenes y los Caballeros de Hábito en el siglo XVII* (Soria, 1988), pp. 118, 197.

24. Amelang, *Honored Citizens*, pp. 66–7; Elliott, 'Provincial aristocracy', p. 129; Casey, *Kingdom of Valencia*, pp. 45–6.

practical importance, fiscal or governmental, nobody might know or care who was *hidalgo* and who was not.[25] Elsewhere it generated a deep hostility among *pecheros* to its fiscal and administrative privileges. The Cortes in 1593 talked of 'the natural hatred they have towards the *hidalgos*', and again in 1598 of 'the great disturbances and outrages between the *caballeros* and *hidalgos* and the *pecheros* . . . on account of the natural opposition between them'.[26] The development of a new, more demanding nobility was one side of the social devaluation of mere *hidalguía* which, without status honour in itself and, the Reconquest completed, no longer exercising its traditional military rôle, had ceased to have any obvious social function, and may indeed in many places have become dysfunctional.

It was not enough, therefore, simply to be *hidalgo*; to be somebody in the seventeenth century required greater distinction. Thus, from the end of the sixteenth century there was an almost Baroque concern with the public demonstration of rank, and with visible social distinctions: the generalized use of the Don, and of multiple family names, like that of the *regidor* of Utrera, Juan Pérez Moreno de Mesa Cárdenas Alvarez Boorques y Gimeno, which advertised one's lineage sometimes in all four quarters; the application for Habits of the Military Orders, to be worn in public, and in which so many had their portraits painted; the acquisition of titles, and the march up the ladder from viscount, count, marquis, duke, and the three classes into which, for a time, the grandeeship was divided.

A major change was, thus, taking place in the nature of nobility. The relative social openness of 'Renaissance' Spain was passing. A not over-refined, and hence comparatively undemanding, concept of inherited privilege or of royal creation that can be seen as the legacy of the Reconquest nation-in-arms, was being redefined and tightened by the later sixteenth century with the conflation of the previously separate criteria of honour: lineage, legitimacy, *limpieza de sangre*, occupation and wealth. *Hidalguía* was becoming increasingly ascriptive, and the criteria for ennoblement progressively narrower and more rigid. From the mid-sixteenth century *probanzas* become more complex and more demanding: from proof on the paternal side for three generations to immemorial proof on both sides; *limpieza*, which had been largely irrelevant in the early sixteenth century, becomes increasingly important from 1550 or so, and by the 1570s it is practically always referred to – that in turn threw the spotlight onto the maternal line as well, and onto all four parental lineages. From the 1580s and 1590s, the justifications of applicants for *privilegios* also reveal a similar shift of emphasis towards 'sangre', lineage, *limpieza* and the remote origins of the family; and the formula of the grant becomes 'declaratory', a substitute for the judgement of the court, rather than the voluntarist 'making' of the *hidalgo* which had been common before.

---

25. See, I. A. A. Thompson, '*Hidalgo* and *pechero*: the language of "estates" and "classes" in early-modern Castile,' in P. J. Corfield, ed., *Language, History and Class* (Oxford, 1991), pp. 53–78, at p. 60, n. 25.

26. *Actas de las Cortes*, vol. 13, pp. 65, 77–9, vol. 15, p. 639; see also Salomon, '*Relaciones topográficas*', p. 295.

The same is apparent in the Military Orders. In the fifteenth century, a *caballero* of the Military Orders did not in practice have to be *hidalgo*. From 1440 the Order of Santiago required 'nobleza' in the male line, but for the mother only *limpieza de sangre*; however, the requirement was not rigidly enforced as long as the applicant was legitimate, and there was no formal requirement of suitable occupation ('limpieza de oficios') or good repute ('buen nombre'). By the third quarter of the sixteenth century the applicant had to be 'hijodalgo de sangre' on both sides back to his grandparents; his parents also had to be legitimate; and back to the grandparents there was to be no evidence of employment in 'oficios viles', 'or others involving manual labour', or as merchant, money-changer, usurer or other agents or brokers; the applicant himself had to be of 'buen nombre' and his ancestors 'limpio de sangre' and free of condemnation by the Inquisition in all degrees however remote. Until 1652 Santiago accepted wholesale merchants (*mercaderes de por mayor*), but then that provision was revoked also. It was precisely this rigour in authenticating *limpieza* on all five fronts, lineage, legitimacy, office, race and religion, that gave the Habit of the Military Orders its social value in the seventeenth century.

Historians have spoken of this process as a 'closure' of nobility, and they have generally interpreted it as part of a more general 'refeudalization' of society in the seventeenth century, a reaction of the society of orders to a period of excessive social mobility by the reinforcement of traditional caste values, an attempt to provide a new justification for a demilitarized and unmilitary nobility.[27] There was certainly an ideological narrowing, though it is less clear whether there was a real check to social promotion. It was from another point of view a means of consolidating *arrivisme* by exaggeration. However, the increasingly demanding refinement of the standards of nobility is perhaps better seen as an expression of the 'vulgar' concern to prevent the ennoblement of rich tax-payers, than as a conscious closing of ranks by the nobility itself. It was, for example, the *caballero procuradores* of the Cortes who were most persistent in their opposition to the revision of past *executorias* decreed in 1593.

In principle there was no way into *hidalguía* without the right ancestors. Yet, paradoxically, the more caste-like nobility became, the more only those with money could acquire it, by buying witnesses (*linajudos*), genealogists, chroniclers; avoiding registration as *pechero* by buying property in exempt towns and villages; buying municipal offices and so getting control over both the *padrones* and the decision of the *concejos* whether to challenge a claim to *hidalguía* or not. The costs of a case, perhaps lasting seven to ten years, meant that anyone who could afford to fight it usually won; if not, the claim would be abandoned without going to court at all. In Extremadura of 255 cases which went to court (mostly in the second half of the sixteenth century), the claimant won 243; and of 206 appeals, the towns lost every one. It was said in the Cortes in 1624,

27. Maravall, *Poder, honor y élites*, p. 206.

The officials of the towns and villages will not dare list anyone in the tax rolls who is prepared to go to litigation, however notorious a *pechero* he is. Thus he is left exempted as if he were an *hidalgo*, and so becomes one. Contrariwise, if they list an *hidalgo* who is poor, he cannot litigate and loses his *hidalguía*.[28]

As a result, whatever theorists were saying about nobility, the wider opinion (and probably the reality as well) was, in the famous line of Lope de Vega:

> Have no doubt, money is the all in all.
> It is prince, *caballero, hidalgo*;
> it is high birth, it is Gothic ancestry.

The fusion of status and wealth and the widespread ennoblement of the rich have been seen by many historians as the central dynamic of the social history of the sixteenth and seventeenth centuries. The profits of economic growth and the financial problems of government enabled the rich by buying offices, lands and jurisdictions put up for sale by the Crown to seize control of political and economic power in the communities and to engineer their own social elevation. The literary and anecdotal evidence, though always prone to sensationalism, testifies to very considerable mobility.[29] It is doubtful, however, whether this should be seen as a transformation of nobility, and still less as a subversion of traditional nobility by the rise of new monied classes. There was absolutely nothing new about such statements in the seventeenth century. 'Why, do you think, the king is more than the duke, the duke than the marquis, the marquis than the *caballero*, the *caballero* than the craftsman, the craftsman than the peasant?', Feliciano de Silva had enquired in 1534, 'For no other reason than the weight and measure of more or less money?'.[30] And the same comments are to be found in the mid-fourteenth century *Libro de Buen Amor*, and in Juan Pacheco and Diego de Valera in the mid-fifteenth century. These are criticisms of too much social mobility, not of exclusivity but of the facility with which successful merchants could acquire noble status for their sons. The continuing complaints about merchants rising *out* of business suggest that the tighter regulations imposed by many institutions in the later sixteenth century acted not as a barrier but as a sort of initiation rite; a reinforcement of the traditional ethos, a forced conversion of new money to old values, which perhaps helped preserve the ideological oneness of nobility in Castile. Although contemporaries were always fearful of the threat to the structure and values of the society of orders from new money, it was perhaps the controlled openness of that society to money that was the best guarantee of its reproduction.

---

28. Salomon, '*Relaciones topográficas*', p. 300.

29. J. M. Díez Borque, *Sociología de la comedia española del siglo XVII* (Madrid, 1976), pp. 256–8; Gutiérrez Nieto, 'Estructura castizo-estamental', pp. 546–7.

30. I. Atienza Hernández and M. Simón López, 'Patronazgo Real, rentas, patrimonio y nobleza en los siglos XVI y XVII: algunas notas para un análisis político y socioeconómico', *Revista Internacional de Sociología*, 2a época, vol. 45 (1987), 25–75, at 28.

THE HIERARCHY OF ARISTOCRACY

Although there was a single nobility, there were within it gradations of importance and respect. Social esteem, as opposed to legal status, pertained almost by definition only to the real élite of power, connection and wealth within its ranks, the *caballeros*, the *títulos* and the grandees who comprised the lower and upper echelons of the Spanish aristocracy. These were the social and political élites of the cities and of the Court, and at this level Spain's élite was relatively narrow and numerically not out of line with those of other countries. It has been estimated that there were some three to four thousand *caballero* families in seventeenth-century Castile, perhaps one in 300 of the population as a whole, two or three score families in each of the major towns and cities.[31]

The situation of the *caballeros* differed significantly between the Crown of Aragon and the Crown of Castile. Although it would not be entirely true to say that the *nobles* and *cavallers* of Catalonia and Valencia and the *caballeros* of Aragon were predominantly a rural gentry, after all 174 members of the *estament militar* (the noble Estate in the Corts), about a quarter of the total, were resident in Barcelona in 1639, and nearly a third (504) of the 1,623 *caballeros* in 1702 were resident in Zaragoza, their base was much less urban than it was in Castile. Not until the early seventeenth century were nobles able to take part in municipal government in Catalonia, and not until the middle of the century in Valencia.[32]

In the Crown of Castile, on the other hand, the *caballeros* were an urban gentry. Their power base was the corporate authority of the city. They comprised the oligarchy of families which governed the cities, through possession of the hereditary venal office of *regidor*, and which had become increasingly noble during the sixteenth century, either as cities (such as Cordoba, Seville, Toro, Madrid) adopted statutes restricting their *regimientos* to nobles, or simply as more and more of the *regidores* became nobles. Their power derived from their control of the municipal economy and of local administration and justice, and collectively they exercised the city's lordship over the villages of its jurisdiction.

Often relatives or clients of great aristocratic families, the *caballeros* ranged from the richer merchant, lawyer or bureaucrat, not necessarily always *hidalgo* in principle, though increasingly likely to be thought so, and to become so, to the untitled brother of a grandee. Indeed, apart from the title itself, no useful distinction can be made between the *caballero* and the ordinary *título*. As Don Jerónimo de Aguayo insisted in the Cortes in

---

31. The estimate, which is probably on the low side, is by A. Domínguez Ortiz, *La sociedad española en el siglo XVII*, vol. 1 (Madrid, 1964), p. 198; in Cuenca, about one-fifth of *exentos* were *caballeros*, up to 70 individuals in 1600, Carrasco, 'Cuenca', p. 174.

32. Elliott, 'A Provincial Aristocracy', p. 130; González Antón, *Cortes de Aragón*, p. 168; Casey, *Kingdom of Valencia*, p. 177.

1609, the only real distinction to be made should be between the grandees and the rest, not between *títulos* and *caballeros*, since 'there are in these kingdoms many very eminent, very rich, noble and very ancient *caballero* houses, and untitled brothers of grandees, all worthy of the greatest honour'.

Typically the *caballero* would be the possessor of a *mayorazgo* (for the social and economic importance of these entails see below, pp. 195–6), with an income ranging from 1–2,000 ducats at the bottom end to 10–12,000 or more at the top. Though individually they may also have had rural properties, farmlands, pastures and vineyards, and have been sheep-owners, or even lords of vassals, the *caballeros* were the rentier class par excellence, almost all of them having substantial investments of *juros* on the Crown debt, as well as *censos*, or mortgages, against the revenues of the cities or other nobles.

There was thus an economic difference between *caballero* and *hidalgo*. As Peñalosa wrote, 'Now, incorrectly, we call "caballeros" those noted *hidalgos* of ancient house and distinguished name who are of a more eminent and wealthy estate than other *hidalgos*.' But the difference between them was not simply, or even primarily, economic; it was a difference of 'quality and estimation'. Unlike *hidalguía* which was a formal, legal status, *caballero* was an informal designation, a mark of esteem, a standing with one's peers. The *caballero* is identifiable by the way he was addressed: 'El Señor', 'El Ilustre Señor', or in the sixteenth and seventeenth centuries, before it became almost totally devalued, by the title 'Don', and increasingly by the Habit which the rules of the Military Orders obliged their knights to wear.[33] Commonly in cities, listings distinguished between 'hidalgos simples' and 'hidalgos notorios' (Cordoba), or between 'hijodalgo' and 'caballero hijodalgo' (Cáceres), 'as a clearer distinction and designation of the quality of each individual'.[34] As Madame d'Aulnoy observed at the end of Charles II's reign, 'Here it is not enough to be rich; it is necessary also to be of quality.' Wealth was secondary to social position. Indeed, though uncommon, there are cases of *caballeros* of good families who claimed to be registered paupers. More important, although the *caballeros* dominated urban society, they were not necessarily the wealthiest members of that society. In the city of Cuenca, when in 1664 a *donativo* was assessed on 114 'wealthy householders regardless of status or privileges', of the thirty-three Dons only six, and included in them only five of the nineteen *regidores*, were in the top thirty-four assessments, and not one was in the top eight.[35] That suggests that there were social barriers which effectively prevented even the richest members of the community from entering the

33. M. Lambert-Gorges, 'Images de soi et de la noblesse ou un programme iconographique à l'usage des *hidalgos*', in Lambert-Gorges, *Hidalgos et hidalguía*, pp. 125–47, at pp. 135–7.

34. Aranda Doncel, *Historia de Córdoba*, p. 213; 'Calificación de la nobleza de Don Diego Antonio de Ovando', Cáceres, 26.6.1623, AHN [Archivo Histórico Nacional, Madrid] Ordenes Militares Calatrava, leg. 1901, f. 23v.

35. AM Cuenca, legajo 286 exp. 1, f. 108v–111 (22.10.1664).

charmed circle of the ruling oligarchy, or cultural inhibitions which disinclined them to do so.

Caballero denoted not just wealth and substance, but ostentation. This was the aim of the ambitious, wrote Cabrera in 1719, 'to live with the sumptuousness and splendour of the *caballeros*'. For acceptance into the ruling oligarchy of Cordoba, for example, it was thought necessary to be a '*caballero* of good intelligence, a good Christian, fearful of God and of his conscience, equable and peaceable, of great virtue, the owner of one of the richest entails in this city', and from a family recognized

as *caballeros hijosdalgo* and of the nobility of this city, having a mansion decorated with their escutcheons and servants and horses to accompany them, and participating with the other leading *caballeros* of the city in the cane jousting and fiestas held in the public squares.[36]

The cane jousts (*juego de cañas*) and the bullfights, described in meticulous detail by contemporary chroniclers, such as Granada's Henríquez de Jorquera, were not only an urban mode of chivalric exercise, a simulacrum of the nobility's military justification for its place in society, and displays of skill, horsemanship and personal bravery, for not uncommonly noble participants were killed by the bulls or their expensive horses destroyed under them, but also forms of self-identification and association by which the quality of a family was publicly accepted by its peers and the noble élite marked out from the rest of urban society.

Though related differently to the means of production, some as lords of vassals, some as owners of land or of urban real estate, others as beneficiaries of tithes, royal revenues and private *censos*, many as holders of *juros*, some as tax farmers, others as ministers of the Crown, agents of the aristocracy, or members of learned professions (lawyers, professors), the *caballeros* were almost exclusively an urban élite, sharing a common rôle in local power, and, in the seventeenth century as mercantile backgrounds receded and *letrado* values began to be absorbed into the cabalerresque, a common lifestyle, common attitudes to consumption, family and culture. They were usually interrelated, and married, almost entirely endogamously, with *caballero* families of their own and other cities.

The *caballeros* were also the body which provided almost the entirety of the middle and much of the upper cadres of the central administration, the judiciary, the army and the Church, the royal governors of the cities (the *corregidores*), the king's secretaries, councillors, and so on. They were thus a mediating group articulating country and Court, the chief beneficiaries of social and political circulation and the main forces of aristocratic renewal.

As has been said, the ordinary titled nobility (*títulos*) cannot be distinguished in any useful way from the *caballeros*, and recent researches have

36. AGS Cámara de Castilla, leg. 2299, 'Ynformacion y diligencias de las calidades de Don Francisco de Corral por ser 24° de Cordoba' (21.3.1591).

Table 6.1

	títulos	dukes	marquises	counts	revenues
1506	53	10	7	36	620,000
1530	69	14	14	41	1,340,000
1557	64	11	10	43	830,000+
1577	105	22	37	46	2,806,000
1597	127	23	46	58	4,145,000
1615	193	26	73	94	5,000,000
1630	212	27	81	104	5,833,000
		[41 *grandes* 1627]			
1665	236	[93 *grandes* 1659]			7,000,000
1700	533	[113]	334	171	
1787	654*	[119 *grandes*]			
1797	1,323				
1896	1,413	[207 *grandes*]			

in this respect confirmed the contemporary view.[37] As can be seen from the table, the titled nobility of the seventeenth and eighteenth centuries was a very new aristocracy. Some seven out of eight titles existing in 1700 had been created since 1550.[38]

That expansion, by quadrupling the number of titles in Spain in less than a century, was necessarily a cheapening of the *título*, not least in the very literal sense that it cost less in real terms to buy vassals than it had in the mid-sixteenth century, and peerages in Charles II's reign were – so it was said – going for an eighth of their cost earlier in the century. Nevertheless, it still required an acceptable level of wealth to be made a count or a marquis. The viscount of Casa Palma was refused a higher title by Philip IV because his income of 2,000 ducats a year was thought insufficient, and an adequate income, together with *hidalguía* and *limpieza de oficios*, was demanded of anybody who bid for one of the twenty-one titles put up for sale in Seville in 1679.[39] The explosion of titles in the seventeenth and eighteenth centuries was brought about mainly by the elevation of leading *caballeros*, for money, or for military and administrative services. One tentative analysis of new creations by Philip IV, estimated that about one-third were either already titled, or the sons of *títulos*, one-quarter granted for military and 30 per

37. S. Aragón Mateos, *La nobleza extremeña en el siglo XVIII* (Mérida, 1990), p. 98.

38. Numbers vary considerably depending on how courtesy titles are treated and as titles are absorbed. Figures for 1506 and 1557 from E. Albèri, *Le relazioni degli ambasciatori veneti* (15 vols; Florence, 1839–63), serie I, i. 23, iii. 263; for 1530 (probably on the high side), 1597, 1630 and 1700, from I. Atienza Hernández, *Aristocracia, poder y riqueza en la España moderna. La Casa de Osuna siglos XV–XIX* (Madrid, 1987), p. 41, and Atienza and Simón, 'Patronazgo Real', pp. 50–63; for 1577, BL Harleian MS 3315, f. 72; for 1615, BL Sloane MS 1573, f. 3; the mid-seventeenth century figures from Domínguez Ortiz, *Sociedad española en el siglo XVII* p. 200; the 1787 figure is for the Crown of Castile, A. Domínguez Ortiz, *Sociedad y Estado en el siglo XVIII español* (Barcelona, 1976), p. 349; 1797 for the whole of Spain, Anes, *Antiguo Régimen*, p. 48; 1896 207 *grandes* and 1206 *títulos*, R. Herr, 'Spain', in D. Spring, ed., *European Landed Élites in the Nineteenth Century* (Baltimore, Md., 1977), pp. 98–126, at p. 99.

39. Domínguez Ortiz, *Sociedad española en el siglo XVII*, p. 127; Atienza and Simón, 'Patronazgo', p. 32.

cent for administrative services of the recipient or his family.[40] There were some promotions of financiers, merchants and government contractors, and these are the ones which have received most attention, but they were a very small minority. That was certainly the case in Valencia, and in Extremadura, where, as a recent study has shown, of the thirty-eight resident *títulos* at the end of the eighteenth century, thirty-six had been created after 1621, all of them for accredited *caballeros*.[41] Therefore, although we still lack a full sociological analysis of this mass of elevations, it would be wrong to see in it evidence of a *social* revolution in the structure of the peerage. It was rather a clarification of existing social distinctions and economic power. As in England, the increase in the number of noble titles in the seventeenth century was in the first instance a response to a pent up demand that had been left unsatisfied in the later sixteenth century.

The significance of these new creations is not social but political. They were part of a process of the compression of nobility, a separation of the *caballero* from the *hidalgo*, a gradual transformation of nobility into aristocracy, and a devaluation of the 'natural' nobility of *hidalguía* in face of a 'Bartolist' honour, awarded as a royal grace at the will of the sovereign prince for services to the Crown. It was a process that was to find expression in the eighteenth century in the granting of non-territorial titles, not attached to lordship which implied a delegation of government over vassals, titles. which were purely honours, taking their names from the surnames of the grantee, or commemorating the very fact of the service itself – count of the Real Piedad, marquises of the Real Defensa, the Real Tesoro, the Real Transporte, preceded in that case by the viscountcy of the Buen Viaje, the honour awarded to Gutierre de Hevia for bringing the royal family from Naples in 1760.[42] The title, in other words, from being a ratification of the distribution of power within the state, was being transformed into a simple exaltation of service to the Crown.

At the top of the noble hierarchy were the grandees, originally, at the time they were so distinguished by Charles V in 1520, the heads of the great, extended families, like the Velascos, the Enríquez, the Manriques, the Mendozas, or the Zúñigas, a family which in the seventeenth century held some fifteen different titles among them. As Aguayo put it, the grandees 'are distinctive in everything', in wealth, in vassals, in their special relationship with the king. They alone had the right of access to the king, to remain covered in his presence, to carry his coffin, to be addressed as 'cousin', to be informed personally of the great events of State. They also stood at the summit of the hierarchy of aristocratic wealth, with revenues in 1597 put at between 50,000 and 170,000 ducats. A process of differentiation within the upper aristocracy had been going on throughout the sixteenth century: in 1520 the average income of the dukes

40. Fayard, *Conseil de Castille*, p. 338, from José Berní y Catalá, *Creación, antigüedad y privilegios de los Títulos de Castilla* (Valencia, 1769).

41. Casey, *Kingdom of Valencia*, p. 152 and n. 1; Aragón Mateos, *Nobleza extremeña*, p. 96.

42. A. Morel-Fatio, *Études sur l'Espagne*, 2ème série, *Grands d'Espagne et petits princes allemands au XVIIIe siècle* (Paris, 1890), p. 6.

Table 6.2

		dukes	marquises	counts
dukes	50–170,000 ducats			
marquises	10–110,000			
counts	4–120,000			
100,000 ducats or more		8	3	1
50–100,000		9	4	1
20–50,000			17	13
20,000 and under			16	27

of Spain was some 20 per cent more than that of the next rank of the peerage, the marquises; in 1620 it was 200 per cent more. The breakdown of aristocratic revenues at the end of the sixteenth century, according to the compilation made in 1597 by Pedro Núñez de Salcedo, is shown in Table 6.2.[43]

'Your Lordship may create as many *títulos* as you like,' advised Iñigo Ybáñez, in his forthright paper of advice to the duke of Lerma in 1599, 'but very few grandees'.[44] By the eighteenth century, they had risen from the forty-one in 1627 to more than one hundred, but only a score or two at the most were really of the first rank – Alba, Arcos, Béjar, Benavente, Cardona, Frías, Infantado, Medinaceli, Medina de Rioseco, Medina Sidonia, Nájera, and so on – most of them creations of the Trastamaran usurpation of the later fourteenth century.

The grandees represented great family complexes rather than individual titles. Their influence thus spread out through the entire noble hierarchy to link with the *caballeros* of cities like Cordoba and Seville, who were in great number related to one or more of the great Andalusian grandees, Alcaudete, Cardona, Alcalá, Arcos, Medina Sidonia. By the eighteenth century, however, the great nobility, whose origins antedated the mass creations of the seventeenth century, had coalesced through the accumulation of *mayorazgos* by inheritance and marriage, into a small number of multi-titled magnates. By the mid-nineteenth century, the dukedom of Osuna, from a modest beginning in 1460 as lord of Olvera, had come to accumulate a gigantic 22 per cent of all the noble revenues of Spain. The eleventh duke was also count-duke of Benavente, duke of Gandía, Béjar, Arcos, and a long list of other titles; the death of his uncle in 1841 then added the duchy of Infantado, with the dukedoms of Pastrana, Lerma, Medina de Rioseco, Estremera and Francavilla to the Osuna patrimony.[45]

43. From García España and Molinié-Bertrand, *Censo de Castilla*, pp. 86–7.
44. RAH [Real Academia de Historia, Madrid] Salazar y Castro K8, ff.30 et seqq., arguing that there should be no more than one grandee in any one *linaje*, 'nor should the king of Spain think so little of letting them who are not heads of lineages or lords of many vassals and great substance be covered in his presence. For this title Your Lordship could certainly require 40,000 ducats of income from vassalage' . . . 'everything I say is what the people are saying' ('todo lo que digo es la voz del pueblo').
45. Atienza, *Casa de Osuna*, pp. 71, 75 n. 10.

In 1902 the tenth duke of Berwick, seventeenth duke of Alba, thirteenth count-duke of Olivares, was a grandee of Spain thirteen times over. The formation of mega houses through this coalescence of titles set the grandees apart from the rest of the titled nobility as a group of national scope and importance. The duke of Cardona had the great patrimonial estates of his duchy in Catalonia, as duke of Segorbe in Valencia, as marquis of Comares in Andalusia. The duke of Osuna had estates from Andalusia and Valencia to Cantabria. With that progressive assimilation the old provincial aristocracies of Aragon, Catalonia and Valencia, always small in number, had ceased to exist, as such, by the end of the seventeenth century. There were only nine native Catalan *títulos* in attendance at the Corts of 1626. After 1623 only two of the eight great magnates of Valencia were resident in the kingdom, the duke of Gandía and the marquis of Guadalest, and Gandía moved to Madrid in the 1690s. Even lesser titles were merged in the same way, so that by the later part of the eighteenth century genuine provincial nobilities survived only at the lowest levels.

Though the grandees were never more than one-fifth even of the titled nobility, by the eighteenth century the *grandeza* was no longer what it had been at its institution in the early sixteenth century, a mark of the pre-eminence of the head of a great family, recognized by the Crown. Now extended to over 100 titles it was an honour bestowed on an individual or on a title by the king, another aspect of the shift from a family to a personal basis of éliteness.

Distanced from the local roots of its power, the greatness of the aristocracy resident at Court and in the capital could only be measured by appearances. Grandeur and the extravagant display of wealth were a necessary public manifestation of political and social standing. Aristocratic dispendiousness was a metropolitanised form of señorial power. The entire existence of the grandee has been described as 'consciously living as a spectacle'. When the duchess of Alburquerque visited Lady Fanshawe in Cadiz in 1665 she was a walking display cabinet for some 2,000 pearls, 'the roundest, the whitest, and the biggest that ever I saw in my life'. The Fanshawes were then entertained in the Puerto de Santa Maria by the duke of Medinaceli,

tables being plentifully covered every meal for above three hundred persons. The furniture was all rich tapestry, embroideries of gold and silver upon velvet, cloth of tissue, both gold and silver, with rich Persia carpets on the floors; none could exceed them. Very delicate fine linen of all sorts, both for table and beds, never washed, but new cut out of the piece, and all things thereunto belonging. The plate was vastly great and beautiful, nor for ornament were they fewer than the rest of the bravery, there being very fine cabinets, looking-glasses, tables, and chairs.[46]

46. B. Marshall, ed., *Memoirs of Lady Fanshawe* (London, 1905), pp. 157, 161.

Grandee culture, manners, economics and politics were paradigmatic of the aristocracy as a whole, though imitated by its lesser members in descending levels of emulation, the provincial nobility buying their French fashions in Madrid, or Seville, for example.[47]

LORDSHIP: *MAYORAZGO* AND *SEÑORÍO*

Aristocracy was an institution which subordinated the transitory individual to the lineage, the house and the family. The perpetuity of the aristocratic family was institutionalized in the *mayorazgo*. The *mayorazgo*, the legal basis of which was developed in the late Middle Ages and codified in the Laws of Toro of 1505, was a perpetual and hereditary property entail, unbreakable except with a specific royal licence, which in its passage through the generations left each possessor the enjoyment of its fruits, but without access to the tree. Its purpose was in the broadest sense political, to maintain the economic existence and hence the social functions of the family and its ability to meet its historical, moral and legal obligations to serve the Crown, and to perpetuate the memory of its founder and his, or her name, for women also could and did found *mayorazgos*.

It provided, therefore, the legal framework for the stability and cohesion of the family and for the regulation of its internal relations. Because most *mayorazgos* were inheritable in the female line as well, it was the instrument by which family growth was maintained and, consequently, for the gargantuan expansion in the size of the great Houses during the seventeenth and eighteenth centuries, and the corresponding reduction in their numbers. It was also one important reason why the aristocracy was obsessed with preventing any of their daughters from marrying beneath them. But, at the same time it was a source of dispute and expense. As different rules applied to different *mayorazgos* the accumulation of titles might only be temporary – the duchies of Osuna and Uceda were split in 1694, for example, because the former could only be inherited in the male line – and there was hardly a major *mayorazgo* that was not the object of protracted litigation or costly family settlements over the terms of its inheritance. At the same time, by making possible through the instrument of the *censo consignativo* massive interest-only borrowing against unliquidizable assets, it provided the means by which these and other irregular expenditures could be harmonized with income and the resources of the family mortgaged in perpetuity to fund individual dispendiousness, not merely for private luxury, but for the maintenance of the visible manifestations and justifications of social dominance, religious and charitable endowments,

47. Aragón Mateos, *Nobleza extremeña*, p. 380.

buildings, retinues, funerals, dowries, the establishment of second *mayorazgos* and independent titles for younger sons, and service to the Crown. The mayorazgo was thus a bond between Crown and aristocracy. The aristocracy needed the cooperation of the Crown to licence the individualization of the resources of the *mayorazgo*; the Crown needed to preserve the long-term institutional capital of the *mayorazgo* in the interests of its own service.[48]

The wealth and power of the aristocracy was based on lordship and land, on the exercise of the administrative functions of the state in the localities, and on influence and office at Court. The aristocratic hierarchy was essentially a hierarchy of wealth; but wealth of a certain sort, wealth that was solid, abiding and, most of all, visible (titles, land, property, offices, rights to Crown revenues and *censos* and *juros*, tapestries, furnishings, plate and jewellery); wealth that could be perpetuated and entailed in the *mayorazgo*.

The characteristic institution of aristocratic dominance in Spain was the *señorío*. Though most *señoríos* were of medieval origin, the process of señorialization continued throughout the Habsburg period and culminated in the first years of Charles II. In the Province of Toledo, four-fifths of the *señoríos* were in place before the sixteenth century. Whereas until that time they had almost always been royal donations, given for political purposes to the king's adherents, in the Habsburg period they were sold, for reasons that were purely financial. In the sixteenth century they were created largely by transfer from the Military Orders and the Church; in the seventeenth by the alienation of vassals from the royal domain.

At the end of the eighteenth century (1797 census) only half the cities, towns and villages, and roughly half the population of the kingdom were in the royal domain (*realengo*). Of the remainder, two-thirds were in lay lordship (*señorío*), and the rest under ecclesiastical jurisdiction. Although the great majority of cities were royal (126 of 148), the same was true of barely more than a third of the towns (1,700 of 4,700). In terms of area, according to a survey in 1811, just over half the land was in private, lay jurisdiction. In view of the chronological pattern of alienations and reincorporations of the royal domain, these figures are not likely to have changed much since the later seventeenth century. The importance of lay lordship varied considerably. It was weakest in the Basque Provinces and Murcia, where nearly 90 per cent was in the *realengo*; strongest in the provinces of Guadalajara, Toledo, Galicia, La Mancha, Valencia, Extremadura, Andalusia and Palencia, where less than 25 per cent was.[49]

The greatest nobles were lords of hundreds of towns and tens of

---

48. See C. Jago, 'The Influence of Debt on the Relations between Crown and Aristocracy in Seventeenth-Century Castile', *Economic History Review*, 2nd series, 26 (1973), 218–36.

49. The relative importance of the *señorío* at the end of the *ancien régime* is set out province by province in S. de Moxó, *La disolución del régimen señorial en España* (Madrid, 1965), pp. 6, 9, and G. Anes, *Los señoríos asturianos* (Madrid, 1980), p. 20.

thousands of vassals. The duke of Infantado was reputed to have some 800 towns and villages and the appointment of over 500 officials. In the province of Toledo alone, the count of Oropesa was lord of eighteen towns and villages and 100,000 hectares of territory; and in 1787 about 5 per cent of the total population of Extremadura, 20,821 vassals, was in the duchy of Feria. However, these holdings were often very dispersed – the seventy-five or more lordships of the duke of Béjar stretched from Cartaya in the extreme south-west of Spain to Navarre in the extreme north – and local lordship was frequently quite fragmented. In the Province of Toledo, in addition to the Archbishop and Oropesa, another seventy titled and untitled nobles shared the lordship of 137 towns and villages.[50]

The original form of the *señorío*, the *señorío solariego*, was territorial, a grant of land, with rights of jurisdiction; but from the fourteenth and fifteenth centuries, lordship was increasingly divorced from landownership. Of 335 *señoríos* in the Province of Toledo in the eighteenth century, the *señor* owned no land at all in 117; in 76.6 per cent of them he owned less than one-tenth of the territory; in only 15 per cent did he own over half. The territorial extent of the *señorío* should not, therefore, be confused with the ownership of the land within that *señorío*. The *señorío jurisdiccional* which was the preponderant form of lordship by the early modern period was purely a delegation of government and public functions giving rights and jurisdiction over *vasallos*, or over a territory. The *señorío* was in essence a piece of the administrative fabric of the state. The *señor* was a sort of 'perpetual *corregidor*'. He was, therefore, the intermediary between the king and the king's subjects, but always subject himself to the supervision and supreme jurisdiction of the Crown.[51]

Although there was enormous variation in the *señorío* over both time and space, with marked regional, and even local differences, the *señorío* consisted typically of three elements. First, jurisdiction and government. The lord had the right to appoint the justices and governing council of the towns of his *señorío*, usually by choosing from a list submitted by the town itself, though practice varied widely in this respect. The lord also had jurisdiction over both civil and criminal cases committed within his *señorío* ('jurisdicción civil y criminal, alta y baja, mero y mixto imperio'), appointing an *alcalde mayor* (chief justice) to review cases first sentenced by the justices of the towns, with appeal from him to the lord himself, or his judicial tribunal. Supreme jurisdiction, however, remained with the king, and all sentences of señorial courts could be appealed to the royal *chancillerías* in Valladolid or Granada, though not without some cost to the appellants. Only in Aragon, where the duke of Híjar had four officials of Belchite hanged without trial in 1599, did the lord claim virtually absolute

50. Toledo figures from, J. M. Donézar Díez de Ulzurrun, *Riqueza y propiedad en la Castilla del Antiguo Régimen. La provincia de Toledo en el siglo XVIII* (Madrid, 1984), p. 53, and S. de Moxó, *Los señoríos de Toledo* (Madrid, 1972), p. 38.

51. A. M. Guilarte, *El régimen señorial en el siglo XVI* (Madrid, 1962), p. 216.

judicial power over his vassals.[52] Although the right of life and death was falling into disuse, it was not formally eliminated until the eighteenth century. Secondly, rights of lordship. These included a variety of other señorial rights, both fiscal – small tributes in recognition of lordship, and economic – monopolies over mills, wine presses, butcheries, bakeries, the inn, or, in the case of Osuna, the brothel, exclusive fishing or hunting rights, sometimes market, entry or transit dues. Third, land rents of medieval origin. The value of these and the way they were exercised depended on where they were, when they had been granted, and how the land had been allocated by the original lords. In Old Castile the usufruct of the land (*dominio útil*) had generally been ceded in perpetuity to communities or individuals for a fixed charge, in money or in kind (*censo enfitéutico, foro*), an arrangement that by the early modern period was highly favourable to the tenant and of only modest return to the lord. In Andalusia, where the lords had established extensive señorial estates, the land was leased in large *cortijos* on revisable leases to large-scale, agrarian capitalists who worked the land with day labour. In Valencia lands and rents were leased in smaller units both to hereditary peasants and to more substantial farmers. The expulsion of the *moriscos* in 1609 had enabled a number of the lords to tighten their grip by imposing harsh terms on the new tenants who moved in to replace the *moriscos*, extending their manorial lordship into lordship over the land, shifting from fixed payments in coin (*censos*) to a share of the crop (*particiò*), and appropriating ex-*morisco* shops and ovens. Here also, in contrast to Castile, señorial dues and land rents had become confused, labour services continued in the seventeenth century, and regalian rights were in some places increased by 50 per cent. Thus the burden of señorialism in Valencia was always seen to be peculiarly oppressive. In Castile, on the other hand, there were hardly any traces remaining in the early modern period of personal services and the burden of the *señorío per se* was insignificant. Whereas in Valencia, which with one-twentieth of the population paid almost half the total of all señorial dues owed in Spain, the ordinary vassal household handed over 112 *reales* a year to its lord, in Asturias señorial dues averaged less than 1 *real* per person, per year, and in Alba de Tormes, the entire señorial element was no more than three-quarters of 1 per cent or so of the total product.[53]

Señorial jurisdiction, though directly of no great material value, could, however, be an indirect source of great economic power. It enabled the lord (through pressure, or control of the *concejo*, or town council) to encroach upon and privatize wastes, common lands and pastures; and it reinforced his powers of extraction of royal revenues alienated to him by

52. González Antón, *Cortes de Aragón*, p. 166; Colas Latorre and Salas Ausens, *Aragón bajo los Austrias*, p. 116.

53. A. Domínguez Ortiz, 'El fin del régimen señorial en España', in J. Godechot, et al., *La abolición del feudalismo en el mundo occidental* (Madrid, 1979), pp. 72–7, at p. 75; Anes, *Señoríos asturianos*, p. 121; J. P. Amalric in discussion in Godechot, *Abolición del feudalismo*, pp. 224–6.

the Crown or usurped during the political crises of the Trastamaran era. The appropriation of royal taxes, predominantly *alcabalas* and *tercias*, was the ideal solution to the crisis of stagnant señorial rents in the late Middle Ages, enabling the lords to increase their revenues at the expense of the Crown without the need to risk intensifying the pressure of the *señorío* on their own vassals. Tithes and royal taxes, though not properly part of the *señorío* and not always a monopoly of the *señor*, thus became by far the most important component of lordly incomes in Castile, though less so in Andalusia, and only the tithe applied in the Crown of Aragon. Already by 1499 the count of Benavente was getting over 70 per cent of his income from *alcabalas*. In the eighteenth century, 85 per cent of the income of the *señorío* of Alba de Tormes came from *alcabalas* and *tercias*, and 57.4 per cent of the total revenues of the estate of Osuna, compared with 37.6 per cent from land rents.

The nobility, whether *señores* or not, were also powerful landowners in their own right. Of the ninety-five richest private landowners in the Province of Toledo, with 12.9 per cent of total agricultural income, forty-nine were titled nobles with 10.14 per cent, thirty-four were Dons with 2.21 per cent, and only twelve mere *labradores* with the 0.55 per cent remaining. However, the nobility as a group did not entirely dominate proprietorship of the land. Nearly half the land area in Toledo was in institutional or communal ownership; but even of the share in private hands, the 157 members of the titled nobility who had properties in the Province owned less than a fifth; a further 3,189 Dons and lesser nobles owned another quarter.[54]

Given the dispersed nature of his landholdings, the titled nobleman was almost inevitably an absentee landlord who did not normally exploit his estates or his rights directly but leased them out on short-term contracts, generally of three to six years, or in the case of revenues in annual farms. All but one-fiftieth of the 11.5 per cent of the agrarian revenues of Toledo which pertained to the titled nobility went outside the province, almost entirely to Madrid. It was not, of course, always the case that there was no direct exploitation of the land; the most widespread exception, particularly in New Castile, Extremadura and Andalusia, being the ownership of flocks of sheep which were grazed on the lord's own pastures, or on those he expropriated from his villages, and the direct exploitation of olives by great *latifundistas*, like the dukes of Medinaceli and Alba, in Andalusia.[55] The *señorío* was not, however, primarily a unit of production and enterprise, but a unit of imposition and rent, and it was that balance

54. Donézar, *Provincia de Toledo* for all my information about the distribution of land and wealth in the Province of Toledo, esp. pp. 263 ff., 291–9.

55. In the mid-eighteenth century, the *señorío* of Buitrago (Guadalajara) was worth nearly 450,000 *reales* to the duke of Infantado, of which 365,000 was from the clip from 35,760 sheep owned by the duke; *alcabalas* and *tercias* (53,837) and señorial dues (18,502) together came to only 16.15 per cent, Grupo '73, *La economía del antiguo régimen. El señorío de Buitrago* (Madrid, 1973), pp. 155–8; M. A. Melón Jiménez, *Extremadura en el Antiguo Régimen. Economía y sociedad en tierras de Cáceres, 1700–1814* (Mérida, 1989), p. 386; A. M. Bernal, *Economía e historia de los latifundios* (Madrid, 1988), pp. 175–8.

which very much determined the strategy the lord was likely to adopt towards his vassals.

The breakdown of the estate revenues of the duke of Béjar demonstrates the relative importance of royal taxes, land and lordship for a substantial Castilian grandee in the early seventeenth century. Of his 98,100 ducats of income, something like half came from *alcabalas* and *tercias*; about one-third from land rents; 9 per cent from other real estate and *juros* on the Crown debt; and a mere 5 per cent or so from señorial dues.[56] That profile is perhaps not untypical of Castile; but there is in reality no typical *señorío* and thus no single 'señorial' attitude. The different structures and modes of exploitation of aristocratic economies in different regions of the country, and consequently the diversity of their economic interests, is illustrated nicely in the case of the late eighteenth-century duchess of Almodóvar, whose estates were spread across Valencia, Andalusia and Old Castile. Whereas in Valencia three-quarters of her income derived from señorial dues, in Andalusia and Castile over 85 per cent came from land rents.[57]

In Castile señorial authority as such was rather limited. It was widely regarded by the eighteenth century as largely symbolic, a vanity, for status rather than for revenue; as the marquis of San Felipe insisted, a 'jurisdición de dignidad', without the power to dispose of the lives or property of the vassals.[58] This contributed to what seems to have been a generally low level of hostility to the *señorío* in Castile. The murder of the Señor de Lozoya by fifteen of his vassals in 1646 was, as far as can be judged, a rather uncommon instance of anti-señorial violence, which contrasts with the repeated and widespread outbursts of anti-señorial revolt in the Crown of Aragon, and especially in Valencia, from the fifteenth to the nineteenth centuries.[59] There were a number of riots against señorial monopolies and grain profiteering in the crisis years of the middle third of the seventeenth century, but the ability of señorial communities to pursue their lords in the royal courts contributed to a generally more orderly settlement of the not infrequent disputes that arose.

Because in the *señorío* the lord confronted and negotiated not with individuals, but with organized communities of vassals with legal personalities, townships and village councils, the balance of power between lord and vassal was by no means always one-sided. Moreover, because local power was not exercised directly by the lord, but through the internal hierarchy of the local community, the *señor* could also emerge as the benefactor of those

56. C. J. Jago, 'The "Crisis of the Aristocracy" in Seventeenth-Century Castile', *Past and Present* no. 84 (1979), 60–90, at 65.

57. P. Ruiz Torres, 'Patrimonios y rentas de la nobleza en la España de finales del antiguo régimen', *Hacienda Pública Española* 108/109 (1987), 293–310, at 301.

58. Moxó, *Disolución*, p. 51.

59. A. García Sanz, *Desarrollo y crisis del antiguo régimen en Castilla la Vieja. Economía y sociedad en tierras de Segovia de 1500 a 1814*, 2nd edn. (Madrid, 1986), p. 374; J. M. Palop Ramos, *Hambre y lucha antifeudal. Las crisis de subsistencias en Valencia (Siglo XVIII)* (Madrid, 1977), pp. 111, 142–60; Colás Latorre and Salas Ausens, *Aragón bajo los Austrias*, pp. 134–50.

oppressed by the local *poderosos*. When in 1776 the justices of Zahinos petitioned the Crown for the right to nominate to offices which their lord, the marquis of San Juan, had previously appointed directly, they were opposed by the majority of the town who argued that he would be without the interests of family and friendship that would motivate the justices and would act as 'a true paterfamilias watching over everyone with prudent care'.[60]

The *señorío*, with the possibility of a protectionist and more indulgent fiscal regime, also offered an escape from the mounting pressure of the royal fisc. Indeed, in 1651 the Cordoban towns of the marquis of Priego and the dukes of Cardona and Sessa owed the treasury nearly 500,000 ducats in tax arrears which the opposition of their lords was making it impossible to collect.[61] The village of Navalperal, in Avila, certainly seems to have preferred the marquis of Las Navas as its lord, rather than as its landlord, petitioning the king in 1597 to allow the marquis to buy its jurisdiction and *alcabalas*, because as the owner of all the land he was squeezing their rents and leases so much that they were in debt and declining, but, they believed, 'If they were the marquis's vassals, he would help and relieve them, and they would not then be brought to depopulation and ruin.' From the reply of the Council, there were clearly other villages in a similar position.[62]

We have no way of knowing how many lords behaved as a *paterfamilias*, and how many did not. But it was the historic function of the *señor*, not as a great landed proprietor, but as a 'lord of vassals', as the founder, patriarch and protector of the community, that legitimated his social dominance and control, and it was to the maintenance and the public manifestation of that dominance that the economics, the getting and spending, of the aristocracy was geared.[63]

THE ARISTOCRACY, THE STATE AND THE COMMUNITY

It was the political rôle of the nobility which changed most over the course of the period. Royal policy from the Catholic Kings onwards was conventionally seen by contemporaries as designed to weaken the independent power of the aristocracy by destroying their military capability and impoverishing them with the high costs of Court and royal service, while relying on men of middling origins and professional formation for the real

---

60. 'Un verdadero padre de familias que atiende a todos con prudente economía', Aragón Mateos, *Nobleza extremeña*, p. 484.

61. A. Domínguez Ortiz, *El régimen señorial y el reformismo borbónico* (Madrid, 1974), p. 10.

62. AGS CJH [Consejo y Juntas de Hacienda] 254 (359), Council of Finance, 24.3.1597.

63. When the duchess of Almodóvar died in 1814, she left her entire personal wealth to provide dowries for the orphans of her towns and to found primary schools in each parish, Ruiz Torres, 'Patrimonios y rentas', p. 298.

work of government. If this interpretation carried an implicit criticism of the disruptive rôle of the aristocracy in preceding periods, it was often also more explicitly a criticism of absolutist attitudes that seemed to be subverting the traditional 'constitution' of the society of orders in which the nobility, standing between king and vassal, was the essential check on unlimited and arbitrary power.[64] The prescriptive right of the nobility as a body to advise, consent and command was part of the natural order which it was the duty of the king to defend and whose reputation, power and wealth it was politic to preserve as essential instruments for his own service and good government.

The restoration of royal authority at the end of the fifteenth century had a profound impact on the rôle of the aristocracy in the State. In a variety of ways during the sixteenth century many of the nobility's traditional sources of power were gradually eroded or weakened. Their capacity for large-scale organized violence gave way to litigation in the royal courts as the means of resolving conflicts with vassals, neighbouring cities, and baronial rivals. Although separate noble representation survived in the increasingly infrequent parliaments of the Crown of Aragon, in Castile, the aristocracy ceased, after their dismissal from the Cortes in 1539, to have a common forum for political action except within the play of factions at Court; while their rôle in counsel was challenged by the growing complexity and professionalization of government and the increased importance of judges and *letrados*. The extension of their influence in the cities was checked both by legislation and by the increased size and venality of the oligarchies, which made the cities steadily more difficult and more expensive to control.

The various contemporary representations of the gross incomes of the peerage between 1520 and 1630 point inescapably to a real change in the balance of power between aristocracy and Crown. At the accession of Charles V in 1516 the total income of the titled nobility was about the same as that of the king; by the accession of Philip II in 1556 it had fallen to about one-half, and by his death to about one-third; under Philip IV it was down to about one-fourth, despite the numbers of the peerage having tripled since the early sixteenth century.[65] That shift was related on the one side to an inability to keep revenues abreast of inflation, especially after 1580, and on the other to the restoration of a monarchical power capable both of checking the gratuitous dismemberment of the royal domain, which had sustained aristocratic rents in the fifteenth century, and of extracting an increasing proportion of the national product in centralized taxation.

Faced with this multiple challenge, the aristocracy had little option but to make its accommodation with the Crown if it was to get a share of the massive resources of the State. That meant the acceptance of a new

---

64. García Pelayo, 'El estamento de la nobleza en el despotismo ilustrado español', p. 52.
65. See Table 6.1 above, p. 191.

framework of order, not only in its relations with the Crown and in the directing of its own internal conflicts through the law and other institutional channels, but also in the regulation of personal behaviour and in the management of family affairs in ways which ranged from restraints on gambling to control of marriages and vetting of the terms of marriage settlements, in the interests of the honour and reputation of the families involved and of the preservation of their patrimonies, and hence of the king's service.

This new order was by no means entirely unacceptable to the aristocracy in general, even if not to particular individuals, so long as it was postulated on the enforcement of the values of the society of orders and reinforced the pre-eminence of aristocracy within that society. It offered a welcome escape from violence into mediation or litigation, which though not cheap was cheaper than war, and, if more protracted, could also be made more predictable. When in 1590 the duke of Alcalá appealed to the king to act as the instrument of his 'venganza y satisfacion' after the duke of Alba had jilted his daughter, he was explicitly asking not to have to come with all his relatives to seek leave 'to pursue in person justice for his daughter and for the insult done to his house and relatives'.[66] It served to buttress the authority of the family, the father, and of the lord, for the royal courts were in practice more likely than not to find in favour of lords against their vassals. Finally, it provided protection against the meltdown of the family's finances. Long before the last resort was reached the Crown would step in to defend the *mayorazgo* from its creditors, defer interest payments, reduce rates, put the estate into administration, arrange a settlement, and restrain the expenses of the individual in order to preserve the integrity of the House.[67]

The challenge to the authority of the aristocracy came less from the king and his inner circle of advisers, who had every practical interest in a rich, powerful, respected, but obedient aristocracy, than from judges and lawyers who, much more than the king himself, embodied a regalist conception of jurisdiction and authority. The duke of Medinaceli's complaint about the treatment of the duke of Cardona after his clash with a judge on his estate of Lucena – 'The authority of his grandees is more important to the king than the formalities of his judges'[68] – exemplified the inherent contradiction between two different conceptions of government. The repeated clashes between the aristocracy and the judges reflected the fact that the capacity of the great lord to extricate not only himself but also

---

66. IVDJ [Instituto Valencia de Don Juan, Madrid] envío 43, f. 122, *junta* of 27.7.1590.

67. Typical was the opposition of the Cámara to the duke of Infantado's request for leave to take a *censo* on his *mayorazgo* to meet his expenses for the visit of the Prince of Wales in 1623: 'the less encumbered the *mayorazgos* are the better it is for Your Majesty's service whenever occasions for great expenditures arise, both within and without the Kingdom, otherwise when these occur they will not have anything' ('que quanto más desempeñados están los mayorazgos, biene a arredundar en mayor servicio de Vuestra Magestad por las ocasiones que, así en el Reyno como fuera del, se ofrezen de tan grandes gastos, pues quando estas subcedan no allarán'), AHN Consejos leg. 4422, 1623, n. 191 (1.10.1623).

68. B L Egerton Ms 347, f. 170, copy Medinaceli to D. Luis de Haro, 29.8.1655.

his clients and retainers from the due process of the law was, in the post-baronial world, a visible mark of his effectiveness as a patron and a protector.

The problem for the Crown was how to keep the grandees simultaneously powerful but dependent. The massive patronage of the worldwide Spanish Monarchy – with its 183 *encomiendas* of the Military Orders, its *patronato* over the Church and eighty-one bishoprics and archbishoprics, its *tercios* and *armadas*, its twenty-odd viceroyalties and forty-six captaincies general, its governorships, *audiencias, corregimientos,* conciliar, Court and household offices – was one instrument; the legal powers of the Crown to modify *mayorazgos* and to licence the long-term mortgaging of their revenues, to set interest rates and control the judicial process was another. These were powerful weapons to which it was rare for a great nobleman to be entirely indifferent, and there were few grandees who did not depend to a greater or lesser extent on the rewards of royal service or royal favour. But at the same time the resources of the aristocracy in followers, money and, above all, authority were not yet easily dispensed with while the Crown lacked an adequate machinery of local administration and control. The dependence of the aristocracy on the Crown did not thereby liberate the Crown from need of its aristocracy, and did not either threaten the general pre-eminence of aristocracy within society or make ineffective their domination of their particular localities.

If in the past the interests of the Crown and the aristocracy have tended to be seen as antagonistic, the more recent perception among Spanish historians, frequently following the lines suggested by Perry Anderson in his *Lineages of the Absolutist State*, is of Crown and aristocracy in a more or less tacit alliance in which the early modern monarchical state acted as the centralized instrument of feudal domination and extraction, or alternatively as the paymaster whose resources were an unavoidable recourse for an aristocracy in crisis. Whether that relationship is regarded as a 'monarcho-señorial regime', as a domestication of the aristocracy, or as an unresolved struggle between absolutist monarchy and feudal nobility for control of the surplus product of the land, the formal supremacy of the Crown was not at issue, however much the actual political balance had to be regulated by a series of transactions which preserved for the nobility its social dominance whilst asserting the ultimate authority of the Crown over the State as a whole.

Within that framework, therefore, aristocratic power emerged from the initial challenge of the 'modern state' altered, but not necessarily weakened. Contemporaries were fairly cynical about the capacity of the great nobility to manipulate the machinery of government and justice. The Savoyard ambassador in 1711, for example, was one who commented on the subservience of justice to the 'grandees, whose power and estimation have been till now excessive', partly because under a weak king ministers fearful of factions needed their support. At Court, in government, war and diplomacy, and, though less absolutely, in the Church, all the most prestigious posts were given to men with the prestige to match them. Most of the councillors of State and of War, and many of the presidents of the other councils as well – and even more so in the seventeenth than in the sixteenth century – were titled noblemen, as were almost all the viceroys, generals and plenipotentiaries. Of course, these were not always the posts most influential in the inner processes of policy-making, but that had ever been the case. The grandees wanted to share the presence of the king, to be counsellors, governors, or generals, not secretaries, or judges.

Nevertheless, it would be wrong to imagine that the aristocracy refused *tout court* to equip itself, or at least its younger sons, with the skills required for a professional rôle in government. Kagan estimates that 5–10 per cent of the aristocracy had sons enrolled in the universities, mostly studying law; not many in his view, but the evidence is very incomplete. In any case, the education of the aristocracy mostly took place privately, outside the universities, and was not on that account necessarily less satisfactory. The 302 judges of the Council of Castile between 1621 and 1746 were *hidalgos* almost without exception; some 10 per cent of them were directly descended from the titled nobility; in excess of another 30 per cent came from *caballero* families, a substantial minority of which had a tradition of administrative service. The aristocracy was a long way from having a leading rôle in this most learned and technical area of government, but it was by no means excluded from it.[69] It was part of a much wider diversification of the traditional military and conciliar functions of the great nobility.

Nor was the decline of the aristocracy's military power as complete or as rapid as is sometimes imagined. Although the demilitarization of the nobility and the abandonment of violence by the aristocracy as an instrument of politics have been seen as a key element in their subordination to the new absolutist state, the great nobility maintained a continuing military potential and associated capacity for violence during the sixteenth and seventeenth centuries. As late as 1638, the duke of Medina Sidonia, leading a force into Portugal to suppress the revolt in Evora, entered Ayamonte with 300 horse and 8,000 infantry raised on his estates and those of his cousin, the marquis of Ayamonte. Not only did the Crown not seek to undermine this capacity of the grandees to mobilize the men of their estates, but royal policy was consistently directed to preserving and exploiting it – under strict control – partly as a covert form of taxation and partly to offset the inadequacies of its own military administration.

Similarly, it was almost obsessively concerned with the personal re-militarization of the nobility through the formation of a series of social or educational establishments to promote the military spirit and the requisite

69. R. L. Kagan, *Students and Society in Early Modern Spain* (Baltimore, Md., 1974), pp. 128–9, 178, 227–8, and 'Olivares y la educación de la nobleza española', in J. H. Elliott and A. García Sanz, eds, *La España del Conde Duque de Olivares* (Valladolid, 1989), pp. 225–47; according to J-M. Pelorson, *Les 'Letrados' juristes castillans sous Philippe III* (Le Puy-en-Velay, 1980), p. 216, it was very uncommon to find sons of the highest nobility at Salamanca in the reign of Philip III, but a conversion to letters was apparent at the level of *títulos* and *caballeros*; for the Council of Castile, Fayard, *Conseil de Castille*, pp. 334–9, 281–2, 553.

expertise – guilds in the 1570s, noble academies under Olivares, *maestranzas* and the militia in the reign of Charles II, cadetships in that of Philip V, military colleges under Charles III. The commonplace notion of an aristocracy that was abandoning its historic function of *defensores* is not well established. The reality is that we have no adequate basis for comparing the personal military activity of the nobility across centuries. Early modern warfare was more demanding of time and commitment. A remarkable number of noblemen participated in the glamour campaigns of Tunis, Lepanto and the Armada, with no intention of pursuing a military career. The apparent crisis of aristocratic demilitarization in the seventeenth century was the result in part of a need for a larger military participation ratio, and in part of an attempt to remilitarize the nobility and revive the military functions of institutions like the Military Orders, which had become purely political and social in function, just at the moment when military service was being demeaned and proletarianized by conscription. It may be, as foreign commentators reported, that in the second half of the seventeenth century the grandees derided those who went to the wars,[70] but the real problem was not so much an aversion to the profession of arms, as the nobility's demand for the social hierarchy of status to be imposed upon the professional hierarchy of the soldier. As the Council of Castile complained in 1654, 'the *hidalgo* requires a substantial wage with a gentleman's bonus before he will go to war; the *caballero* a post that would flatter him even after several years of service; and those higher up will not begin without rewards that would be honours worthy of a victory they had won for Your Majesty'.[71] Yet for untalented and unmarriageable younger sons of the lesser nobility, military service remained, with the Church, one of the few openings available. Even in the eighteenth century, something like one in three adult, male nobles in Extremadura followed a military or naval career, despite the high costs, the irregular pay, and promotion prospects which were only attractive for the more powerful, titled families.[72]

It was partly because it still held a virtual monopoly of armed force at the local level that the nobility continued to retain so much of its power in the country. Surveys of weapons held in the cities and their regions in the late sixteenth century show the *caballeros* to have had almost all the horses and arquebuses in private hands, and the old, castled aristocracy to have veritable arsenals of cannon, firearms and armour. Even in the mid-seventeenth century, the marquis of Las Navas had twenty-five pieces of artillery in Las Navas which he donated to the king (1637); as they were worth 30,000 ducats they must have been very substantial pieces. The duke of Medina Sidonia had even more, forty-two in 1639. The duke of

70. J. García Mercadal, ed., *Viajes de Extranjeros por España y Portugal*, vol. 2 *Siglo XVII* (Madrid, 1959), p. 651 (Bertaut, 1659); J. M. Díez Borque, *La sociedad española y los viajeros del siglo XVII* (Madrid, 1975), p. 192 (Grammont, 1659).

71. BL Egerton Ms 332, f. 286, Council of Castile, November 1654.

72. Aragón Mateos, *Nobleza extremeña*, pp. 430, 457, 465.

Infantado's armoury in Guadalajara in 1643 contained nearly 400 muskets and arquebuses. Great lords, like the duke of Medina de las Torres who had with him 270 attendants when he left for Naples to take up his vice-royalty in March 1636, could still summon entourages of hundreds of men in the mid-seventeenth century, and leading local families muster armed men in their scores.[73]

Organized inter-noble violence, though on a much smaller scale than in the fifteenth century and generally contained within specific regions, such as the remote corners of Murcia and Asturias, had still not entirely died out, even if, as in Valencia and Catalonia, it concealed itself behind the surrogate of banditry. Moreover, just as local nobles provided the only real forces of law and order against popular disturbance in the cities, so, as often as not, armed resistance to royal officals, tax-collectors, or justices came from cadets of the local nobility, making the cooperation of that local nobility indispensable for effective royal government. In Jerez de la Frontera in 1660, the Villavicencios and the Avilas had over 200 men protecting their relative, the ex-*corregidor* and administrator of taxes, against judicial investigation. In Malaga, in 1683, the son of the count of Puertollano and his uncle headed a gang of contrabandists, which included two knights of the Military Orders, eight other Dons and 'one of the leading gentlemen of the city'. There were similar reports from other cities in Andalusia, such as Andújar and Jaén.[74] The nobility of the seventeenth century was still a violent, if not a military élite, slow to be brought under control. The tightening of anti-duelling legislation in the late seventeenth century, after two hundred years of legislative silence, and the fierce new prohibitions imposed by Philip V are perhaps indications of a recrudescence even of aristocratic violence and of a new reluctance by the nobility to surrender itself and its right of private satisfaction for injury to the common justice of the king and his ministers.[75]

Nevertheless, the armed *bandos* and affinities through which the aristocracy in the fifteenth century had tried to control the cities in which they lived and had an interest, had lost much of their force and cohesiveness. The great nobles were having to find more discreet ways of infiltrating their adherents into city government. Influence at Court was now the key to procuring the reissue of escheated *regimientos* and to buying for their clients the local offices being put up for sale by the Crown. In the longer term, however, the continued increase

---

73. A notable example being the affray in Cordoba in May 1642 between two companies of soldiers of the Inquisition and the followers of D. Pedro de Cárdenas, who assembled all his relatives and other *caballeros* to prevent by force of arms his son being ejected from a house, the lease of which was disputed by the Inquisition; the *corregidor* had to intervene to warn the Inquisition against 'exposing the poor militiamen of the Tribunal to the fury of the *caballeros* who were awaiting them armed and angry', *Memorial Histórico Español*, xvi.366.

74. For Jerez, Philip IV to D. Juan de Góngora, 16.9.1660, AGS CJH 806 (1109); Council of Finance, 13.10.1682, AGS CJH 1069 (1462); for Malaga, *Oidor* D. Luis Francisco de Villamarín, 2.2.1683, 'Memoria de los metedores más principales de la ciudad de Málaga', AGS CJH 1069 (1462).

75. *Novísima Recopilación* (1805), v. 393, lib. 12, tit. 20, leyes 1–3, decrees of 29.8.1678, 16.7.1716, 21.10.1723, 28.4.1757.

in the number of new *regimientos* created and sold by the Crown made it more difficult and more expensive to preserve a majority in the councils. By the seventeenth century, offices were no longer allocated equally between the *bandos*, which had either atrophied or were serving a largely ceremonial function. This must have been a serious blow to the influence of the local aristocrat because it ruptured the link between Court influence and local patronage, and in effect made the grandee have to pay for whatever local influence he wanted to exert. This was something not restricted to municipal government. The division of the cathedral chapter of Pamplona between Agramonteses and Beamonteses, of whom the duke of Alba was still regarded as the head in 1592, had also disappeared in 1628.[76] There were places, particularly in the former frontier regions of Extremadura, Andalusia and Murcia, where the old aristocratic *bandos* still survived as effective power blocs, covering a wide geographical area and extending vertically down through the nobility to embrace the common people as well, as Bennassar found in Andújar.[77] In Extremadura, especially in Trujillo, Cáceres and Plasencia, it was said in the early seventeenth century that 'it is not only the important people who are factious, but even the ordinary people and the commons are divided between Carvajales and Ovandos', the former related to the counts of Osorno, the latter to the marquises of Mirabel.[78] But even here a hundred years later, the *bandos* had ceased to be either a political or a social reality.

By the seventeenth century there were only a few royal cities where a single great nobleman directly controlled the government by means of a bloc of his clients on the council. The duke of Infantado in Guadalajara and the marquis of Mirabel in Plasencia, where the marquis owned no less than nineteen voting offices in the *ayuntamiento*, as well as both the clerkships of the council, were perhaps the outstanding examples. In many other royal cities and towns the aristocracy still had a presence in the government but usually on an individual basis, as holders of their most honorific hereditary offices (*alférez mayor, alguacil mayor*). The personal influence of the local great lord – Cañete in Cuenca, Chinchón in Segovia, Cerralbo in Ciudad Rodrigo, Santisteban in Jaén, Alba de Aliste in Zamora – so often called upon to support the king's causes in the cities, continued to be powerful, though perhaps less effective than in the sixteenth century, and in some regions more than in others. Of the Almirante de Castilla it was said that 'in Valladolid, he is king and lord, adored and revered as such, and applauded by all'.[79] In Galicia the influence of the counts of Lemos, Altamira and Monterrey, who all had *regimientos* in each of the

76. Junta in Valladolid, 17.7.1592, IVDJ envío 45, f. 475; A. Domínguez Ortiz, *La sociedad española en el siglo XVII*, vol. 2 *El estamento eclesiástico* (Madrid, 1970), p. 46.

77. B. Bennassar, 'Contribution à l'étude des comportements en Andalousie à l'époque moderne: vivre à Andújar au début du XVIIe siècle', *Les mentalités dans la Péninsule ibérique et en Amérique latine aux XVIe et XVIIe siècles* (Tours, 1978), pp. 85–100.

78. Francisco Núñez de Velasco (1614), quoted in J. Caro Baroja, 'Honour and Shame: a historical account of several conflicts', in J. G. Peristiany, ed., *Honour and Shame. The Values of Mediterranean Society* (London, 1965), pp. 81–137, at p. 127 n. 36.

79. Jago, 'Crisis', p. 87.

seven cities with a vote in the Cortes, as well as that of the Archbishop of Santiago, seems to have been much greater than that of their peers in other parts of Castile. Lemos was able to persuade the Orense city council to change its voting procedures in order to elect him as its *procurador* to the Cortes of 1646, and when he was elected by Mondoñedo for the same Cortes, got them to put his fourteen-year-old son in his place. In the Crown of Aragon, the fact that municipal offices were neither hereditary nor venal, but balloted every year, meant that magnate influence in the towns and cities could not operate as easily as it did in Castile. That is not to say that the arteries of clientage did not reach into the cities, but that they were more complex, and perhaps more tenuous, than they were in Castile.

It was the lesser nobility, however, the *caballero* oligarchies of the cities, who really dominated municipal government. Their relationship with the great Court nobility was ambiguous. In places such as Cordoba, where so many of the councillors were related to one or more of the great Cordoban grandees, the marquis of Priego, the counts of Alcaudete and Palma, the dukes of Sessa, Maqueda and Cardona, marquis of Comares, the city was an aristocratic redoubt. But in other cities there are indications that the ennoblement of the councils from the end of the sixteenth century, with the presence of knights of the Orders, lords of vassals and new *títulos*, was reflected in a greater assertiveness and a new resistance to the dominance of the great noble, seen in the opposition to his acquisition of honorific offices, rejection of aristocratic brokerage of services to the Crown, hostility to penetration of the city councils by courtiers and to the appointment of *regidores* in the employ of the aristocracy. In Plasencia, for example, there were many lawsuits between royal *regidores* and those of Mirabel, who unashamedly employed his influence at Court in the 1670s to block resumptions of offices and other attempts by opposing *regidores* to curb his power.

Despite some exceptions, the decline of direct aristocratic influence in the cities by the mid-seventeenth century was palpable. This was, however, a crisis of the local community and of the political rôle of the city as much as of aristocratic power. The aristocratic affinity had been, as Bennassar puts it, an 'astonishingly powerful force of integration of urban society'.[80] Its disappearance was a major step in the rearticulation of the community from a society of vertical bonds to one of horizontal bands.

The brokerage of power between Court and country by the great Court nobility, by means of the patronage they exercised in the cities and over *regimientos* of the city councils, had been the key to the functioning of the Lerma and Olivares regimes in the first half of the seventeenth century through the establishment of ministerial parties in the major Cortes cities. Influence in the cities enabled grandees to participate in the Cortes, either for their own personal interests or as part of a ministerial management team. But after the fall of Olivares in 1643, and with the failure of representatives of the cities to assemble in the Cortes after 1664, the cities

80. Bennassar, 'Vivre à Andújar', p. 86.

became disconnected from central power in the capital, and the great aristocracy, almost never resident in the cities any longer, abandoned them as power bases. The *regimientos* that they owned were served by substitutes, or even rented out, possibly on a purely commercial basis. By the later seventeenth and eighteenth centuries the aristocracy seems to have lost interest in controlling the cities which had ceased to have a national political rôle, and to have concentrated their attentions on the capital. Symptomatic was the transfer by the duke of Béjar, among the most provincial of the grandees, of his main residence to Madrid in 1656. The lesser titled nobles often remained in the provinces, but the more important aristocracy was almost entirely metropolitanized. The city council of Cordoba is a striking example. Of the twenty offices held by titled noblemen in 1746, all but four were vacant, and only one was being served actively.[81] The need for a voice for the aristocracy as a whole, which in 'absolutist' periods was expressed in thoughts of a restoration of a noble chamber in the Castilian Cortes, was satisfied in the reign of Charles II through grandee first ministers and the Council of State. Under the Bourbons, with the emasculation of the conciliar system, the Court and, perhaps even more important, Madrid society were to serve as substitutes for the loss of direct involvement in government decision-making.

THE 'CRISIS OF THE ARISTOCRACY'

The seventeenth century has been characterized as a period both of 'aristocratic crisis' and of 'refeudalization'. The aristocracy was faced with a concurrent economic, financial and political crisis from which, paradoxically, the señorial regime emerged permanently extended and reinforced and the aristocracy temporarily with a controlling position within the State.[82]

The equilibrium of the sixteenth century had been sustained by a long period of economic growth which both kept señorial incomes buoyant and enabled the Crown to increase its revenues directly from trade and taxation. The cessation of growth, while it did not reduce costs, particularly the fixed obligations to which both royal and señorial incomes had become subjected, forced the Crown to demand financial and military contributions from an aristocracy whose rents were rapidly falling behind the movement of prices. If one can trust the not always well-based lists of contemporary commentators, the gross revenues of the dukes extant in 1520, after more than tripling in sixty years, barely did more than stagnate between 1580 and 1620, during which time the general price level rose by some 40 per cent.

Already by the early seventeenth century, well before the collapse of

81. M. Cuesta Martínez, *La ciudad de Córdoba en el siglo XVIII* (Córdoba, 1985), p. 48.
82. I owe a great deal of what follows to Charles Jago's superb article on 'The "Crisis of the Aristocracy" in Seventeenth-Century Castile', *Past and Present* no. 84 (1979), 60–90.

their incomes in the 1630s and 1640s, a large part of the aristocracy was heavily in debt. Two-thirds of the 747,309 ducats mortgaged against the rents of the *mayorazgo* of Benavente between 1531 and 1612, had been imposed prior to 1574. In 1623 the duke of Infantado claimed that his House had debts of over 800,000 ducats, and in the same year the duke of Feria was paying 59,000 ducats in interest on loans that must have exceeded one million ducats. Commonly about a third, and sometimes as much as two-thirds of a grandee's revenues was being spent to service his debts. At the start of Philip IV's reign, the Luccan ambassador, Burlamacchi, attributed the visibly parlous state of aristocratic finances to the expenses of their rank and their services to the Crown. However, by far the most important part of the debt was created by dowries and other investments for the improvement of the *mayorazgo* and the maintenance or advancement of the status of the House. Only after 1580 did military expenditures and other costs in the service of the Crown come close to matching what was spent on dowries. But only by ignoring the social, economic and political functions of aristocratic marriages can that indebtedness be thought of as the penalty for maladministration and economic incompetence rather than, as Bartolomé Yun puts it, a consequence of the 'contradiction between the social legitimizing function of the *señorío* and the nature of the specific rhythm of señorial revenue'.[83]

The 'crisis of the aristocracy' was thus the combination of a legacy of indebtedness from the sixteenth century exacerbated by falling agricultural revenues and simultaneous fiscal pressure from the Crown, aggravated in Valencia by the expulsion of a third of the population in 1609 and for lords with Extremaduran, Leonese and Galician estates by the war on the Portuguese frontier in 1641–68. The decline of rents, however, pre-dates 1641 and is general everywhere except in Andalusia, where Bernal argues adaptation by increasing product specialization stopped señorial revenues from falling and provided the material basis for the political predominance of the Andalusian aristocracy in the seventeenth century.[84] Elsewhere, the economic crisis of the aristocracy was the result of a long-term decline in agricultural output going back to the end of the previous century, together with a series of deflations, the first for 100 years, beginning in 1628–9 and introducing a long period of monetary instability which was not ended until the 1680s. Where leases and tax-farms were short, as they were on the Béjar estates, rents were sensitive to the movement of prices and output. In the duchy of Feria, after a modest increase of 7 per cent in 1623–35, revenues fell by 44 per cent by 1641; leases of pasture, in particular, were down 76 per cent. The 1640s, 1650s and 1660s were decades of almost total financial collapse from which a sustained recovery began only in the 1670s. Between 1635 and 1670 rents were barely a third

---

83. B. Yun Casalilla, 'Consideraciones para el estudio de la renta y las economías señoriales en el reino de Castilla (s. XV–XVIII)', in *Señorío y feudalismo en la Península Ibérica (siglos XII–XIX)* (Zaragoza, 1993), pp. 1–35, at p. 15.

84. Bernal, *Latifundios*, pp. 40, 44, 167.

of the 50,000 ducats of 1600; between 1706 and 1725 they did not much exceed 20,000; and not until after 1762 did they surpass in real terms the 1600 figure. Though less spectacularly, the duke of Béjar's revenues fell between 1628 and 1660 by 17 per cent, and the count of Benavente's by 20 per cent between 1638 and 1643. Given that Benavente's gross revenues of 61,000 ducats in 1638 left him with an income net of fixed obligations of less than 12,000 ducats, it is easy to see that this was a crisis caused not by profligacy or mismanagement, but by the problem of servicing the debt on encumbered estates in a time of economic adversity. The *mayorazgo* ensured capital stability but restricted the liquidity needed in such circumstances to meet the high fixed expenses of the aristocratic economy. Of the 99,102 ducats that the duke of Béjar spent in 1642, 23,200 was earmarked for the servicing of the debt, 21,000 for contractual family stipends, 13,000 for the administration of the estate, 27,100 for household expenses, including the seventy plus domestic servants, and 12,000 for personal spending; he was left with a deficit of 8,000 ducats.[85]

On top of this the aristocracy had to face unprecedented demands on their resources from the Crown, in the form of donatives, the commutation of knight service (*lanzas*), dues on offices and pensions (*medias anatas*), the retention of interest payments on *juros*, personal military service, the raising of *tercios*, compositions for the recovery of *alcabalas* and jurisdictions, as well as the huge increases in indirect taxes on meat and wine, and on luxuries like chocolate, brandy and ice, which were contained in the services of the *millones*, and a tax on rents introduced in 1642. The belief that because the Castilian nobility enjoyed the immunity of the *hidalgo* from the *personal* taxation of the *servicios* they were unaffected by these taxes on consumption and wealth is quite wrong. It was the privileged and the wealthy who were the immediate victims of the fiscal arbitrariness that was at its height during the ministry of Olivares. It could be that as much as 60 per cent of the 140 million ducats, or so, of new royal income raised between 1621 and 1640 came from the pockets of the upper classes. The count of Chinchón paid over 70,000 ducats in forced loans between 1633 and 1645; the duke of Osuna spent over 100,000 in sixteen years on the raising of regiments and other services; the marquis of Poza was owed 277,000 for *medias anatas*, retained and unassigned *juros*, costs of military levies, and losses on alterations of the coinage, all incurred between 1647 and 1664. Some, like the count of Oropesa, who sold a town of 300 households, together with its *alcabalas* and its mill, had to be given permission to sell off part of their inheritances to meet the charges; others, it was said, asked to relinquish their titles, or to be allowed to sell them. As one of the bitterest opponents of the Olivares regime complained, the Crown was in effect depriving the nobility of its fiscal immunity:

85. Jago, 'Crisis', p. 75.

Nobles and villeins, the great and the humble, all paid and were taxed at whatever sums were asked of them, or they were assessed for. That was done with the full rigour of the law, sequestrating their property and sending bailiffs against them in the same way as against the most ordinary husbandman.[86]

The crisis was thus also a political crisis for the aristocracy. The emergence of the *valido* as an instrument of government in the seventeenth century, the revivification of the Councils of State and War at the accession of Philip III, the adolescent militarism of the new king, the expansion of the size and cost of the Court had all signalled a recapture of royal government by the great nobility (or a recapture of the great nobility by royal government) after the death of Philip II. But with the ministry of Olivares, what under his predecessor, the duke of Lerma, had been an internal conflict of aristocratic factions became a political crisis of the aristocracy as a whole. The attempt of Olivares to isolate the king, by-pass the aristocrat-dominated councils, reform, remilitarize and reeducate the aristocracy, together with the fiscal and military demands to which they were subjected, enforced by special judicial commissioners (*jueces de comisión*), undermined the entire political standing of the great nobleman as broker of patronage and as patron and protector of his vassals. Symptomatic of the perceptions of the aristocracy was the comment (by no means isolated) of the duke of Béjar's brother, made in 1641 in support of his desire for a university education, 'If before, grandees were greater than *letrados*, now *letrados* have become the grandees.' As the context makes clear, this was a political not a social comment. The threat from the *togado* was ideological; it denied the 'aristocratic constitutionalism' of the society of orders, and asserted a legal authoritarianism which overrode all privileges and prescriptive rights.

The aristocracy reacted to this cumulation of pressures in a variety of ways. Some made determined efforts to sharpen the management of their properties and revenues, to improve their *mayorazgos*, cut down expenses, and consolidate their *censos* in order to reduce interest charges. The dukes of Cardona and Infantado were reputed to be diligent landowners. The duke of Béjar immediately responded to the decline in his revenues by sending an accountant to investigate, though his attempts to secure stricter administrative control, not helped by the wide dispersal of his estates, produced only limited results. Central control was difficult when a necessarily absentee aristocracy had to depend on estate treasurers, themselves substantial peasants or *hidalgo* 'poderosos', with their own interests as local proprietors, usurping ducal lands and rents.

Another response was to screw up the exploitation of estate rents and *alcabalas*, pursuing debts with greater vigour, enforcing monopolies more rigorously, attempting to transform their *dominio eminente* or jurisdiction into a right of property, or to assume rights of jurisdiction where they only had ownership, and rejecting the authority of local officials to intervene in their appropriation and enclosure of common lands and pastures.

86. Matías de Novoa, *Historia de Felipe IV* (Madrid, 1881), vol. 2, p. 103.

The extent of this 'señorial reaction' is suggested by the aggravation of conflict between the lord and the communities of his *señorío*. There is some evidence of a partial breakdown in relations between *señores* and vassals in the middle decades of the seventeenth century. It was partly, as one Venetian ambassador observed, a loss of respect for lords who were unable to defend their vassals against the fisc, partly a loss of confidence in royal justice which left a choice between submission and violence. There were anti-señorial riots in a number of places in central Andalusia in 1647, where lords, like the duke of Cardona and the marquis of Priego were notorious speculators in wheat and wine.[87] On the Béjar estates no less than seven riots, led for the most part by the local *alcaldes ordinarios*, took place between 1628 and 1673, and during the years 1628–60 the duke was engaged in major litigation with the city of Béjar over the appointment of officials, the use of the commons and jurisdiction over its villages, and with other towns of his estate over rights to *alcabalas*, the enforcement of local ordinances, and so on. It was not individuals, but the community, the *concejo* of the town, that resisted *señorial* encroachment in the courts, hence the numerous disputes over the right to appoint to municipal offices. It is not surprising then that the duke of Béjar employed a permanent legal staff of five in Valladolid, nine in Granada and ten in Madrid. It was as much the cost of litigation as its outcome that limited the success of señorial responses and, in so many cases, resulted in compromise settlements out of court.

But the evidence for real hostility against the *señor* is in the present state of our knowledge sparse – the great waves of rioting in the 1640s and 1650s were overwhelmingly anti-fiscal rather than anti-señorial – and it may be that on balance vassals were drawn into greater dependence on their lords by the demands of the State and the calamities of the times. Despite their own difficulties, the position of the lords was assisted enormously by the fact that everybody else was in similar, or worse, financial difficulties, and for much the same reasons, *caballeros*, communities, peasants and Crown. The bankruptcy of the *concejos*, which made it difficult to pursue cases through the courts, and the weakness of the royal *chancillerías* in the seventeenth century contributed a good deal to the advance of señorial power. The patronage and support of a great lord, therefore, became more necessary rather than less: to provide career opportunities for *caballeros* forced into service in aristocratic administrations; to lobby for the alleviation of taxes in their areas of influence; to succour their vassals when the resources of the municipal granary failed. In many cases it was the town itself which surrendered its independence to a lord in order to acquit itself of a mountainous burden of debt, or, as Yepes had to in 1674, sell municipally owned offices, rents and properties to the marquis of La Rambla to redeem the 10,000 ducat *censo* they owed him.

So often success or failure at this level depended on influence at Court,

---

87. A. Domínguez Ortiz, *Alteraciones andaluzas* (Madrid, 1973).

that is to say political considerations took precedence over narrowly financial or judicial ones. In 1640, the duke of Arcos was able to buy his way out of the opposition of the *concejos* of the Serranía de Villaluenga to his acquisition of the woods, pastures, wastes and commons of the area, because the Crown preferred to sell to him, 'taking into account His Excellency's commitment to His Majesty's service and to the needs of the war, and his many and distinguished services . . . which are worth very much more than the price of those woodlands'. Similarly, in 1664, the Constable was able to block the judicial exemption sought by villages subject to his towns of Haro and Cerezo, despite the abuses they alleged and the financial inducements they offered the Crown, in the king's own words, 'in view of the Constable's injunction against these exemptions and of the consideration his house and person deserve'.[88] It was, therefore, crucial, as Charles Jago has shown, for even the greatest of nobles to have a connection or a protector at Court, and to have an agent representing his interests, defending his lawsuits and promoting his petitions with the councils and tribunals.[89]

But more than anything, the 'crisis of the aristocracy' was overcome by means of the very royal demands that had contributed so much to produce it. The fiscal exactions of the Crown on the aristocracy were on the scale they were only because they were underwritten by the greatest extension of señorialism since the fifteenth century. The late medieval crisis of señorial rents had been overcome in the fourteenth and fifteenth centuries by the extension of señorial power at the expense of the Crown by royal donation. In the sixteenth century, the financial needs of the Crown enabled señorial expansion to continue at the expense of the Church and the Military Orders by purchase, and aristocratic revenues to increase by investment in alienated royal taxes. In the seventeenth century the señorial regime was extended by the dismemberment of the *realengo* through a sort of compulsory purchase. The funds extracted from the nobility were technically loans that were recycled directly into increased señorial power and revenue by being used as credits for the purchase from the Crown of jurisdictions, vassals and revenues. This was almost the only way that the compensation due for those 'loans' could be collected, and it is that which explains the paradox of a debt-ridden aristocracy apparently investing simultaneously in lands, rents and offices. In 1657 the marquis of Aguilar-count of Castañeda bought off a lawsuit by the Crown for the recovery of *alcabalas* he held without title at ten years' income (a concessionary rate in itself) for 42,100 ducats; however, only 15,000 ducats was paid in cash, the rest was offset against compensation owed for the *medias anatas de juros* that had been withheld from him. In 1660 the marquis of

88. For the duke of Arcos, R. Benítez Sánchez-Blanco, 'Expulsión de los mudejares y reacción señorial en la Serranía de Villaluenga', in *Andalucía Moderna (Siglos XVI–XVII)* (Córdoba, 1978), vol. 1, pp. 109–17, at pp. 116–17; for the Constable, AHN Consejos leg. 4438–9, 1664, n. 33, Cámara 30.5.1664 and 20.7.1664.

89. C. J. Jago, 'La Corona y la aristocracia durante el régimen de Olivares: un representante de la aristocracia en la Corte', in Elliott and García Sanz, *La España del Conde Duque de Olivares*, pp. 373–97.

Camarasa made a similar settlement for the *alcabalas* of Castrojeriz and Astudillo for some 56,000 ducats, paying 20,000 in cash, 23,400 in *medias anatas de juros*, and 12,800 in other credits against the Crown. In 1661, the Vizconde de la Puebla de los Infantes (Sevilla) bought the *tercias reales* of Puebla, which he paid for entirely in *medias anatas de juros*.

In this way, the nobility was able to transform exactions into power, taking advantage of the multitude of fiscal expedients and sales of offices, rights, taxes and jurisdictions by the Crown, both to buy offices of government and supervision within their own towns, and to acquire administrative offices, particularly of a fiscal nature, outside them. Thus, when the duke of Béjar paid 24,000 *reales* to suppress the functions of the *alcaldes ordinarios* in eight of his towns, or the Constable 5,000 ducats for six *regimientos* of the town of Haro for his nominees, or the count of Aguilar bought the posts of gaoler, market factors, inspector of weights, dues and measures, and clerk of flour weighing in Entrena, their judicial powers and their control of the government and economic life of the towns of their *señoríos* were very substantially increased. There are literally hundreds of cases of this kind which, as much as the direct sale of royal vassals into *señorío* and the alienation of revenues, were an enormous potential reinforcement of señorial power.[90]

But if re-señorialization is an accurate enough term for this process, one should also be talking of an increase of aristocratic power over a much wider area. The same fiscal expedients opened up access to offices of honour, influence and profit in royal cities and in their provinces, which were served by substitutes, agents, or simply leased out, offices such as the chief clerkships of taxes (*escribanías mayores de rentas*) which, for example, the count of Villamediana owned in Avila, Medina del Campo, Campóo, Carrión, Monzón, Saldaña and Palencia and their districts, and the count of Gondomar for the whole of Asturias and Galicia. These were key posts of supervision, inspection and control, not of much direct financial value, but others were important contributors to noble incomes. In 1636 the duke of Medina Sidonia bought the brandy monopoly of Sanlúcar, Jerez de la Frontera and Puerto de Santa María – though in the event he had to dispose of it again, piecemeal in 1662 and 1672. The count of La Roca owned the office of chief inspector of measures for the city and kingdom of Seville, and with it dues of four *maravedís* for every *arroba* of wine, vinegar and oil measured; in 1643 the office was worth 200,000 *escudos*.

The seventeenth century, and the reign of Philip IV in particular, thus witnessed a massive señorialization in Castile. In the Crown of Aragon, where the king did not have the same rights over offices nor the same fiscal instruments, señorialization could not occur in the same way, although in Valencia it was advanced by a different process through the resettlement that took place after the expulsion of the *moriscos* in 1609.[91] Already by 1637 there were 3,671 places in Castile whose *alcabalas* had

---

90. Numerous examples can be found catalogued in F. Gil Ayuso, *Junta de Incorporaciones* (Madrid, 1934)
91. Palop, *Hambre y lucha antifeudal*, pp. 110–11.

been alienated to private individuals, and it has been calculated that between 1625 and 1668 169 new *señorios* were created and upwards of 80,000 vassals sold by the Crown, so transferring some 15 per cent of the population of the royal domain into private jurisdiction. More than 70 per cent of the *alcabalas* and *tercias* and over 50 per cent of jurisdictions and vassals sold in Andalusia went to the titled nobility. By the eighteenth century the duke of Alba had a quarter more vassals in Extremadura than in the sixteenth, and between 1599 and 1721 the duke of Osuna increased the amount of land he owned in his estates by one-sixth.

The importance of these alienations and the very legitimacy of talking about a 're-señorialization' or 'refeudalization' have been denied by historians for whom these transfers had not much more than formal or honorific meaning, neither weakening the authority of the Crown nor diminishing the Crown's capacity to intervene in señorial jurisdictions in a corrective or mandatory capacity.[92] Technically it is true that the *señorio* always remained subject to the supreme jurisdiction of the king, and that in some respects the encroachment of royal agents, particularly in a fiscal and military capacity, reached new levels in the mid-seventeenth century, but it is clear that in the main the *señorio* enjoyed considerable operational autonomy from royal supervision. Furthermore, by exploiting their responsibility for billeting, recruiting and the other administrative duties that were devolved upon them and by collusion with the royal governors, local lords, like the count of Balazote in Alcaraz (La Mancha), could exercise what their victims claimed was a 'Machiavellian tyranny'. The count of Valparaiso, indicted before the Council by Almagro and other towns of La Mancha in 1712, had, they said, succeeded in making himself 'so absolute in this district and so powerful, with the judge in his pocket and the backing of his relatives at Court, that there was nothing he wanted that he did not get'.[93] Throughout the seventeenth century the royal councils were unequivocal in their denunciations of the extension of señorial jurisdiction at the expense of the Crown. The ownership of *alcabalas* and clerkships of the revenues by lords with señorial jurisdiction was regarded as a guarantee of fraud and abuse with no means of control or correction, while the competence and authority of the royal *corregidores* were being eroded by the continuous alienation of jurisdictions. The need to check this continuing señorialization and to restore the authority and effectiveness of royal justice was one of the central pillars of reform propounded by the Council in the 1650s and 1660s.[94]

---

92. Bernal also argues against the validity of the concept of 'refeudalization', but on different grounds. What he sees going on in seventeenth-century Andalusia is a sort of 'modernización capitalista': 'la intensificación del régimen señorial respondía a ese doble afán de ampliación del patrimonio territorial y maximalización de los beneficios netos obtenidos de la tierra', as well as increased bourgeois ownership, *Latifundios*, pp. 167, 60.

93. J. Díaz Pintado, *Conflicto social, marginación y mentalidades en La Mancha (Siglo XVIII)* (Ciudad Real, 1987), pp. 168–72.

94. For example, Cámara, 30.10.1660, AHN Consejos leg. 4437, 1660, n. 84; Council of Castile, Nov. 1654 and 26.3.1669, BL Egerton Ms 332, ff. 286–92v, 299.

There was also a political dimension to the señorial reaction of the seventeenth century. The link between Court influence and the resolution of the economic crisis of the *señorío* and the *mayorazgo* made access to a favourable hearing in government decision-making essential. The conspiracy of the duke of Medina Sidonia and his cousin, the marquis of Ayamonte, designed to remove Olivares, restore the rights of the aristocracy and their place in the Cortes, and alleviate the burdens on Andalusia, rather than to establish an independent kingdom there, which the rest of the Andalusian aristocracy would have opposed, was merely the extreme form of a near united aristocratic opposition to the arbitrariness of the minister.[95] The fall of Olivares, which the grandees procured in January 1643, signified a restoration and a reassertion of the traditional monarcho-señorial system. Some of the most objectionable aspects of the ex-minister's 'anti-aristocratic' policies were withdrawn – the rent tax, the capitation tax, actions for the recovery of alienated *alcabalas*, the exclusion of the grandees from the king's presence. After Olivares, and during the reign of Charles II, observers even spoke of a sort of aristocratic republicanism, operating through a series of grandee premiers (not *validos* according to Tomás y Valiente, for they were placed there by an 'imposición nobiliaria y cortesana'[96]), Don Juan José de Austria, the duke of Medinaceli, the count of Oropesa, or a dominant Council of State composed almost entirely of grandees. 'Power is entirely in the hands of the grandees', wrote the Venetian Cornaro in 1683. 'Bound together by family ties and by their own private interests, they care neither for the public weal nor for the interests of the Crown. So much has their power increased, and so much has that of the king diminished, that if he wanted to rule in an absolute and despotic manner, I doubt if he would succeed.' This was less an attempt to govern directly than to limit government, to prevent a repetition of the 'tyranny' of the count-duke and to ensure the continuation of an advantageous system of patronage and fiscal redistribution, for as one writer in the minority of Charles II observed, 'Nowadays, either because their estates have declined or because their expenses at Court have forced them into receivership, the lords cannot survive without military or government posts or offices in the Royal Household, so they are applying even for lesser positions and depriving the *caballeros*.'[97] The blocking of administrative and fiscal reform was a crucial element in the response of the aristocracy to the seventeenth-century crisis, for it provided the grandees, as the Genoese ambassador, Spinola, observed in 1688, with patronage over an infinity of unnecessary ministers accustomed to live in luxury at the expense of the Crown. It was a success achieved and sustained so long

95. A. Domínguez Ortiz, 'La conspiración del duque de Medina Sidonia y el marqués de Ayamonte', *Archivo Hispalense* 106 (1961), 133–59; L.I. Alvarez de Toledo, *Historia de una conjura* (Cadiz, 1985).

96. On the aristocratic coup that put Don Juan José de Austria into power, for example, see BL Egerton Ms 353, f. 278, 'La Unión de los Grandes y Nobleza con el Señor Don Juan de Austria sobre poner en libertad a Don Carlos II', 21.12.1676.

97. Atienza and Simón, 'Patronazgo', p. 48.

as the Crown remained dependent on the administrative and military services of the nobility, and was unable to establish and maintain for itself an autonomous monarchical administration.

The aristocracy thus came through the crisis of the seventeenth century very much at the expense of the Crown, though some would argue even more at the expense of the further proletarianization of the peasantry, the loss of communal rights, and the sacrifice of the Castilian agrarian economy to the interests of pastoralism and the demands of the international market. In some cases recovery was spectacular. The duke of Pastrana, whose estates of Pastrana and Infantado in 1662 were in receivership (*concurso*), with obligations of 90,000 ducats a year to their creditors, died in 1693 not a penny in debt. Pastrana was exceptional. For others recovery was a good deal slower. The revenues of the duchy of Feria in the first quarter of the eighteenth century were scarcely a fifth more than at their low point of 1635–70, and it was not until the second half of the century that they exceeded their peak in 1600 in real terms. In the eighteenth century, however, agricultural prices and land rents were booming. There is evidence of a 50 per cent increase in señorial incomes in Andalusia during the first half of the century. In Extremadura, the Feria revenues tripled between the first and the third quarters. The ordinary income of the Cuéllar estates in Segovia province, 70,000 *reales* in 1646, had risen by over 75 per cent to 123,000 by the mid-eighteenth century, and to 190,000 by its end. Similar increases were recorded on the Alcañices estates in Zamora.[98]

Nevertheless, the political power of the old aristocracy was dealt a mortal blow with the end of the Habsburg dynasty in 1700. The new Bourbon monarchy revealed the power of the grandees in the reign of Charles II to have been something of an illusion. The death of Charles II had caught the aristocracy still low down on the recovery curve and economically dependent on their control of government. The French who arrived in 1701 expected a powerful and wealthy aristocracy that would present serious resistance to the reestablishment of royal authority. They were soon reporting that the grandees were powerless, disunited and not to be feared. As Toby Bourke, the Stuart representative in Madrid in 1705, wrote, 'They are not as formidable as is believed in other countries; they have neither credit, money, nor influence over the people . . . their only ability consists in the petty intrigues they conduct through the secret channels of the Court.'[99]

Their activities in the War of Succession exposed a political and military impotence that is a remarkable contrast to the rôle they had played under Philip IV. There was a good deal of plotting, dissidence and disloyalty, but only the renegade count of Cifuentes in Aragon seems to have been capable of raising a following to lead into the field. The nobility of

98. Aragón Mateos, *Nobleza extremeña*, pp. 88–92; Bernal, *Latifundios*, p. 172; Yun Casalilla, 'Consideraciones para el estudio de la renta y las economías señoriales', pp. 1–35, at p. 28.

99. H. Kamen, *The War of Succession in Spain 1700–15* (London, 1969), pp. 89, 92.

Valencia were not even able to defend their own towns against their peasantry.

The policy of Bourbon absolutism was not to undermine the aristocracy as an Estate, but to break the political power of the grandees by removing them from control of the central administration of government. The new dynasty, with its own slate of ministers and courtiers and its reform of the conciliar system, ruptured the link between the political and the socio-economic functions of the incumbent Court aristocracy. 'The opinion that His Catholic Majesty [Philip V] holds in general of the grandees of Spain', wrote ambassador Bonnac in 1711, 'is that so long as they are not in office they will be incapable of harm, hated as they are by their subjects and odious to the lower nobility.'[100]

The Bourbons regarded the grandees, through their dominance of the councils, as the major barriers to efficient administration. Charles II's Council of State had been totally dominated by the Court aristocracy; 90 per cent of its Spanish lay members were grandees or inherited *títulos*. Philip V began symbolically by suppressing the historic offices of Constable and Admiral of Castile, and reformed the central administration along a French-modelled ministerial style that had the effect of marginalizing the Council of State. The eighteenth-century Council of State was both very different from that of Charles II and an expression of the social principles of the Bourbon monarchy. Only one-third of its eighty-two Spanish lay members were grandees or old inherited *títulos*, 28 per cent had new titles (twenty-three), but over 35 per cent were untitled; lawyers, the military and those with a background in government or the administration were almost equally represented.[101] The composition of the Council of State reflected the consolidation of a new type of administrative aristocracy that had been in the process of formation during the later seventeenth century. To that extent Henry Kamen goes too far in claiming that it was the Succession War that saw the death of one concept of nobility and the birth of another. Some outstanding bureaucratic figures had always succeeded in rising into the aristocracy on an individual basis, but the virtually automatic rewarding of central bureaucratic service with *hábitos*, *encomiendas* and *títulos* on a regular and systematic basis was something new to the second half of the seventeenth century. This new service aristocracy was reinforced by the more than 200 new titles created by Philip V; clearly not an attack on 'aristocracy', but a fundamental shift in its conceptual basis, a renovation of the aristocracy by the aristocratization of the bureaucracy.

In a more general way, the bureaucratization of the administration – again the acceleration of a much longer process – also tended to reduce the influence of the old aristocracy by blocking the informal channels through which noble patronage and employment had operated. Under Charles III

100. Kamen, *War of Succession*, p. 107.
101. F. Barrios, *El Consejo de Estado de la Monarquía Española 1521–1812* (Madrid, 1984), Part 3.

corregidores, for example, were increasingly professional lawyers, the number of non-*letrado corregidores* being limited in 1783 to one in four. In an attempt to demonstrate the continuing importance of the nobility in royal service in the eighteenth century, the Marqués del Saltillo compiled a list of 196 nobles in major military and civilian office; of those only 37 per cent were titled, and two-thirds of the titles were eighteenth-century creations, very often in reward for the service itself.[102] The old aristocracy was pushed out of government to become purely an aristocracy of the Court and of the capital. That did not necessarily destroy aristocratic influence, but it forced it to flow through social, cultural and financial rather than administrative channels. That imperative had much to do with the nature and the social mix of high society in eighteenth-century Madrid.

The aristocracy was thus not entirely without influence nor was the vision of aristocratic constitutionalism totally dead in the eighteenth century. The so-called 'partido aragonés', led by the count of Aranda and linked with the Prince of the Asturias (the heir-apparent) in the early years of Charles III's reign, combined an aristocratic faction and a group of military malcontents hostile to the civilian administration and adhering to the traditional belief that absolutism needed to be restrained by the *fueros* of the regions and the rights of the nobility. Again, some forty years later the 'partido fernandista', which included the dukes of Infantado, San Carlos and Sotomayor, and the counts of Orgaz, Oñate and Altamira, embraced similar positions and brought down the chief minister, Godoy, in 1808, in ways that are reminiscent of the fall of Olivares 165 years before.

The Bourbon reform of local government also had its impact on the administrative autonomy of the *señorío*. The *señorío* had always been part of the territorial organization of the monarchy. *Señoríos* had been seats of treasuries of the *millones*, for example, and even in Philip IV's reign royal *corregidores* and *sargentos mayores de milicias* had acted indiscriminately in *realengo* and *señorío*. But the development of the Province as the key unit of fiscal administration with the unification of the revenues into *rentas provinciales* and the appointment of *intendentes* as provincial supremos from 1718 and their definitive establishment in 1749 further absorbed señorial into royal government. The decree of the Council of Finance in 1742 that the subdelegates of the *intendente* of Seville were to act as judges in fiscal suits not the duke of Osuna's *corregidor*, is just one example of the frequent encroachment of *intendentes* and their *subdelegados* into señorial jurisdictions.[103] However, although Philip V had quickly been successful in eliminating the political influence of the grandees, for a long time nothing effective was done to check their ability to pervert the course of justice, or to remedy señorial abuses in the countryside.[104] The sporadic threats to reincorporate alienated royal rights were almost entirely fiscal in motivation, and it was

102. Marqués del Saltillo, 'Nobleza española en el siglo 18'.
103. Atienza, *Casa de Osuna*, p. 116.
104. C. Morandi, ed., *Relazioni di ambasciatori sabaudi, genovesi e veneti (1693–1713)* (Bologna, 1935), p. 58.

not until the municipal reforms of Charles III and the support given to peasant litigants against their lords that there was any sort of move against the domestic power of the *señor*.

With the cessation of alienations of vassals and rents from the *realengo* after the 1670s halting the expansion of señorialism and the bureaucratization of the Bourbon State stopping up the pork-barrel of Court and office patronage, the financial viability and hence the social dominance of the aristocracy in the eighteenth century depended almost entirely on their own economic resources, and thus on the general state of agriculture.

With señorial incomes buoyant during a sustained period of economic expansion, fewer demands from the Crown for military services, an official interest rate cut to 3 per cent in 1705, and, in the middle decades of the century, actual rates of interest even lower, the aristocracy embarked on a new round of borrowing to finance the extravagant manifestations of their status which were the only sources of influence left to them at Court. Whereas in Catalonia credit was used to finance productive activity, there was in Castile a superabundance of credit without a productive outlet. It was a good time to borrow, and it made sense to borrow to spend, and of course to redeem old debts at higher rates.[105] Most of the *censos* still extant in the nineteenth century originated in the second half of the eighteenth. It was the money-market that sustained the social rôle of the Castilian aristocracy in the eighteenth century, bereft of their other traditional functions, as cataracts of (admittedly a selective) splash-down economics: gamblers, spendthrifts, patriarchs supporting thousands of domestics, palace builders – Piedrahita cost the duke of Alba 7–11 million *reales* in 1755; Moncloa and Buenavista cost Berwick y Liria 9 million *reales*; the duke of Medina de Rioseco had three mansions in Madrid, and Medinaceli's palace, spread over several acres, was said to house 3,000 people.[106]

The Indian summer of the *señorío* came to an end in the 1780s with the end of the agrarian boom. This time there was no relief to be got at the expense of the State, from *mercedes*, alienations, or opportunities in State service. With the contraction of señorial rents, the *mayorazgos* were unable to support the volume of *censo* debts undertaken during the easy years of the eighteenth century. In many cases it was necessary to alienate properties from the *mayorazgos* – the count of Altamira had to sell 3 million *reales* of pasture in Avila in 1800–2, but still had to take on more debt. Faced with competition from royal *vales* at 4 per cent and the massive demand for capital generated by the *desamortizaciones*, deficit financing in the old form was becoming impossible. It was replaced with new forms of borrowing – 'obligaciones' – secured on personal wealth and not subject to

105. R. Robledo, 'El crédito y los privilegiados durante la crisis del antiguo régimen', in B. Yun Casalilla, ed., *Estudios sobre capitalismo agrario, crédito e industria en Castilla (Siglos XIX y XX)* (Salamanca, 1991), pp. 238–65.

106. Robledo, 'Credito', p. 240 n. 11; Aragón Mateos, *Nobleza extremeña*, pp. 357, 360.

the legal interest limit, but imposing different disciplines, for whereas interest on the old *censos* could be paid late with relative impunity, essentially enabling the borrower to control his debt, this was not true of the 'obligaciones'. The lords had perforce to attend to maximizing their incomes from their rents like other private landowners, and to try to expand their own private property within their *señoríos*, especially those more recent lords with minimal legal rights over the land who used their judicial authority to seize waste, scrub and communal lands, enclose them and turn them over to pasture, as a number of great lords were doing in Extremadura and La Mancha.[107]

All this contributed to a sharper sense of proprietorship and the transformation of vassal into tenant relationships. As lords became more businesslike, familiar relationships with their estate treasurers and agents became more professional and managerial. This facilitated permanent absenteeism, the emotional as well as economic abandoning of the estate, the increasing tendency to give up the direct exploitation of estates and for the *señorío* to become a purely financial unit.[108] Where, as in Andalusia and Catalonia, the absentee lords sub-contracted the exploitation of their estates to the substantial agrarian 'bourgeoisie' of the district (Dons, *regidores*, landowners), the local bosses, the *poderosos* of the villages, were drawn into a symbiotic relationship with the *señorío*.[109] The greatest resistance to señorialism occurred in areas such as Valencia where the *señorío* remained 'feudal' and where the local *poderosos* were not middlemen, but vassals on the same basis as the peasantry, uniting in a common hostility to the *señor*.[110] To the scissors of stagnating rents and rising interest rates was thus added a growing resistance to señorial charges as peasants and local institutions responded to the pressure of lords who sought a greater commercialization of the agricultural output of the *señorío* and looked to increase their control over agrarian resources by an extension of landownership.

While the War of Independence after 1808 merely accelerated an aristocratic crisis that had been gathering pace from about 1780 or 1790, the transformation from *señor* to landlord enabled the aristocracy both to overcome the crisis of the *señorío*, which culminated in the first abolition of señorial jurisdictions in the Cortes of Cadiz in 1811, and to move into the nineteenth century on a new capitalist footing. If in places, in parts of Valencia for example, the final abolition of the *señorío* in 1837 resulted in a wider spread of landownership, in the bulk of Castile-León it did nothing to reduce the territorial power of the old aristocracy. On the contrary, the

107. Moxó, *Disolución*, p. 47; Díaz Pintado, *Conflicto social en La Mancha*, pp. 168–72.

108. Melón, *Extremadura en el Antiguo Régimen*, pp. 391–2.

109. J. Vilar, 'El fin de los elementos feudales y señoriales en Cataluña en los siglos XVIII y XIX, con algunas referencias comparativas al resto de España y al Rosellón', in Godechot, *La abolición del feudalismo*, pp. 78–93, at p. 87.

110. Palop, *Hambre y lucha antifeudal*, pp. 124, 131; P. Ruiz Torres, 'La fi de la noblesa feudal al país valencià', in N. Sales, et al., *Terra, treball i propietat. Classes agràries i règim senyorial als països catalans* (Barcelona, 1986), pp. 166–85, and *ibid.*, 'Los motines de 1766 y los inicios de la crisis del "Antiguo Régimen" ', in B. Clavero, et al., *Estudios sobre la revolución burguesa en España* (Madrid, 1979), pp. 49–111.

cash compensations paid for the abolition of ancient señorial rights, many of which had been effectively uncollectable, were an infusion of oxygen for an aristocracy in financial crisis, restoring liquidity at the very moment when the land market was being burst open by the dissolution of ecclesiastical mortmain and the relaxation and eventual abolition of the *mayorazgo* in 1836, which enabled them to shift out of entails in order to reinvest in free properties ('bienes libres'). Something like one and a half million hectares of land went onto the market in nineteenth-century Castile, and the traditional aristocracy was one of the main groups of purchasers, confirming their position at the summit of the pyramid of landed wealth.[111] In a survey of the Osuna estates undertaken in 1863, the surveyor concluded, 'His Excellency, the duke of Osuna, is today, in truth, an ordinary property owner. His properties are completely free of entail, and that is due to the achievements of the revolution.'[112] As he was very much aware, the nineteenth-century liberal-bourgeois reforms did as much for the embourgeoisified aristocracy as they did for the bourgeoisie.[113]

THE TRANSFORMATION OF NOBILITY

The abolition of the *señorío*, though not finalized until 1837, and of the *mayorazgo*, in the previous year, was in a very real sense the end of the *ancien régime* in Spain. It capped an intellectual challenge to traditional concepts of nobility that was as crucial in the transformation of the aristocracy as the economic and military crisis that preceded it.

The creation of jurisdictional *señoríos* had been opposed by the councils and the Cortes in the sixteenth and seventeenth centuries because they believed they had adverse consequences for the effective administration of justice. The alienation of jurisdictions was also at odds with the political programme of the Bourbons, but although the repeated proposals for reincorporation did no more than reduce the number of *señoríos* very marginally (Moxó's estimate is about thirty resumptions), there was no further addition to the high point that señorialism had reached in the minority of Charles II. However, the reincorporationist regalism of the royal *fiscales*, especially during the reigns of Charles III and Charles IV, helped to generate a climate of hostility to the *señorío* that, backed by a current of popular anti-señorialism, above all in Valencia and Galicia, was to contribute to its abolition.

111. R. Robledo Hernández, *La renta de la tierra en Castilla la Vieja y León* (1836–1913) (Madrid, 1984), p. 44.

112. Robledo, 'Crédito', p. 262: 'El Excmo. Señor Duque de Osuna es hoy, a la verdad, un propietario particular; sus bienes son completamente libres, pero esto se debe a las conquistas de la revolucion.'

113. Domínguez Ortiz, 'Fin del régimen señorial', p. 77, 'So, at the cost of giving up some archaic rights and a few generally insignificant revenues, the lords transformed an uncertain and shared ownership into an absolute property right, and a multitude of settlers with perpetual title were turned into leaseholders with insecurity of title, or into simple labourers.'

What was new about this rising wave of hostility in the late eighteenth century was that it was not merely a demand for reform, a call for the better administration of justice, it was ideological. As long as sovereignty was thought of as a private prerogative of the king, the delegation of royal jurisdiction was a purely administrative matter. Once sovereignty was viewed as an expression of the Nation, any alienation of that sovereignty was a diminution of the Nation. The demand in the Cortes of Cadiz in 1811 for the immediate reintegration of *señoríos* into the Crown declared it repugnant 'that there should be partial states implanted within the national state' ('que existan imperios parciales ingeridos en el imperio nacional'); as a dismemberment of sovereignty 'it is unlawful, unjust and self-contradictory that there should be Spaniards who recognize and are subject to any other lordship than that of the Nation of which they are an integral part' ('es ilegal, injusto y contradictorio que haya españoles que reconozcan y estén sujetos a otro señorío que el de la Nación de que son parte integrante').[114] The lack of resistance to the abolition of the *señorío* by the lords themselves, who preferred to concentrate on the defence of their 'property rights' over the land, speaks volumes for the transformation that had taken place in the valuation of lordship in the previous decades.

The ideological onslaught against the *señorío* fell upon an institution weakened by the more general intellectual critique of nobility that was part of the social rationalism of the Enlightenment. Criticism of hereditary nobility was not new to the eighteenth century, but the critique of the Enlightenment was targeted very differently from what has been called the Baroque critique that preceded it.[115] Whereas the former was essentially utilitarian, the latter had been principally ethical. The honour values of nobility of lineage had always had distinguished critics, on the one hand for disassociating nobility from virtue and on the other for elevating the tenets of honour, chivalry and illicit love above those of Christianity. The vain pretences and the empty honour of the uneducated, pauper *hidalgo* were ridiculed by writers like Quevedo. Equally severe were the strictures against a titled nobility that demanded positions and rewards beyond its experience, application or capacity. The seventeenth century criticized the 'mania' for ennoblement and for the establishment of *mayorazgos* primarily as vanities, vehicles for the ambitions of upstarts which led to distortions of the social order and which also had unjust fiscal and deleterious economic consequences. The concern of the early seventeenth-century *arbitristas* for economic regeneration was expressed mainly in an opposition to social mobility. The fault was not so much nobility, but the vaulting ambition of the merchant, artisan, or *labrador* who, having accumulated enough to establish a small entail for his eldest son, found all his other sons too proud to continue in the humble crafts which had made the money in the first place. It was this that Cellorigo, Fernández Navarrete, López Bravo,

---

114. García Herrera, 5.6.1811, in Moxó, *Disolución*, pp. 16, 19.
115. Aragón Mateos, *Nobleza extremeña*, pp. 35, 70.

Saavedra Fajardo, and others blamed for the abandoned fields, the lack of skill in the mechanical arts and the general downturn of trade.

With the *arbitristas*, but most of all in the eighteenth century, the balance of criticism shifts from the *hidalgo* to *hidalguismo*, to the *hidalgo* ideal, and to the damaging consequences for the economy of the cult of 'ociosidad', the notion of an idle, useless and reactionary nobility, disparaging of productive activity, yet having abandoned its ancient military ethos (Jovellanos) and its political function as a check on despotism (Blanco White). The eighteenth-century critique, though not without the moral undertones of the Baroque, was preponderantly economic. Characteristic was the objection to the *mayorazgo* not so much as a facilitator of social mobility than as a constraint on the free market in land, which thus gave marriages, offices, jurisdictions and administrative authority a distorted value as means of gaining control of land, deprived the state of revenues from land sales, and tied up capital that could not therefore be released for improvements.[116] At the core of the criticism was a view of señorialism as an economics of rent rather than production, of negligent absentee latifundism and depopulating pastoralism, of the dead hand of the entail which blocked the market in land and the incentive to improvement.

The utilitarian critique of the Enlightenment has been the dominant influence in the overwhelmingly negative historiographical assessment of the rôle of the nobility and the noble ethos in Spanish history. Manuel Colmeiro took a typically nineteenth-century liberal stance when he wrote, 'The sterile vanity of *hidalguía* gave us a propensity for the idle life, impoverished the nation and by diminishing individual initiative retarded our industrial education.' *Hidalguismo* was condemned as a reactionary social ethos that placed purity and antiquity of blood before individual merit, discouraged achievement, drove families into the safety of obscurity and locked all levels of society into the values of the country's history, an embattled religiosity, a militarist anti-intellectualism and a rigid and deterministic code of honour. As Michel Devèze writes:

The Spain of Philip IV was marked above all by the existence of a numerous body of noblemen who had succeeded in imposing on the whole of the rest of society their particular view of life, a Christian view, but a narrow Christianity, a concept of honour, but a mistaken honour, a belief in hierarchy, but one based on 'purity of blood', in other words on the religious origins of one's ancestors, a view of life unadapted to the economic situation from which the capitalist bourgeoisie of northern Europe were to derive such benefit.

---

116. See the legislation of 28.4.1789 restricting the foundation of *mayorazgos* without royal licence as an evil 'which foments idleness (*la ociosidad*) and arrogance in its possessors and their children and relatives, and deprives the army, the navy, agriculture, commerce, the crafts and trades of many hands'; the legislation was designed to promote the 'free movement of real property' ('libre circulación de bienes estables'), *Novísima Recopilación* (1805), v.114 (ley 12, tit.17, lib.10).

For Díez Borque, 'The *hidalgo* has the fundamental responsibility for economic decline.'[117]

Yet it is arguable that this critique has been insufficiently sensitive to the degree of openness and change in the system during the early modern period. There has also been an unwillingness to recognize the implications of the fact that nobility was a formal, legal status. We are not free to make our own definitions. Nobility cannot be confined to the grandees or to the titled aristocracy. Groups defined as 'bourgeois' by the forms of their economic activity, or as 'middle class' professionals, are not infrequently noble in legal terms. Conversely, the élites, defined, for example, by the number of their servants, are not always nobles. If *hidalguía* cuts across other behavioural criteria, then it is the *a priori* assumptions about the *hidalgo* and *hidalguismo* that must be reexamined.

In many ways the Enlightenment critique was pushing at an open door, or at the wrong door. Traditional *hidalgo* values and the dysfunctional extended nobility of *hidalguía* were already on the way out in the second half of the eighteenth century as new social pressures in different economic circumstances ruptured ideological constraints. After the death of Philip IV the rôle of the fisc in social promotion declined rapidly, and for two or three generations the shell of the social order hardened. With the stricter documentation required by the early Bourbons, the more rigid regulations introduced in cities like Cordoba and guilds like the Cofradía de Santa María la Mayor of Zaragoza, or the increasingly formal requirement of nobility for military commissions, for example, in the early eighteenth century, it became increasingly difficult to establish *hidalguía* and less easy for the *nouveaux riches* to manipulate the necessary proofs. There was at best a stagnation of *hidalgo* numbers in the eighteenth century and then a rapid dissolution of *hidalguía*, a collapse into commonalty, at one end, and an assimilation of nobility with aristocracy, at the other. The Don ceased to be a mark of nobility, the number of lawsuits to prove nobility in the courts declined, formal office sharing (*mitad de oficios*) was falling into disuse, and in Cáceres by 1806 the *hidalgo* had disappeared as a category.[118]

But the renewal of economic growth and the rise of new wealth after the Succession War, revived the pressure for social promotion damped down by the economic difficulties of the later sixteenth and seventeenth centuries. The blockages to that promotion under the old rules forced a radical rethinking of the nature of nobility and the opening up of new modes of access, like the *maestranzas*, and the Order of Carlos III, established in 1771 to reward political, military and administrative service without the constraints of the old Military Orders.[119] In a buoyant economy the ennoblement of the wealthy was coming

117. M. Devèze, *L'Espagne de Philippe IV (1621–1665)*, 2 vols (Paris, 1970), p. 267; Díez Borque, *Sociología*, p. 296.

118. Pérez de Guinea, *Soria*, pp. 72, 74; Aragón Mateos, *Nobleza extremeña*, pp. 70, 75, 77, 113, 132.

119. See R. Liehr, *Sozialgeschichte spanischer Adelskorporationen: die Maestranzas de Caballería, 1670–1808* (Wiesbaden, 1981) for the *maestranzas*; J. Moreta i Munujos, 'Los Caballeros de Carlos III: Aproximación social', *Hispania* 41 (1981), 409–20. These new modes of access, as well as secret societies like the Freemasons, have been seen as responses to the need for a counterweight to the upper aristocracy in the eighteenth century, J. Velarde Fuertes, 'Datos empíricos sobre el papel económico de la baja nobleza española', *Revista de Trabajo* 20 (1967), 85–114, at 94.

to be seen less as a fiscal injustice than as an economic and political desideratum. Rather than condemning the ambition for social advance, writers in the reign of Charles III were actually arguing for a greater and more automatic access to nobility for the new rich both as an economic incentive and to palliate disaffection.[120] The celebrated decree of 1783 empowering the ennoblement of families that remained active in commerce or manufacturing for three generations was the official response to this rethinking, its aim not so much to ennoble manufacturers as to keep ennobled manufacturers in industry. A not dissimilar decree, issued a hundred years before, in 1682, had been ignored; but the fact that the 1783 decree was used as the basis for a number of petitions for grants of *privilegios* in the 1780s and 1790s and its wording cited directly, is evidence of the way ideas of nobility had been transformed during the eighteenth century.[121] The justifications for nobility in the eighteenth century put far less emphasis on blood, lineage and feats of arms than they had in the seventeenth. Whereas in the mid-seventeenth century over 90 per cent had claimed association with a known, noble manor of the mountains of Cantabria (*solar conocido*), only one quarter were doing so after 1720; one-third made no family claim to nobility at all; and fewer than 30 per cent offered any sort of military justification. There was also a greater willingness to confess to honest *labrador* origins, and to present success in commercial and industrial undertakings as both honourable and socially meritorious. The merits that were beginning to be adduced were 'bourgeois' qualities (application, diligence, zeal, integrity, education, incessant work), social utility, public works and service to the community, and personal wealth ('bienes de fortuna').[122] In Cordoba, *hidalguía* was becoming less 'noble' and more 'bourgeois'; 'simple' *hidalgos*, nearly two-thirds of whom were merchants, rose from 62 per cent to 76 per cent of the total between 1715 and 1775, and increased by one-fifth in absolute numbers, while the *hidalgos notorios* were reduced by nearly 40 per cent. Similarly, in Extremadura, simple nobles were becoming less reticent in involving themselves in economic activity, while at the same time active businessmen were being accepted as *hidalgos*.[123] Parallel changes can also be seen at other levels of the noble hierarchy. The composition of the *maestranzas* was much altered after 1765 by a huge leap in admissions (twelvefold in places), fewer entrants related to old members, more foreign to the city, much higher entry fees, and more ostentatious and extravagant contributions to civic welfare. At the same time, the titled nobility of the eighteenth century was much more an aristocracy of merit and public service than it ever had been before, and the landed nobility was being transformed into something that can reasonably be called an aristocratic bourgeoisie.

120. Miguel Avilés Fernández and Jorge Cejudo López, eds, *Pedro Rodríguez de Campomanes. Epistolario*, vol. 1 (*1747–1777*) (Madrid, 1983), p. 383, Rodrigo Ponce to Campomanes, 14.9.1772, 'Proyecto para multiplicar el número de gente noble en España' – arguing that entails should be distributed among all sons; p. 402, Campomanes 26.10.1772, 'con dificultad se les pueden negar sin caer en el inconveniente de desmayar su industria'.

121. The background to the 1783 decree and its effectiveness have been analysed in detail by W. J. Callahan, *Honor, Commerce and Industry in Eighteenth-Century Spain* (Boston, Mass., 1972), and by J. Guillamón Alvarez, *Honor y honra en la España del siglo XVIII* (Madrid, 1981).

122. Thompson, 'Neo-noble Nobility', pp. 392–5.

123. Aranda Doncel, *Historia de Córdoba*, pp. 214, 217; Aragón Mateos, *Nobleza extremeña*, pp. 113, 129.

The simplistic portrayal of the nobility as idle leeches, indifferent to the management of their estates, careless of the long-term productivity of the land and of the welfare of their vassals, and spurning commerce and business, is thus by no means a recognizable picture of the immensely varied economic interests of the nobility as a whole. Practically every study we have of the mid-eighteenth-century *catastros* shows the local economies to have been dominated by nobles – exploiting estates, offices, rents, taxes, lending and leasing on harsher terms than the *labradores* themselves, selling grain, wine, even setting up commercial companies, and by no means unconcerned with the modernization of the economy. The Economic Societies that sprang up after 1765 to foment agricultural and industrial improvement were founded for the most part by local nobles inspired by the Physiocrats and with an immediate interest in returns from the land. Indeed, it is the central thesis of Richard Herr's monumental new study of agrarian change in late-eighteenth century Spain that commercial agriculture was almost always associated with local *hidalgo* families.[124] In Buitrago (Guadalajara), in 1752, of seventeen families of graziers with in excess of 10,000 *reales* a year, only three were not *hidalgos*. In Ciudad Real, the majority of the forty nobles owned oil presses and flour mills and were active in commerce and transportation. In Logroño, only two of the dozen top 'comerciantes' were not noble. And we are not just talking about simple *hidalgos* and *caballeros*. Indeed, Antonio Miguel Bernal has argued powerfully that the great Andalusian latifundist landlord had always been a 'nobleza negociante', actively involved in agribusiness, consolidating, enclosing, converting as economic conditions demanded, notably to the direct exploitation of the olive and the vine, to sheep, and in the eighteenth century to the breeding of fighting bulls, controlling productivity by means of short-term leases, and marketing the product he received from the land. The *latifundia* was managed in accordance with rational economic criteria, and rather than archaic and unproductive, increased wheat yields by 50 per cent and barley yields two and a half to three fold between 1611 and 1710, and unit land rents by 183 per cent during the eighteenth century.[125] The liberal condemnation of the *mayorazgo* and the *latifundia* may thus be misguided, not only because they were both being even more commercialized in the eighteenth century, but because, although they entailed the *dominio eminente* of the land, they did not exclude others from its usufruct, and indeed served as a bridge across which the local agrarian bourgeoisie moved into capitalist landownership in the nineteenth century.

Titled noblemen too were tax-farmers, factory owners, exporters, money lenders. One in ten of the investors in the Extremadura Company were titled nobles (including the dukes of Alba and Liria); the *Consulado de Comercio* of Seville included fifteen marquises and two counts; the Malaga *consulado* also included grandees, *títulos*, and *caballeros* of the *maestranza*;

---

124. R. Herr, *Rural Change and Royal Finances in Spain at the End of the Old Regime* (Berkeley, Cal., 1989).
125. Bernal, *Latifundio*, pp. 31, 59, 200, 131, 172.

while from 1732 the Cadiz Guild of Indies Merchants required proof of nobility for membership.[126] It is nevertheless true that in most cases the involvement of the upper nobility in commerce was only in the sale of the produce of their estates and their investment in company shares very marginal. Members of the Seville *maestranza*, for example, were involved in the Indies trade, but none was in manufacturing, or retailing, in a craft, in any of the liberal professions, or even exclusively in commerce or banking.[127] The economic norm of the upper aristocracy may still have been rent- rather than production-orientated, but the number and the quality of the exceptions raises methodological questions about the comparative economic behaviour of different regional and national nobilities and the effect of institutionalized values on that behaviour that are not easy to answer.

The ordinances against manufacturers and tradesmen exercising positions of honour are a case in point. Too often they have been interpreted as absolute social exclusions which contributed to the economic backwardness of Spain by discouraging men from following productive occupations, when what was really at issue was a conflict of interests between two functions, marketing and market-regulation. In Salamanca, for example, merchants were statutorily excluded from holding the office of *regidor* in the city; but on 19 May 1660, Miguel Conde de Avila was admitted as a member of the city council, following the testimony of the notary that that same day he had gone to the premises from where Conde had traded as a cloth merchant, and found them shut and that there was no intention of reopening them. Conde's office had in fact been renounced to him by his brother eleven years before, during which time he had presumably continued to run the store rather than take up the *regimiento*.[128] His case is an example of how variously social rules were operated, even from one town to another, and an indication that the apparently ferocious exclusions of the ordinances were not always what they seemed. Forced to choose between honour and business, individuals did not always choose honour.

Even in Spain bourgeois *activity* and noble *values* were by no means inevitably antithetical. Rich and not so rich merchants and lawyers of sixteenth- century Valladolid, as well as the bourgeoisie of eighteenth-century Santiago de Compostela, also participated in the more traditional aspects of 'noble' economic activity, with its focus on land, rent and entail. Manufacturers and merchants were proud to conduct their businesses 'con el mayor honor', and seem to have inhabited a culture in which religiosity, traditionalist literature, the desire for title and ostentatious consumption were as prominent as they were among the aristocracy. Don Pedro Eloy de la Porta, a dealer in wool and *regidor perpetuo* of Logroño, put three of his five sons

---

126. Domínguez Ortiz, *Sociedad y Estado*, pp. 350–1.

127. In Seville, the *títulos* confined themselves to shipowning and the wholesale trade, R. Pike, *Aristocrats and Traders. Sevillian Society in the Sixteenth Century* (Ithaca, NY, 1972), p. 33; L. C. Alvarez Santaló and A. García-Baquero González, 'La nobleza titulada en Sevilla 1700–1834', *Historia, Instituciones, Documentos* 7 (1981), 1–43, discuss the different structures of aristocratic and commercial wealth.

128. A. M. Salamanca, Libro de Actas 44 (1660), f. 258v (19.5.1660).

into the Church, and a fourth into the army. The servant-employing élite of Santiago de Compostela 'lived nobly', whether noble or not, owning their own residences in the centre of the city, having country houses, private tombs, endowing a large number of Masses, and monopolizing public office.[129] Manuel Peset argues that this homogeneous social bloc formed from the union of lesser nobility, bourgeoisie and city élite was at the core of the eventual 'bourgeois revolution'. Undoubtedly the emergence of a business-orientated lesser *nobility*, in places in conflict with the great señorial aristocracy, as Ruiz Torres has identified in Valencia, and as is implied in Richard Herr's findings in the province of Jaén (though not in Salamanca), was one of the dynamic forces of the later eighteenth century.

The view that the noble ethos was responsible for the economic decline of Castile has also to take account of the fact that the justifications for nobility in the Crown of Aragon were no less concerned with *limpieza de sangre* and perhaps even more with *vileza de oficios* than they were in Castile, yet Catalonia and Valencia were the seats of booming commercial and industrial economies that sprang into life in the second half of the eighteenth century. Where the Aragonese differed strikingly was in a much more willing association of nobility and wealth – petitions for grants of nobility to the Council of Aragon were supported by specific evidence of wealth, which was not the case in Castile – and in their earlier and more frequent acceptance of education, and involvement in commerce and manufacturing as meritorious public services. Indeed, whereas *hidalguía* was declining in Castile, in Catalonia the number of *hidalgos* was on the increase, serving to bring merchants and rich farmers into the nobility.[130] What was distinctive in Catalonia and Valencia was a positive evaluation of *homo oeconomicus*, rather than the negative attitude to racial impurity and the mechanical trades which they shared with the Castilians.

Ideas and ideals of nobility were not, however, simply an external imposition upon society, they were a functional part of it, and reciprocated with it. If in some ways they constrained, they also helped define, integrate, perhaps even sustain. Baroque ideals of *hidalguía* asserted that distinctions between men were intrinsic, not extrinsic, that the essence was more real than the appearance. They were an assertion of the values and the importance of the past over the present; they were both an expression of and an escape from the moral crisis of seventeenth-century Spain, a manifestation of a loss of confidence in the present and a flight back to past glories and traditional values. A concept of *hidalguía* as a perpetual reward for the preservation of Spain and the maintenance of its religious and racial integrity against the infidel 900 years earlier had something to say to a 'disenchanted' generation desperately seeking new saviours and El

129. A. Eiras Roel, 'Las élites urbanas de una ciudad tradicional: Santiago de Compostela a mediados del siglo XVIII', in *La Documentación Notarial y la Historia*, 2 vols (Santiago de Compostela, 1984), i.117–39; Melón, *Extremadura en el Antiguo Régimen*, p. 389.

130. P. Molas Ribalta, 'La nobleza del corregimiento de Mataró en 1830', *Anuario de Historia Económica y Social* 3 (1970), 481–90.

Cids.[131] *Hidalguía*, together with its attendant panoply of genealogies and family chronicles, was a lesson in history, a key element in the transmission of the myth of Spain, its provenance, and its providence; but it was a lesson with much less meaning after 1700.

By defining and delimiting what values were worthy of social approval, nobility forced administration, letters and money to translate their merits into those values.[132] The extensive nobility of *hidalguía* and the obligatory adherence of new nobles to common lineage and military values into the eighteenth century may thus have had a positive function in preserving the ideological unity of nobility and helping to bridge the fault lines between different layers of the noble hierarchy. There were no steep *social* barriers between titled and untitled nobles, rich and poor, old and new, sword and robe nobility. Nor was political conflict so acutely socialized and hatred of 'base-born' ministers such a significant element in political discourse in Spain as it was elsewhere. The pool of *hidalguía* was large enough to staff councils, secretariats, judiciary, *corregidurías*, the upper levels of the legal profession and the governing cadres of the State without the need for them to become the Trojan horses of commoner power and social infiltration. The fact that judges, *letrados* and bureaucrats were nobles does not mean that it is legitimate to talk of a 'noblesse de robe' in Spain as some sort of parallel nobility; they were part of a single nobility. Letters did not automatically ennoble, and – unlike France – judicial office was not venal and therefore could not be inherited. Arms and letters were acceptable alternatives for the younger sons of aristocrats. Differences between sword and robe were rather professional, temperamental and cultural, than social. Ideological rigidity can thus be said to have had an integrative function in Spain, permitting social mobility without fracturing élite unity.

It may also be that this integrative function extended from the nobility to other levels of society. The shared acceptance of primary social values and the apparent absence of sharp lines of social differentiation may have contributed to the relative lack of violent social animosity in Castile in the early modern period, just as in Catalonia the sharing of a more learned 'culture' served to unite *ciutadans* and *nobles*.[133] The attribution of honour to the plebeian, and the common link of *limpieza*, which enabled it to be said that 'the lackey carries in his breast his own deed of honour, which is his certificate of baptism, and he is as good as the master he serves, even though he be a grandee of Spain,'[134] helped maintain a reciprocity of esteem between 'lackey' and 'grandee' and a plebeian pride, even presumption, which was commented on by so many foreign travellers (Joly, Brunel, Fanshawe, Muret, d'Aulnoy). There was 'nowhere with greater

131. Francisco Santos, *El No Importa de España y La Verdad en el Potro*, ed. J. Rodríguez Puértolas (London, 1973), p. lxix.
132. Pelorson, '*Letrados' juristes*, p. 238, 'la abogacía que también es milicia'.
133. Amelang, *Honored Citizens*, p. 118.
134. Santos, *El No Importa de España*, p. lxii ('El Arca de Noé', 1697).

equality', in Brunel's opinion.[135] One expression of this was the modish *majismo* of the later eighteenth century, a sort of public-school cockney affectation of lower-class manners and dress by the Court aristocracy, a frustrated and functionless group's rejection of the 'civilizing process'.[136] Evidence for shared values has been found in the wide popularity of chivalric fantasies, or in the way the working classes acted the noble, the men wearing swords, the women painting their faces white and red, 'from the Queen to the cobbler's wife, old and young'.[137] They also observed their own hierarchy of disdain, husbandmen having nothing to do with 'vile' tanners, for example, and refusing to allow their children to marry them.[138] Indeed, late eighteenth-century intellectuals believed it was vulgar opinion that adhered most obtusely to traditional values. As Antonio de Campany complained, 'Ideas have changed, but only among the writers; the people remains as ever immutable.'[139]

The seeming universality of the criticism of the *hidalgo* ethos from intellectuals, theologians, men of literature and government ministers raises the question whether the extreme *hidalguismo* they were attacking was really ever the dominant social ideology, rather than their own negative social myth, or counter identity. Indeed, it may be that the '*hidalgo* ideal' was not the ideal of the *hidalgo* at all, but the vulgar, popular image of what the *hidalgo* should be, artificially kept alive by the fantastic adventures of books of chivalry and the literary topoi of the theatre. That is what writers like Moreno de Vargas and the count of Fernán Núñez argued, and both the 'Bartolist' critique of the sixteenth and seventeenth centuries and the 'utilitarian' critique of Enlightened thinkers in the eighteenth can be seen as concerted attacks on popular opinion by an élite, for whom, in the judgement of a reformer like Pedro Antonio Sánchez in 1781, 'Todo el mal reside en la persuasión vulgar'.[140]

Concepts of nobility were also clearly related to concepts of the State. A nobility of blood and lineage beyond royal creation belonged to a *Ständestaat*, to a 'judicialist' monarchy limited by the natural order of society and the 'consultative' rights of its aristocracy; here the *señorío* was the instrument by which the aristocracy shared in government as lords and protectors of their vassals; in the same way the influence of the *caballerato* was tied in with the economic and political vitality of the city *señoríos*. The exaggerated indefeasibility of the blood line was a more or less explicit reaction against the emergent absolutism of the Crown, as manifested in

135. García Mercadal, *Viajes de Extranjeros*, vol. 2, p. 412 (1655). See also, Domínguez Ortiz, *Sociedad y Estado*, p. 326, on familiarity between the classes.

136. Charles E. Kany, *Life and Manners in Madrid, 1750–1800* (Berkeley, Cal., 1932), pp. 172, 178.

137. Fanshawe, *Memoirs*, p. 193; on the 'mimetismo' of the lower classes, A. Domínguez Ortiz, 'Notas sobre la consideración social del trabajo manual y el comercio en el Antiguo Régimen', *Revista de Trabajo* (1945) 673–81, at 677.

138. Guillamón, *Honor y honra*, p. 157; V. Palacio Atard, *Los españoles de la Ilustración* (Madrid, 1964), pp. 51, 53, 55.

139. Palacio Atard, *Los españoles de la Ilustración*, p. 59.

140. Guillamón, *Honor y honra*, p. 108.

a policy of royal 'creations' in the sixteenth century, and, in its extreme form, the ethnic patriality of *hidalguía* in Guipúzcoa and Vizcaya served both as the expression of a 'national' self-pride and as a form of local resistance to the spread of power from Madrid.[141] The developed, centralized absolutism of the 'administrative' or 'executive' monarchy of the Bourbons, with local power undermined by the decline of the cities, produced a nobility of Court and capital, a non-territorial, service nobility of royal creation that was not so much part of the natural order as an assertion of absolute authority. Restrictive traditionalist concepts of nobility had to be eradicated, as Pedro Antonio Sánchez recognised in 1781, by 'calling in aid the voice of the sovereign'.[142] Finally, in the atomistic, universalist, liberal nation-State, where there was no place for lordship over men or the delegation of sovereignty, the values of nobility became utilitarian, materialist and quantitative; aristocracy was plutocracy.

Clearly the framework of the traditional society of orders survived until the liberal revolution of the early nineteenth century. The question is, what had survived within that framework? A hereditary aristocracy remained the dominant élite and the ruling class, but it was a different aristocracy in 1800 than it had been in 1600. Exactly how different and in what ways has still to be definitively established. It was much more numerous – that at least is certain; more varied in lineage and origins, less clannish, less related by group loyalties, more disparate in wealth and weight. The *mayorazgo* was giving ground in the eighteenth century as fathers, preferring family to lineage, left their free property to their younger sons rather than to the entail.[143] The aristocracy was at its upper levels preponderantly metropolitan, more national, and perhaps international.[144] It was a Court and administrative 'service' aristocracy that was more divorced from the minor *títulos* and lesser nobility of the provincial capitals than had been the case in 1600. That concentration was as true of the local Aragonese and Catalan noblities in Zaragoza and Barcelona, as it was of Madrid. It was an aristocracy that was, to a much greater extent, a creation of the State and dependent upon it, and its power, exercised through government and office, or as patrons, landlords and employers, was less the power of an estate, or of houses, than of families and individuals.

Within, or rather alongside, that aristocracy many, if not most, of the great grandee families of 1600 still remained powers in the land in 1800 and for a long time after, though on more limited terms than in 1600. The

141. P. Fernández Albaladejo and J. M. Portillo Valdés, 'Hidalguía, fueros y constitución política: el caso de Guipúzcoa', in Lambert-Gorges, *Hidalgos et hidalguía*, pp. 149–65.

142. Guillamón, *Honor y honra*, p. 109.

143. Legislation of 28.4.1789 permitted the division of a *mayorazgo* among all children; Robledo, *Renta de la tierra*, p. 30 on increased amounts of 'bienes libres' for personal legacies; Ruiz Torres, 'Patrimonios y rentas', pp. 298–9; Aragón Mateos, *Nobleza extremeña*, p. 318.

144. Non-Castilian titles made up about 20 per cent of the total in 1597 (on Núñez de Salcedo's figures, twenty-three out of 127), about 50 per cent at the end of the eighteenth century (654 Castilian titles in 1787, 1,323 for whole of Spain in 1797), and 38 per cent of appointments to the Order of Carlos III between 1771 and 1808 were non-Castilian (Moreta, 'Caballeros de Carlos III', p. 417).

old grandees, with a few exceptions – the duke of Arcos and the count of Aranda in Charles III's reign are the most notable examples – had no significant rôle in central government after the successful establishment of Bourbon rule and much less direct influence or involvement in local government. It may also be that their position in their own domains was coming to depend less on authority than on personality. The contrast between the humiliation of the duke of Arcos in Elche in 1765, by the refusal of a group of civic dignitaries to pay their respects to his wife, and the endless round of receptions, parades, dances and bonfires that greeted the enlightened and philanthropic marquis of Santa Cruz when he visited Santa Cruz de Mudela, Valdepeñas, El Viso and the rest of his estates in 1774 is suggestive.[145] More and more the grandees were, though never simply, great landlords. The House of Alba remained the largest landed proprietor in nineteenth-century Castile and León.[146] The fact that of the thirty grandees in 1931 owning in excess of 4,000 hectares of land only three had been created after 1802, and nineteen had titles that dated back to the seventeenth century, indicates not only a real degree of continuity, but also an obvious success in adapting to juridical and economic change.

What is apparent before the end of the *ancien régime* is a significant 'modernization' of the social hierarchy in Spain. The successive devaluation of the *hidalgo*, the Don, the Habit of the Military Orders, the provincial *caballero*, left a simplified nobility that by the nineteenth century was in effect equated with title, and title was equated with wealth and power.[147]

The compression of nobility was thus a passage from status to class; from blood to wealth and office; from a closed, natural ideal of nobility deriving from the lineage, to an open, meritocratic, individualist élite centring on the family; from personal service to the prince to public service to the State. The chronology of that transition, always of course partial and incomplete, is confused by the mutual adjustments between social and ideological processes. Nobility in the seventeenth century had been open to money but only at the cost of accepting the framework of the society of orders and the 'Visigothic' values of *hidalguía*, and therefore of the denial of social and status change. The utilitarianism and bureaucratism of the eighteenth century both attributed to the State social welfare functions which had once defined aristocratic paternalism and provided new justifications for nobility more conducive to élite circulation. The doctrine of selflessness that had legitimized fiscal privilege, ceased to matter once the privileged were seen to be creators rather than consumers of wealth; the principle of heredity was threatened once a breeding for leadership and martial spirit was exposed as a less effective way of producing military success than experience, organizational ability and technical knowledge, and when what the progress of the nation seemed to need were the skills

145. Ruiz Torres, 'Los motines de 1766', p. 69, for Arcos; Morel-Fatio, *Etudes sur l'Espagne*, pp. 389–416, for Santa Cruz.

146. Robledo, *Renta de la tierra*, p. 50.

147. García Pelayo, 'El estamento de la nobleza', p. 57.

learned in the bourse (Stock Exchange), the factory and the university. 'Blood' was irrational; history a lesson, not a justification. Material differences were the sole philosophically legitimate basis for social differentiation (Feijóo, Campomanes). These changes came late in the eighteenth century and were more an acceptance of new values into the traditional canon than a wholesale replacement of that canon, but they opened the way to the survival of the old élite beyond the *ancien régime*, as well as to the transformation of the élite.

CHAPTER SEVEN

The Italian Nobilities in the Seventeenth and Eighteenth Centuries

Claudio Donati*
University of Milan

INTRODUCTION

An analysis of the size, characteristics and internal composition of the Italian nobility during the seventeenth and eighteenth centuries must be preceded by a brief summary of the political, economic, cultural and religious situation of the peninsula and the adjacent islands at this time. This will underline one essential fact: the existence not of a unified Italian nobility, but of a number of different nobilities, each distinct yet at the same time possessing certain characteristics in common with élites elsewhere in the peninsula.

This diversity was a long-standing characteristic of Italy's political physiognomy; it became even more marked during the seventeenth and eighteenth centuries. Elsewhere in Europe, large-scale States were coming into existence during this period, but no such evolution took place in the peninsula, where even the separate geographical regions were often themselves divided into smaller territories. Moreover, the constitutional characteristics of these various states were also diverse: there were city-States with limited territorial possessions; aristocratic republics; principalities which had retained many of the characteristics of the Renaissance State; the Papacy – an elective monarchy, but of an unusual kind; and the provinces of major European powers, above all Spain and later Austria, which enjoyed considerable autonomy from their foreign overlord.

In a work published in 1722, *L'Italia nobile* by Ludovico Araldi, the whole peninsula and the surrounding islands were divided into the following 'countries': Piedmont (that is to say, the most important territory of the Savoy dynasty); the State of Milan; Monferrato; the Duchy of Parma; the Duchy of Modena; the Duchy of Guastalla; the Duchy of Mirandola; the

---

* Translated by Helen Hyde.

Duchy of Mantua; the Republic of Venice; the Republic of Genoa; the Republic of Lucca; the Duchy of Massa; the Grand Duchy of Tuscany; the Papal State; the Kingdom of Naples; the Kingdom of Sicily and the Kingdom of Sardinia. This list can be completed by the inclusion of some other small independent States such as: the Republic of San Marino, situated between the Romagna and the Marches; the island of Malta, from 1530 the seat of the Order of the Knights of St John of Jerusalem (the so-called Knights of Malta) and considered one of the islands 'adjacent to Italy'; the Tuscan *presidi* (the *presidios de Toscana*), created in 1557 to guarantee Madrid's control of the Tyrrhenian sea coasts through the Spanish garrisons stationed there, and entrusted to the Appiani family; and the Bishopric of Trent, an ecclesiastical principality of the Holy Roman Empire tied politically to the Austrian province of the Tyrol, but economically and culturally inclined towards the Veneto and Lombardy. Nor can we omit other small – even in some cases quite minute – territories which claimed to be fiefs of the Holy Roman Empire and enjoyed *ius statuendi*, the right to legislate over their own subjects. These fiefs were especially numerous in the territory of the Apennines (between Piedmont, Lombardy, Liguria, Tuscany and the Romagna), but also existed in other parts of Italy.

Even from an economic point of view, the nobility in Italy was not homogeneous. The majority of nobles in the south drew a large part of their incomes from the land. Yet in many towns of northern and central Italy (such as Venice, Genoa, Lucca, Florence and Ancona) during the seventeenth and eighteenth centuries a considerable proportion of the nobilities' incomes continued to derive from 'commerce': that is, from international trade, foreign exchange transactions and financial speculation. It is certainly true, as will be shortly seen, that these cases were rather unusual and that, overall, the Italian nobility in this period was more concerned with exploiting the resources of the land than with trade or manufacturing. Throughout the early modern period, however, not even the near-universal status of landowner was capable of unifying the nobilities of the various parts of the peninsula.

This lack of unity arose from marked differences in the forms of agricultural leases and in the methods by which the land was exploited. From the end of the seventeenth, and above all during the eighteenth century, in some regions of northern Italy (especially the irrigated plains of the Po valley) there was an increase in commercial farming involving substantial investment and the employment of hired labour: usually these estates were not run directly by the noble owners themselves, but by their tenants who were well provided with both money and stock. Over a somewhat wider area, concentrated in central Italy and in the hilly or dry regions of the north, family smallholdings were the agricultural norm, with the landowners employing either leases with rent paid in kind, or *métayage* (share-cropping) agreements, or a mixture of both. Finally, there was an extensive agricultural area, concentrated in central and especially southern

Italy, in Sicily and in Sardinia, in which feudal *latifundia* predominated. These consisted of vast expanses of land used alternately for the grazing of livestock and for the cultivation of cereals by hired labour and by peasants tied to short-term and particularly onerous leases. Since the great majority of landowners were either noblemen or clergy of noble origins, this tripartite division of the land system in Italy established certain economic differences within the nobility: between those who lived off the profits of large capitalistic estates, others whose incomes derived from renting out smallholdings to tenant farmers, and finally the great feudal lords with their vast *latifundia*.

The formation of a single and homogeneous nobility was hindered by these economic and political divisions within the peninsula during the seventeenth and eighteenth centuries. At the same time, however, it must be remembered that factors tending towards cohesion and unity were as plentiful and as important as those tending towards division.

The first of these was the influence exerted by Spain. Until the final decades of the seventeenth century, the Spanish Monarchy directly or indirectly controlled a large part of the Italian peninsula and adjacent islands. Spain's own possessions (Milan, Naples, Sicily, Sardinia and the Tuscan *presidi*) covered almost half of the Italian territories; the rulers of Savoy and Tuscany owed their titles and subsequent consolidation of their position to Charles V and Philip II; Genoa was closely linked to Madrid by financial interests; the principalities of the Farnese, Gonzaga, and Este families were too small to develop an important rôle; and, given Spain's rôle as the strongest bastion of Catholicism in both Europe and the Mediterranean, the Papal State was inevitably inclined to seek alliance with the Spanish king, even if some popes did try to free themselves from this bond. This circumstance profoundly influenced the way of life and the mode of thought of the Italian nobles, who strongly felt the influence of Spanish customs and the attraction of the Court at Madrid. In particular, all the Italian nobilities, with the notable exception of the Venetian patriciate, derived from Spain the hierarchical system on which the noble class was built. At the apex of this pyramid stood the *Grandes de Espana* and the titled nobles (*duchi, marchesi, conti, visconti, baroni*); in the middle were the *caballeros*; and at the bottom the large mass of the *hidalgos*, the Italian equivalent of the latter being the world of the simple *gentiluomini* (gentlemen), defined by Giovanni Botero at the beginning of the seventeenth century as 'those who have sufficient property to support themselves from its revenue'.

Around 1700, however, Spain's influence was eclipsed by that of France. In the eighteenth century, political hegemony in Italy was not wielded by one single foreign State, but by the two power blocks of the Bourbon monarchies (France and Spain) on one side and by Habsburg Austria on the other. From the cultural viewpoint, however, one unifying factor was the diffusion of the French language and French culture and civilization throughout the upper classes of all the Italian states. Thus in the seventeenth century, Spanish customs, and in the eighteenth century, the civilization of France were two powerful elements of integration for the various nobilities of the peninsula.

From the sixteenth century onwards, moreover, the Italian upper classes had developed and refined a common culture based on the Aristotelian, humanistic, chivalrous and Catholic values of *virtù* (virtue), *cortesia* (courtesy), *onore* (sense of honour) and *dignità* (dignity or rank). Therefore, during the Renaissance a strong ideological and cultural identity had arisen among all the nobilities of the peninsula, regardless of their origins or political and economic situations. Within this historical context, a powerful element of cohesion was to be found in the formulation and diffusion of a learned language which derived originally from the *volgare* (vernacular) of fourteenth-century Florence, but which spread among the ruling classes of all the regions of the peninsula, above all through its use in Counter-Reformation Rome.

In fact, Rome, or more correctly the Roman Curia, constituted the most important place for the meeting and amalgamation of the various Italian nobilities at least until the beginning of the eighteenth century. The seventeenth-century Curia, from the minor offices through to the congregations of cardinals and the Pope himself, was almost exclusively both noble and Italian: as were the approximately fifty governors of the towns and provinces of the Papal State and the twelve Nuncios (Papal diplomats) permanently resident in the Catholic monarchies and republics throughout Europe. Those who pursued careers in the Curia came from the entire peninsula: from Florence, Genoa, Siena, Milan, Como, Naples, Venice and the towns of the Veneto, Piedmont, Modena, Parma and Piacenza, the Papal towns of the March and the Legations and Rome itself. As is clear from this list, the entire Italian nobility was represented in the Curia to the almost complete exclusion of nobles from other Catholic countries. From this point of view, the Papal Curia was not merely the largest but also the most representative Italian Court. The 'italianization' of the College of Cardinals, the Papal bureaucracy and, indeed, the Papacy itself created an enduring alliance between the Roman Catholic Church and the Italian nobility, which was only undermined by the reforms of the second half of the eighteenth century.

LEGAL CHARACTERISTICS AND NUMERICAL SIZE

Until the mid-eighteenth century a great many Italian States did not possess detailed laws defining the status of noble. Some rulers tried to link nobility to the possession of offices and fiefs conferred by themselves and to create a hierarchy of titles at the top of which they stood as territorial sovereigns (see below, pp. 244–9). Another very different concept of nobility was also to be found, especially in the principalities of Northern and Central Italy, and was peculiar to those towns which were heirs to the traditions of the medieval City-States. In these towns, for the most part during the sixteenth century, a *chiusura* (closure of noble ranks) or distinction of classes had come into effect, as a result of which the chief civic offices had been made hereditary in certain leading families, to the exclusion of the *popolari* (lower classes). The members of these families maintained that a town which had effected a *chiusura*, with either the explicit or tacit consent of the ruler as superior authority, had become a noble 'body' which could also transfer its own nobility to its 'limbs', the civic magistrates. These two opposing concepts coexisted for a long time. In fact, it was not difficult to find a solution – all that was needed was for the urban élites to ensure that they had noble titles conferred on them by the ruler, while he could choose his own nobles mostly from amongst the civic magistrates. It will be seen that in Tuscany, just such a process took place. But in theory the absence in a state of one single authority appointed to confer and recognize individual nobility was the source of considerable unease for the many noblemen who wanted a confirmation of their 'status' which could also be of value outside their own homeland. As a result, some supranational institutions, which adopted particularly rigorous criteria when examining the quality of would-be members, enjoyed great prestige amongst all the Italian nobilities and saw their judgements accepted as indisputable proof of the individual's noble status.

Throughout the early modern period, the most authoritative of these was undoubtedly the religious-military Order of the Knights of Malta. From the second half of the sixteenth century onwards, a would-be knight of the *Lingua dell'Italia*, one of the eight national groupings into which the Order was divided, had to undergo an investigation by two commissioners. This was based on a questionnaire of twenty-two points and examined very thoroughly the places of origin of the candidate and his 'quarterings' (his father, mother, paternal and maternal grandparents). The commissioners had to ascertain, among other things, the following: if the males of the four families from which the candidate descended had always lived *more nobilium*, that is to say separately from the common people; if these same men had held town offices normally reserved for the nobility; if lower class (*popolari*) families became members of the nobility in their town; if the candidate and/or his ancestors had ever personally been involved in any trade in wool, silk or other goods and if they had stood behind a counter or practised other humble vocations (among which the office of notary was specifically mentioned). In one clause, it was specified that the ban on 'trade' did not apply to the nobles of Genoa, Florence, Siena and Lucca, which demonstrates how even an international institution such as the Knights of Malta recognised that the situation in Italy was both complicated, and quite distinct from that of other European nobilities.

The political and social implications of this situation will become clear subsequently. Here it is important to note that the diversity of criteria by which different authorities could bestow or recognize the nobility of an individual makes it very difficult to determine either the total numerical size of the Italian nobility before the legislation of first the eighteenth and then the nineteenth centuries, or the relationship between the number of nobles and the total population and the trajectory of this relationship over time. Among other things, it is necessary to bear in mind that the data for the nobility of a particular place as a rule only refers to male adults, and it is thus difficult to gain a reliable picture of its overall numerical size. A further difficulty arises from the ambiguous meaning of the term *famiglia* ('family'): in certain cases this includes all individuals with the same surname, in others only those living under one roof or *casa* ('household'). At the present stage of research it is impossible to arrive at a comprehensive estimate of the number of nobles in Italy during the seventeenth and eighteenth centuries. Only some incomplete figures can be given, beginning with the city republics, where problems of interpretation are fewer because the only nobility recognized by law was identical with the ruling class of the main town or city.

From 1528 to 1797 at Genoa 10,856 names of male nobles were entered in the *Libro d'oro* ('Golden Book') of the nobility: of these approximately 10,000 were the descendants of nobles already inscribed in the book. For the beginning of the seventeenth century a very rough count gives a total of 2,500 Genoese noblemen, even if considerably fewer were actually present and able to take part in the magistracies. The total population of the Republic in 1608 was approximately 360,000, of which the city of Genoa held only 67,000. By 1630, the number of male nobles in that city had fallen to 1,802 of whom 306 were absent; by 1725, this figure had fallen further to 804, of whom seventy-three were absent from the city. By the mid-eighteenth century, the total population of the Republic had risen to 450,000. If the absence of many nobles from Genoa was a result of their emigration to Spain, the Spanish American Empire, Naples, Sicily, Rome, France and Flanders for military, commercial and financial motives, the progressive and accelerated numerical decline of the nobility was, as noted by Edoardo Grendi[1], a result both of demographic factors such as the increase in celibacy, the reduction in the number of remarriages of widows and widowers and the diminution in the number of children, and of a political decision, namely the ever-tighter restriction placed on the number of entries made in the *Libro d'oro*. Thus within this context, it is significant that the 289 family names of the Genoese nobility in 1621 had shrunk to 128 by 1797.

From the end of the sixteenth century onwards access to the two main magistracies at Lucca (the *Consiglio Generale* [General Council] of ninety members in office for one year and the *Anzianato* [Council of Elders] of ten members with a tenure of two months) was restricted to a limited number of families: in 1628 this closure (*chiusura*) was formalized by a law

---

1. Edoardo Grendi, *La repubblica aristocratica dei genovesi* (Bologna, 1987), esp. pp. 13–48.

which recognized 211 families as noble. Yet in the period from 1608 to 1627, some 144 families featured in the *Consiglio Generale* and 105 families in the *Anzianato*. In the following two decades, from 1628 to 1647, the numbers remained practically unchanged: 141 families were represented in the *Consiglio Generale* and 105 in the *Anzianato*. Before the plague of 1630, the population of the city of Lucca numbered approximately 22,000, a figure which subsequently fell to 13,500; it is more difficult to determine the population of the rural regions of the Republic which may have been as high as 80,000. All the sources concur in their emphasis on the population growth in the State of Lucca during the eighteenth century and the parallel decline in the number of noble families who in 1787 numbered a mere eighty-eight, while male nobles totalled no more than 200.

From the end of the thirteenth century onwards, the patriciate of the Republic of Venice formed a clearly defined class. In the fifteenth and sixteenth centuries, the legal devices were perfected which were to maintain the exclusivity of the patrician families in relation to the burghers of Venice and the nobles of the towns on the Venetian mainland. From an examination of the registration of the births, marriages and accessions to the *Maggior Consiglio* (Great Council) of all the legitimate male patricians, very precise figures can be given for the nobility of Venice.[2] At the beginning of the seventeenth century, there were approximately 2,090 male patricians over the age of 25, of whom between 1,300 and 1,600 were members of the *Maggior Consiglio*. After the devastation of the plague of 1630–31, the number of patricians fell to 1,660. From the mid-seventeenth century to the early years of the eighteenth century, 127 new families were admitted to the patriciate yet the number of nobles never again equalled that of the earlier period: in 1775 they numbered 1,300, but by the end of the Republic in 1797 this figure had dropped to 1,090. At the beginning of the seventeenth century, the population of the city of Venice was approximately 150,000, a figure which the plague reduced to 102,000; by 1696 the population had climbed again to 138,000 and it then stabilized for a century. From the census of 1766, it can be seen that 2,249,000 people lived on the mainland, yet the number of these who, even if they did not belong to the Venetian patriciate, could be described as noble on the basis of customary local laws is unclear. The number of adult male nobles in the large and medium sized towns of the mainland (namely Padua, Vicenza, Verona, Brescia, Bergamo, Treviso, Belluno, Feltre, Crema and Udine) can be calculated at approximately 9,000, although this figure would be considerably increased by the inclusion as nobles of the members of families who ran the smaller towns of the mainland. It should also be noted that patriciates similar to those of the mainland existed in the maritime territories of the Republic, in particular in Istria and Dalmatia.

Information concerning the nobility of the principalities of northern and central Italy before the second half of the eighteenth century is often

2. James C. Davis, *The Decline of the Venetian Nobility as a Ruling Class* (Baltimore, Md., 1962).

unreliable. Until 1720, the constitution of the nobility in the territories of the House of Savoy was regulated by two parallel bodies: the *Chambre des Comptes* based at Chambéry dealt with the transalpine regions and the *Camera dei Conti* at Turin covered the cisalpine territories. These two bodies kept copies of all letters or patents of nobility and feudal investitures granted by the sovereign and received the oath of loyalty from the titled noblemen (*marchesi, conti, baroni*) and the 'vassal' holders of fiefs with power of jurisdiction. They also evaluated the proofs of nobility necessary to enjoy certain privileges and to occupy some public offices. The cisalpine feudal nobility was to be found overwhelmingly in Piedmont and at the beginning of the seventeenth century it consisted of approximately 800 families. By 1724, this had risen to 1,246 at a time when the population of Piedmont was 1,075,000. In 1702, the families of noble rank in Savoy numbered 795 with a total of 3,400 individual members, compared to Savoy's total population of 337,000 in 1734. During the seventeenth century, 186 patents of nobility were granted in Savoy.[3] There were also various public offices which conferred personal nobility upon their holders. But the picture is not completed by the mention of the titled and untitled feudality and those ennobled by holding office (who often purchased fiefs and thus merged with the old nobility). In reality, the situation was far more complex, especially in Piedmont, because in many towns, local patriciates existed who were neither holders of fiefs nor in the service of the prince, but who nevertheless claimed nobility.

In the eighteenth century various changes occurred. From 1720 onwards the island of Sardinia was part of the Savoyard State. Her feudal lords, mostly of Spanish origin, numbered 360 out of the island's total population of around 300,000. In the same year the *Camera dei Conti* was merged with the *Chambre des Comptes*, with the headquarters of the new organization at Turin, and the sole jurisdiction of the *Camera* in matters of ennoblement was established. In this context, it should be remembered that the Savoyard monarchy was the first Italian State to set down in law the three single legitimate sources of transmissible nobility.

These were: the purchase of a fief; a royal letter of ennoblement; and the holding of an office suitable for the foundation of a noble line (for example, the post of senator). In fact, a law of 1733 which reformed the municipal administrations also greatly limited the privileges of the patriciates of the smaller towns and brought to an end their claims to constitute a nobility autonomous from the sovereign. Even the old patrician families resorted to purchasing feudal titles. These titles continued to be in great demand throughout the whole of the eighteenth century, both because they guaranteed fiscal immunity and because of the prestige and authority they bestowed.

In the Duchy of Mantua, the formation of a titled nobility dated back to the second half of the sixteenth century when the Holy Roman Emperor

3. Jean Nicolas, *La Savoie au XVIIIe siècle: noblesse et bourgeoisie,* 2 vols (Paris, 1978).

granted Duke Guglielmo Gonzaga the right to create *conti* and *marchesi*. However, precise data on the Mantuan nobility is lacking before 1775, when the *Tribunale Araldico* (Heraldic Tribunal) set up by the Austrian government recognized 161 noble houses: five *principi*, thirty-five *marchesi*, sixty-two *conti*, fifty-two untitled nobles and seven noble burghers. As a whole the nobility must have consisted of about 700 people, out of the duchy's population of approximately 218,000 inhabitants.

It is not possible at the present stage of research to give reliable figures for the number of nobles in either Parma or Modena during the seventeenth century. In these duchies the picture is especially confused because of the existence side-by-side of feudal lords of ancient origin, those who had been newly created by the Duke, and noble citizens of the capital city and of the smaller towns. The ducal courts of the Farnese and Este were certainly the places where all these gentlemen mixed, although these same courts were never to become the only institutions authorized to ratify a family's noble status.

Even after the establishment of the principality of the Medici, the influence of the republican tradition remained very strong in Tuscany. In the fifteenth century, the major offices of the Florentine Republic were held by the members of approximately 1,000 families, of which 150 were the most frequent holders of office and were conspicuous by their wealth and prestige. As will be seen in the following paragraphs, this republican nucleus continued to wield considerable political influence even under the new Medicean regime, and it did not suffer a serious diminution in numbers. At the end of the seventeenth century, Florentine families descended from the Republican élite numbered 385, giving a total of approximately 2,000 members. By around 1760, 314 of these families were still in existence: in the same period Florence boasted a population of around 80,000 inhabitants. It is more difficult to estimate the overall number of nobles living in the Grand Duchy before the promulgation of the law of 1750 which laid down the conditions under which inscription in the *Libro d'oro* of the Tuscan nobility was permitted. The definition of 'nobility' had not previously been seriously examined in the Grand Duchy: the reason for this is perhaps to be found in the deliberate wish of the Medici not to disturb the politico-constitutional balance within which certain aspects of the old republican structure and the new practices typical of an absolutist state happily coexisted. According to these new rules, the Tuscan nobility consisted of the officers and courtiers of the Grand Duke, the Knights of the military Order of Saint Stephen, and Tuscany's feudal lords. But in a broad sense and by general consensus, all the families descended from those citizens who had held the main offices in the city-states of medieval Tuscany were included in the aristocracy, which thus meant not only Florence and Siena but also Pistoia, Arezzo, Pisa, Volterra, Cortona and even Sansepolcro, Montepulciano, Colle, San Miniato, Prato, Livorno and Pescia. In the seventeenth and eighteenth centuries, this more archaic definition of nobility was still very much common currency and thus the most important distinction was not between nobles and non-nobles but between those who lived in the towns and those who lived in the countryside.

It is even more difficult to provide comprehensive and reliable figures for the nobility of the Papal State where each province had its own local laws and the central government provided no effective coordination. Naturally, such a situation did not encourage the development of a homogeneous nobility. For example, Bologna was characterized by a type of 'patrician totalitarianism'[4]; the rule of approximately 300 families was virtually absolute and was exercised through the city's Senate which both looked and behaved like the government of an autonomous state in its dealings with both Rome and foreign governments. In the Papal March[5] there was a large number of urban communities which followed their own particular laws, and there was thus a wide variation from community to community as to those who were allowed to hold municipal office. In some places, such as Ancona and Camerino, the lower classes (*popolari*) were totally excluded from government. Elsewhere, municipal office included some posts which were open only to nobles and others which could be held by the lower classes. Consequently, the March can be seen as one of the regions of Italy in which the political traditions of the medieval communes had largely been maintained. A completely different situation was to be found in the provinces of Lazio – Patrimonio, Campagna and Marittima – where the great fiefs of the powerful Roman baronage predominated. There the rulers included both the old seignorial families of the Colonna, Orsini, Savelli, Caetani and Conti, and the new dynasties comprising relatives of the Popes, such as the Barberini, Borghese and Pamphili, who had moved to Rome and been invested with fiefs and other privileges. The old and new baronage also formed the nucleus of the nobility of Rome which, however, also included the descendants of the urban patriciate downgraded in importance in the fifteenth and sixteenth centuries by the pope, and above all the prelates of the Papal Curia which (as noted earlier) was drawn from all parts of Italy. In short, the peculiar characteristics of the Roman nobility were a result of the presence in Rome of a sovereign as distinctive as the pope.

It remains to consider the three main territories of the Spanish Crown in Italy: Milan, Naples and Sicily. In the Duchy of Milan during the seventeenth century, the richest and most politically influential group of nobles was the patriciate of the capital city, and it was from this group that the Spanish Governor chose the members of the *Consiglio dei Sessanta Decurioni* (the 'Council of the Sixty Decurions'). This Council was the highest civic office and had a wide jurisdiction over all the Duchy's territory. From 1535 to 1796, there were 789 Decurions, drawn from 293 families: of these, 182 resigned their position in favour of their brothers, nephews and, especially, their sons, thus ensuring that their own family remained

---

4. Angela De Benedictis, *Patrizi e comunità: Il governo del contado bolognese nel '700*, (Bologna, 1984), esp. p. 19.
5. Bandino Giacomo Zenobi, *Ceti e potere nella Marca pontificia: formazione e organizzazione della piccola nobiltà fra '500 e '700* (Bologna, 1976).

continuously in the Council.[6] It is noteworthy that seventy-five families produced at least four Decurions and thirty-one families were present in the Council for five generations or more. This smaller group was the cream of the patriciate and had its stronghold in the *Collegio dei Conservatori degli Ordini*, founded in 1621 and not subject to the Governor's approval. New patricians were only admitted by the *Collegio* according to very strict criteria.

Another institution closely linked to the patriciate was the *Collegio dei dottori giureconsulti*. Admittance to this body was also gained by an examination of the 'proofs' of nobility, with the onus on the would-be member to prove that he lived nobly and was not descended from anyone who had ever practised a humble craft. Between 1535 and 1796, there were 939 admissions to the College. The majority of the members of this College were called on to fill the upper and middle posts of the municipal and State administrations throughout the period of Spanish rule and then during the early years under Austrian control. The Milanese Senate was the most important tribunal of the Duchy and it, too, was dominated by members of the Milanese patriciate. Senators were chosen by the sovereign and comprised members of the Spanish nobility (later to be replaced by the Austrian nobility, after Vienna's acquisition of the province at the beginning of the eighteenth century), the Milanese patriciate and the patriciates of the Duchy's smaller towns such as Cremona, Pavia, Como and Lodi.

These figures also include the titled nobility, that is to say men who obtained noble titles from the reigning sovereign. Between 1554 and 1706, the kings of Spain granted 276 titles of *conti* and *marchesi*, of which 118 went to Milanese patrician families. The titles were tied to the purchase of fiefs in the Duchy. Between 1707 and 1740, the new Austrian sovereign, Charles VI, sold a further 124 titles. In addition, many titles were granted to families of the Duchy by foreign sovereigns such as the Holy Roman Emperors, and the Dukes of Parma, Mantua, Modena, Savoy and Bavaria. Naturally, this brought about a progressive decline in the status of noble titles. In any case, the possession of a title was not in itself sufficient to ensure entry into the patriciate: for the most part, a title was either an official recognition of a previously established position or signified the beginning of a rise in social status. A law of 1769 which set out to prescribe the exact form of the nobility within the Duchy instituted three levels of nobility: royal officials with their own personal nobility; feudal lords given jurisdiction over at least fifty *fuochi* (households); and chamberlains and other courtiers of the Archduke Ferdinand of Habsburg (from 1771 governor of Milan), placed on a level with the patricians of the towns of Austrian Lombardy. A Heraldic Tribunal was to revise the list of the nobles of the State. Between 1770 and 1796, the register of the Heraldic Tribunal recorded 284 lineages of the Milanese patriciate, with 195 different surnames.

6. Franco Arese, 'Nobiltà e patriziato nello Stato di Milano', in S. Pizzetti, ed., *Dallo Stato di Milano alla Lombardia contemporanea* (Milan, 1980), pp. 71–96.

Various criteria can be adopted to describe the nobility of the Kingdom of Naples. In the capital, Naples, and the larger cities of the provinces there was the patriciate or the *nobiltà di seggio*. The *seggi* were the administrative districts into which the city of Naples was traditionally divided and which had come to be dominated by the high nobility who resided there. They were an increasingly exclusive means by which aristocratic power was organized and exercised. The status of *nobiltà di seggio* was transmissible only in the direct line and carried the right to take part in the administration of the city. At Naples, there were five noble *seggi* (with a sixth reserved for the lower orders), and they only admitted new families by unanimous consent and royal ratification: in fact, after 1553, the *seggi* successfully opposed any admission of new members. From 1629 to 1703, the total number of families belonging to the *seggio* groupings remained fairly constant, at between 126 and 132. The patriciate of the provincial towns numbered in total approximately 1,200 families. There was also the so-called *nobiltà fuori piazza* (literally the 'nobility outside the piazza'), made up of families of the local nobility excluded from the *seggi*, foreign nobles who had recently settled in the Kingdom, and families of mercantile origins who were holders of fiefs periodically offered for sale by the Spanish government. It is difficult to estimate the size of the *nobiltà fuori piazza*; it was perhaps one-third of the size of the whole *nobiltà di seggio*. Both types of nobility took part in the general Parliaments of the Kingdom which met until 1642. Such representative institutions had emerged in Italy between the eleventh and the sixteenth centuries. Their main function was to vote the 'gifts' (in effect, taxation) demanded by the sovereign. The oldest and most important Estates were those of Sicily and Sardinia, while the general Parliaments of the State of Savoy and those of the Papal State no longer met after the sixteenth century.

Up to this point, the structure of the nobility in the Kingdom of Naples could well appear similar to that of Milan. There is, however, one fundamental difference caused by the preponderant influence of feudal power in the south. Between 70 and 80 per cent of the entire population of the Kingdom (which numbered approximately 2,850,000 inhabitants in the mid-seventeenth century) was, in fact, subject to feudal control. The feudal lords were divided into two groups: the families of the 'titled nobility' who exercised civil and criminal jurisdiction in the provinces, had palaces in Naples and for the most part also belonged to the *seggi* of the capital; and the families of the 'untitled baronage' who owned feudal communities of less than 500 households. In the mid-sixteenth century, there were seventeen families which formed the élite of the titled nobility and between them they owned a total of 199 domains containing 190,000 households, in other words more than half of the population which fell under feudal control. This aristocratic élite formed a very close-knit group due to frequent inter-marriage and the sharing of military offices and posts in the government of the capital city. The group consisted of the old families of the Kingdom, such as the Carafa, Sanseverino, Caracciolo and Pignatelli, along with members of the Italian and European aristocracy who were part of Spain's imperial power structure such as the d'Avalos, Gonzaga, de Lannoy and Piccolomini. At the beginning of the reign of Philip II (1556–98), the feudal nobility as a whole contained 245 surnames. In the seventeenth century, its ranks swelled enormously, above all as a result of the policy of enfeoffment and the sale of State lands through financial necessity on the part of the Spanish government. Thus by 1675, the feudal nobility comprised in total 937 families, of which 444 were titled.

To conclude, if one takes into account the nobilities *di seggio* and *fuori piazza* and the titled and non-titled nobles, in the seventeenth century the nobility of the Kingdom of Naples must have included approximately 2,500 families in total. Yet it is all but impossible to determine the number of individual nobles because of the great variation in the size of the families involved. For example, from a document of 1605 on the *seggi* of Naples, it emerges that some noble households were made up of only one or two individuals while others even comprised as many as fifty-one members of the same lineage. Yet any discussion of the Neapolitan nobility cannot end here. In reality, in Naples as in France and in other European monarchies, there was an intermediate 'rank' between the nobility and the lower classes which can be defined as the '*ceto civile*' (civil class) and included magistrates, lawyers, officials and university professors. Within the 'civil class' there existed a more exclusive and close-knit group, the *ministero* (ministry), made up of the supreme judges of the courts of Naples: this was a true *nobiltà di toga* (*noblesse de robe*), whose power lay in their control of the law. The estimates of the size of this 'civil class' vary immensely: for the beginning of the eighteenth century, figures of 26,000 and 50,000 individuals are quoted, which can be compared to the contemporary population of 215,000 inhabitants in the city of Naples and 3,300,000 in the Kingdom as a whole.

A similar situation existed in Sicily where the great feudal lords with their political stronghold in the Parliament also constituted the most important part of the nobility. In the larger cities and especially at Messina, there also existed a patriciate of mercantile origin. Nevertheless, during the seventeenth century, the Spanish Crown decidedly favoured the feudal nobility, and in particular the titled nobles, generously granting them licences for the construction of new villages within their large 'feudal states' and extending their legal jurisdiction over their subjects: in exchange, the *conti* and *marchesi* settled at Palèrmo at the Court of the Viceroy. In this way, the Sicilian nobles assumed their characteristic double life of refined aristocratic courtiers at Palermo and oppressive and violent overlords at home in their fiefs. As for the size of this class, it is known that there were eighty parliamentary nobles at the end of the sixteenth century.

This analysis of the legal characteristics and the numerical size of the Italian nobilities has touched upon two topics which must now be explored at greater length: in the first place, the structure of the patrimonies on which the social pre-eminence of the aristocracy was founded and the methods by which these same patrimonies were built up, consolidated and then passed on to subsequent generations; and, secondly, the political rôle of the nobles with respect to other groups in society and when confronted with the development of absolutist states.

SOCIAL AND ECONOMIC POWERS

The identification between nobility and the land which has been proposed by many historians, economists and sociologists is sustainable if one is to understand from this that the essential characteristic peculiar to the medieval and early modern European nobilities was dominion over the land and the men who worked it. In the same way, it is correct to maintain that until the eighteenth century, and in many countries even during the nineteenth century, the majority of large landowners were noblemen. Yet given that many noble patrimonies exhibit wide variations in their sources of income, it would be mistaken to believe that during the *ancien régime* agriculture constituted the aristocracies' only source of wealth. This is particularly true for the Italian patriciates of the fifteenth and the first half of the sixteenth centuries. In their family balance sheets the income and produce from the land and sometimes the seigneurial dues were certainly of considerable importance; but of no less significance were the income and profits from the families' activities in manufacturing, commerce, shipping, insurance and banking.

In this context it is remarkable that during the sixteenth and seventeenth centuries the patrician families of northern and central Italy were the leaders in a widespread movement away from trade and manufacturing and towards the purchase and exploitation of landed estates. This wide-ranging social and economic development has been variously called 'a race to the land', 'the reorientation of society to the land' and 'refeudalization'. Even in earlier centuries, however, the capital accumulated through industry, commerce and banking had at times been used to purchase landed estates. One well-known case springs immediately to mind: that of the Borromeo family who, in the fifteenth century, were involved in Milanese high finance yet a hundred years later drew most of their income from agricultural and feudal revenues. From the second half of the sixteenth century onwards, however, there was a further development. New families did not emerge to replace those merchant-entrepreneurs who abandoned commerce and industry in favour of living off income from their estates, from investments in the public debt, from the possession of fiefs and from usurious loans to peasants. Many historians have argued that the reasons for the reversion to the land lie in the broader economic context, with high prices in grain and other agricultural products and with a crisis in the commercial and manufacturing sectors which worsened throughout the peninsula from

1619–20 onwards, as a result of a long succession of wars, plagues and famines. It has also been claimed, however, that the economic downturn had devastating effects on Italian society because the nobilities exploited the opportunity offered by the crisis to close their ranks, thereby preventing that social mobility which, to a greater or lesser extent, had always occurred in earlier periods. In fact, it was in the seventeenth century that the rules previously alluded to (see above, p. 241) which excluded from the nobility the sons and grandsons of those who had practised the 'mechanical arts' were made more rigorous and inflexible. In this climate, being a merchant not only involved making less profit than two centuries earlier, but also carried a social condemnation of present and future generations against which there was no right of appeal.

There were, however, some exceptions within this general picture. In certain instances, the unfavourable economic situation did not lead to the abandonment of industry and commerce. The case of seventeenth-century Lucca is typical.[7] Throughout this period, its young nobles were urged to seek employment in the silk industry which was declared to be 'a suitable business for people of their position'. During the seventeenth century, at least 154 mercantile companies were active at Lucca and many of the shareholders belonged to old patrician families, such as the Arnolfini, the Buonvisi, the Burlamacchi and the Guinigi. Faced with the sharp contraction in exports to Germany as a result of the outbreak of the Thirty Years War, the great patrician families sought new markets in Sicily, Poland, Lithuania and Russia. The failure of these attempts does not detract from the fact that throughout successive generations, the nobility of Lucca remained faithful to their commercial inclinations.

To a certain extent a similar pattern can be found in the Genoese nobility and especially among the group of 'innovatory' patricians led by Agostino Pallavicini, who was elected Doge in 1637. These nobles were politically hostile to Spain and hoped to free Genoa from its economic tutelage, aiming instead to revitalize the Republic's shipping industry, and form trading companies with public membership and investment based on the English and Dutch models: in short, to restore to their former prosperity the two sources of Genoa's fortune and its position as a commercial and maritime power. The scheme failed for many reasons, but principally due to the united opposition of all the other maritime states. The project itself, however, underlines that the seventeenth-century Genoese nobility were anything but resigned to the unfavourable economic situation.

In other parts of the Italian peninsula, the signals were contradictory and ambiguous. At Florence, following the banking and industrial crisis of 1573–75 and the slow but continuous decline of the wool industry after 1616, the patrician families chose to invest in land either in Tuscany or in the Papal State or the Kingdom of Naples.[8] In some cases, such as that

---

7. Rita Mazzei, *La società lucchese del Seicento* (Lucca, 1977).
8. Paolo Malanima, *La decadenza di un'economia cittadina* (Bologna, 1980).

of the Ricasoli, this reversion to the land was total. The Florentine patricians also managed to obtain the feudal titles pertaining to the estates which they purchased: by the mid-seventeenth century, the titles of *conti* and *marchesi* preceded the surnames of some famous families from the republican era, such as Niccolini, Guicciardini, Albizi, Ridolfi and Capponi. At the same time, the personal investments for which the Florentine nobility had been well known for centuries throughout Italy and Europe diminished. But a reduction does not mean a complete disappearance: throughout the seventeenth century and the early decades of the eighteenth century a high proportion of the nobility continued to maintain their own personal investments: furthermore, in the same period 10 or even 20 per cent of Florentine business partnerships were headed by noblemen. In any case, the diverse economic strategies of the various families is striking. In 1720, the patrimony of the Riccardi, who by their wealth were the foremost House of Florence, consisted of 58 per cent property and 6 per cent shares in commercial companies. The comparable figures for the second wealthiest House, that of the Salviati, were 78 per cent and 0.7 per cent respectively.

The Venetian patriciate was the oldest and most famous of all Europe's mercantile aristocracies. From the second half of the sixteenth century onwards, the distancing of the patricians from commerce was a gradual process which then gathered pace in the eighteenth century. Yet for Venice's leading families it was probably military defeats by the Turks together with the Republic's ever more apparent weakness in international affairs, rather than the unfavourable economic climate, which caused their withdrawal from commerce. A brief study of the Donà family illustrates the patriciate's dilemma.[9] Giambattista Donà (1488–1568), a merchant and the governor of Cyprus, was very active in the Mediterranean trade and for several years personally served as captain of the family ship. His eldest son, Andrea, an agent of his father's trade company at Tripoli in Syria, died in 1571 at the battle of Lepanto. Another son, Girolamo, was sent to the trade fairs at Lyon and after his father's retirement became captain of the family ship. Giambattista's third son, Nicolò, was the only one to father children and is a transitional figure: he had known the prosperity of Venetian trade with the East, but had also experienced the decline and gradual withdrawal of the patriciate from 'trade' and shipping. It is significant that the sea-faring days of the Donà ended in 1602 when a ship laden with sugar and under the command of Antonio, a son of Nicolò, was captured by English pirates. Another son of Giambattista, Leonardo, typified the new leanings of the patriciate. He resolutely pursued a political career and was, in fact, elected Doge in 1606, and purchased properties on the mainland with equal determination. The account books of Leonardo for the thirty years before his election as Doge show that his

---

9. James C. Davis, *A Venetian Family and its Fortune, 1500–1900: The Donà and the Conservation of their Wealth* (Philadelphia, Pa., 1975).

wealth came principally from the agricultural revenues of his estates in the province of Verona and from his investments in the Venetian public debt. These two entries alone comprised more than two-thirds of his income: the rest was made up of profits from the running of a ferry which linked the two banks of the Grand Canal near the Rialto bridge and from the salaries and perquisites of the public offices he held. There is no mention whatsoever in these accounts of any investment in trading companies. Two problems which are always present in these case studies remain unresolved: to what extent can the Donà family be regarded as typical of the Venetian patriciate as a whole? and could the different economic choices of the brothers of the same noble family have been influenced primarily by the practices followed to preserve and pass on the family patrimony? This latter question will be examined shortly (see below, pp. 254–7).

The Milanese patriciate was without doubt the noble class which most quickly and thoroughly transformed its economic outlook as a result of the crisis of the seventeenth century. From 1620 to 1650, some patrician families of long-standing mercantile origins (the d'Adda, Arese, Melzi, Arconati, Litta, Crivelli and so on) invested large amounts of capital in the purchase of landed property and even of fiefs, and in the following period made so many further purchases that large consolidated estates were formed. This strategy undoubtedly reflected the patriciate's refusal to risk capital in commercial ventures during times of crisis and its willingness to make do with the low but secure returns (around 3 per cent per annum) which investment in land guaranteed. But as time passed, this course of action became so rooted in the patriciate's mentality that it changed its basic characteristics: what had previously been one of Europe's most active commercial groups became during the seventeenth century an élite of *rentiers*. Some recent researchers have argued that the decline of seventeenth-century Lombardy was limited to the urban economy whilst rural areas were unaffected by the slump and the manufacturing enterprises which had existed there since the previous century remained intact.[10] Yet this new and more optimistic interpretation of the situation in Lombardy during the seventeenth century does not really alter the negative assessment of the transformation which the patriciate experienced and simultaneously encouraged. It is not simply a question of a 'race to the land', but of a far deeper and more fundamental transformation. In 1593, more than a decade before the onset of the industrial and commercial crisis, the aforementioned *Collegio dei giureconsulti* decreed the exclusion from membership of those whose families had devoted themselves to commerce. Milan, a city which had been so proud of its 'industry', prepared to celebrate the *ozio onorato* (honourable idleness) of those gentlemen who lived off private incomes. Furthermore, from the early years of the seventeenth century onwards, the patricians adopted the two institutions of the *maggiorascato* (primogeniture) and the *fedecommesso*

---

10. Domenico Sella, *Crisis and Continuity: The Economy of Spanish Lombardy in the Seventeenth Century* (Cambridge, Mass., 1979).

(entail or *fideicommissum*) which tied up a family's landed patrimony and concentrated it in the hands of one single heir. The general spread of these inheritance practices within the nobility helped to change radically the relationships between the various members of a family and deeply affected marital strategies. However, this was not a development which only influenced Milan and Lombardy. An examination of the ties between a noble family and its property will thus be useful both in order to understand the mechanisms of this economic and social structure and the transformations these same mechanisms were undergoing.

The first area to be examined will be the ways in which wealth was passed on to the next generation. Until the mid-sixteenth century, the favoured method of the upper classes throughout Italy had been the patrilinear division of the inheritance, which gave equal shares to all the male children and brought about the rise of *fraterne* (fraternal partnerships) among the mercantile patriciates. Within these partnerships brothers lived together and thus kept intact the family's property while dividing between themselves the profits from any industrial and commercial enterprises. In the south and in other regions where feudalism remained strong, the division of fiefs between all the sons led to a strong sense of the solidarity of the 'lineage' between the various branches of a family which often intermarried so as to be able to hand down the fiefs within the 'lineage' and thus avoid their ever escheating to the Crown. From the second half of the sixteenth century and above all during the seventeenth century, the favoured method by which wealth was handed down was by patrilinear unity of the inheritance. In this way all a father's property and wealth passed to only one of his sons with the entire transaction being recorded in great detail in the will of the head of the family. The principle of primogeniture meant that the family estate passed from eldest son to eldest son through to the end of the male line, at which point it passed to the collateral male lines listed in order of precedence. In the absence of any males in all the lines stated in the will, a female member of the family could inherit the estate on condition that she changed the surname of her own son to that of the testator. Primogeniture was often combined with entail, which provided that the whole patrimony had to pass undivided from one heir to another *in perpetuum*. It is important to note that entail had been both known and used in earlier centuries, but only for a part of the inheritance such as the ancestral palace which, as a symbol of the antiquity of the family, had to remain within the same family name. A study of sixteenth-century Lucca cites the 1515 will of Nicolao Balbani in which he specified that the palace where he lived was to remain *alicui seu aliquibus de domo et familia de Balbanis* (in the possession of the house and family of the Balbani); a similar stipulation with the added clause of *in perpetuum* was dictated in 1535 by another Lucchese patrician, Stefano Bernardi.[11] Moreover, this type of simple *fideicommissum* was not tied to

---

11. Marino Berengo, *Nobili e mercanti nella Lucca del '500* (Turin, 1965), pp. 32–3.

primogeniture and was used by both nobles and non-nobles: for example, in 1568, the Florentine merchant Giovanni Riccardi entailed 78 per cent of his landed wealth while leaving his three sons as his joint heirs.

Studies of the various regions of Italy make clear that it was only during the second half of the sixteenth century and the early seventeenth century that *fideicommissum* began to be applied together with the practice of primogeniture to all the landed patrimony of a noble family. Yet this inheritance strategy enjoyed anything but immediate and total success. Extensive research has been published on the Kingdom of Naples[12] and the example of the Capua family from Altavilla may be cited. Within this family, the first entail was established in 1588 by Giovanni, but only in 1691 did Bartolomeo extend it to the whole feudal and allodial inheritance. The Sanseverino family of Bisignano had adopted the practice of primogeniture at an early stage but the first entail was only set up in 1645 by Luigi and was limited to the allodial property. In 1704, it was extended by Carlo to cover the old feudal property and in 1726 Giuseppe Leopoldo included recently purchased lands. For the Caracciolo family of Martina, it was only in 1655 that Francesco established an entail in primogeniture covering some one-third of the patrimony: in 1703, his son Petraccone extended it to cover all the family goods including the silverware. At the other end of Italy, in Piedmont, Carlo Lodovico Falletti of Barolo in his wills of 1675, 1690, 1695 and 1705 fixed a succession of ever-wider and more definitive entails in primogeniture on his property.[13] In Venice, the cases of the Donà[14], the Pisani[15] and the Querini[16] show how in the eighteenth century the entail was still considered a tool with which to keep the patrimony intact along the lines of the old model of the fraternal partnership (*fraterna*). The case of the Querini family is particularly significant. From 1552 to 1808, they kept their patrimony undivided by severely restricting the number of marriages to one per generation. This made it possible to comply with the hereditary egalitarianism peculiar to Venetian customary law without risking the dispersal of the family estate. From time to time, all the brothers inherited the property left by the father and uncles which then returned to the sons of the only brother who had been allowed to marry, and so it continued.

As this last example shows, until more detailed research is available on all the different nobilities of the peninsula it is necessary to exercise caution when discussing the success of entail and primogeniture in Italy. It can be claimed in general terms that in the eighteenth century this inheritance

12. Maria Antonietta Visceglia, *Il bisogno di eternità: i comportamenti aristocratici a Napoli in età moderna*, (Naples, 1988). See also Gérard Delille, *Famille et propriété dans le Royaume de Naples (XVe–XIXe siècles)* (Rome-Paris, 1985).

13. Stuart J. Woolf, *Studi sulla nobiltà piemontese nell'epoca dell'assolutismo* (Turin, 1963).

14. Davis, *A Venetian Family and its Fortune.*

15. Giuseppe Gullino, *I Pisani dal Banco e Moretta. Storia di due famiglie veneziane in età moderna e delle loro vicende patrimoniali tra 1705 e 1836* (Rome, 1984).

16. Renzo Derosas, 'I Querini Stampalia. Vicende patrimoniali dal Cinque all'Ottocento', in G. Busetto and M. Gambier, eds, *I Querini Stampalia. Un ritratto di famiglia nel Settecento veneziano* (Venice, 1987), pp. 43–87.

strategy was widespread and had important consequences for the structure of the family and on the behaviour of its various members. Above all, the position of the first-born son, or if applicable the only male child, as the designated heir of the household's patrimony made it imperative that he should continue the family line. This meant that the only important marriage was that of the heir, whereas the other children could remain celibate: and naturally the choice of bride for the heir was something to be considered with great attention. In fact, she had to be of noble standing equal to that of the groom so that the honour of future generations would not be tarnished; at the same time, she had to bring to the marriage a handsome dowry which would increase the patrimony of the house she was entering. The other 'younger' sons had two choices: either to live in the home of the elder brother when he became the head of the family and to receive an allowance, or to leave home and pursue a career. A variant of the first choice can be found in a figure very familiar in noble Italian families of the seventeenth and eighteenth centuries, the 'uncle priest', a brother of the family's head who lived in the house and acted as tutor to his nephews, administered the family estate and, of course, celebrated Mass in the family chapel.

For those sons who left home, the choices were many: either a military career, in the service of his own State, a foreign sovereign, or an Order of Knights; or a secular ecclesiastical career which could be followed either locally or in the Roman Curia and in the happiest cases might lead to a Cardinalship, a source of pride and material benefit to the whole family. Alternatively, there was entry into a religious order, or the study of law or letters which could secure judicial office or a teaching post in a university. Finally, there was the possibility of a profession 'on the edges of the nobility' such as medicine or the office of notary which in some places were also allowed, although with a hint of disapproval. In reality, the choice was rarely left to the individual involved, but was either part of a wider family strategy which assigned a different rôle to each son or was dictated by contingent necessities. The sons were merely pawns in a game which had at its centre the family: if the eldest son died before having produced a male heir, another son had to marry and guarantee the continuity of the line; if there were no other sons, the family turned to the members of earlier generations. A typical case is the Milanese patrician family of the Trotti.[17] Giambattista Trotti, who lived from 1569 to 1640, had by his first marriage only one son who reached adulthood and who then produced two sons, one of whom died at an early age, while the other married but died without heirs. By a second marriage, Giambattista fathered, at the age of 65, another son, Luigi, and it was he who finally continued the family line by marrying when over 50 and siring in 1686 a son named Giambattista after his grandfather.

17. Dante E. Zanetti, *La demografia del patriziato milanese nei secoli XVII–XVIII–XIX* (Pavia, 1972), see pp. 55–6.

The predicament of daughters was even worse. Given that a marriage dowry constituted an impoverishment of the family patrimony and that on the other hand the so-called 'spiritual dowry' (the alms demanded by a convent for the acceptance of a nun) were decidedly lower, naturally only one or at most two daughters were allowed to marry; all the others were either pushed into monastic life or kept at home as spinsters. As for the wife, if she became a widow she had a choice: either to continue living with her children and if they were still minors to administer in usufruct the family patrimony; or (and this was the norm if there were no surviving children) to return to her father's house and attempt to recover all or part of her dowry; or to remarry, which, however, meant that she had to leave the children of her first marriage in their father's home to be raised by an uncle or other relative.

Among the professions suitable for younger sons, the study of letters and the sciences merits further mention. In Italy, the bond between nobility and culture was both intimate and enduring, and it profoundly influenced the form and content of learning. It has been calculated that between the mid-fifteenth and the mid-seventeenth centuries more than 60 per cent of Italian men of letters were of noble origin which, in this case, included both the feudal nobility and the urban patriciates. For the following period, figures are available on the members of the *Accademia dell' Arcadia* during the years 1690–1728, the first phase of the *Accademia's* activity.[18] This institution is important for many reasons, including the fact that its members were from all parts of Italy, above all from the Papal State, the Grand Duchy of Tuscany and the Kingdom of Naples; then from the Republic of Venice, the Republic of Genoa, the Duchy of Modena, the Duchy of Milan, the Duchy of Parma, the Kingdom of Sicily, the Duchy of Savoy, the Republic of Lucca, the Duchy of Mantua, the Duchy of Massa, the Tuscan *presidi* and the Bishopric of Trent. Of the 2,619 members, 543 or some 20 per cent were defined as 'nobles', but in all probability a significant proportion of the ecclesiastics (33 per cent) also belonged to the nobility as well as all the *dottori*, *cavalieri* and *senatori* (who totalled 11 per cent of the membership). In addition, one cannot fail to be struck by the fact that throughout the eighteenth century and during the first half of the nineteenth, the Italian nobility continued to lead in all fields of culture, and in particular in the two great intellectual movements of Enlightenment and Romanticism. A roll-call of just a few names will suffice: Scipione Maffei, Pietro Verri, Cesare Beccaria, Gaetano Filangieri, Alessandro Volta, Vittorio Alfieri, Ugo Foscolo, Alessandro Manzoni, Federico Confalonieri, Gino Capponi and Giacomo Leopardi.

18. Amedeo Quondam, 'L'istituzione Arcadia: sociologia e ideologia di un'accademia', *Quaderni Storici*, 23 (1973), 389–438.

POLITICAL POWER

As noted at the beginning of this chapter (see above, p. 237), at no time during the early modern period did the Italian peninsula constitute one single state. This division profoundly affected the nobilities in many ways but its influence was most apparent in the manner in which they wielded political power. For this reason the power of the nobles and the various institutional structures within which it operated – the independent principalities, the provinces of imperial states whose centre of power was outside Italy, and the aristocratic republics – will be considered separately and in turn. For reasons of space, it will not be possible to cover all the Italian states, and only two of the independent principalities (Savoy and Tuscany), one of the territories under foreign control (Milan) and one of the republics (Venice) will be examined.

During the early modern period, the Italian principality which was closest in political structure to the absolute monarchies found elsewhere in Europe was undoubtedly the Duchy of Savoy, which during the eighteenth century was known as the Kingdom of Sardinia. During the reign of Charles Emmanuel I (1580–1630), members of the feudal nobility were given positions of command in the Duchy's army which was mostly made up of mercenary troops. Other nobles were appointed to the provincial governorships, which in Piedmont numbered twelve (during the seventeenth century the total rose to eighteen). Generals and governors also formed the core of the Court nobility who lived alongside the Duke and received prebends and honours from him. All the other feudal lords lived in their own strongholds and in financial circumstances which ranged from moderate wealth to real poverty. They were excluded from a Court to which bourgeois families, ennobled through their tenure of the highest administrative, legal and financial offices (Secretaryships of State, Controller General of Finance, positions in the Courts of Counts and Senates) gained immediate and easy access. These families of *roturiers* (commoners) integrated very easily with the older feudal nobility. There was considerable social mobility within the administration and the dukes certainly did not encourage the formation of dynasties of officials, but preferred to choose their own staff from the provincial bourgeoisie. This is perfectly illustrated by the actions of Duke (later king) Victory Amadeus II (1675–1730).[19] Almost none of this ruler's close advisors were of noble birth: Giambattista Gropello, the Chancellor of the Exchequer, was of humble origins and lacked formal academic qualifications; Pietro Mellarede, the Secretary of State for Internal Affairs, was a lawyer at Chambéry in Savoy; Giovanni Zoppi, from Alessandria, was professor of law at the University of Pavia when the king called on him to write the text of the Constitutions of Savoy and then named him President of the *Camera dei Conti*. All three men were raised to the titled nobility: Gropello and Mellarede became

---

19. Guido Quazza, *Le riforme in Piemonte nella prima metà del '700*, 2 vols (Modena, 1957); Geoffrey Symcox, *Victor Amadeus II: Absolutism in the Savoyard State, 1675–1730* (London, 1983).

conti and Zoppi a *marchese*. Even more famous is Carlo Ferrero, who replaced Gropello at the Exchequer and Mellarede at Internal Affairs and under the new king, Charles Emmanuel III, united the Secretariats of both Foreign and Internal Affairs in his own hands. In fact, he is not known nowadays by his surname of Ferrero, but by his title of marchese d'Ormea which he received in 1722 when a large number of other royal officials were also ennobled. In short, it can be said that in the Savoyard State, the nobility enjoyed the unquestioned status of the first 'rank' of the country, but did not as such have any monopoly on the exercise of political power. For the most part, this lay in the hands of jurists who came from the bourgeoisie of provincial towns and who, due to their rôle in the State bureaucracy, then became part of the nobility. It was thus the ruler who, by filling the offices of State from the ranks of the bourgeoisie, transformed the very structure of the nobility as the class of government.

The evolution of another leading independent principality of early modern Italy, the Grand Duchy of Tuscany, was quite different. During the early period of the new State, and in particular under the government of Cosimo I (1537–74), the most important political offices, such as *Primo Segretario* (Chief Secretary), *Auditore delle Riformagioni* (Auditor of Reforms), *Auditore Fiscale* (Fiscal Auditor) and *Auditore della Giurisdizione* (Auditor of Ecclesiastical Affairs) were for the most part entrusted to 'provincials' from Tuscany's small towns, or to lawyers from outside the Grand Duchy. Examples can be found in the figures of Francesco Campana, a citizen of Colle in Sienese territory; Lelio Torelli, a jurist from Fano in the Papal March; Pier Francesco Riccio from Prato and Bartolomeo Concini from the small village of Terranuova in the countryside around Arezzo.[20]

Up to this point, developments closely resembled those in the Savoyard State, but the picture changes if we consider the Grand Duchy's corporate bodies such as the *Senato dei Quarantotto* (Senate of the Forty-eight), the *Consiglio dei Duecento* (Council of Two Hundred) and the *Magistrato Supremo* (Supreme Magistracy) to which Cosimo himself gave purely formal duties but which under his successors increased their powers. These institutions contained a very substantial number of members of those families from the old Florentine patriciate who, from the fourteenth century onwards, had held political power in the Republic's corporate bodies: the Albizi, Capponi, Cavalcanti, Corsini, Guicciardini, Machiavelli, Niccolini, Pitti, Pucci, Ricasoli, Ridolfi, Rucellai, Salviati, Strozzi, Vettori and so forth. The patriciate similarly predominated in local government and above all in the legal bureaucracy of the *podestà* and the *vicari*.

This compromise between the old and new régimes influenced later developments. The group of officials who owed their rise to the Grand Duke's favour was neither sufficiently numerous nor homogeneous to bring about any transformation within the ruling élite. In any case, a public office in Tuscany did not automatically bestow on its holder personal

20. Furio Diaz, *Il Granducato di Toscana: I Medici* (Turin, 1976); Raymond Burr Litchfield, *Emergence of a Bureaucracy: the Florentine Patricians 1530–1790* (Princeton, N.J., 1986).

nobility as it did in the Savoyard State.[21] It was thus easy for patrician families gradually to take over positions previously occupied by the 'new men'. The percentage of senior posts (Secretaries, Auditors and Directors of various departments) held by Florentine patricians was 15 per cent under Cosimo I and 43 per cent at the beginning of the seventeenth century, rose to 53 per cent by the end of that century and at the moment of the Medici's extinction in 1736 had peaked at 68 per cent. The increasingly close ties between the patriciate and the principality's administration helped to ensure the survival of many old patrician families, as these same posts offered employment and income to those who had difficulties making a career in commerce. Moreover, the essential continuity of political power in the hands of the very families which had governed the Republic, meant that constitutional structures which had existed before the establishment of the principality survived to a significant extent, above all the supremacy of the state capital over the rest of the territory.

This situation was partially modified by the reforms which the new dynasty of Habsburg Lorraine carried out in Tuscany, beginning with the law concerning the nobility and townspeople of 1750. This defined as 'nobles' all owners of fiefs, the members of the Order of the Knights of Saint Stephen (founded by Cosimo I in 1562), those who had been granted certificates of nobility by the Grand Dukes, and finally 'the majority of those who have enjoyed or are enjoying at this moment the highest and most distinguished ranks in the noble towns of their homelands'. Below the nobles were the 'burghers', that is those 'who have or are suitable to have all the positions of the city, except the highest': they had to enjoy a certain taxable income which was fixed by law, otherwise they were excluded from the rank of 'burghers'. This law was a kind of compromise between the hierarchic and feudal vision of the Lorraine ministers and the oligarchical aspirations of the patrician families. In fact, the communal Tuscan tradition which had always associated nobles and burghers was rejected: but at the same time the supremacy of the patriciates of the larger towns over the Grand Duchy's other burghers was sanctioned by law.

Many Italian territories were part of foreign empires, but the Duchy of Milan was the only one which for almost three centuries (from 1535 to 1796) was continuously subject to foreign rule: that of Spain until the beginning of the eighteenth century and that of Austria until the end of the eighteenth century, and again from 1814 to 1859. In this situation, there were many restrictions upon the exercise of political authority by the local nobility, who (as discussed earlier) for the most part consisted of the patriciates of Milan and the smaller towns of Lombardy. The most important decisions concerning military and foreign policy were taken at Madrid by the *Consejo de Estado* (Council of State), a body with vast

21. Enrico Stumpo, 'I ceti dirigenti in Italia nell'età moderna. Due modelli diversi: nobiltà piemontese e patriziato toscano', in A. Tagliaferri, ed., *I ceti dirigenti in Italia in età moderna e contemporanea* (Udine, 1984).

consultative powers which unified the Spanish Monarchy's interests and was presided over by the king himself, and by the *Consejo supremo de Italia* (Supreme Council of Italy). This Supreme Council had a Spanish president and 'regents' of whom half were Spanish and half native Italians (representatives from Naples, Sicily and Milan). At Milan, ultimate civil and military power was held by the Governor who was appointed by the king of Spain and from 1558 was always a titled Spanish nobleman. The *Consiglio Segreto* (Secret Council) was convened by the Governor and discussed matters of the highest importance. This Council included the *Gran Cancelliere* (High Chancellor) who was appointed by the king and after 1561 was always Spanish; the *Castellano di Milano* (Milan's military governor), who was a Spanish army officer; the Presidents of the two *Magistrati Camerali* (Exchequers: Ordinary and Extraordinary) who could be Lombards or Spaniards; and the President of the *Senato* (Senate), who was chosen by the king without exception from among the local patricians. The latter's participation in the Secret Council underlines that the support of the local nobility was necessary to Spanish rule in Milan. In fact, the Senate, which was made up of twelve Lombard magistrates (*togati*) each chosen by the king from a shortlist of three candidates, and three Spaniards, was not only the highest of all the Courts of Appeal in the Duchy for civil and criminal cases: it was also the only authorized interpreter of the Duchy's own law, which dated back to Milan's period of independence under the Visconti and the Sforza and had been included in the *Nuove Costituzioni* granted in 1542 by Charles V. Like the French *Parlements*, the Senate of Milan possessed the right of 'ratification', that is the authority to suspend the registration of a royal order if that edict was considered to go against the *Nuove Costituzioni*.

The power of the Milanese patriciate could be seen not only in their possession of the majority of the seats in the Senate, but also in the numerous royal posts they held in the Duchy and in their monopoly of the municipal offices which at various times had jurisdiction over Milan's entire territory. An example is the important royal post of *Tesoriere Generale* (Treasurer General) which was held from 1642 to 1692 without interruption by Milanese patricians of the Visconti, Airoldi and Arese families. These patrician officials tended to consider themselves representatives of their city rather than agents of the Spanish king.[22] In this context, it is significant that it was more often the younger sons who were steered towards a career in the Senate and the royal government, whereas the highest municipal office, that of Decurion, was reserved for the eldest sons of the leading patrician clans. Hence that peculiar relationship, which was theoretically dependent but in practice dominant, between the Milanese Decurionate and the Duchy's magistracies.

This discussion would be incomplete without a mention of the extraordinary integration between the patrician oligarchy and the Roman Catholic

22. Carlo Capra, *La Lombardia austriaca nell'età delle riforme* (Turin, 1987).

Church in the Duchy. Through its members, the patriciate controlled many Lombard dioceses (above all the immense Archbishopric of Milan), the chapters of collegiate churches and cathedrals, the richer monasteries and the 'charitable offices' (schools, charitable institutions, hospitals and so on). These extremely close ties with the ecclesiastical hierarchy gave the patriciate great economic power and a profound influence over all of society, given that the Church controlled and organised the daily life of the entire population. This intimate relationship was not peculiar to Lombardy but was common to all regions of Italy. It should thus be emphasized that until the second half of the eighteenth century the power of the nobility was constantly supported by the authority of the Church.

During the first half of the eighteenth century, the situation in Milan changed very little, in spite of the arrival of a new foreign ruler with the Duchy's acquisition by Austria during the War of the Spanish Succession. At Vienna, a *Consejo de Españá* (whose very name showed the desire of Emperor Charles VI to keep alive claims to the Spanish throne) was founded, later to be replaced by a *Consiglio d'Italia* from which came the Governors of Milan who were Austrian or Bohemian nobles but had powers similar to their Spanish predecessors. In this period, the Senate and the Milanese patriciate retained most of their dominance. The situation changed only when Maria Theresa's government embarked on a wide-ranging series of reforms in the Duchy. These initiatives began in the 1740s and gathered pace from the 1760s onwards. It would be a lengthy task to describe these measures in detail: they largely originated in Vienna but a contribution was also made by a group of young Lombard patricians such as Pietro Verri, Cesare Beccaria, Alfonso Longo and Luigi Lambertenghi, who were critical of the established order. It will suffice to state that one of the fundamental consequences of the reigns of Maria Theresa and Joseph II in Lombardy was the progressive downgrading in authority of those bodies in which the power of the patriciate was most apparent (the Senate was, in fact, formally suppressed in 1786) and the creation of a cadre of career officials who were, in birth and training, foreign to the local ruling class and were instead tied to the Habsburg Monarchy. In short, in the space of a few decades, the patriciate as a 'body' was excluded from the government of the city and duchy of Milan.

In the aristocratic republics political authority resided in the hands of the nobility to the extent that the public offices and the holding of supreme power were reserved for this class. In the *Dizionario del diritto comune e veneto* by Marco Ferro, published in 1778, the entry for '*aristocrazia*' reads: 'a form of government in which the supreme authority lies with the Optimates, namely in a Council composed of Nobles and from which all the Boards and Magistracies are drawn'. This was certainly the case in Venice. Justice and administration were both a right and a duty of the Republic's patriciate, a type of 'hereditary vocation' which was perfected not so much by the academic study of law as by membership from an early age of the Republic's corporate bodies and by participation in their deliberations. This was an integral part of the 'myth' of Venice's political perfection, but the situation in practice was rather different. In the first place, because of their lack of legal expertise the patriciate needed the support of a group of officials who were trained lawyers; secondly, the number of adult noblemen could at times be insufficient to fill the public offices; thirdly, an excessive disparity of wealth within the patriciate was capable of destroying the principle of political equality among those inscribed in the *Libro d'oro*, giving rise to the dominance of the wealthiest. During the seventeenth and eighteenth centuries, all these problems became very serious and also interlinked with the decline in numbers of the patriciate, the widening of the economic inequalities between the patrician families and the failure of every attempt at constitutional reform. The problem of finding men able to fill the Republic's most important offices became the subject of public debate in the 1630s and remained a matter of serious concern at the end of the seventeenth century. The most difficult posts to fill were the governorships of the most important towns ruled by Venice on the mainland, and the embassies in foreign capitals which not only did not carry salaries but involved substantial expenditure for their holders. In contrast, the minor posts in the provinces which offered only a small remuneration were greatly sought after by the poorest patricians, known as the *barnaboti* after the parish of Venice (san Barnaba) in which they mostly lived. They were consequently very much opposed to the idea of the re-opening of the *Libro d'oro*, that is, to the admission of new families to the patriciate who would then be able to compete for these salaried posts. The *barnaboti* showed even greater ill feeling towards the *cittadini originari* (original citizens) of Venice: this was a closed group of officials who had the exclusive prerogative of assisting the patricians in the chancelleries of the magistracies and colleges, in the 'governorships' and the embassies, with the right to hold the minor offices themselves (for example the posts of diplomatic *attachés* in foreign cities). But the dispute which exploded in 1582, 1628, 1761 and 1780 pitted the patrician families who were least important in terms of wealth and prestige against the *Grandi* (the Great Families) who had their stronghold in the two powerful magistracies: the *Consiglio dei Dieci* (Council of Ten) and the *Inquisitori di Stato* (State Prosecutors). It was a struggle between the patrician oligarchy and the lesser nobles claiming equality of opportunities.

In fact, this conflict was not solved, but the situation continued to be stable until the fall of the Republic in 1797 because fundamentally all the patricians agreed that political power should be monopolized by those families who were inscribed in the *Libro d'oro*, to the exclusion of all others. This is crucial to an understanding of the relationship between power and nobility in the Venetian Republic which cannot be viewed solely in terms of the internal disputes of the patriciate. The Republic contained many other gentlemen who did not believe themselves inferior in any way to the patricians: the nobilities of the mainland towns who could claim a glorious past under the communes and seignories but who submitted with bad grace to their exclusion from all the Republic's municipal and military offices.[23] During the eighteenth century there were some who, like the Veronese noble Scipione Maffei, conceived the idea of amalgamating the Venetian patriciate and the mainland nobility into one ruling class based on the English model. Proposals of this nature, however, were not even contemplated by the patriciate. The nobles of the mainland were excluded from any participation in the Republic's government and had to make do with running the government of their own locality.

This analysis of the different constitutional structures of the various Italian states has necessarily emphasized the continuing rôle of the higher nobility. Yet the picture is incomplete without mention of the rôle of the lesser nobles in local government. In the Grand Duchy of Tuscany as in the Duchy of Milan and the Republic of Venice, the majority of posts in central government were held by the patriciates of the leading city (Florence, Milan and Venice). But in the smaller towns, there existed a number of bodies and institutions which were controlled and run by the local nobilities. These were the courts of first instance, purveyors' offices, the fiscal administration, hospitals and pawnshops. The power of the local nobilities over other town-dwellers and the inhabitants of the surrounding countryside was perpetuated by their rôle in the operation of these institutions, yet it was also a frequent source of abuse, malversation and extortion. The corruption of the local ruling classes of the Venetian mainland came to light not as a result of the intervention of central government, which generally avoided meddling in such matters, but when one of the factions into which the local nobility was split evicted the other nobles from local offices.[24] At that point, the conspiracy of silence was broken and the ousted nobles would denounce the wrongdoings of their opponents. This situation changed during the eighteenth century, but only where there were radical reforms of local government, such as in Milan and Piedmont. Through such reforms a political order which had come into being under the city-states and Renaissance seignories and was characterized by urban structures with strong parasitical elements came under critical examination for the first time.[25]

PERCEPTIONS AND PRIVILEGES

Throughout the peninsula, and especially in northern and central Italy, the concept of nobility itself was the subject of an intense and prolonged debate. This had its origins in a fundamental contradiction rooted in the

---

23. Marino Berengo, 'Patriziato e nobiltà: il caso veronese', *Rivista Storica Italiana* 87 (1975), 493–517.
24. Angelo Ventura, *Nobiltà e popolo nella società veneta del '400 e '500* (Bari, 1964).
25. Giorgio Chittolini, ed., *La crisi degli ordinamenti comunali e le origini dello stato del Rinascimento* (Bologna, 1979).

historical evolution of a large proportion of the ruling class of seventeenth- and eighteenth-century Italy and was difficult to resolve. The urban patriciates who had greatly influenced the political, economic and cultural life of the Italian *ancien régime* had secured their power through successful struggles against those who in the Middle Ages had been the nobles *par excellence*: the seigneurs and castellans of the countryside. In cities such as Florence, 'anti-magnate' laws had been passed excluding these nobles from holding offices unless they abandoned their surname and enrolled in artisans' guilds. In addition, the seventeenth- and eighteenth-century patriciates who dominated city-states were based on statutes and laws which had earlier been set up as rivals to the authority of the Emperor who was, nevertheless, the foremost member of the Christian nobility. The medieval bourgeoisies, from which the patriciates later emerged, had been distinguished by their involvement in industry and commerce, while one of the basic tenets of the ideology of nobility was the superiority of land-owning over all other forms of economic activity. To sum up, the Italian patriciates had an 'original sin' which had to be erased or justified in the eyes of the world, especially after the fall of the peninsula to a foreign power such as Spain, where the definition of nobility was a problem which bordered on the obsessive. The vindication of the genuine and legitimate nobility of those who in Italy constituted the ruling élite was the principal aim of a large number of the many treatises on the subject of nobility which were published in Italy, for the most part during the second half of the sixteenth and early seventeenth centuries. The two fundamental concepts of this plethora of treatises, which enjoyed great publishing success, were *onore* (honour) and *virtù* (virtue), both linked by a conflicting relationship which was not easy to resolve. A hereditary component was present in the concept of *onore*, while *virtù* was eminently personal. Through a skilful integration of Aristotle's texts, the works of the fourteenth- and fifteenth-century Humanists and the elaborations of the commentators on Roman law together with the support of the Counter-Reformation Church, each contradiction was overcome or at least smoothed over to the extent that the ideology of nobility expounded in Italy could even be exported to France, Germany and England where the treatises of such Italians as Baldassare Castiglione and Stefano Guazzo enjoyed extraordinary and enduring success. These authors did not limit themselves to a simple definition of nobility but also gave advice on the way in which the noble should behave towards rulers, equals and inferiors. In this way, a sense of common belonging was formed and manifested itself through gestures, language and behaviour peculiar to the nobles and from which the lower classes were peremptorily excluded. Some of these manifestations of the exclusivity of nobility were codified in law and thus became privileges in their own right.

The political division of the peninsula influenced the privileges enjoyed by the Italian nobilities in the seventeenth and eighteenth centuries, in that many of these were linked to the *consuetudo loci* and thus changed not only from state to state but even from province to province and from town to town. Among these, so to speak, 'variable' privileges, the first was the exemption from taxation, which as a rule was very generous but neither applied to all possessions nor equally favoured all the nobles of one country. There was then the right to carry weapons, which was not always a privilege exclusive to the nobility. Exemption from the sumptuary laws was a privilege at times given to only certain categories of nobles and could thus be seen as a manifestation of the prince's determination to redefine noble hierarchies within the State. More general and uniform was the immunity of all the nobles of the peninsula from certain judicial penalties. For example, shortly after 1600, Giambattista Baiardi, a jurist from Parma, wrote that in Italy, unlike France, the gallows were seen as an ignominious punishment for nobles who, if found guilty of murder, were sentenced to a punishment deemed more honourable: decapitation. The monopoly of membership of certain societies was one of the most important noble privileges, both because this ratified the fact that they belonged to the highest class of society and because other privileges resulted from this one. Mention has already been made of the Order of the Knights of Malta, in addition to which there were other religious-military orders created by Italian rulers during the sixteenth and seventeenth centuries: the Order of Saint Stephen in Tuscany; the Order of Saints Maurice and Lazarus in Savoy; the Order of the Redeemer at Mantua; and the Constantine Order of Saint George at Parma. Highly prestigious institutions from other European countries were also important, above all the Order of the Golden Fleece created by the Duke of Burgundy in 1431 and bestowed by the Habsburg sovereigns: up to the year 1700, more than 200 Italians, for the most part princes of the ruling dynasties (such as the Este and the Gonzaga), Roman barons and the great feudal lords of Naples, were admitted to this Order. In this way, a symbol of honour became also a mark of hierarchy within the Italian nobility, placing on a higher level those who could call themselves noble in every respect because they enjoyed the 'mero e misto imperio' – jurisdiction over their own subjects.

For nobles of different geographical origins, participation in the same institutions was both a sign of distinction and a means of acquiring common modes of thought and behaviour. A very important rôle in the evolution of a common deportment was played both by the literary Academies which until the end of the seventeenth century in Italy had a strongly aristocratic tone and by the 'colleges of education' for young nobles, which for the most part were run by Jesuits. From 1600 to 1773, there were 9,500 boarders at the four colleges of Parma, Modena, Bologna and Siena. More than 20 per cent of these came originally from the towns of the Venetian mainland, 10 per cent from the Hereditary Lands of the Habsburgs of Austria (Vienna, Styria, Carinthia, the Tyrol, Croatia, Bohemia and Moravia, and so on) and from other territories of the Holy Roman Empire, such as Bavaria and the Bishopric of Trent, and then smaller percentages from the various Italian territories: Savoy,

Parma, Modena, Mantua, the Republics of Genoa and Lucca, the Papal State and the Kingdom of Naples; also present, albeit in far smaller numbers, were nobles from Switzerland, Portugal, England and even Sweden, Poland and Russia.[26] These colleges with their emphasis on communal living, a common curriculum, a type of training steeped in baroque religiosity and at the same time designed to encourage worldly aplomb (fencing, dancing and theatrical performances numbered among the colleges' activities) were important places for the integration of nobilities of very different origins and descent. For many young French, English and German aristocrats, a sojourn at a college was part of the Italian stage of the 'Grand Tour' or *Kavalierreise*, which during the seventeenth century became very fashionable. Relatively few young Italian noblemen made this journey in the opposite direction and travelled to countries beyond the Alps. Those Italian nobles who did travel to foreign lands usually did so for one of three reasons: to seek sanctuary from religious or political persecution (which was still current even during the seventeenth and eighteenth centuries, albeit less intensely in comparison with the numbers who had escaped to Geneva in the sixteenth century); to secure employment at a Court or in a foreign army; or to carry out a diplomatic mission on behalf of his own sovereign. Only during the Age of Enlightenment did an increasing number of Italian noblemen undertake the Grand Tour: the preferred destinations were Paris and other French cities, closely followed by Holland, England, the German territories and Eastern Europe. The majority of travellers were not young nobles but officials and men of science and letters anxious to become personally acquainted with the most culturally and politically advanced centres of eighteenth-century Europe.

CONCLUSION

During the seventeenth and for part of the eighteenth centuries, the Italian nobilities preserved much of their economic and political supremacy within the different states of the peninsula. The emergence of absolutist governments tended to limit the autonomy traditionally enjoyed by the urban patriciates and the feudal lords, but overall the Italian nobilities succeeded in preserving the positions they had acquired and defended in earlier time until the middle of the eighteenth century both against princely absolutism and occasional challenges from the lower classes of society. A very important change for the nobilities occurred with the arrival first of the reforms of the second half of the eighteenth century and then the spread

26. Gian Paolo Brizzi, *La formazione della classe dirigente nel Sei-Settecento: I 'seminaria nobilium' nell'Italia centrosettentrionale* (Bologna, 1976).

of the ideas and laws of Revolutionary and Napoleonic France. The new State structures began to exert increasing control over those areas of power, such as finance and the administration of law in the localities, where the influence of the nobility had hitherto been preponderant. The vast estates of the Church and the widespread influence of the clergy were both severely curtailed and this, albeit temporary, decline of ecclesiastical power also spelt the end of the secular alliance between the Italian nobilities and the Papacy. New bourgeois classes of industrial and agricultural entrepreneurs and above all of officials and intellectuals emerged. They held values antithetical to those of *onore* (honour), *sangue* (blood) and *privilegio* (privilege) on which the noble ideology of the *ancien régime* had been established.

This break would not be healed by the Restoration. In 1833, Monaldo Leopardi, a member of one of the established patrician families of Recanati in the Papal March, pointed out that the return of the pope to Rome and the re-establishment of the Papal State within its old borders had not meant the extinction of the Napoleonic legacy. On the contrary, he claimed, the 'abolition and extermination of the nobility' had been sanctioned. Before the deluge caused by the French Revolution, the nobles had held in their hands the exclusive right both to run and to represent their countries. Now, however, the communal magistracies were open to all classes, 'including the pallbearers'. In such a situation, to be able to enjoy, by the kind permission of the government, the title of *marchese* Leopardi was a joke 'as it would be to grant someone the privilege of calling themselves Bartolomeo'. The sense of the ineluctable end of an era was obvious in this disconsolate observation by one of the most intelligent Italian reactionaries of the nineteenth century. Balzac's comment on the France of Louis-Philippe was equally applicable to Italy: 'Il n'y a plus de noblesse aujourd'hui, il n'y a plus qu'une aristocracie.'

Guides to Further Reading

Readers should note that the guides give especial prominence to books and articles in English and, to a lesser extent, to works in the more familiar European languages.

1. INTRODUCTION: THE CONSOLIDATION OF NOBLE POWER IN EUROPE, c.1600–1800

The essential starting point is the work of Michael Bush, who is producing a three-volume survey of 'The European Nobility', of which the first two have been published: *Noble Privilege* (Manchester, 1983) and *Rich Noble, Poor Noble* (Manchester, 1988); a third will be devoted to noble power. His approach is distinctive and his perspective extends from the Roman Empire to the twentieth century. Though this is not without its drawbacks, these volumes are a mine of fascinating information and the one truly indispensable work. Dr Bush has also edited a lively collection of essays on *Social Orders and Social Classes in Europe since 1500* (London, 1992) which provides a valuable context for the study of the nobility during the seventeenth and eighteenth centuries, as does Jonathan Powis's elegant brief survey of *Aristocracy* (Oxford, 1984). The seminal work of Otto Brunner, first published in German in 1939, has now been excellently translated by Howard Kaminsky and J. V. H. Melton: *'Land' and Lordship: Structures of Governance in Medieval Austria* (Philadelphia, Pa., 1992). Recent work on the family, especially among the higher nobility, can be approached through James Casey, *The History of the Family* (Oxford, 1989) and Roger Chartier, ed., *A History of Private Life: Passions of the Renaissance* (1986; English trans., Cambridge, Mass., 1989), while the crucial subject of inheritance and landed power is examined for Western Europe and especially Britain in a long essay by J. P. Cooper, 'Patterns of Inheritance and Settlement by Great Landowners from the Fifteenth to the Eighteenth Centuries', in Jack

Goody, Joan Thirsk and E. P. Thompson, eds, *Family and Inheritance: Rural Society in Western Europe 1200–1800* (Cambridge, 1976); this collection also contains a valuable survey by Joan Thirsk of 'The European Debate on Customs of Inheritance, 1500–1700'. On the nobility's economic activities, there is nothing more recent than the symposium in *Explorations in Entrepreneurial History* 6 (1953–54), which included a general survey by Fritz Redlich, 'European Aristocracy and Economic Development'.

There are some valuable recent discussions of the nature of the early modern 'State' and of the continuing rôle of the nobility: see especially Gerhard Oestreich's incisive survey of 'The Structure of the Absolute State' in B. Oestreich and H. G. Koenigsberger, eds, *Neostoicism and the Early Modern State* (Cambridge, 1982); J. H. Elliott, 'A Europe of Composite Monarchies', *Past and Present* no 137 (1992), 48–71; and several of the articles collected together in H. G. Koenigsberger's *Politicians and Virtuosi: Essays in Early Modern History* (London, 1986), especially '*Dominium Regale* or *Dominium Politicum et Regale*: Monarchies and Parliaments in Early Modern Europe'. Perry Anderson's *Lineages of the Absolutist State* (London, 1974) is important for its emphasis on the nobility's continuing political importance and especially its rôle in government, while the best guide to some crucial developments is now John Miller, ed., *Absolutism in Seventeenth-century Europe* (London, 1990). A lively collection of essays edited by Mark Greengrass, *Conquest and Coalescence: the Shaping of the State in Early Modern Europe* (London, 1991) views the process of State-building from the periphery, while Dietrich Gerhard's dense but seminal discussion of 'Regionalism and Corporate Order as a Basic Theme of European History' appears in an English translation in Ragnhild Hatton and M. S. Anderson, eds, *Studies in Diplomatic History: Essays in Memory of David Bayne Horn* (London, 1970). There are some suggestive remarks in J. H. Shennan, *Liberty and Order in Early Modern Europe: the Subject and the State 1650–1800* (London, 1986). The nobility's enduring military rôle is surveyed in C. Storrs and H. M. Scott, 'The Military Revolution and the European Nobility 1600–1800', *War in History* (forthcoming, 1994), while the best introduction to the aristocratic diplomacy of the *ancien régime* is now that contained in chapter two of M. S. Anderson, *The Rise of Modern Diplomacy 1450–1919* (London, 1993). On the nobility at Court, there is much of interest in the recent collection edited by R. G. Asch and A. M. Birke, *Princes, Patronage and the Nobility: the Court at the Beginning of the Modern Age c. 1450–1650* (Oxford, 1991) and in the lavishly-illustrated A. G. Dickens, ed., *The Courts of Europe* (London, 1977), while Norbert Elias, *The Court Society* (1969; Eng. trans., Oxford, 1983), has been widely influential, though its approach increasingly seems rather crude and schematic. The nobility's enduring rôle in the Roman Catholic Church is made clear by the essays in W. J. Callahan and D. Higgs, eds, *Church and Society in Catholic Europe of the Eighteenth Century* (Cambridge, 1979). Finally, the extent and continuity of aristocratic power after 1800 can be gauged from three recent works: Dominic Lieven, *The Aristocracy in Europe, 1815–1914* (London, 1992), a valuable synthesis of much specialized research; A. J. Mayer, *The Persistence of the Old Regime: Europe to the Great War* (New York, 1981), stimulating and controversial, though it can now be seen to be overdrawn; and G. Delille, ed., *Les noblesses européennes au XIXe siècle* (Paris-Rome, 1988), an impressive collection of conference papers.

2. THE BRITISH NOBILITY, 1660–1800

For individual peers, the indispensable reference work is the *GEC Complete Peerage* in thirteen volumes. This was an impressive collective endeavour, which began publication in 1910 and was brought to a conclusion in 1940. Much additional information is contained in numerous appendices which, for the first ten volumes, are listed at the end of Volume XI.

The best general introduction is J. V. Beckett, *The Aristocracy in England, 1660–1914* (Oxford, 1986). It is particularly good on the economic side, though its conclusion that the nobility is 'alive and well' seems questionable. The overall picture is continued chronologically by D. Cannadine, *The Decline and Fall of the British Aristocracy* (New Haven, Conn., 1990) which argues that the aristocracy was in good shape until the 1880s. Three other admirable foundation volumes are G. E. Mingay, *English Landed Society in the Eighteenth Century* (London, 1967), Mingay, *The Gentry: the Rise and Fall of a Ruling Class* (London, 1976), and F. M. L. Thompson, *English Landed Society in the Nineteenth Century* (London, 1963).

A rather more specialist work is M. L. Bush, *The English Aristocracy: a Comparative Synthesis* (Manchester, 1984), which offers a longer time span and, among much of value, includes a very useful bibliography. L. Stone, *The Crisis of the Aristocracy, 1558–1641* (Oxford, 1965) offered the thesis of noble financial disarray in the decades before the Civil War: I have indicated in the footnotes to the text where challenges to Stone's views may be found. Two books which came out close to each other questioned the peculiarly liberal character of the English nobility and its willingness to mix: they were L. Stone and J. C. F. Stone, *An Open Elite?: England, 1540–1880* (Oxford, 1984) and J. A. Cannon, *Aristocratic Century: the Peerage of Eighteenth-century England* (Cambridge, 1984). Two recent volumes by P. Langford, taking a rather different view, are *A Polite and Commercial People: England 1727–1783* (Oxford, 1989) and *Public Life and the Propertied Englishman, 1689–1798* (Oxford, 1991).

A good deal of attention has been paid to the functioning of the House of Lords. Older works which are still of value are C. H. Firth, *The House of Lords During the Civil War* (London, 1910) and A. S. Turberville, *The House of Lords in the Reign of William III* (Oxford, 1913), *The House of Lords in the XVIIIth century* (Oxford, 1927), and *The House of Lords in the Age of Reform, 1784–1837* (London, 1958). The claims for the House of Lords as a balancing mechanism in the constitution are examined in two works: C. C. Weston, *English Constitutional*

Theory and the House of Lords, 1556–1832 (London, 1965) and M. W. McCahill, *Order and Equipoise: the Peerage and the House of Lords, 1783–1806* (London, 1978). Much of the most interesting recent work on the Lords has been published in journals. Two volumes which perform a most valuable service by bringing together some of the more important articles are C. Jones and D. L. Jones, eds, *Peers, Politics and Power: the House of Lords, 1603–1911* (London, 1986) and C. Jones, ed., *A Pillar of the Constitution: the House of Lords in British Politics, 1640–1784* (London, 1989). The first of these prints an excellent bibliography, pp. xvii–xxix.

Lastly, there are many studies of individual peers and aristocratic families. The following are of particular interest: C. C. H. and M. I. Baker, *The Life and Circumstances of James Brydges, 1st Duke of Chandos* (London, 1949); J. Wake, *The Brudenells of Deene* (London, 1953); A. L. Rowse, *The Early Churchills, an English Family* (London, 1956); A. N. Newman, *The Stanhopes of Chevening: a Family Biography* (London, 1969); R. J. S. Hoffman, *The Marquis: a Study of Lord Rockingham, 1730–82* (New York, 1973); R. Kelch, *A Duke Without Money: Thomas Pelham-Holles, 1693–1768* (London, 1974); R. A. C. Parker, *Coke of Norfolk: a Financial and Agricultural Study, 1707–1842* (Oxford, 1975); E. A. Smith, *Whig Principles and Party Politics: Earl Fitzwilliam and the Whig Party, 1748–1833* (Manchester, 1975); P. Jupp, *Lord Grenville, 1759–1834* (Oxford, 1985); J. J. Bagley, *The Earls of Derby, 1485–1985* (London, 1985); J. M. Rosenheim, *The Townshends of Raynham: Nobility in Transition in Restoration and Early Hanoverian England* (Middletown, Conn., 1989).

3. THE DUTCH NOBILITY IN THE SEVENTEENTH AND EIGHTEENTH CENTURIES

There is, unfortunately, very little in English on this subject. Even Sherrin Marshall, *The Dutch Gentry, 1500–1650: Family, Faith and Fortune* (New York, 1987) deals only with the province of Utrecht and ends by the middle of the seventeenth century. The recent translation of van Nierop's book (below) under the title *The Nobility of Holland: from Knights to Regents 1500–1650* (Cambridge, 1993) is thus especially welcome. There is a useful survey of the rôle of the princes of Orange in H. H. Rowen, *The Princes of Orange: The Stadholders in the Dutch Republic* (Cambridge, 1988), and their Court is discussed in essays by H. Schilling and O. Mörke in Ronald G. Asch and Adolf M. Birke, *Princes, Patronage and the Nobility: The Court at the Beginning of the Modern Age c.1450–1650* (Oxford, 1991), but none of these have much to say about the nobility as a whole. Jan de Vries, *The Dutch Rural Economy in the Golden Age 1500–1700* (New Haven, Conn., 1974), pp. 35–41, gives a brief account of the nobility but for the sixteenth century only. Matters are a little better with regard to the regents: there are helpful discussions of central issues in D. J. Roorda, 'The Ruling Classes in

Holland in the Seventeenth Century', in J. S. Bromley and E. H. Kossmann, *Britain and the Netherlands* II (Groningen, 1964), pp. 109–33, and H. van Dijk and D. J. Roorda, 'Social Mobility under the Regents of the Republic', *Acta Historiae Neerlandicae* 9 (1978), 76–103, and an alternative view of the process of aristocratization to the one given in the text can be found in P. Spierenburg, *Elites and Etiquette* (Rotterdam, 1981), pp. 19–30.

There have been a number of important recent studies of the nobility in Dutch, but the coverage is still rather patchy. The essays in J. Aalbers and M. Prak, eds, *De bloem der natie: adel en patriciaat in de Noordelijke Nederlanden* (Meppel, 1987) provide an interesting introduction to the nobles and patriciate in general, but studies of individual provinces have produced the most interesting results. On Holland there is the seminal work of H. F. K. van Nierop, *Van ridders tot regenten* (Amsterdam/Dieren, 1984) which covers the sixteenth and early seventeenth centuries, but also has much which is relevant for the *ancien régime* as a whole. S. W. Verstegen, *Gegoede ingezetenen: jonkers en geërfden op de Veluwe tijdens Ancien Régime, Revolutie en Restauratie (1650–1830)* (Arnhem, 1990) is an interesting brief treatment of one of the quarters of Gelderland, largely in the eighteenth century, while the nobility of Groningen is dealt with in the pioneering works of H. Feenstra, *De bloeitijd en verval van de Ommelander adel* (Groningen, 1981), and *Adel in de Ommelanden. Hoofdelingen, jonkers en eigenerfders van de late middeleeuwen tot de negentiende eeuw* (Groningen, 1988). The same author has also produced a short study of the economic position of the nobles in Drente, *Drentse edelen tijdens de Republiek* (Meppel, 1985). Friesland is rather less well-served, but there is Y. Kuiper, 'Uitsterven of uithuwelijken? Een analyse van het demographische gedrag van de adel in Friesland in de 18e en 19e eeuw', *Tijdschrift voor sociale geschiedenis* 12 (1986), 269–99, on the effects of endogamy, and J. A. Faber, 'De oligarchisering van Friesland in de tweede helft van de zeventiende eeuw', *Afdeling Agrarische Geschiedenis Bijdragen* 15 (1970), 39–65, on the growth of oligarchy. There is also much useful material in J. A. Faber, *Drie eeuwen Friesland* (Wageningen, 1972). The nobility of Overijssel is placed in its economic and social context in B. H. Slicher van Bath, *Een samenleving onder spanning: geschiedenis van het platteland in Overijssel* (Assen, 1957).

The modern literature on the regents is discussed in D. J. Roorda, 'Het onderzoek naar het stedelijk patriciaat in Nederland', in W. W. Mijnhardt, ed. *Kantelend geschiedbeeld* (Utrecht/Antwerp, 1987). Three studies of local regent groups in the eighteenth century are indispensable: J. J. de Jong, *Met goed fatsoen. De elite in een Hollandse stad, Gouda 1700–1780* (Dieren, 1985), L. Kooijmans, *Onder regenten. De elite in een Hollandse stad, Hoorn 1700–1780* (Dieren, 1985) and M. Prak, *Gezeten burgers. De elite in een Hollandse stad, Leiden 1700–1780* (Dieren, 1985). A rather different perspective is given by a study of a single regent family: C. Schmidt, *Om de eer van de familie. Het geslacht Teding van Berkhout 1500–1950* (Amsterdam, 1986).

4. THE FRENCH NOBILITY, 1610–1715

The best description of how the hierarchical society of *ancien régime* France was structured, in theory if not always in practice, is to be found in Roland Mousnier, *The Institutions of France under the Absolute Monarchy, 1598–1789*, 2 vols (London/Chicago, Ill., 1979–84). On the idea of *noblesse* in the seventeenth century, F. E. Sutcliffe, *Guez de Balzac et son temps: littérature et politique* (Paris, 1959), remains the most extended study, which should be supplemented by Davis Bitton, *The French Nobility in Crisis, 1560–1640* (Stanford, Cal., 1969), Antoine Adam, *Grandeur and Illusion: French Literature and Society, 1600–1715* (London, 1972) and Roger Mettam, 'Definitions of Nobility in Seventeenth-century France', in Penelope J. Corfield, ed., *Language, History and Class* (Oxford, 1991). Moving from the theorists to the world of the Court, the controversial and stimulating work by Norbert Elias, *The Court Society* (Oxford, 1983) is essential reading. The rôle of the nobility in government and society is revealed in some excellent provincial studies, notably William Beik, *Absolutism and Society in Seventeenth-century France: State Power and Provincial Aristocracy in Languedoc* (Cambridge, 1985), James B. Wood, *The Nobility of the Election of Bayeux, 1463–1666: Continuity Through Change* (Princeton, N. J., 1980), and Sharon Kettering, *Judicial Politics and Urban Revolt in Seventeenth-century France: the Parlement of Aix, 1629–1659* (Princeton, 1978). A different approach, examining aristocratic power in a number of French provinces, is adopted by Robert R. Harding, *Anatomy of a Power Elite: the Provincial Governors of Early Modern France* (New Haven, Conn., and London, 1978) and J. Russell Major, *Representative Government in Early Modern France* (New Haven, Conn., and London, 1980). Centred on Court faction, but with a provincial dimension, are Roger Mettam, *Power and Faction in Louis XIV's France* (Oxford, 1988), A. Lloyd Moote, *Louis XIII, the Just* (Berkeley/Los Angeles, Cal., 1989) and two books by Joseph Bergin – *The Rise of Richelieu* (New Haven, Conn., and London, 1991) and *Cardinal Richelieu: Power and the Pursuit of Wealth* (New Haven, Conn., and London, 1985). The ecclesiastical, sword and robe nobilities reveal their priorities and strategies in a number of short-term crises, which are well described by J. Michael Hayden, *France and the Estates General of 1614* (Cambridge, 1974), A. Lloyd Moote, *The Revolt of the Judges: the Parlement of Paris and the Fronde, 1643–1652* (Princeton, N. J., 1971), Albert N. Hamscher, *The Parlement of Paris after the Fronde, 1653–1673* (Pittsburgh, Pa., 1976) and Richard M. Golden, *The Godly Rebellion: Parisian Curés and the Religious Fronde, 1652–62* (Chapel Hill, N. C. 1981). Finally Jean-Pierre Labatut, *Les ducs et pairs de France au XVIIe siècle* (Paris, 1972), examines the fortunes, marriages and strategies of the peerage, André Corvisier, *Louvois* (Paris, 1983), reveals the continuing influence of the nobility in the army under Louvois and Louis XIV, and Daniel Dessert, *Argent, pouvoir et société au grand siècle* (Paris,

1984), shows that the nobility were active participants in the world of finance.

5. THE FRENCH NOBILITY, 1715–1789

The essential starting place for any study is the work of Guy Chaussinand-Nogaret, *The French Nobility in the Eighteenth Century: From Feudalism to Enlightenment* (Cambridge, 1985), but F. Bluche, *La vie quotidienne de la noblesse française au XVIIIe siècle* (Paris, 1973), and J. Meyer, *La noblesse française à l'époque moderne (XVI–XVIIIe siècles)* (Paris, 1991), are also useful. Chaussinand-Nogaret emphasises the dynamism of the noble élite and builds upon the classic work of H. Carré, *La noblesse française devant l'opinion publique au XVIIIe siècle* (Paris, 1920). Other important revisionist studies include: J. McManners, 'France' in A. Goodwin, ed., *The European Nobility in the Eighteenth Century* (London, 1953); G. V. Taylor, 'Types of capitalism in Eighteenth-century France', *English Historical Review* 79 (1964), 478–97, and his 'Non-capitalist wealth and the origins of the French Revolution', *American Historical Review* 72 (1966–67) 469–96; C. Lucas, 'Nobles, Bourgeois and the Origins of the French Revolution', *Past and Present* no. 60 (1973), 84–126; and G. Richard, *La noblesse d'affaires au XVIIIe siècle* (Paris, 1974). The case for the fusion of *épée* and *robe* was put by F. Ford, *Robe and Sword: The Regrouping of the French Aristocracy after Louis XIV* (Cambridge, Mass., 1953), although continuing social frictions have been detected by B. Stone, 'Robe Against Sword: the Parlement of Paris and the French aristocracy, 1774–1789', *French Historical Studies* 9 (1975), 278–303. R. Forster, *The House of Saulx-Tavanes: Versailles and Burgundy, 1700–1830* (Baltimore, Md., 1971), offers a fascinating insight into the life of a successful Court family. Amongst many excellent studies of the social and political world of the *robe* see: F. Bluche, *Les magistrats du parlement de Paris au XVIIIe siècle* (Paris, 1960); W. Doyle, *The Parlement of Bordeaux and the End of the Old Regime, 1771–1790* (London, 1970); M. Gresset, *Le monde judiciaire à Besançon de la conquête par Louis XIV à la révolution française* 2 vols (Paris, 1975); and M. Cubells, *La Provence des lumières. Les parlementaires d'Aix au XVIIIe siècle* (Paris, 1984). The purchase of ennobling offices is discussed by W. Doyle, 'The Price of Offices in Pre-revolutionary France', *Historical Journal* 27 (1984), 831–60, and D. D. Bien, 'Manufacturing Nobles: the chancelleries in France to 1789', *Journal of Modern History* 61 (1989), 445–86. An influential study of *finance* is that of Y. Durand, *Finance et Mécénat: les fermiers généraux au XVIIIe siècle* (Paris, 1976). For the army, see: D. D. Bien, 'The Army in the French Enlightenment: reform, reaction and revolution', *Past and Present* no. 85 (1979), 68–98. Among the many studies of the provincial *noblesse*, the most helpful are: P. de Vaissières, *Gentilshommes campagnards de l'ancienne France* (Paris, 1903); R. Forster, *The Nobility of Toulouse in the Eighteenth Century* (Baltimore, Md., 1960), and his 'The Provincial Noble: a reappraisal', *American Historical Review* 68 (1963), 681–91; and J. Meyer,

La noblesse bretonne, 2 vols (Rennes, 1966). Much can also be gained from reading G. Bossenga, *The Politics of Privilege: Old Regime and Revolution in Lille* (Cambridge, 1991). The relationship between the *noblesse* and the peasantry has been discussed by: W. Doyle, 'Was there an Aristocratic Reaction in Pre-revolutionary France?', *Past and Present* no. 57 (1972), 97–122; G. V. Taylor, 'Revolutionary and Non-revolutionary Content in the cahiers of 1789: an interim report', *French Historical Studies* 7 (1972), 479–502; and J. Q. C. Mackrell, *The Attack on Feudalism in Eighteenth-century France* (London, 1973). The peasants' perspective is provided by P. M. Jones, *The Peasantry in the French Revolution* (Cambridge, 1989). The debate about the *noblesse* and taxation begins with C. B. A. Behrens, 'Nobles, Privileges and Taxes in France at the end of the Ancien Régime', *Economic History Review* 2nd series, 15 (1963), 451–75, although her work has been criticized by G. J. Cavanaugh, 'Nobles, Privileges and Taxes in France. A revision reviewed', *French Historical Studies* 8 (1974), 681–92. Differing interpretations of the rôle played by the *noblesse* in the Revolution are offered by: D. Wick, 'The Court Nobility and the French Revolution: the example of the Society of Thirty', *Eighteenth-Century Studies* 13 (1980), 263–84; P. Higonnet, *Class, Ideology and the Rights of Nobles During the French Revolution* (Oxford, 1981); M. Price, 'The "Ministry of the Hundred Hours": a reappraisal', *French History* 4 (1990), 317–39; and A. Patrick, 'The Second Estate in the Constituent Assembly, 1789–1791', *Journal of Modern History* 62 (1990), 223–52.

6. THE NOBILITY IN SPAIN, 1600–1800

Surprisingly, although there has been a great deal written in Spain about *hidalguía* and *hidalguismo*, that is about the concept, the meaning and the ethos of nobility, and also, more recently, about the *señorío*, that is about the economics and the socio-political reality of lordship, there has been very little work on 'the nobility', as such, in this period. Our knowledge of the nobility and its long-term dynamics as a social group, and in particular of the aristocracy as a politically active body at specific junctures, has suffered both from the absence of a mainstream tradition of serious political history and political biography in Spanish historiography, and from the nature of the sources generated by the *mayorazgo*, which fragment the study of the noble House into its separate component *estados*, and make it difficult to reconstruct the fortunes even of the individual aristocrat. There has, therefore, been no general history of the nobility in the early modern period prior to the very recent and very brief survey by D. García Hernan, *La nobleza en la España Moderna* (Madrid, 1992). A. Domínguez Ortiz, *La sociedad española en el siglo XVII*, vol. 1 (Madrid, 1964) – reprinted in part in *Las clases privilegiadas en la España del Antiguo Régimen* (Madrid, 1973), is a mine of information on all aspects of the subject for the seventeenth century; while M. García Pelayo, 'El estamento de la nobleza en el despotismo ilustrado español', *Moneda y Crédito* 17 (1946), 37–59, though old, remains a valuable general overview of the eighteenth century. More recently, stimulating reappraisals of the rôle of the eighteenth-century nobility have been proposed by A. Morales Moya, in 'Una interpretación del siglo XVIII español a través de la perspectiva nobiliaria', *Revista de Estudios Políticos* 40 (1984), 45–58, and his doctoral dissertation, 'Poder político, economía e ideología en el siglo XVIII. La posición de la nobleza' (Universidad Complutense de Madrid, 1983).

However, the focus of most of the work that is being done is local, and at this level useful contributions are being made on individual aspects of noble culture, mores and lifestyle. At present, however, the only region for which we have a 'total' study of the nobility is Extremadura, where M-C. Gerbet's *La noblesse dans le royaume de Castille. Étude sur ses structures sociales en Estrémadure de 1454 à 1516* (Paris, 1979) has recently been matched by a massive study of the eighteenth century by Santiago Aragón Mateos, *La nobleza extremeña en el siglo XVIII* (Mérida, 1990), a splendid work of scholarship and a model it is to be hoped will be followed by historians of other regions.

The study of nobility as a concept must inevitably start with the numerous contemporary treatises which multiplied from the mid-fifteenth century on in an attempt to make sense of the ideological confusion which reigned as the Reconquista was completed. Perhaps the best known, most comprehensive and, since its republication in 1971, most accessible, is Bernabé Moreno de Vargas, *Discursos de la nobleza de España* (Madrid, 1622). The popular literature, and particularly the drama of the period, is also an essential source for ideas of nobility and honour, which has been usefully mined by J. M. Díez Borque, *Sociología de la comedia española del siglo XVII* (Madrid, 1976). Of the many relevant histories of Spanish literature, one of those with the most historical sense is O. H. Green, *Spain and the Western Tradition. The Castilian Mind in Literature from El Cid to Calderón*, 4 vols (Madison, Wisconsin, 1963–66), especially Volume 1. Foreign travellers and diarists in Spain have also a good deal to say about noble manners both from direct observation and from hearsay. An extensive, though by no means exhaustive, collection of their accounts has been put together by J. García Mercadal, *Viajes de Extranjeros por España y Portugal*, 3 vols (Madrid, 1952–62). Of modern works, I have not seen the PhD dissertation of Armand Arriaza, 'Nobility in Renaissance Castile: the formation of the juristic structure of nobiliary ideology' (University of Iowa, 1980), but there is a useful introduction to ideas of nobility and *hidalguía* at the end of the Middle Ages in R. Boase, *The Troubadour Revival: a Study of Social Change and Traditionalism in Late-medieval Spain* (London, 1978), and an excellent survey for the early modern period in J. Fayard, *Les membres du Conseil de Castille à l'époque moderne (1621–1746)* (Geneva-Paris, 1979), pp. 181–219. J. A. Maravall, *Poder, honor y élites en el siglo XVII* (Madrid, 1979) is an important attempt to explain shifts in the ideology of nobility within the framework of a reaction of señorial society to the rise of a middle class. Attempts to reconstruct an internal ideology of nobility on the basis of Court and administrative records have been made by J. Fayard and M-C. Gerbet, 'Fermeture de la noblesse et pureté de sang en Castille à travers les procès de *hidalguía* au XVIe siècle', *Histoire, économie et société* 1 (1982), 51–75, and I. A. A. Thompson, 'Neo-noble Nobility: concepts of *hidalguía* in early-modern Castile', *European History Quarterly* 15 (1985), 379–406; while the latter has also endeavoured to trace the evolution of social terminology over the period, in '*Hidalgo* and *pechero*: the language of "estates" and "classes" in early-modern Castile', in P. J. Corfield, ed., *Language, History and Class* (Oxford, 1991), pp. 53–78, and to calculate the importance of the purchase of royal patents as a means of access to nobility, in 'The Purchase of Nobility in Castile, 1552–1700', *Journal of European Economic History* 8 (1979), 313–60. These three articles have been brought together in I. A. A. Thompson, *War and Society in Habsburg Spain* (Aldershot, 1992). M. Lambert-Gorges, et al., *Hidalgos et hidalguía dans l'Espagne des XVIe-XVIIIe siècles* (Paris, 1989), contains a number of interesting essays (mainly in French), political, sociological and cultural, as well as literary, in orientation. The economic attitudes and activities of the nobility have been examined for their different periods and fields by R. Pike, *Aristocrats and Traders. Sevillian Society in the Sixteenth Century* (Ithaca, N. Y., 1972), W. J. Callahan, *Honor, Commerce and Industry in Eighteenth-Century Spain* (Boston, Mass., 1972), C. R. Phillips, *Ciudad Real 1500–1750. Growth, Crisis and Readjustment in the Spanish Economy* (Cambridge, Mass., 1979), and R. Herr, *Rural Change and Royal Finances in Spain at the End of the Old Regime* (Berkeley, Cal., 1989). Of the institutions of nobility, there is a solid work of scholarship on the *Maestranzas* by R. Liehr, *Sozialgeschichte spanischer Adelskorporationen: die Maestranzas de Caballería, 1670–1808* (Wiesbaden, 1981), and two good studies of the Military Orders by L. P. Wright, 'The Military Orders in Sixteenth and Seventeenth Century Spanish Society', *Past and Present*, no. 43 (1969), 34–70, and E. Postigo Castellanos, *Honor y Privilegio en la Corona de Castilla. El Consejo de las Ordenes y los Caballeros de Hábito en el siglo XVII* (Soria, 1988). The association between the nobility and the law, and aspects of the nobility's involvement in government and administration are dealt with in R. L. Kagan, *Students and Society in Early Modern Spain* (Baltimore, Md., 1974), J-M. Pelorson, *Les 'Letrados' juristes castillans sous Philippe III* (Le Puy-en-Velay, 1980), and Fayard's *Les membres du Conseil de Castille à l'époque moderne*. The military-administrative rôle of the nobility and the demands made on them in the reign of Philip IV are the subjects of A. Domínguez Ortiz, 'La movilizacíon de la nobleza castellana en 1640', *Anuario de Historia del Derecho Español* 25 (1955), 799–824, and chapter five of I. A. A. Thompson, *War and Government in Habsburg Spain 1560–1620* (London, 1976). What little there is on aristocratic faction and Court politics has to be extracted from more general political studies, such as P. L. Williams, 'Lerma, Old Castile and the Travels of Philip III of Spain', *History* 73 (1988), 379–97, 'Lerma, 1618: Dismissal or Retirement?', *European History Quarterly* 19 (1989), 307–32, and his forthcoming study of the duke of Lerma, for the reign of Philip III; J. H. Elliott, *The Count-Duke of Olivares. The Statesman in an Age of Decline* (New Haven, Conn. and London, 1986) for the first part of Philip IV's reign, and R. A. Stradling, *Philip IV and the Government of Spain, 1621–1665* (Cambridge, 1988) for the rest; and H. Kamen, *Spain in the Later Seventeenth Century, 1665–1700* (London, 1980), for the reign of Charles II. For the eighteenth century, A. Morel-Fatio has an account drawn from the original correspondence of a leading grandee, the count of Fernán Núñez, *Etudes sur l'Espagne*, 2e série (Paris, 1890), *Grands d'Espagne et petits princes allemands au XVIIIe siècle, d'après la correspondance inédite du comte de Fernan Nuñez avec le prince Emmanuel de Salm Salm et la duchesse de Béjar.*

For the nobility of the Crown of Aragon, the essential works in English are J. H. Elliott, 'A Provincial Aristocracy: The Catalan Ruling Class in the Sixteenth and Seventeenth Centuries', *Homenaje a Jaime Vicens Vives*, 2 vols (Barcelona, 1967), II, 125–41, reprinted in Elliott, *Spain and its World 1500–1700: Selected Essays* (New Haven, Conn., 1989), pp. 71–91; J. S. Amelang, *Honored Citizens of Barcelona. Patrician Culture and Class Relations, 1490–1714* (Princeton, N.J., 1986); and J. Casey, *The Kingdom of Valencia in the Seventeenth Century* (Cambridge, 1979).

The economic history of the nobility, on the other hand, is attracting an increasing amount of attention. B. Clavero, *Mayorazgo. Propiedad feudal en Castilla (1369–1836)* (Madrid, 1974) is the now classic and near definitive study of the *mayorazgo* as a legal institution. H. Nader, 'Noble Income in Sixteenth Century Castile: the case of the marquises of Mondéjar, 1480–1580', *Economic History Review*, 2nd series, 30 (1977), 412–28, sets out the legal and financial structure of one aristocratic *mayorazgo*, while C. J. Jago, 'The Influence of Debt on the Relations between Crown and Aristocracy in Seventeenth-Century Castile', *Economic History Review*, 2nd series, 26 (1973), 218–36, is an important article showing the political implications of royal authority over *mayorazgo* law. For the *señorío*, A. M. Guilarte, *El régimen señorial en el siglo XVI* (Madrid, 1962) is an institutional study which is relevant to the seventeenth and eighteenth centuries as well. But fundamental for the study of lordship as an institution is Jerónimo Castillo de Bovadilla's *Política para corregidores y señores de vasallos*, first published in 1597, with many subsequent editions, and a modern facsimile published by the Instituto de Estudios de Administración Local, Madrid, in 1978.

Historical work on the *señorío*, greatly facilitated by the Ensenada Catastro of the 1750s, a massive nationwide survey of taxable property and income in Castile, has tended to concentrate on the second half of the eighteenth century and the demise of the señorial regime in the early nineteenth century. The sixteenth and seventeenth centuries are rather less fully covered, though the numerous essays of B. Yun Casalilla, notably his splendid, 'Consideraciones para el estudio de la renta y las economías señoriales en el reino de Castilla (s. XV–XVIII)', *Señorío y feudalismo en la Península Ibérica (siglos XII–XIX)* (Zaragoza, 1994), pp. 1–35, are both major original contributions and essential guides to the issues. In English, chapter 4 of D. E. Vassberg, *Land and Society in Golden*

Age Castile (Cambridge, 1984) is a helpful general outline. The crisis of the seventeenth century is the subject of a magnificent article by C. J. Jago, 'The "Crisis of the Aristocracy" in Seventeenth-Century Castile', *Past and Present* no. 84 (1979), 60–90, and important contributions on the question of 'refeudalization' have been made by I. Atienza Hernández, ' "Refeudalización" en Castilla durante el Siglo XVII: ¿Un tópico?', *Anuario de Historia del Derecho Español* 56 (1986), 889–920, and B. Yun Casalilla, 'La aristocracia castellana en el seiscientos. ¿crisis, refeudalización u ofensiva política?', *Revista Internacional de Sociología*, 2a época, vol. 45 (1987), 77–104, of which there are English translations in I. A. A. Thompson and B. Yun Casalilla, eds, *The Castilian Crisis of the Seventeenth Century* (Cambridge, 1994). Of the economics of individual aristocratic Houses, the only in-depth study across the entire period is I. Atienza Hernández, *Aristocracia, poder y riqueza en la España moderna. La Casa de Osuna siglos XV–XIX* (Madrid, 1987). Atienza also writes extensively about the culture and anthropology, as well as the material life of the aristocracy. More chronologically limited but wider in scope is Charles Jago's exemplary PhD dissertation, still unpublished, 'Aristocracy, War and Finance in Castile, 1621–65. The Titled Nobility and the House of Béjar during the Reign of Philip IV' (Cambridge University, 1969). There is also a dissertation by L. Jury Gladstone on 'Aristocratic Landholding and Finances in Seventeenth-century Castile: the case of Gaspar Téllez Girón, duke of Osuna (1656–1694)', (University Microfilms International, Ann Arbor, Mich., 1977). For the developing climate in the eighteenth century that was to lead to the dissolution of the señorial régime, A. Domínguez Ortiz, *El régimen señorial y el reformismo borbónico* (Madrid, 1974); and for the dissolution itself, *La disolución del régimen señorial en España* (Madrid, 1965) is perhaps the most important of the many works by the doyen of the subject, Salvador de Moxó. Finally, R. Herr, 'Spain', in D. Spring, ed., *European Landed Elites in the Nineteenth Century* (Baltimore, Md. 1977), pp. 98–126, takes the *señorío* into the modern world of capitalist landownership.

7. THE ITALIAN NOBILITIES IN THE SEVENTEENTH AND EIGHTEENTH CENTURIES

Though there are a significant and growing number of titles in English and French, the most important studies of the nobility in the peninsula are inevitably in Italian. Five recent volumes are especially important and together provide a composite picture of the present state of research: Claudio Donati, *L'idea di nobiltà in Italia. Secoli XIV–XVIII* (Rome-Bari, 1988) is a wide-ranging survey of the concept of 'nobility' throughout the early modern period; while the following edited volumes all contain detailed studies of importance: Cesare Mozzarelli and Pierangelo Schiera, eds. *Patriziati e aristocrazie nobiliari. Ceti dominanti e organizzazione del potere nell'Italia centro-settentrionale dal XVI al XVIII secolo* (Trent, 1978); Elena

Fasano Guarini, ed., *Potere e società negli stati regionali italiani del '500 e '600* (Bologna, 1978); Amelio Tagliaferri, ed., *I ceti dirigenti in Italia nell'età moderna e contemporanea* (Udine, 1984); and Maria Antonietta Visceglia, ed., *Signori, patrizi, cavalieri in Italia centro-meridionale in età moderna* (Rome-Bari, 1992).

There are some important studies of nobilities of particular States in English and French. These are especially abundant for Venice: see the essentially demographic James C. Davis, *The Decline of the Venetian Nobility as a Ruling Class* (Baltimore, Md., 1962) and the large-scale social study by Jean Georgelin, *Venise au siècle des lumières* (Paris, 1978), chapters 11, 13 and 14 of which contain detailed material on the nobility. A crucial transformation is examined by S.J. Woolf, 'Venice and the terraferma: problems of the change from commercial to landed activities', in B. Pullan, ed., *Crisis and Change in the Venetian Economy in the 16th and 17th Centuries* (London, 1968), pp. 175–203: this is a convenient introduction, for English readers, to the fundamental study of Daniele Beltrami, *La penetrazione economica dei veneziani in terraferma: forze di lavoro e proprietà fondiaria nelle campagne venete dei secoli XVII e XVII* (Venice-Rome, 1961). The same theme is taken up by R. T. Rapp, 'Real estate and rational investment in early modern Venice', *Journal of European Economic History* 8 (1979), 269–90, which provides a case study of Alberto Gozzi, who was admitted to the Venetian nobility in 1646. The Tron family estate near Rovigo is the subject of Jean Georgelin, 'A Great Estate in Venetia in the eighteenth century: Anguillara', in Marc Ferro, ed., *Social Historians in Contemporary France* (New York, 1972), pp. 100–30. A key phase in the evolution of the patriciate of one rich city on the Venetian mainland is the subject of Joanne M. Ferraro, *Family and Public Life in Brescia, 1580–1650* (Cambridge, 1993). The recent study of Peter Musgrave, *Land and Economy in Baroque Italy: Valpolicella, 1630–1797* (Leicester, 1992), offers some sidelights on the nobility in Verona. For Milan, see Dante E. Zanetti, 'The *patriziato* of Milan from the domination of Spain to the unification of Italy. An outline of the social and demographic history', *Social History* 1 (1977), 745–60 and Domenico Sella, *Crisis and Continuity. The Economy of Spanish Lombardy in the Seventeenth Century* (Cambridge, Mass. 1979).

The position of the nobility in Savoy-Piedmont has attracted considerable attention: see S. J. Woolf, 'Economic Problems of the Nobility in the Early Modern Period: the example of Piedmont', *Economic History Review*, 2nd series, 17 (1964–65), 267–83, and the same author's more detailed study, *Studi sulla nobiltà piemontese nell' epoca dell' assolutismo* (Turin, 1963); for the eighteenth century there is the impressive and large-scale Jean Nicolas, *La Savoie au XVIIIe siècle: noblesse et bourgeoisie* (2 vols, Paris, 1978); while Geoffrey Symcox, *Victor Amadeus II: Absolutism in the Savoyard State. 1675–1730* (London, 1983) examines the position of the nobility, particularly in chapters 2, 9 and 14. For the Grand Duchy of Tuscany and especially Florence, see R. Burr Litchfield, *Emergence of a Bureaucracy. The Florentine Patricians 1530–1790* (Princeton, N. J., 1986), Jean-Claude Waquet, *De la corruption: morale et pouvoir à Florence aux XVIIe et XVIIIe siècles* (Paris, 1984), now translated as *Corruption, Ethics and Power in Florence 1600–1770* (Cambridge, 1991), which casts some light on this subject and the same author's book, *Le Grand-Duché de Toscane sous les Derniers Médicis* (Paris-Rome, 1990). The distinctive situation of the nobility in Rome is outlined, for the mid-seventeenth century, in chapter 6 of Laurie Nussdorfer, *Civic Politics in the Rome of Urban VIII* (Princeton, N. Y., 1992). For Naples and Sicily, see – in addition to the works of Gérard Delille and Tommaso Astarita cited below – the discussion of a central theme by Maurice Aymard, 'The Transition from Feudalism to Capitalism', *Review* 6 (1982–83), 131–208 [this is a translation of Aymard's fundamental 'La transizione dal feudalesimo al capitalismo', in the Einaudi *Storia d'Italia, Annali I* (Turin, 1978)]; Gérard Labrot, 'Le comportement collectif de l'aristocratie napolitaine du 16e au 18e siècle', *Revue historique* 101 (1977), 45–71; Rosario Villari, *The Revolt of Naples* (English trans., Cambridge, 1993; original Italian edn, 1967), which contains material on the situation of the Kingdom's nobility in the early decades of the seventeenth century; and Timothy Davies, 'Changes in the Structure of the Wheat Trade in Seventeenth-century Sicily and the Building of New Villages', *Journal of European Economic History* 12 (1983), 371–405, for one example of noble initiative. Two recent surveys of the Peninsula both contain a significant amount of material on the nobility: Y.-M. Bercé, G. Delille, J.-M. Sallmann and J.-C. Waquet, *L'Italie au XVIIe siècle* (Paris, 1989), parts 1 and 2, and D. Carpanetto and G. Ricuperati, *Italy in the Age of Reason, 1685–1790* [*Longman History of Italy*, vol. 5] (London, 1987), esp. chap. 5.

There are some important studies in English and French of individual noble families: Gérard Delille, *Famille et propriété dans le Royaume de Naples (XVe–XIXe siècle)* (Rome-Paris, 1985); Maurice Aymard, 'Une famille de l'aristocratie sicilienne aux XVIe et XVIIe siècles: les ducs de Terranova, un bel exemple d'ascension seigneuriale', *Revue historique* 96 (1972), 29–66; James C. Davis, *A Venetian family and its Fortune, 1500–1900. The Donà and the Conservation of their Wealth* (Philadelphia, Pa., 1975); Pierre Hurtubise, *Une famille-témoin: les Salviati* (Vatican City, 1985); and Tommaso Astarita, *The Continuity of Feudal Power: the Caracciolo di Brienza in Spanish Naples* (Cambridge, 1992). This last work is the most impressive detailed study in English and contains a notably full bibliography of the abundant recent work on the nobilities of the Italian peninsula.

Notes on Contributors

John Cannon is Professor Emeritus at the University of Newcastle upon Tyne, where for many years he held the chair of Modern History. His publications include: *The Fox-North Coalition: Crisis of the Constitution 1782–84* (Cambridge, 1969); *Parliamentary Reform, 1640–1832* (Cambridge, 1972); *The Letters of Junius* (Oxford, 1978); *Aristocratic Century: the Peerage of Eighteenth-century England* (Cambridge, 1984); *The Oxford Illustrated History of the British Monarchy* (with Ralph Griffiths) (Oxford, 1988); and, as editor, *The Historian at Work* (London, 1980) and *The Whig Ascendancy: Colloquies on Hanoverian England* (London, 1981).

Claudio Donati is Professor of early modern Italian history at the Università Statale di Milano. His publications include *L'idea di nobiltà in Italia, secoli XIV-XVIII* (Rome-Bari, 1988) and studies of the Bishopric of Trent and of the Papacy in the seventeenth and eighteenth centuries.

Roger Mettam is Reader in History in the University of London, where he teaches at Queen Mary and Westfield College. His publications include *French History and Society: the Wars of Religion to the Fifth Republic* (with Douglas Johnson) (London, 1974); *Government and Society in Louis XIV's France* (London, 1977); *Power and Faction in Louis XIV's France* (Oxford, 1988), and articles on seventeenth-century French history.

J. L. Price is Senior Lecturer in History at the University of Hull. His publications include *Culture and Society in the Dutch Republic during the seventeenth century* (London, 1974), *Holland and the Dutch Republic in the seventeenth century* (Oxford, 1994), and articles on seventeenth-century Dutch and Anglo-Dutch history.

H. M. Scott is Senior Lecturer in Modern History at the University of St Andrews. His publications include *The Rise of the Great Powers 1648–1815* (with Derek McKay) (London, 1983), *British Foreign Policy in the Age of the American Revolution* (Oxford, 1990), and numerous articles on eighteenth-century international history, and, as editor, *Enlightened Absolutism: reform and reformers in later-eighteenth century Europe* (London, 1990).

Christopher Storrs has taught in the Universities of London and Reading and in 1991–92 was a Leverhulme Research Fellow at the University of St Andrews. His publications include articles on international and Italian history in the later seventeenth century and on the early modern nobility. He is now working on eighteenth-century Piedmont. He is now Lecturer in Modern History at the University of Dundee.

Julian Swann is Lecturer in History at Birkbeck College, London. His publications include several articles on eighteenth-century French history, and the forthcoming *Politics and the Parlement of Paris, 1754–1774* (Cambridge, 1995).

I. A. A. Thompson is a University Fellow in the Department of History at the University of Keele, where for many years he was Senior Lecturer in Modern History. His publications include *War and Government in Habsburg Spain, 1560–1620* (London, 1976) and numerous articles on early modern Spanish history; these have now been collected together in two volumes: *War and Society in Habsburg Spain* (Aldershot, 1992) and *Crown and Cortes: Government, Institutions and Representation in early modern Castile* (Aldershot, 1993).

Thematic Index

Proper names and place-names which occur primarily in the survey of one national nobility have not been indexed.